Polish Surnames: Origins & Meanings

THIRD EDITION

WILLIAM F. HOFFMAN

VOLUME I

POLISH GENEALOGICAL SOCIETY OF AMERICA®
984 NORTH MILWAUKEE
CHICAGO IL 60642-4101
– An Illinois Not-For-Profit Corporation –

This edition is dedicated to

Edward A. Peckwas

who inspired this book

Kazimierz Rymut

who made it possible, and

Daniel J. Kij

who helped me "polish" it.

Niech spoczywają w pokoju!

Cover designed by Annmarie Bochenek Utroska

ISBN 978-0-924207-13-6

Published by:

Polish Genealogical Society of America®
984 N. Milwaukee Ave., Chicago IL 60642-4101
http://www.pgsa.org

Printed and bound in the United States of America

Table of Contents

Volume I

Introduction—Or, How Did I Get Roped Into This?

One evening in 1991, Edward A. Peckwas, founder and long-time president of the Polish Genealogical Society (now called the Polish Genealogical Society of America®, or PGSA), called me to discuss publications the Society ought to consider producing. We exchanged several ideas we thought promising; but the one for which Ed had the most enthusiasm was an English-language book on the origins and meanings of Polish surnames. He wasn't proposing an encyclopedic compilation of surnames, but rather a relaxed, almost chatty prose exploration of different kinds of names and how they came from such varied sources: names of trees, names of coats of arms, names of animals, and so on. Ed felt such a book would be quite popular; and he felt I was the one to write it.

I must admit that the idea left me cold. Oh, I liked it in principle. But I had doubts as to how many people would buy such a book, especially if it didn't contain all the names they were researching and didn't provide extensive information on each name's precise origin. There are so many Polish surnames, however, that only a massive, multi-volume set could be that comprehensive. The book we envisioned would only have space for perhaps 10,000 names, with brief indications of each name's etymological origin.

Besides, I had some notion how much work writing any book on surnames would involve, and I absolutely hated the suggestion that I be the one to write it! Put in words, my attitude was "Let some other idiot write it—this idiot has enough to do already."

Once Ed had made me aware of the idea, however, I couldn't help but notice whenever anyone expressed interest in a book about Polish names; and I was surprised at how much interest there was. For one thing, in a survey of members of the Polish Genealogical Society of America on potential book subjects, a book on Polish surnames was one of the two publications they most wanted to see. I had also joined an on-line computer service, Prodigy, and its genealogy bulletin board featured a surprising number of queries on the origins and meanings of Polish surnames. One evening I decided to conduct an experiment, so I answered one of those questions. My answer led to more questions, and soon I found myself answering several notes a night (sometimes as many as twenty), almost every night, for the better part of two years. I could no longer doubt that there was real interest in the subject.

By this point, I had agreed to survey the available literature and see if I could work up a respectable book. I found that Polish scholars had produced a sizable body of work, so lack of sources was not a problem. Getting my hands on those sources, and shaping their material into something accessible to non-specialists (and non-Polish-speakers), remained formidable obstacles.

I did not know it yet, but a slim volume published in Poland in 1991 would change all that. The noted Polish onomastic expert, Professor Kazimierz Rymut, had produced a work entitled *Nazwiska Polaków,* and in 312 pages he supplied an incredible amount of information about the most common Polish surnames. A friend with whom I was corresponding—Rafał T. Prinke of Poznań, an expert in genealogy and heraldry—knew of my efforts and was kind enough to present me with a copy of Rymut's book as a gift.

Professor Rymut's book not only inspired me, it filled in major gaps in my knowledge and suggested a methodology for my own book. I decided to devote Part I to prose discussion of the history and origin of surnames—much as Ed Peckwas had suggested—and Part II to an index of names organized by the root from which they derived—somewhat as Professor Rymut had done. In that way the reader can look for particular names in Part II, see the roots they came from and the category they belong to, and then consult the relevant chapters in Part I for general background on how names of that category typically arose.

Once I had a clear idea of how to proceed and a reliable source of basic information, I began work on the book. I could not simply re-hash what Professor Rymut had written, of course. I needed to explain for non-Polish-speaking Americans a great many points that Rymut, writing for Poles, could afford to ignore or discuss briefly. It also seemed advisable to incorporate more information on German names than he had given, because so many Polish-Americans have names of German origin. But there's no question my book owed an enormous debt to his from the very beginning; and I advise anyone with a real interest in Polish surnames to get hold of *Nazwiska Polaków* (Chapter Twelve of this book contains bibliographical information on this and all the sources I used).

By mid-1993, I had finished my *magnum opus* and delivered it to the printer so it could be unleashed on an unsuspecting world. There were no reports of book-shops being overrun by hordes clawing desperately to procure precious copies (go figure!); but I was gratified to hear that the book sold steadily and received unanimously favorable reviews. Since then I've lost count of how many kind folks have taken the time to send me letters or e-mail notes telling me how much they enjoyed reading *Polish Surnames: Origins & Meanings,* and how much they learned from it. Apparently I had done something right!

I realized I had better figure out what, because before long there was talk of issuing a second, revised edition. By late 1996 I got word that the first edition was almost sold out and I'd better get to work.

The Second Edition

When I sat down to work on the second edition, I realized that minor revisions would not do. By then, I had accumulated so much more material than I had back in 1993; it would be a crime not to use it to improve my work.

After the first edition was published, I had the privilege of striking up a correspondence with Professor Rymut, and he was incredibly helpful, especially in enabling me to buy copies of scholarly works on onomastics published in Poland. Those works are listed in Chapter 12, but one in particular needs to be mentioned here: the *Słownik nazwisk współcześnie w Polsce używanych* [Dictionary of Surnames in Current Use in Poland]. This 10-volume set listed virtually every surname borne by Polish citizens as of 1990, the number of Poles bearing each name, and a breakdown of where they lived by province. It was a massive amount of raw data, incredibly useful in some ways, maddeningly useless in others. But for me, it meant that when I went to work on the second revision, I could draw on hard data telling me which names were most common and what areas they lived in.

The Third Edition

Once the second edition went to press, I felt for quite a long time that it was good enough to leave alone for a while. As the years passed, I noticed some errors, but not sufficient to justify a new edition. In the meantime, I continued to collect books and articles on surnames whenever I could. Sadly, Professor Rymut died in November 2006—but not before completing a final edition of his *Nazwiska Polaków*, which I obtained. His colleague, Professor Aleksandra Cieślikowa, graciously continued to provide me with books published by Polish experts, and also offered to advise me on specific questions.

By 2010, I was beginning to feel I had enough additional information to justify work on a third edition. The folks at the Polish Genealogical Society of America® asked if I could provide them with a file suitable for offering my surname book on a print-on-demand basis. I explained that the files I'd used for the second edition would require extensive reworking to produce a reliable digital file for printing. Since it would take quite a bit of work anyway, I suggested we hold off while I put together a third edition.

I knew it would take a while to accomplish this, but I never thought I'd still be plugging away at it in mid-2012! As time passed, PGSA wanted more and more to have the book back in stock, as considerable demand for it had developed. I finally promised to have the third edition ready to turn over by September 1, 2012.

This means the book is not as complete as I would like it to be. But I realize now, I could go on revising it till I drop dead, and I'll never be satisfied that it's ready. I am satisfied that this edition is ready to publish. It corrects a number of errors in the previous edition, and includes a lot of additional information I received from Professors Rymut and Cieślikowa, plus the numerous books that have been published on surnames of all kinds in recent years.

I wanted to include most surnames borne by more than 100 Poles as of 2002 in the Index of Surnames by Root that makes up Part II. Part II ran 156 pages in the first edition and covered about 10,000 surnames. In the second edition, it ran more than 380 pages and included about 30,000 surnames. In this edition, it runs almost 1,000 pages and includes some 50,000 surnames. Do you see a pattern here? And do you see why I'm not promising a fourth edition?

You might ask if I've aspired to produce a work giving detailed derivations for every Polish surname. No, I long since concluded that wasn't practical. The 2002 data I used as my source listed *341,055 surnames!* And that covers only those areas that are within the current borders of Poland—no data from those parts of Lithuania, Belarus, and Ukraine that were formerly part of the Polish-Lithuanian Commonwealth, but which of necessity must be given some attention if the book is to prove useful to Polish genealogical researchers. It also does not take into account the many surnames that existed at one time but have since died out. I have no basis on which to estimate how many names that covers, but I'm sure it's no small number.

So even if I wanted to cover every single Polish surname in my book, it wasn't feasible to do so—there are just too many!

Derivations: Custom-Made, or Off-the-Rack?

Besides the issue of sheer numbers of names, another factor affected the size and scope of this book: the depth and detail of the derivations. By necessity, this book—like the one by Kazimierz Rymut on which it is partly based—has to provide "off-the-rack" derivations, rather than "custom-made." I use those terms because the distinction involved is much like the one familiar to anyone who buys clothes: "off-the-rack" clothing won't fit as well, but is adequate and affordable, whereas "custom-made" fits beautifully but costs an arm and a leg. A surname expert can offer "off-the-rack" derivations that are basically correct, reasonably-priced (50,000 in one book!), but not very specific as regards your particular ancestors; or he can offer "custom-made" derivations, specific, detailed, and very expensive.

Once, when I asked Polish genealogy expert Rafał T. Prinke for his opinion on some suggested derivations from place-names, he answered as follows: "My 'intelligent' guess would be that all the possibilities you mention are valid, and *it is not possible to pinpoint just one place without actual genealogical investigation. There can obviously be same-sounding surnames of different etymological origin.*" These are words of wisdom, and ones you need to understand so you can take this book for what it's worth, not too much, not too little.

You see, to do a really good job of tracing the origin of even one surname, you have to know exactly where the family in question came from, study old records to see if there's any surviving information that sheds light on the origin of the name (often there isn't), study the language as it existed centuries years ago when surnames were being established, take into account dialect terms and regionalisms that might have been involved, pore over old maps and records to see if the surname might have come from a long-forgotten name of a nearby locality, and so on, and so forth. All those factors can be involved, and any or all can vary from one instance to the next. Your *Kowalski* ancestor might have gotten that name because he was a *kowal,* a blacksmith; the *Kowalski* ancestor of that guy over there might have been an innkeeper who received that name because he lived in a place named *Kowale;* yet another *Kowalski* might have acquired that name because his ancestor originally had a name meaning "sniveling rat-faced geek" and changed it at the first opportunity to the much less embarrassing *Kowalski.* All you can really know for sure, without tracing the name and the family as far back as possible, is that the word *kowal,* smith, is involved somehow. Most of the time, the connection will be a fairly direct and obvious one; most Kowalski ancestors either were smiths or lived in a place that was named because of a connection with smiths. But you cannot possibly know what unique and unforeseeable circumstances in a family's past might have affected the form of the name they went by—unless you study that past in detail.

I wish I could offer "custom-made" derivations. I estimate, however, that a researcher who does really first-rate work would be a phenomenon if he compiled accurate analyses for, oh, 100 surnames a year. This edition of my book contains about 50,000. So you see, I had no choice but to give "off-the-rack" derivations, and hope that the material in the first part of the book will help folks flesh out the very sketchy info given in the second part.

Lo, The Oracle Speaks!

All of this leads me to feel I should say something on the stance I take as the author of this work. I am not the omniscient, infallible Polish expert, ladling out truth to the masses; nor am I the wise mentor who resolves all your doubts and questions with a word. Consider me, rather, a partner in your research, one who's spent quite a bit of time studying the origins of Polish surnames and who now offers you the best information he could find on a selection of those names. Sometimes those insights will prove incorrect; but for the most part they're pretty reliable, as far as they go.

I've agonized at length about possible errors in this book. As I've already explained, it's impossible to be certain about a name without doing far more detailed research than I've been able to do. This engenders uncertainty, which disturbs me because I am cautious by nature and would prefer to keep quiet when I'm not positive, rather than risk perpetuating error or inaccuracy. For me, writing this book was like dancing drunk in a minefield! No matter how much research I did, I was always aware there was more I needed to know. But I think the book will help you, as long as you remember this: if you conduct your research well, and have a little luck, you will become far more expert on the origins of your particular names than I can ever hope to be.

In fairness, I must also point out I have done nothing original here—I have not dug through ancient manuscripts, traced names as they evolved through the centuries, puzzled over archaic spellings, investigated local dialects to see how they affected the forms of names. My only contribution is to study work others, true experts, have done, and try to present it in a way non-specialists can use. Scholars such as Kazimierz Rymut, Aleksandra Cieślikowa, Józef Bubak, Jan Stanisław Bystroń, Zofia Kaleta, Genowefa Surma, Maria Malec, Hans Bahlow, and so on—they've done the real work and deserve the real credit. I have tried to give them the credit they deserve.

As long as I'm acknowledging those whose help made it possible to write this book, I might as well be complete. I mentioned already that the book was Ed Peckwas's idea, and that Rafał Prinke's gift of a copy of Rymut's *Nazwiska Polaków* was instrumental in making it a reality. James Czuchra of the Polish Genealogical Society of America® was magnificent in supplying me with copies of various hard-to-find sources. PGSA past-president Stan Schmidt and his wife Joan proofread the manuscript and provided excellent editorial advice. Michael Chonoles and Bernard Kouchel, two friends I met by way of Prodigy, provided material to educate me on the subject of Jewish surnames—the errors I've undoubtedly made on that score would have been far more numerous without their help. Pat Bretan and Krzysztof Ignatowicz, two more Prodigy contacts, offered useful suggestions on some of the more difficult derivations. David Zincavage and Robert G. Mazeika's help with sources on Lithuanian, and Jonathan D. Shea's expertise in Polish, were very welcome. Eileen Carter, Kathy Glowacz, David Haskell, Roman Kałużniacki, Teresa Lach, Rosalie Lindberg, and Cynthia Piech all volunteered vital assistance. I particularly want to recognize the late Daniel J. Kij, who read the manuscript of the first edition, suggested editorial improvements, and helped me get hold of several extremely useful reference sources. I thank them, and anyone who finds this book useful will want to thank them, too.

But Seriously, Folks...

What really bothers most of us about the origin of surnames is that, looking back from our perspective toward the time when they were being established, we would like to think the formation of surnames was an orderly process guided by rational rules. It was nothing of the kind. We're dealing with millions of people spread out over a vast region, speaking a language (several languages, in many cases) by no means homogeneous (dialectal variation was far more pronounced back then than it is today). These people chose names, or had names thrust on them, as circumstances dictated, and seldom stopped to ask "Will my great-great-great-grandson be able to figure out where this name came from?" As with all things human, the process was sloppy, catch-as-catch-can, and downright chaotic. But it worked, and anything that works has method hidden somewhere in the madness. Let's see if we can discover some of the method.

William F. Hoffman
Houston, Texas, USA
September 2012

VOLUME I

Chapter One:

"Where Did My Name Come From?"

When I first got online, back in 1990, I subscribed to a popular service, Prodigy. Before long, I began posting notes on some of its public bulletin boards. Whenever Prodigy posted such a note, it automatically identified the sender by his or her registered first name and surname, which made me "William Hoffman." That irritated me just a little because I generally go by my middle name, "Fred." My father, William Lee Hoffman, had a claim to the names "William" and "Bill" that predated mine by twenty years. My family called me by my middle name, and that's what I grew up answering to. Still, I've long since accepted that for standard purposes, our society regards one's first and last name as the ones that count. So it's never really bothered me to be called "William."

Anyway, back in the good old Prodigy days, I was browsing through the bulletin board devoted to genealogy when I was astonished to see a note on some aspect of German genealogy signed "William Hoffman"—but for the life of me, I couldn't remember writing or sending that note! A day or two later a message appeared from "William Hoffman" to "William Hoffman." It turned out there was another William Hoffman, in California, who was interested in some of the same things I am. He'd seen my postings and contacted me to compare notes on the Hoffman surname.

I checked Prodigy's membership list and found that there were at least two more William Hoffmans signed up as members. I realized that a lot of potential for confusion existed, so I started signing all my notes "Fred Hoffman, in CT" or "William F. 'Fred' Hoffman, in CT" (I was living in Connecticut at the time). After that, no one seemed to have trouble keeping the various William Hoffmans straight (although some people remain confused why a guy named "William" insisted on calling himself "Fred").

As I was beginning work on the first edition of this book, it occurred to me that I had personally experienced on that computer service the same thing that originally caused surnames: the need to distinguish individuals of the same name. When I was a child and my only community was my family, even then, some way was needed to distinguish me from my father, so that when my mother called "Bill, would you like me to bring you a beer?" I wouldn't break out in a big grin. Later, as I took an adult's place in a larger community, "William Hoffman" generally sufficed to distinguish me, while "Fred Hoffman" further defined me within the narrower sphere of my friends and family. But when I joined a community as large as the computer service's membership, numbering well over a million, the need for further differentiation arose. There were too many William Hoffmans; which one was I? It struck me that these were the same basic considerations that led European societies to insist that members add to their given name, which originally was sufficient, a second name to single them out and make them identifiable legally and socially.

The parallel goes further. I realized there was no point simply calling myself "Fred Hoffman" on my computer notes, because there are more than a few people by that name in this country. In fact, years later, when I wanted to set up a personal website, I discovered that <www.fredhoffman.com> was already taken, by a physical fitness expert. Well, no danger anyone will confuse me with him! But even back in 1990, I realized "Fred Hoffman" might not be sufficient identification; so I often added a localizing identifier, "in CT."

In time, the growing use of screen names and e-mail addresses online put an end to the confusion, and these days it's not much of an issue. But imagine if Prodigy had acquired another member named Fred Hoffman living in Connecticut. I might have found it necessary to change my signature again to specify the town I was living in. Or I might have identified myself as the Fred Hoffman born in Kansas. Or I might have abandoned geographical considerations entirely and called myself "Bill's son," or "the translator."

All these are old solutions to an old problem; and when you study the origin and development of surnames, you see that there is, indeed, nothing new under the sun. Whether you're an American middle-class writer of German descent living in Connecticut or a Polish peasant living near Kraków, the same basic processes are at work. Similar social needs, and fundamental linguistic similarities, produce similar solutions to problems. This is a phenomenon often encountered in the study of names, which is called *onomastics*; and surnames represent a particularly fascinating branch of onomastics.

To someone studying surnames for the first time, they can seem absolutely bewildering. They originated in dozens of different ways, in thousands of different places; and subsequent changes in history, language, and economic status have so jumbled them that the mental picture we get is a blur. Yet these names did make sense when they first arose, and they stuck for a reason. With a bit of learning and a lot of patience, we can hope to unjumble the picture enough to get the main contours right; then we can hope to clear up individual details, such as our own surnames.

At one time, Europeans possessed only given names. They began using second names as the population grew, settlements sprang up, roads were built to connect the settlements, and people came into contact with other communities and regions more and more often. The Poles were no exception. The earliest records show no use of surnames, only occasional use of nicknames or bynames. As the Polish realm grew, however, and the nobles increased in number and began to move around, the need to distinguish one from another arose. The main motivation was to establish a legal identity, to ensure that property ownership passed from one generation to the next with a minimum of bloodshed and disorder, to keep straight the levying and paying of taxes on that property, and to avoid confusion in organizing martial activities.

Remember that this was a time when Turks threatened Poland (and all of Europe) from the southeast; also from the southeast, ferocious Cossacks came riding over the steppes of Ukraine to wreak general havoc; to the east, the Russians were reaching out from Moscow to carve an empire of their own; to the northeast, the Lithuanians proved decidedly pugnacious, until Poland and Lithuania agreed to join forces and become a commonwealth consisting of two independent nations; and to the north and west, the Teutonic Knights, and later the Prussians, raised hell from time to time. In other words, there was no real lack of turmoil all around Poland—and the last thing the Poles needed was bloody internal fights over who owned what piece of land. Assuring undisputed property ownership was an essential way to keep the land in order, regulate taxation, and organize defense of the realm. And no matter how you slice it, none of these desirable goals was advanced if, every time the king called "Stanisław," a dozen different nobles said "Who, me?"

So Polish nobles, like their counterparts in other European countries, began to assume additional names. At that point, most records were kept in the language of scholars, Latin, and the first formative process was the use of Latin *de*, "of, from," to indicate where an individual came from, e.g., *Joannes de Grabowo,* "Jan [John] from Grabowo." This usage—like that which spawned German names with *von* and French names with *de*—produced a vernacular equivalent: Polish names with the preposition *z*, as in *Jan z Grabowa,* "Jan from Grabowo." That formula was common until the 15th century. But then adjectival names, formed typically by adding the suffix *-ski* to the name of a noble's primary estate, became popular. *Jan Grabowski* means the same thing as *Jan z Grabowa,* but Poles seemed to like the flow of *Jan Grabowski* better. From the 15th century on, *-ski* names became more and more popular.[1]

Another option was the **patronymic**, a name formed from one's father's name, for instance, the English surnames *Johnson* and *Davidson*. In Slavic languages, patronymics are easily formed by adding a suffix: Poles used *-owicz,* for instance, to mean "son of," so that *Kazimierz syn Jana,* "Kazimierz, Jan's son," could also be rendered *Kazimierz Janowicz.* (Actually, at first Poles preferred using the suffix *-icz* in patronymics; eventually, under Belarusian influence, they came to prefer *-owicz,* and it became standard). In time, that suffix, along with others such as *-czyk,* became more common than the expressions with *syn*. Patronymics actually made good second names, because they stressed the basis on which one inherited: legitimate descent from a father who acknowledged paternity.

In early days, a single name plus an occasional patronymic provided adequate information, partly because Polish drew on a large array of Slavic roots and suffixes for a rich store of personal names. In his book *Nazwiska Polaków,* Kazimierz Rymut cites records from the 12th and 13th centuries that display the variety of names nobles went by: "Stanoch, Pizla (or Pizła), Boruch, Wojan, Dargorad, Radost, whose firstborn [son] is Rpisz, Niezda, Wilkosz, Żerzucha, Radosz, Rusowic...."[2] With so many names to choose from, the chance that a given noble's name and patronymic would match those of another noble from the same general area was low enough to be acceptable.

But as time went on, it became standard practice for Polish Catholics to name their children primarily after saints—the Church usually insisted on this—and this rich variety of names diminished perceptibly. In modern times the records show page after page of *Jan, Stanisław, Kazimierz, Piotr, Paweł,* and so on. You almost get the impression that Poles were required by law to choose from no more than a dozen names! That impression isn't really accurate; but it did become far more common for different people to go by the same name. Other ways of distinguishing people were sought, not in any sort of official way, but as a spontaneous response to a perceived need.

Patronymics worked fairly well, but were not the only option chosen. Another was to cite the office or ceremonial position a noble held. It is very common to read that so-and-so was a court standard-bearer *(chorąży)*, chamberlain *(podkomorzy)*, master of the horse *(podkoniuszy)*, master of the pantry *(stolnik)*, sword-bearer *(miecznik)*, and so on. One also sees many nobles with Church titles. While the clergy of the Roman Catholic Church was an institution in which a medieval commoner could hope to advance by merit, the higher offices were reserved for nobility. The Church, in fact, supported efforts to identify nobles' lineage more clearly because illegitimacy was supposed to disqualify one from taking Holy Orders.[3]

These additional names—the patronymics and the names derived from estate or position—were not true surnames in the modern sense. The names changed as their bearers' circumstances changed; children did not necessarily inherit them from parents; and the same person might be called by different names in different contexts (on tax rolls, in birth records, in court proclamations, and so on). The names were merely conveniences to help identify individuals for purposes of law and protocol.

Eventually, however, unchanging names handed down from generation to generation—that is, surnames—began to be established for the nobles because that particular kind of name proved useful. This happened over the course of the 14th through the 16th centuries. Once surnames became *de rigueur* for nobles, wealthier non-nobles decided they had to have them, too. Eventually the practice spread throughout Polish society, although peasant surnames did not become firmly fixed until about the 17th and sometimes even the 19th century.[4]

It was not practical to enforce any strict set of rules regarding surnames. Calling yourself by a title derived from a place name, e.g., *z Grabowa* or *Grabowski*, was originally a privilege reserved for nobles because only they could own estates; but how do you enforce such a rule? Polish scholar Jan Stanisław Bystroń pointed out that a popular impression arose that *-wicz* names were lower-class, while *-ski* names were noble. As middle-class Poles started going by surnames, and eventually peasants began to do so as well, this impression caused a decided preference for names ending in -*ski,* to such an extent that they seem almost universal among Poles.[5]

More functional than aristocratic pretensions were surnames derived from the given names of a prominent ancestor, from one's profession, or a distinguishing feature of one's body or environment. Somewhere along the line, something about a family or its most prominent member came to be associated with the family as a whole, and that something stuck as a surname. Interestingly, however, eventually these names, too, often took the -*ski* suffix, so that one sees not just *Młynarz* (miller) but *Młynarski* (Sir Miller?!), not just *Kupiec* (merchant) but *Kupiecki* (Sir Merchant?!).

The many Jews living in Poland proper and in regions historically under Polish rule or cultural and linguistic influence (including much of Belarus, Lithuania, and Ukraine) had a slightly different onomastic history. They had done just fine using patronymics; a fellow named *Mojsiej* whose father was *Lewko* was called *Mojsiej Lewkowicz,* and then his son *Berko* in turn was called *Berko Mojsiejewicz*, and so on. Some Jews also used a third name that functioned much like a surname, but this usage was far from universal. When Russia, Prussia, and Austria overran and divided up the Kingdom of Poland and the Grand Duchy of Lithuania, near the end of the 18th century, the Jews found themselves living under foreign emperors who regarded their new subjects as little more than tax-paying cannon-fodder. All three partitioners mandated the use of surnames with decrees aimed primarily at the Jews, because most other inhabitants of Poland and Lithuania had surnames by then. The timing and approach of the mandates differed from one empire to another; but by the late 1800s, virtually all Jews living in what used to be Poland and Lithuania had surnames, either adopted freely or imposed by the authorities.

In many cases, Jews' patronymic -*wicz* names become frozen as surnames. That's one reason such names as *Moskowicz* and *Leibowicz* and *Lewkowicz* are so common today, especially in German-influenced spellings, e.g., *Moskowitz* and *Leibowitz* and *Lefkowitz*. Other Jews chose to adopt surnames based on their professions or other features, much as Polish Christians had done; but often, those names came from Yiddish words and were Germanic in origin, or sometimes Semitic, rather than Slavic.

Finally, a time came when everyone had surnames; but that didn't mean those surnames were always spelled the same way. Standardized spelling is a product of widespread education, a comparatively recent development in the West. You don't feel there's a "right" way to spell something till most of the people around you can read and write; up to that point, there's no real emphasis on spelling. Even when a Pole kept the same surname for most of his life, he might never spell it the same way twice; and many Polish peasants never learned to write, so those who wrote for him might spell the name however they saw fit. By the 19th century, Prussia, Russia, and Austria had divided Poland among themselves, and now foreigners were trying to spell Polish names, with spectacularly dismal results. Poles who emigrated to the United

States usually came by way of German ports, so the Germans filling out paperwork got another crack at mangling Polish emigrants' surnames. American officials got their shot at Polish names when Poles tried to settle down in their new home. Even when all concerned tried to get the names right, there was a lot of potential for mishearing, misspelling, and misunderstanding.

Even supposing Poles made it all the way to their new homeland with names intact, they then had to put up with people of every nationality trying to figure out how on earth you pronounce *Szczelągiewicz* or *Wojciechowski.* Frequently, a Pole trying to earn a living would realize he was losing business to competitors whose names English speakers could pronounce, and he would simplify his name. I remember reading an editorial in the Chicago Polish-language daily newspaper *Dziennik Chicagoski* in which the writer lamented a family's decision to change their beautiful name *Sandomierski* to *Sands* because it helped the members fit in better in America.

Now, years later, along come the Polish immigrant's American descendants, who don't speak the language, intent on trying to figure out what the family name was and what it meant. Good luck!

I don't want to discourage anyone from studying Polish surnames—this would be a pretty strange book if it began by saying "Why bother?" But before I can define the book's goals, I must describe the difficulties it seeks to address; and the difficulties are formidable. Polish names in their original form are hard enough for those who don't speak the language. What's more, many of the names Polish-Americans bear are not "pure." Over the years, spelling variations and even deliberate changes can make their original forms difficult to recreate. In addition, many Polish names are not Polish in origin at all, but ultimately of German, Russian, Czech, Ukrainian, Latin, Greek, Italian, French, Belarusian, Lithuanian, Yiddish, or Hebrew linguistic origin—and that's only a partial list! Even names that are of Polish linguistic origin have often been subjected to modification because of the influence of these or other languages, including English.

As an example, my wife's maiden name is *Holowak*, and her family is of Polish origin; but *Holowak*, believe it or not, is an Americanized form of the original surname! Her ancestors were ethnic Poles living in Lithuania, and the Polish form of their name was *Chołochwość*, pronounced something like "hoe-woke´-voshch." In Lithuanian, it is generally spelled *Galachvoščius* or *Golochvoščius*. Inasmuch as Lithuania was long under Russian and Soviet control, their name was often given in Cyrillic forms such as *Галахвощ* and *Голохвощ*; we'd render those names as *Galakhvoshch* and *Golokhvoshch*, respectively, in our alphabet. We know exactly where the family comes from, we have corresponded with surviving relatives living near Alytus in Lithuania—but which is the "correct" form of the name, and what does it mean?

A family story suggests it is related to the Polish word for "dove," which is *gołąb*; that is, in fact, the root of many Polish surnames, including *Golembiewski*. But from *gołąb* to *Chołochwość* is a bit of a reach, and I don't find that theory convincing. Also possibly relevant are Polish surnames from the root *cholewa*, "boot-top," or names from Ukrainian *голова* [*holova*], "head," including *Holowiak* and *Holowka*.[6] I suspect those had nothing to do with the original surname. They may, however, have influenced the family's choice of *Holowak* to replace *Gołochwość,* a name which sounds rather foreign even to Poles; *Holowak* is closer to "more normal" names such as *Holowiak* and *Holowka.*

The best idea I've heard on this name came from Aleksandra Cieślikowa, Ph.D., of the Polish Language Institute, an outstanding scholar. In her review of the first edition of this book, she suggested the name could be a compound of the Slavic roots seen in Belarusian *голы* [*holy*], "bare" (compare Polish *goły* and Ukrainian *голий* [*holyi*]) and *хвост* [*khvost*], "tail, back" (compare Polish *chwost* and Ukrainian *хвіст* [*khvist*]).[7] Information from the *Dictionary of Surnames in Current Use in Poland at the Beginning of the 21st Century* (more on this source in Chapter Eleven) makes this conjecture look even more plausible. It shows that as of 2002, there were Polish citizens with similar names, for example, *Gołofit* and *Gołokwast.* Even so, the only way to settle the matter would be to do careful research in written records on the spot—assuming any have survived—to determine whether the name has changed over the years, what its earliest form was, and what it meant in Polish, Lithuanian, Russian, or Belarusian, whichever was relevant. The family traditionally considered itself to be pure Polish, but that doesn't necessarily mean much in regard to their name's linguistic origin.

And yet sometimes names mean exactly what they seem to mean. My mother's maiden name was *Elmer.* I've heard people who considered themselves wits (and they were half right) speculate about my possible kinship to Elmer Fudd. This name meant little to anyone in the family, however, until one of my aunts developed an interest in genealogy. She realized that in German names the -*er* suffix often means "native of," as in *Berliner*, "native of Berlin." Before long, she established that the family came from Elm, Switzerland; she visited the town and met numerous distant relatives. In this case, the surname pointed straight back to the family's place of origin. So you never know.

It may well be that the greatest value of learning about your surname lies not in how much the information advances your search—quite frankly, determining the origin and meaning of most Polish surnames may not provide much real help—but rather in reinforcing a feeling of closeness to your ancestors. Finding out your surname comes from a word meaning "ash tree" does not necessarily illuminate the whole course of your family's past! Yet it somehow lifts your spirits to know your surname isn't just a jumble of sounds; it means something, it touches your ancestors' lives. Tracing genealogy is a long and often discouraging task, and anything that strengthens your sense of closeness to your ancestors is useful. It may help you get through all those letters saying "Sorry, we never heard of your family, please send money" till you finally get the one that says "Yes, your great-grandfather was born and baptized right here on such-and-such a day (please send money)."

Having suggested the dimensions of the problems involved with Polish surnames, let me explain how this book tries to help with those problems. Volume One studies different categories of surnames and discusses some of the ways they originated, citing representative examples. The chapters on these categories are preceded by a brief look at Polish orthography and grammar, because many surnames cannot be understood without a little background in those subjects. Volume II consists of an index to common surnames, arranged by the roots from which the names derive. Readers can use that index to look for specific names or categories relevant to their interests.

I wish I could have made this book an exhaustive study of all Polish surnames, so that it could help every Polish-American who picks it up; but that just is not feasible. The number and variety of Polish surnames are staggering. To keep the book from bogging down in jillions of names, I had to confine my attention to those seen most often, and to specific ones I've encountered that illustrate useful or interesting points. If that means your name doesn't appear here, I am truly sorry for the omission. Chapter Twelve provides a bibliography and other sources to lead you to all the valuable onomastic research Polish scholars have done that may enlighten you on your particular name, whether it appears here or not. Some of these sources are easier to get hold of than others; but at least it may encourage you to know that there are people out there who can help you answer one of the most basic questions of genealogy: "Where did my name come from?"

Endnotes

[1] Zofia Kowalik-Kaleta, *Staropolskie nazwy osobowe motywowane przez nazwy miejscowe,* Zakład Narodowy im. Ossolińskich—Wydawnictwo, Wrocław, 1981, pp. 6–8.

[2] Kazimierz Rymut, *Nazwiska Polaków,* Wydawnictwo Naukowe DWN, Kraków, 2001, Vol. I, p. XVI.

[3] Prof. Władysław Chojnacki, "American Polonia Seeks its 'Roots,'" English translation in the *Polish Genealogical Society Newsletter,* Spring 1985, p. 3.

[4] Włodzimierz Dworzaczek, *Genealogia,* Warsaw, Państwowe Wydawnictwo Naukowe, 1959; English translation of Chapter Three in the *Polish Genealogical Society Newsletter,* Fall 1985, pp. 23ff.

[5] Jan Stanisław Bystroń, *Nazwiska Polskie,* 2nd ed., Lwów-Warsawa, Książnica-Atlas, 1936, pp. 70ff.

[6] Rymut, *Nazwiska Polaków,* Vol. I, pp. 241–242.

[7] A. Cieślikowa, "W. F. Hoffman, *Polish Surnames: Origins & Meanings"* (review), *Onomastica,* Kraków 1995.

Chapter Two:

"Properly Polished Polish"

It irritates grammarians no end, but any language spoken by humans is a sprawling, untidy thing—sort of the linguistic equivalent of a teenager. No matter how insistently we lay down the rules, the language itself goes its own way, sometimes following the rules, sometimes ignoring them, sometimes smashing them to bits. For every hour honest language teachers spend explaining rules of grammar, they have to spend at least two pointing out all the exceptions.

Yet the rules are useful because they summarize useful patterns. A language must have observable patterns to be coherent, and speakers of that language can't ignore those patterns too drastically without becoming unintelligible to others. (Consider Humpty Dumpty's conversation with Alice in *Through The Looking Glass* if you doubt this.) So the patterns apply most of the time, and rules summarize how they apply; with any luck, they help you figure out enough to make sense even of parts that aren't properly polished.

A discussion of Polish surnames requires a look at Polish *orthography*— the rules that govern how Polish words, including names, are spelled and written—and at Polish grammar. I know many readers approach this discussion with the kind of spontaneous glee usually visible in a dentist's waiting room. But a grasp of the essential points of Polish spelling can pay off handsomely when it comes time to make sense out of real, live Polish surnames. Until you understand how *Rządca* and *Żonca* can be different spellings of the same name, you can literally pass right by vital information without even suspecting that you just missed the payoff to years of research.

These are the letters of the Polish alphabet:

$$a \; ą \; b \; c \; ć \; d \; e \; ę \; f \; g \; h \; i \; j \; k \; l \; ł \; m \; n \; ń \; o \; ó \; p \; r \; s \; ś \; t \; u \; w \; y \; z \; ź \; ż$$

Every one of these letters is considered an integral part of the Polish language, and you ignore the differences between them at your peril. Alphabetical order is as shown, with *ą* after *a*, *ć* after *c*, and so on, so that *Ćwik* comes after *Czyż*, *Ścibak* after *Szymkiewicz*, and so on. I have not observed that order in this book, to avoid confusing those not fluent in Polish; but be advised that modern Polish-language dictionaries, indexes, and the like follow it religiously. (Older Polish works may vary slightly in this regard.)

The Polish letters derive from the same alphabet we use—the alphabet the Romans and the Church spread throughout Europe—and most of the familiar ones sound at least reasonably like ours. The unfamiliar characters were added because certain sounds common in Polish didn't match up well with any of the existing letters, so certain letters were modified to make new ones that could stand for those sounds. This may seem complicated, but it actually makes better sense than the approach used in English, where we just pronounce the same letters many different ways. Try helping a foreigner say this sentence, which appears on various Web pages: "Though a rough cough and hiccoughs ploughed through him, he houghed the horse with thorough thoughtfulness." (In case you're wondering, "to hough," pronounced "hock," means "to hamstring.")

Any attempt to represent the sounds of Polish on a printed page is doomed. To get them right, you really need to listen to and imitate native speakers. But it is possible to give you a rough idea how the letters sound.

Vowels

a   as in "f*a*ther"

ą   a nasalized vowel, like "own" without quite finishing the *n*; before *b* or *p* the *ą* sounds more like "om" in "h*om*e"

e   as in "l*e*d"

ę   generally like "en" in "m*en*," without quite finishing the *n*; before *b* or *p* it sounds like "em" in "m*em*ber"

i   as in "mach*i*ne"

o   somewhat like the "o" in "m*o*th," "s*o*ft"

ó   Polish *u*, like "oo" in English "f*oo*t"

u   Polish *ó*, like "oo" in English "f*oo*t"

y   like the "i" in English "b*i*n," "p*i*n"

The *i* requires more attention: it serves not only as a vowel but also as a sign that the preceding consonant is palatalized or softened (like *ni* in "onion" as opposed to plain *n* in "net"). The consonants *ć, ń, ś,* and *ź* are spelled that way when they do not precede vowels; before vowels they are written *ci, ni, si,* and *zi,* respectively. In a word like *cichy,* "quiet," the *i* not only softens the first *c* to a "ch"-sound, it also supplies the following vowel.

Consonants

c   (when not followed by -*h*, -*i,* or -*z*) – like "ts" as in "fi*ts*"

ch   = Polish *h* – like the "ch" in German *ach* but a bit less guttural

ć   = *ci* – somewhat like English "ch" in "*ch*eese"

cz   more or less like "ch" in "*ch*alk," but a bit chunkier

dz   like "ds" in "wor*ds*,"sometimes like "ts"; *dź* = *dzi* – like "j" in "*j*ail"

g   always as in "*g*ive," never as in "*g*eometry"; at the end of words, like *k*

h   = *ch* – like the "ch" in German *ach* but a bit less guttural

j   like "y" in "*y*ield" (but *aj* sounds like "I," *ej* like "ay" in "h*ay*," *oj* like "oy" in "b*oy*," and *uj* or *ój* sounds a little like "uey" in "**H**uey")

l   lighter than in English, more as in "mi*ll*ion" than in "hi*ll*"

ł   like English "w," sometimes barely pronounced

ń   = *ni* – like "ni" in English "o*ni*on"

r   like the trilled *r* in Italian

rz   like "s" in English "pleasure"

ś   = *si* – somewhat like English "sh" but softer, almost hissing

sz   like English "sh," but a bit chunkier

w   like English "v"

ź   = *zi* – a voiced *ś*, like "s" in English "pleasure" but softer

ż   = Polish *rz*, like "s" in English "pleasure"

b, d, f, k, m, n, p, s, t, and *z* – more or less as in English

Unfortunately, due to considerations that fascinate linguists and put everyone else to sleep, many Polish letters have come to represent more than one sound. This list shows some letters and combinations that can be pronounced similarly and so are often interchanged.

Examples of Possible Equivalents

ą ↔ on ↔ om ↔ ę	**Dąbek ↔ Dombek; Piątek ↔ Piontek**
b ↔ p	**Dzió́b ↔ Dzió́p**
c ↔ tz ↔ dz ↔ dc ↔ cz	**Kac ↔ Katz ↔ Kacz; Kocur ↔ Koczur**
ć ↔ ci ↔ cz	**Ścibiorski ↔ Szczybiorski**
ch ↔ h ↔ g	**Cholewa ↔ Holewa ↔ Golewa**
cz ↔ c ↔ ć ↔ ci ↔ sz	**Szczybiorski ↔ Ścibiorski; Kacz ↔Kac**
d ↔ t	**Badkiewicz ↔ Batkiewicz**
dz ↔ c ↔ ts ↔ tz ↔ dc	**Sieradzki ↔ Sieratzke ↔ Sieracki**
ę ↔ en ↔ em ↔ ą	**Kolęda ↔ Kolenda**
em ↔ ę	**Dembiński ↔ Dębiński**
en ↔ ę	**Gens ↔ Gęś**
g ↔ h ↔ ch	**Galachwoszcz ↔ [C]Hołochwość**
h ↔ ch ↔ g	**Harasym ↔ Gerasim; Hudak ↔ Chudak**
i ↔ j ↔ y	**Marjan ↔ Marian ↔ Maryan**
l ↔ ł	**Łąka ↔ Ląka ↔ Lonka**
ń ↔ ni	**Koń ↔ Konia**
ó ↔ u	**Jakób ↔ Jakub**
om ↔ ą	**Dombek ↔ Dąbek**
on ↔ ą	**Piontek ↔ Piątek**
p ↔ b	**Dzió́p ↔ Dzió́b**
r ↔ rz	**Repka ↔ Rzepka**
rz ↔ r ↔ sz ↔ z ↔ ż ↔ ź	**Rzonca ↔ Żonca; Przymusiński ↔ Pszymusiński**
s ↔ z	**Smełty ↔ Zmełty**
ś ↔ si ↔ sz ↔ z ↔ zi ↔ rz ↔ ż	**Ślęzak ↔ Szlęzak**
sz ↔ ś ↔ si ↔ rz ↔ ż	**Stosz ↔ Stoś; Stawasz ↔ Stawarz**
u ↔ ó	**Jakubczak ↔ Jakóbczak**

*$v \leftrightarrow w \leftrightarrow f$	**Varshavski ↔ Warszawski**
$w \leftrightarrow$ *$v \leftrightarrow f$	**Chwałek ↔ Fałek; Wasąg ↔ Fasąg**
*$x \leftrightarrow ks$	**Alexa ↔ Aleksa**
$y \leftrightarrow i \leftrightarrow j$	**Dyak ↔ Diak ↔ Djak**
$z \leftrightarrow s \leftrightarrow ż \leftrightarrow zi \leftrightarrow ż \leftrightarrow$	**Zoppot ↔ Sopot; Ziebro ↔ Żebro**
$rz \leftrightarrow ż \leftrightarrow z$	**Żonca ↔ Rzonca; Żak ↔ Zok**

*The letters *v* and *x* are considered foreign and do not normally appear in native Polish words, but often show up in older spellings (generally because of the influence of Latin) or in words borrowed from other languages. The abbreviation *X.*, for instance, is frequently seen; it is short for *Ksiądz,* "Father" (as when addressing a priest).

I should also mention that proper Polish spelling does not allow *g* and *k* to be followed directly by an *-e*, but interposes an *-i-*. Theoretically, this means you should never see *Gerek* or *Niemkewicz,* only *Gierek* and *Niemkiewicz.* In practice, however, Poles and non-Poles alike often ignored the *-i-* that Polish inserts between softened consonants and vowels, so that *Niemkiewicz* can easily end up as *Nemkewicz* or *Zieliński* as *Zelinski.* Proper Polish also does not allow *y* to follow *g* or *k,* so names spelled *-sky* are usually Czech, Jewish, Russian or Ukrainian, or perhaps just misspelled.

A Sample Surname

Anyone with a flair for math who studied the list on the previous page will faint at the mere thought of how many possible spelling permutations one might encounter in the course of tracing just a few surnames. Fortunately, the situation is not quite that desperate. Almost all the confusion arises due to similar-sounding letters and combinations. As you begin to pronounce Polish words correctly, it becomes easier to recognize possible variants.

Let us take as an example the surnames I mentioned earlier, *Żonca* vs. *Rządca.* The standard form is *Rządca,* which appeared as a surname as early as 1400 and derives from the noun *rządca,* a ruler, governor, or steward of an estate.[1] First take the vowel *ą* and realize that it can easily be spelled *on* because it sounds like *on → Rzondca.* When a *d* is crowded in between consonants, it generally devoices to the sound of a *t,* and the *c* already includes that sound (because Polish *c* sounds like *ts*); so the *d* is superfluous and could easily be dropped → *Rzonca.* Then remember that *rz* and *ż* are pronounced exactly the same, so the name could be spelled *Żonca.* And there you are: *Rządca = Żonca!*

Remember that when someone wrote down names in the records—and since most Polish peasants were illiterate, someone else usually wrote the names for them—that person spelled the names the way they sounded to him. There were only so many common first names, it wasn't hard spelling them consistently, but surnames were another matter. Slight differences in dialect, or pronunciation, or the record keeper's hearing or schooling, could affect the way the names were written down. I've seen records in which the same registrar spelled the same person's name several different ways. It's not surprising that besides *Rządca,* the spellings *Rzeńca* and *Rzońca* are also attested,[2] and other forms such as *Żąca* or *Rzątsa* are possible. Try pronouncing them and you'll see, or rather hear, why: they all sound like "ZHON-tsah."

Chief Troublemakers

Admittedly, *Rządca → Żonca* is a rather extreme example. More often, the variant forms of surnames are not that radically different. Very common is trouble with the nasal vowels: *Piątek* is often spelled *Piontek, Dąbrowski* is often *Dombrowski, Dębiński* can be *Dembiński,* and so on. Also, in certain circumstances, the nasal vowels tend to switch: *Jarząbek* dates from at least 1388, but *Jarzębek* and *Jarzembeck* are also seen.[3]

Another major source of difficulty is confusion of *c, ć, cz,* and of the sibilants *rz, s, ś/si, sz, z, ź/zi,* and *ż.* The *c, ć (ci),* and *cz* are often used interchangeably, even though they're distinguishably different sounds; and as far as *rz, s, ś/si, sz, z, ź/zi,* and *ż* are concerned, all bets are off. *Ziółkowski* frequently is confused with *Żółkowski, Waśko* may appear as *Waszko, Przymusiński* is sometimes spelled *Pszymusiński,* and so on. Non-Poles also stumble over the pairings *ć/ci, ń/ni, ś/si,* and *ź/zi,* because a name ending in one of these pairs can change form when grammar adds or changes declensional endings: so *Łoś* can become *Łosia,* for instance, in certain circumstances. We'll look at this a bit more when we discuss grammar.

Foreign Influences on Spelling

If Poles were the only ones who had ever tried to spell Polish names, much confusion would have been avoided. Oh, there'd be plenty of variant spellings; most European languages show significant spelling changes over the course of the last few centuries, and the last couple of pages prove Polish was no exception. But the worst happened when non-Poles started tackling Polish names. I go into more detail on this in Chapter Nine, but a few remarks on the subject here may be helpful.

German phonetic values often left their mark on Polish names, especially from the 19th century on. After all, once Poland was partitioned, two-thirds of it went to German-speaking countries, Prussia and Austria. Attempts were made in Prussia (and, to a lesser extent, in Austria) to suppress the Polish language; so German names and spellings were crammed down Poles' throats. Once Poles decided to leave for America, most often they went through German ports such as Hamburg and Bremen, where German officials filled out records (temporary residence permits, papers for ship passage, etc.). The Germans got Poles coming and going, and many Polish names show it.

For example, to the German ear, the common Polish suffix *-wicz* sounds like *-witsch* or sometimes *-witz,* so that's how Germans spelled it. Similarly, the suffix *-wic* or *-wice* often became *-witz* in German. Germans didn't know what to make of the *ł* — German has no sound like our *w* or the Polish *ł* — so they usually just spelled it *l* and left it alone. Polish *sz* and *ś* were usually rendered by *sch* in German; *rz* and *ż* baffled Germans, so they usually left them unchanged or used the closest German sound, the *sch*. The *-ów* suffix often became *-off* (this is more common with Russian names, but some Polish names were affected). A Pole named *Kac* would more likely spell his name *Katz* if he'd been around Germans, to whom *-tz* or just *-z* is a normal way of spelling the *-ts* sound Polish spells with *-c* (compare German *Schwartz* with a common Polish spelling of the same name, *Szwarc*).

And, of course, once a Pole reached America, he often found it expedient to let his name be spelled the way it sounded according to English phonetic values. In other words, what's spelled *Łoś* in Polish sounds like "wosh" in English; so it's conceivable the name might be spelled *Wosh* or *Wosch*. If an American bothered looking at how the Pole spelled his name and saw that the name was supposed to begin with a letter that looks like an *L*, he might compromise and spell the name *Losch* or *Losh*. The *cz* and *ć/ci* were likely to be spelled the way they sounded to Americans, as *ch*; *sz* and *ś/si* tended to become *sh*. The *rz* and *ż* perplexed Americans and were often left alone; but over time many Polish-Americans came to pronounce *rz* as *r* and *z*, and the *ż* and *ź/zi* tended to become plain old *z*. (We even see *Krzemień* become *Krezmien!*)

Polish Handwriting

Before moving on to grammar, I should comment on Polish handwriting. Generally speaking, it doesn't give Americans too much trouble, because most of the letters are formed much the same as in English; but a few do cause some real trouble. It's a case of rounding up the usual suspects: *cz, rz,* and *sz*. In Polish the *z* is usually written *ʒ*, rather than as *ʒ*. While good penmanship will distinguish *cz* from *rz* from *sz*, normal handwriting often is sloppy and merges the letters to where all three look something like *u* or *ʉ*. It's best to remember how common *cz, rz,* and *sz* are in Polish and try to spot quickly how the writer formed his or hers.

Another letter that confuses many is *ł*, which in cursive often looks much like *t*. Some Poles cross the *t* and some don't, so a *t* could be either *ł* or *t*. The best bet is to look for words that unquestionably contain a *t* and an uncrossed *ł* so that you can see how the writer formed those letters, then compare them against the mystery letter. This is no minor matter: there are documented instances where Polish surnames changed spelling when someone mistook *ł* for *t* and the mistake stuck, so that a *Ciołek* became a *Ciotek*, and *Marszałek* turned into a *Marszatek*.

The tails on *q* and *ę* usually make them easy to spot. Remember that Polish doesn't use the letter *v*; if you see something that looks like a *v*, it's probably *w*. Poles don't always round and group the humps in *m* and *n*, so, as with German, you often have to stop and count up-and-down spikes to tell which you're dealing with. For the same reason, *u* and *n* can be hard to distinguish.

Pages 16-17 give a reproduction of a handwritten Polish baptismal certificate and a rendering of that writing in a standardized cursive. By comparing the standardized cursive on the left, which should be easy to decipher, with the original cursive, you will become familiar with typical Polish handwriting and thus have an easier time deciphering your own documents. (Both pages are adapted from analysis in the book *Following the Paper Trail: A Multilingual Translation Guide,* and are used with permission.)[4]

Grammar

It would be nice if we could talk about Polish surnames without tackling Polish grammar. It would also be nice if women could have babies without the pain and mess. Welcome back to Planet Earth.

Fortunately, there's no need to wallow in grammar to deal with surnames. A typical researcher needs to grasp only a few points to have a fighting chance with most forms of names that appear.

First, the basics. One of the patterns that dominates Polish is the changing of words' endings to reflect how the words interact in a sentence. This practice of changing endings is called ***inflection*** by grammarians, and historically it's actually the rule, not the exception, in European languages. With the passage of time there has been a pronounced tendency to shed inflectional complexity—modern German and English are far less inflected than their earlier forms—but the Slavic languages still rely a lot on it. This isn't just some professor's notion; if you can't put the right endings on words you'll have a hard time talking to Poles, even though they generally appreciate the attempt and will be as helpful as possible. The feature is just that deeply woven into the language.

Nouns and adjectives change endings according to patterns called ***declensions***. A noun is the name of a person, place, or thing; it can be a common noun, such as "chair," "foot," "sky," or it can be a proper noun, such as "Joe," "Greenland," "Bible." An adjective is a word that modifies a noun, that is, supplies additional information about that person, place, or thing. In the expression "blue sky," the adjective "blue" modifies the noun "sky."

In English, the only common changes to noun endings occur when you make a noun possessive singular *(blue sky's)*, plural *(blue skies)*, or possessive plural *(blue skies')*. No matter what you do to the noun "sky," the adjective "blue" doesn't change.

In Polish, not only can a number of different endings be added to the stem form of a noun, any adjective modifying a noun also has to take an

Here is a rendering in a standardized cursive of the handwriting on page 17:

W języku rosyjskim który w przekładzie na polski brzmi:

"Działo się w mieście Suwałkach dnia dziewiątego Maja
tysiąc osiemset osiemdziesiątego szóstego roku o godzinie trzeciej po południu. Stawił się osobiście Antoni
Kozicz, rolnik zamieszkały we wsi Małe-Pijawne trzydzieści osiem lat mający, w obecności Antoniego Tarlec-
kiego i Adama Kulbackiego po pięćdziesiąt lat mających rolników zamieszkałych we wsi Małe-Pijawne
i okazał nam dziecię płci męskiej urodzone we
wsi Małe-Pijawne drugiego Maja bieżącego roku
o godzinie dziesiątej rano z jego prawnej małżonki
Józefy z Kopiczków, trzydzieści lat mającej. Dziecięciu temu na chrzcie świętym udzielonym w
dniu dzisiejszym przez księdza Wincentego Gry-
ketysa nadano imię Jan, a rodzicami
chrzestnymi byli: Piotr Kujałowicz i Anna
Tarlecka. Akt ten oświadczającemu i świadkom
niepiśmiennym przeczytany, przez nas tylko
podpisany.
(-) Ks. A. Makowski G. S. par.

w języku rosyjskim który w przekładzie na polski brzmi:

„Działo się w mieście Suwałkach dnia dziewiątego Maja tysiąc osiemset osiemdziesiątego szóstego roku o godzinie trzeciej po południu. Stawił się osobiście Antoni Kozicz, rolnik zamieszkały we wsi Małe-Pijawne trzydzieści osiem lat mający w obecności Antoniego Garleckiego i Adama Kulbackiego po pięćdziesiąt lat mających rolników zamieszkałych we wsi Małe-Pijawne i okazał nam dziecię płci męskiej urodzone we wsi Małe-Pijawne drugiego Maja bieżącego roku o godzinie dziewiątej rano z jego prawnej małżonki Józefy z Kopierków, trzydzieści lat mającej. Dziecięciu temu na chrzcie świętym udzielonym w dniu dzisiejszym przez księdza Wincentego Grykietysa nadano imię Jan, a rodzicami chrzestnymi byli: Piotr Kujałowicz i Anna Garlecka. Akt ten oświadczającemu i świadkom niepiśmiennym przeczytany, przez nas tylko podpisany ——

(-) Ks. A. Makowski P. S. par.

appropriate ending. Factors in choosing the right endings are whether the noun is singular or plural and whether it is masculine, feminine, or neuter in gender. Fortunately, in dealing with names of people, the gender is usually just what you'd expect, masculine for males and feminine for females; so we don't have to worry too much about gender. And figuring out whether something's singular or plural isn't too big a challenge.

Both noun and adjective declension patterns are relevant to surnames, because Polish surnames are formed both from nouns and from adjectives: names ending in *-ski, -cki,* and *-zki,* and some ending in *-y* and *-i,* are adjectival in origin and change their endings according to the adjectival pattern. The rest come from nouns and use that paradigm. A typical person's name could be **noun + noun**, as *Jan Mazur,* or it could be **noun + adjective**, as *Jan Grabowski,* or **adjective + adjective,** as in *Jerzy Grabowski.*

Having said this much, let's take a look at the noun and adjective declensional patterns that typically appear in names.

Typical Noun Patterns as Found in Names

	Masc. Sing.	Fem. Sing.	Masc. Plur.	Fem. Plur.
Nominative	-	-a	-owie	-y,-i,-e
Genitive	-a	-y,-i	-ów	-,-i
Dative	-owi	-e,-i,-y	-om	-om
Accusative	-a	-ę	-ów	-y,-i,-e
Vocative	-e,-u	-o,-u,-i	-owie	-y,-i,-e
Instrumental	-em	-ą	-ami	-ami
Prepositional	-e,-u	-e,-i,-y	-ach	-ach

Typical Adjective Patterns as Found in Names

	Masc. Sing.	Fem. Sing.	Masc. Plur.	Fem. Plur.
Nominative	-ski	-ska	-scy	-skie
Genitive	-skiego	-skiej	-skich	-skich
Dative	-skiemu	-skiej	-skim	-skim
Accusative	-skiego	-ską	-skich	-skich
Vocative	-ski	-ska	-scy	-skie
Instrumental	-skim	-ską	-skimi	-skimi
Prepositional	-skim	-skiej	-skich	-skich

The adjectival pattern for names ending in *-ski, -cki,* and *-zki* differ only in the letter preceding *-ki*—so it's *-cka* or *-zka* instead of *-ska,* and so on. Note that the nominative masculine plural for adjectives—a form one often sees—is *-scy* (or *-ccy* or *-zcy*), so that in Polish "the Kamińskis" is *Kamińscy,* genitive *Kamińskich* ("of the Kamińskis"), etc.

The value of familiarizing yourself with these declensions lies in realizing that Polish names can change form without being different names. This means an ancestor named *Jan Grabowski* may appear in Polish-language documents not only under that name, but also possibly as *Jana Grabowskiego, Janowi Grabowskiemu,* and so on. These are not three different names, but one name that changes slightly because of Polish grammar. Similarly, *Czesław Łoś* and *Czesława Łosia* can be the same name. The genitive or accusative singular ending *-a* is added to the given name easily enough, *Czesław → Czesława*; but when the *-a* is added to the surname, *ś* followed by a vowel becomes *si*, producing not *Łośa* but *Łosia.*

This discussion is oversimplified, but will apply reasonably well so long as we focus on proper names. I am not demanding you memorize them (although, of course, it wouldn't hurt to do so); I am simply listing them to help you recognize the forms when you see them.

Other Adjectival Names; Names Ending In Vowels

There are a few names, both first names and surnames, that decline as adjectives but do not end with *-ski-cki/-zki,* and the endings are slightly different. Thus the first name *Ambroży* (Ambrose) has the forms *Ambrożego, Ambrożemu,* etc.; and the first name *Jerzy* (George) is *Jerzego, Jerzemu,* and so on. Surnames such as *Groźny* and *Woźny* do the same (*Groźnego, Groźnemu,* etc.).

Also significant are noun surnames ending in *-a* or *-o,* which decline like feminine nouns in the singular and like masculine nouns in the plural, so that *Lech Wałęsa* is *Lecha Wałęsy* in the genitive, *Lechowi Wałęsie* in the dative, but "the Wałęsas" would be *Wałęsowie, Wałęsów,* and so on.

When Men Were Men And Women Were Women...

A little familiarity with these patterns can also help you avoid changing your ancestors' sex. Many Polish feminine first names were originally formed by just tacking an *-a* onto a corresponding male name: *Władysław → Władysława, Ludwik → Ludwika, Franciszek → Franciszka,* etc. Notice that in the genitive and accusative singular of the noun declension, masculine nouns add that same ending, *-a.* If you see a note that so-and-so is *syn Bronisława i Ludwiki,* you might think it means "son of Bronisława and Ludwiki." In fact, it means he's the son of a man named Bronisław and a woman named Ludwika—the endings are what tip you off. Recognizing this can save you from inventing a whole new set of ancestors who are not only fictitious but also of the wrong sex!

All Polish-Americans researching their roots sooner or later confront the fact that many Polish women don't seem to have the same surname as their husbands. The husband may be "Jan Grabowski" but the wife is "Maria

Grabowsk*a*." If you look at the adjective pattern, you see that a name ending in *-ski* changes to *-ska* in the feminine, and that's the whole solution to the mystery. A Polish wife considers her *-ska* surname to be the same as her husband's *-ski*, just as *-skiego* is—the ending changes are just grammar, nothing more. Eventually Poles in America dropped this distinction because English couldn't accommodate it and Poles got tired of explaining the difference to non-Poles; in Poland it is still standard procedure (though there are some female Poles these days who prefer to go by the masculine form,[5] perhaps finding a separate feminine form discriminatory).

There are several other peculiarities about the surnames of Polish females that perplex researchers. One is the way of expressing maiden names. Often you see *Marianna Grabowska z domu Kwaśniewska,* which means her married name is *Grabowska* and her maiden name was *Kwaśniewska* (*z domu* means literally "from home, from the house"). More common in records would be *Marianna z Kwaśniewskich Grabowska,* which means "Marianna (of the Kwaśniewskis) Grabowska." The maiden name is given with the preposition *z* (from, of) and the genitive plural form; so if Marianna Grabowska's maiden name was *Grabowicz,* a noun-derived surname, the form would be *Marianna z Grabowiczów Grabowska.*

A third way, also seen a lot in records—though it is gradually disappearing in modern Poland—is adding the suffix *-ówna* to noun-derived surnames. In proper Polish, an unmarried Marianna Grabowicz would appear as *Marianna Grabowiczówna.* The suffix *-owa* denoted a married woman, so that Marianna's mother would be *pani* (Mrs.) *Grabowiczowa.* These suffixes apply only to noun-derived surnames; when an adjectival surname is involved, both Mrs. and Miss just take the *-ska* form, e.g., *pani Kwaśniewska* is Mrs. Kwaśniewska and *panna Kwaśniewska* would be Miss Kwaśniewska.

To add to the confusion, noun-derived surnames ending in *-a* dropped the *-a* and added different suffixes: the wife added *-ina* and the daughter added *-(i)anka,* so that Mrs. Zaręba would be *pani Zarębina* and Miss Zaręba would be *panna Zarębianka.* Surnames ending in *-o* added the usual suffixes, as in *Kościuszkowa* and *Kościuszkówna.* In some parts of Poland, the *-anka* suffix was also used to form a married woman's surname, so that Mrs. Karczewska could appear as *Karczewszczanka,* and Mrs. Lewoć could be *Lewocianka.*[6] We also see instances where dialect influence has turned that suffix into *-onka.* It's not "correct," but you do run into it in records.

One more point worth mentioning is that female surname forms ending in *-owa* decline as adjectives, but those ending in *-ówna* or *-anka* decline as nouns. So "Mrs. Grabowicz" is *pani Grabowiczowa,* but "of Mrs. Grabowicz" is *pani Grabowiczowej.* "Miss Zaręba" is *panna Zarębianka,* but "of Miss Zaręba" is *panny Zarębianki.* I would not advise anyone to lose sleep over these details. You need only realize that a surname with the ending *-anka* or *-szczanka* may be a feminine form. To find the standard form of the surname, it's usually enough to drop the suffix and, if applicable, change final

-ci, -ni, -si, or -zi back into ć, ń, ś, or ż. Most of the time this will give you something recognizably close to the nominative masculine singular form that is traditionally regarded as standard.

A researcher needs to recognize these suffixes because they appear a lot in older records. In modern Polish records there is a pronounced tendency to forget about all these suffixes and use the simple noun or adjectival form: *pani Zaręba, panna Zaręba, pani Karczewska,* and so on. Polish-Americans also tended to drop the suffixes, so that female names in Polish-language American newspapers generally did not distinguish a separate female form for noun-derived surnames. The distinctive *-ska* survived longer, remaining in use as long as the name appeared in Polish-language text.

Summary

It's an unfortunate fact that the typical family history researcher can't afford to invest the time and effort necessary to learn a lot about Polish orthography and grammar; yet some of the most basic features of Polish surnames simply cannot be understood without knowledge of those subjects. I hope this chapter provides a satisfactory solution to that dilemma. I have greatly over-simplified some complex subjects, but the points made are true in a general way and should clarify a number of common features that mystify researchers. Those who can afford it should study Polish in depth, preferably with a qualified teacher. But failing that, the information given here may illuminate some aspects of Polish, even if it's not properly polished.

Endnotes

[1] Kazimierz Rymut, *Nazwiska Polaków,* Wydawnictwo Naukowe DWN, Kraków, 2001, Vol. II, p. 381.

[2] Ibid.

[3] Ibid., pp. 338-339.

[4] Jonathan D. Shea and William F. Hoffman, *Following the Paper Trail: A Multilingual Translation Guide,* Avotaynu, Inc., Teaneck, NJ, 1994.

[5] Kazimierz Rymut, *Dictionary of Surnames in Current Use in Poland at the Beginning of the 21st Century,* Polish Academy of Sciences – Polish Language Institute, and Polish Genealogical Society of America®, Kraków and Chicago, 2002, Introduction, p. III.

[6] Constance M. Ochnio, "Don't Let Suffixes Confuse You," *Pathways and Passages* (the publication of the Polish Genealogical Society of Connecticut), Spring, 1992, page 4.

Chapter Three:

Polish Surname Formation

At last, a simple statement: Polish surnames consist of a root plus suffixes.

That felt wonderful! After all the stipulations and qualifications of the first two chapters, it's a pleasure to make a simple statement with no if's, and's, or but's. You probably enjoyed it even more than I did. I hope so—it may be the last one for a while....

I've said this before and will say it again: some Polish surnames are hard to figure out, but that shouldn't discourage you. Most aren't really that tough. If we could go back to the place and time when they first originated, and if we could fit in—that is, believe in the religions, know the economic and social conditions, speak the language(s)—most surnames would make a great deal of sense. The purpose of this book is to give you a hand in going back to the right time and place, in which context many Polish surnames are as simple as "Big-nose" and "Cry-baby" and "New guy in town."

To understand a Polish surname, you must recognize the name's *root* and distinguish it from the suffixes that follow it. There aren't always suffixes; but usually there's at least one tacked onto the root. The roots are what can usually be translated into something simple and comprehensible; the suffixes may or may not be so cooperative. In any case, you can usually get at least a rough notion of what the name meant. There was something about an ancestor that made that name seem fitting.

Some people get a little impatient when it proves difficult to find a concise, accurate English translation of a Polish surname. But should that surprise us? Most of us don't know the derivation of even the most familiar English names. Quick, what does *Brady* mean? How about *Clinton*? How sure are you that the obvious derivation of *Bush* is the right one? Where did the name *Presley* come from (or *Elvis*, for that matter)? If you, a native English-speaker, can't answer these questions about names you hear all the time, why expect Polish surnames to be any more obvious?

Surname Categories

As a rule, students of onomastics classify surnames by origin, the nature of the root from which the name derived. They usually distinguish four basic categories: given names, names of places of residence or ethnic origin, occupations or professions, and individual physical or personal characteristics. Some add ornamental names, such as German *Morgenstern*, "morning star." I certainly have no quarrel with these categories, but it might be helpful to break them down a little further. My analysis of the surname root index in Volume II suggests at least fourteen sources of Polish surnames:

animal names	*growing things*
coats of arms	*objects*
day or time	*occupations or positions*
emotions	*personal names*
features	*sounds*
food or drink	*toponyms (place names)*
foreign words or names	*verb roots*

Of course, I haven't devised new categories; reflection reveals considerable overlapping of these sources, so that they fit—albeit with a bit of massaging—into the standard categories. For instance, a surname formed from an animal's name surely arose because something about the animal was associated with the name's original bearer (e.g., *Orlik*, from *orzeł*, "eagle," or *Baranek* from *baran*, "ram"). A name formed from a verb root must have fit because the bearer typically performed that action (e.g., *Bakacz* from *bakać*, "to yell, scold"). And. of course. the foreign names fit into one of the categories in their languages of origin (e.g., *Adler*, German, from the word for "eagle," points to an association of person with eagle, just like Polish *Orlik*).

So while the index of surname roots in Volume II sorts roots by the categories I indicated above, it seems unnecessary to devote a whole chapter of text to each. Similar sources can be grouped together and discussed in the same chapter. I have grouped those sources as follows:

Chapter 5.   personal names; coats of arms
Chapter 6.   toponyms
Chapter 7.   occupations or offices or positions
Chapter 8.   feature or object associated with individual:
              animals; day or time; emotions; food and drink; growing things; insulting or offensive names; objects; verb roots; sounds;
Chapter 9.   foreign: Czech, German, Hungarian, Jewish, Lithuanian, Ukrainian/Russian/Belarusian, others

Bynames, Nicknames, Surnames

Before we plunge into examination of the different sources of surnames, I think a few remarks on the general processes of surname formation, and on factors that affected those processes, may be useful, and even interesting.

The simplest ways a surname could get started are ones we can all intuitively grasp. Imagine a couple of Polish peasants chatting at the inn after a hard day's work. One says, "Say, that girl of yours is about old enough to have the boys interested. Who's she going to marry?"

The other sips reflectively before answering, "We're planning to marry her off to Janusz."

"Janusz?" the first says in amazement. "I thought he was already married to Dorota's daughter."

"No, you're thinking of Janusz, Piotr's son. My girl's marrying Janusz, the son of that smith, Józef—the one who lives across the river."

"You mean the boy with the crooked leg?"

"Why not? He's learning a good trade, and a crooked leg won't stop him from giving me grandsons."

Considering the quality of brew served at most *karczmy* (inns, often owned by the local squire, who required his peasants to drink there or nowhere), the conversation probably didn't proceed much further before one or both men passed out, got sick, or got into a fight. But we need eavesdrop no longer—we've already seen several usages that could produce a surname.

Two of them are patronymics. "Janusz, Piotr's son" would be a handy tag, and once surnames took root among peasants it would be quite natural to call the lad in question *Janusz Piotrowicz (Piotr + -owicz)*. Similarly, "the smith's son" is a useful name, and either *Kowalczyk (kowal + -czyk)* or *Kowalewicz* could start that way. Note that the second Janusz in our little conversation could go by either *Kowalczyk* or *Kowalewicz,* which both mean "the smith's son," or by *Józefowicz,* "Joseph's son."

Another good source of a surname is derivation from a place, in this case "the one who lives across the river." You can imagine how easily such phrases could slip into conversation; and if that designation proved the handiest for people to use, Janusz might find himself being called *Zarzecki* (from *za,* "beyond, behind, past" + *rzeka,* "river").

In fact, our friend Janusz has at least three surname candidates: *Kowalczyk, Józefowicz,* and now *Zarzecki.* If you think about it, for most folks, more than one of these different ways of deriving names would fit. There's no infallible way of guessing which of several equally appropriate names might end up sticking. A given family might go by several different names before one of them finally won out and became established as their surname. Traces of this abound in the records if one goes back far enough. They're easier to find with nobles, of course, because for centuries the nobles were the only ones considered important enough to talk about in records; but the same thing clearly happened with peasants, too.

Back to our hypothetical conversation. Another potential surname source heard there is "Dorota's daughter." **Metronymics** (names formed from a mother's name) are less common in Polish than patronymics, as one might expect from the patriarchal nature of traditional Polish society. But there were matriarchs, unmarried mothers, and widows in Poland; and they left their traces in surnames. This Dorota might have been an unmarried mother who raised her child herself, or a widow who kept her family together. In either case her children might well come to be called *Dorociak (Dorota + -iak).*

Finally, calling somebody *Krzywonoga,* "crooked-leg," might not be the kindest way of referring to him, but people aren't always kind; and if this particular feature was a person's most obvious trait, the name might stick. If a king could get saddled with a name like Bolesław Krzywousty (crooked-mouth) or Władysław Łokietek (the elbow-high), why should a peasant be immune? It's reasonable to assume that the establishment of some surnames was the occasion of more than one fistfight, but the persistence of those names in records proves that the mouth can be mightier than the fist.

"Smile When You Call Me That!"

Actually, there have been plenty of Polish names that everyone (except the bearer) must have found hilarious. Bystroń's book on Polish surnames cites several examples, drawing mainly from published lists of surname changes officially authorized after their bearers petitioned to have them changed. Sometimes the names were compounds with funny meanings: *Starybrat* (*stary*, "old" and *brat*, "brother"), *Durybaba* (*dur-*, "dolt, fool," and *baba*, "woman"), *Małolepszy* (*mało*, "little," and *lepszy*, "better"). Sometimes the names were insulting: *Oszust* ("cheat, swindler"), *Galgan* ("rag, good-for-nothing, scoundrel"), *Kostera* ("dice-player, surly person"). I'm often amazed at the number and variety of surnames that clearly come from insults!

Bystroń also mentions names that were downright vulgar: *Hujek* (from *chuj*, "dick, prick," plus the diminutive suffix *-ek*—that's really hitting below the belt!), *Burdel* ("brothel"), *Pierdzioch* (from *pierdzieć*, "to fart").[1] I've encountered others of questionable taste that Bystroń didn't mention: *Bolibrzuch* (literally, "belly-ache"), *Kutas* (literally "tassel," also a vulgar synonym for *chuj*), *Mierzwa* ("manure," actually the matted straw you muck out of barns and stables), *Moczygęba* ("mouth-wetter," a heavy drinker), and so on. The term *dupa*, "butt, ass," has provided some interesting names, of which my favorite is *Stodup*, literally "hundred butts"—apparently it meant someone so stupid that calling him an ass once wasn't enough, he was stupid enough for a hundred asses.[2] As of 2002, there were still six Polish citizens who who bore this name! They all lived in Kolno *powiat* of Podlaskie *województwo*, which suggests they may all be members of a single family.[3]

I discuss this subject again in Chapter Eight. For now, let me point out that some prominent citizens have borne the names I've mentioned, so not everyone saddled with an offensive moniker bothered to change it. A good example is Rev. Leopold Moczygemba, a major figure in Polish-American history. His surname may have meant "drunkard," but that didn't appear to slow him down.[4] Maybe he had a thick skin; but I suspect that his name didn't cause him that much grief, because people seldom stopped to think about what it meant.

This is not rare in onomastics, whether Polish or English; I think you could argue that an essential part of a name's becoming a name is the loss of meaning. Clearly names meant something when they originated, but after a while they lost meaning and just became what others called you. I once knew a family named "Leech," some very nice people, and offhand I can't remember ever hearing anyone ridicule them as blood-sucking parasites. I'm sure it must have happened on occasion, human nature being what it is; but obviously not enough to make the Leech family change their name. In fact, it would never occur to most of us even to wonder whether that name did, originally, refer to leeches, or came from some term or place name that has since passed out of common use. Hanks' *Dictionary of American Family Names* says *Leech* is a variant of *Leach*, which can came from an archaic English word for "doctor," a reference to doctors' use of leeches to let blood.[5]

In any case, many of these surnames arose via nicknames or bynames, because the transition from a one-named society to a two-named one did not proceed in a nice, clear-cut manner. So many people had the same first name that the use of bynames or nicknames was common long before surnames were established. And those nicknames can be very deceptive.

Bystroń's book on Polish surnames mentions a man in one village who was called *Rusin* by everyone. *Rusin* means "Ruthenian, Rusyn," referring to the people of Ruś, the historical home of the Eastern Slavs, lying to the east of the Polish homeland. So naturally this Rusin fellow came from Belarus or Ukraine, right? Well, no. It turned out he got that name because when he was unhappy with someone he had the habit of saying *"Tyś taki, jak Rusin!"* (Oh, you're just like a Ruthenian!)[6] What this fellow had against Ruthenians is unclear, but the point is this little quirk of his was so well-known that everybody called him that. If that nickname happened to be preserved in a surname—for instance, *Rusiński*—there may be descendants of that fellow who've been told by "experts" like me that their name proves they came from Belarus or Ukraine! (Actually, in 99 out of 100 cases that is what *Rusiński* would mean; but there's always one in every crowd...)

Nicknames were not, of course, confined to the peasants. Minor gentry living in a particular village, or on an estate identified with a village, often acquired a surname formed from that village or estate's name; so that the Borzyszkowskis, for instance, were the noble family with a nest in Borzyszkowy. But on the face of it, such a name was of limited value for identification because it could apply to all members of the noble family; and these families often came to be extensive, with many branches. There came a point where a separate name was useful to distinguish individuals. In the records we see members of the Borzyszkowski family who went by such names as Chadyn, Chamir, Gawrysz, Kujach, Panic, Szada, Witk, Wyszk, etc. These bynames— "nicknames" doesn't really seem the appropriate term for them—started out as names for an individual; but later we see them handed down from father to son, and at that point they're well on their way to becoming surnames.[7]

What about the peasants who lived in Borzyszkowy? Well, I suspect most members of the *szlachta* (the nobility) were not in the habit of letting the peasants address them as anything other than "master," so the peasant didn't necessarily know or care what his lord called himself. Besides, nobles often had compound names, so that four or five generations might all be officially named *Jan Stanisław Konstanty,* and only when you got to the fourth or fifth name (or a byname) would you come to the one that a particular noble actually went by.[8] A peasant couldn't be bothered keeping track of all that; so when it came time to take a surname, he might just use the name of the estate, rather than his lord's name. Thus some of the less linguistically inventive peasants of Borzyszkowy might take the course of least resistance and choose to call themselves *Borzyszkowski.*[9]

Of course, that may or may not be the surname they finally ended up with. In practice, some might end up with the surname *Borzyszkowski*; others might take a patronymic; still others might go by a name formed from their occupations; and so on. We can feel sure the names they ended up with had some relevance to their bearers that was obvious at the time. Unfortunately, the exact nature of that relevance may not be obvious to us, centuries later!

Variations of Surnames

Even after surnames came to be fairly well established—that is, once the cake-walk of first names and bynames and nicknames and place names and parents' names and trade names and trait names had slowed to a halt and everyone was sitting firmly on a surname—there were plenty of ways that name could vary in form.

For one thing, there was spelling. Over the centuries, minor changes occurred in the way one put into letters the sounds of the language. As an example, the common noun ending now written *-ia* in some words and *-ja* in others—such as *parafia,* "parish," and *Maria,* "Mary"—was written *-ja* for a long time; not that many years ago, you saw educated Poles writing *parafja* and *Marja.* In some words now properly spelled with *-ja*—such as *Rosja,* "Russia," and *Galicja,* "Galicia"—it was once considered correct to use *-ya,* so that reference works from the 19th century refer to *Rosya* and *Galicya.* The point is that consistent spelling relies on a consensus of people who write in a given language; every so often the consensus changes, and spelling does, too. In older records, therefore, one sees *Rayski, Gorayski, Czaykowski,* instead of modern *Rajski, Gorajski,* and *Czajkowski.* Other examples of old-style spelling were *Trąmpczyński* instead of the more modern *Trąbczyński, Brzechffa* instead of *Brzechwa,* and *Thokarski* for *Tokarski.* Quite often bearers of old names were proud of them and insisted on the outmoded spelling as a sign of their family's antiquity; the archaic spelling proved the family had remained prominent since the days when other spelling norms prevailed.[10]

The very common *-owski* suffix has also caused some trouble. For one thing, Polish phonetics often show a link between *o* and *e,* and to this day some names have *-owski* and some have *-ewski.* According to Rymut, in this respect Poland divides into two sections. In one, covering Pomerania, Greater Poland, and Mazovia, roots ending in a hard consonant took the ending *-owski,* while those ending in a soft consonant took *-ewski.* In the other, the ending was *-owski,* regardless of the root's final consonant.[11] I think the point that concerns us is that records show vacillation between the spellings, e.g., *Bartoszowski* vs. *Bartoszewski,* and sometimes the mere appearance of one form in the written records might turn out to be enough to tip the scales in favor of that form.[12]

Another interesting tidbit is the way the *w* in *-owski/-ewski* pops in and out of names. It's not rare to see *Dąbroski* as well as the original *Dąbrowski, Wiśnieski* instead of *Wiśniewski*—in other words, there should be a *w,* but it got dropped. Often this is due to regional pronunciation; in many parts of Poland that *w* is not pronounced, so that *-owski* sounds like *-oski,* and people just spelled the name the way it sounded to them ... On the other hand, it's not rare for people to insert a spurious *w* by force of habit. For instance, *Zaleski* means "of/from Zalesie," but sometimes it has been "corrected" to *Zalewski,* which is a name in its own right, from the root seen in *zalew,* "flood, bay." Similarly, *Pułaski* (of/from Połazie or Pułazie-Świerze) is not the same as *Puławski* (of/from Puławy). Occasionally the bearer of a changed name kept the change to distinguish himself, so that an *Iwanoski* would stand out among all the *Iwanowskis.*[13]

Dialect terms also show up in surnames, and can be very frustrating— even someone who speaks Polish fluently may encounter names derived from terms that are unfamiliar because they are not used in standard Polish, or are used with different meanings. The best way to deal with them is to trace your family to their native region, then inquire locally (from family members or persons in charge of keeping records) about any regional term your name might have come from. Most genealogical research requires contact with the ancestral region anyway; so in practical terms, dialect need not cause researchers insuperable problems.

There is one dialect phenomenon worth noting; Polish linguists call it *mazurzenie,* from *mazur,* "native of Mazury," in the northern part of the region of Mazowsze." It is characterized by the pronunciation of *sz, ż, cz, dż* as *s, z, c, dz.* Say the sounds out loud and you'll hear the pattern. Here's a table to help you compare the standard Polish pronunciation and the Mazurian version, with an indication of how we would write each according to English phonetic values:

Polish	= English	→	Mazurian	= English
cz	*ch*		*c*	*ts*
dż	*j*		*dz*	*dz*
sz	*sh*		*s*	*s*
ż	*zh*		*z*	*z*

So in areas where this dialect affects pronunciation, the name *Szomowski,* which most Poles would pronounce roughly "sho-moff'-skee," would sound more like *Somowski,* "so-moff'-skee". Similary, *Czaczkowski* ("chach-koff'-skee") would sound like *Cackowski* ("tsats-koff'-skee"). Since spelling is sometimes affected by pronunciation, dialect version can affect the spellings in records. Bystroń cites:

> Czaczkowski vel Cackowski 1581 (wieś Czaczki na Podlasiu), Czychrowski vel Cichrowski 1656 (wieś Cychchry pow. warecki)...

He also comments that in *szlachta* names, the form usually was established one way or another fairly quickly; but in middle-class names, confusion might persist for some time before one form emerged as the consensus standard version of the surname.[14]

Well, there's quite a bit more we could say about surnames in general, but after a while generalities become tedious. So on to the next chapter, where we'll start getting into specifics with a look at the suffixes added to Polish roots to form specific surnames.

Endnotes

[1] Jan Stanisław Bystroń, *Nazwiska Polskie,* 2nd ed., Książnica-Atlas, Lwów-Warszawa, 1936, pp. 152–153.

[2] Genowefa Surma, *Nazwy osobowe w opoczyńskiem,* Gdańsk, 1991, p. 32.

[3] Kazimierz Rymut, editor, *Dictionary of Surnames in Current Use in Poland at the Beginning of the 21st Century,* Polish Academy of Sciences, Polish Language Institute, and the Polish Genealogical Society of America®, Kraków–Chicago, 2002, p. 10,720.

[4] T. Lindsey Baker, "The Moczygemba Family of Texas and Poland," The *Polish Genealogical Society Newsletter,* Spring 1988, p. 1.

[5] Patrick Hanks, ed., *Dictionary of American Family Names,* Vol. 2, G–N, p. 408 and 413.

[6] Bystroń, pp. 14–15.

[7] Bystroń, pp. 56–57.

[8] Włodzimierz Dworzaczek, *Genealogia,* Chapter III, translated in the *Polish Genealogical Society Newsletter,* Fall 1985, p. 28. As of 25 July 2012, a revised edition of this translation, by the author of this book, was available here: <**http://www.pgsa.org/PDFs/DworzaczekIII.pdf**>.

[9] Bystroń, p. 36.

[10] Ibid., pp. 132–133.

[11] Kazimierz Rymut, *Nazwiska Polaków,* Wydawnictwo Naukowe DWN, Kraków, 2001, Vol. I, p. LIX.

[12] Bystroń, p. 135.

[13] Ibid., p. 139–140.

[14] Ibid., pp.144–46.

Chapter Four:

A Sufficiency of Suffixes

I realize you may be grumbling to yourself something like, "Chapter Four already, when will this long-winded so-and-so bring on the Polish surnames? That is what the book's about, right?"

Well, yes. But experience suggests that a few unfamiliar features of Polish onomastics simply must be discussed before there's any point looking at the surnames themselves. Otherwise much of what I say when I do start talking about surnames will make no sense. The subject of suffixes is one of those necessary preambles.

The problem is, Polish likes to take one name root and create a jillion different surnames by tacking on suffixes. Of course, many English surnames were formed that way, too; but Polish seems to take it to extremes. To us, "Baker" is a name is a name is a name; in Polish, the word that means "baker," *piekarz,* is just a start. Look at some of the surnames that come from it:[1]

Piekar	*Piekarniak*	*Piekaruś*
Piekara	*Piekarnik*	*Piekarz*
Piekarczuk	*Piekaroś*	*Piekarzewicz*
Piekarczyk	*Piekarowicz*	*Piekarzewski*
Piekarec	*Piekarski*	*Piekorz*
Piekarek	*Piekaruk*	
Piekarewicz	*Piekarus*	

That's nineteen surnames that are currently borne by Polish citizens and were formed from taking the noun *piekarz* as a surname and by adding suffixes or, in some cases, modifying the original ending (*Piekorz, Piekara*). If English had surnames along the lines "Bakerson, Bakerman, Bakerly, Bakerish, Bakerlike, Bakerkin, Bakerama," we wouldn't need to discuss Polish suffixes. But it doesn't and we do.

The first and most discouraging feature of Polish suffixes is that there are so many of them, and often there is no adequate way to translate the differences between them into English. In some instances, there is no real difference in meaning; there's just more than one way to say the same thing, and Poles like a little variety in their names. It seems inconceivable that *Krawcowicz, Krawczak, Krawczuk, Krawczyk,* and *Krawicz* (all from *krawiec,* "tailor") mean pretty much the same thing: "tailor's son." Yet, unless you're willing to wade into some fairly serious discussions of Polish historical linguistics, that's the only general translation one can give. The suffixes do have slightly different origins and connotations, but there is no concise, satisfactory way to reflect them in English.

Often different suffixes point to regional variations: *-czuk* (or the Anglicized spelling *-chuk*) tends to appear in names coming from eastern Poland, Belarus, and Ukraine; *-czok* is more likely to lead back to Silesia; *-czak* and *-czyk* are standard Polish—but they are all patronymics, that is, they all can mean "son of." The suffixes *-icz/-ycz* and *-owicz/-ewicz* are also true patronymics, whereas *-owski/-ewski* is an adjectival suffix that signifies "of, from"; we'll take a closer look at it soon. As was discussed in Chapter One, surnames ending in *-ski* became fashionable, and some families changed their *-owicz* names into *-owski*. In other words, the form of a particular *-ski* name may reflect nothing more than a social fad. In any case, none of these "rules" is reliable enough to deserve much confidence. They are generalizations, and as a profound thinker once observed, "No generalization is worth a damn, including this one."

A second feature of Polish suffixes is that they often influence consonants (and vowels) preceding them to change somewhat. I think it would be a mistake to stress this too much, as it will confuse readers not overly interested in linguistic phenomena. Even an expert of the status of Kazimierz Rymut states that it is hard to tell whether the surname *Janczak*, for instance, derived directly from the first name *Jan* simply by adding the suffix *-czak*, or if it arose when the suffix *-ak* was added to the diminutive *Janek,* with modification of the *-k* sound to *-cz-:* → *Jank-* → *Jancz-* + *-ak*.[2] I suspect you could find instances of either origin—in onomastics, we often find there's more than one way for a particular name to get started. In any case, these consonant changes make it harder for non-Polish-speakers to figure out what their names come from. Here is a brief list of the most common patterns I've found to affect the final consonants of roots when suffixes are added.

Change	*Examples*
c → *cz*	Niemie*c* → Niem*cz*yk
ch → *sz*	Bla*ch* → Bla*sz*ka
d → *dzi*	Wo*d*a → Wo*dzi*ak
g → *ż*	Wi*lg*a → Wi*lż*ak
k → *cz*	Wnu*k* → Wnu*cz*ek
ł → *l*	Ciep*ły* → Ciep*l*ak
n → *ni, ń*	Bo*n* → Bo*ń*czuk
r → *rz*	Wi*r* → Wi*rz*ek
s → *si, ś*	Wrzo*s* → Wrzo*si*ński, La*s* → Le*ś*niak
sk → *szcz*	De*sk*a → De*szcz*ka
st → *ści*	U*st* → U*ści*ech
t → *ci*	Bar*t* → Bar*ci*k
w → *wi*	Wdo*w*a → Wdo*wi*ak
z → *zi, ź*	Dro*z*d → Dro*ździ*k

I should add that experts in Polish linguistics have studied these changes and can explain when, how, and why they take place. The truth is, in presenting this list, I am guilty of grossly oversimplifying a complex subject. But I keep reminding myself that I'm writing this for folks who don't know much about Polish, not for experts (who would hardly need this book anyway). There are detailed, highly technical linguistic treatises that cover the subject far more responsibly than the list above does; but those treatises are thoroughly incomprehensible to non-specialists. So let's all agree that my summary is primitive and superficial, and that's just what you like about it!

Some Common Suffixes Analyzed Structurally

In the Introduction to his book *Nazwiska Polaków*,[3] Prof. Rymut devotes a large section to listing and analyzing the suffixes most often used in forming Polish surnames. I found this passage extremely informative, and have translated it, with some editing, so that you can study it as well. First he goes through the vowels that can be tacked on to the end of name roots; then he analyzes suffixes formed from consonants, with or without addition of vowels. It is not the lightest reading in the world; but if you'd really like to gain some insights into these suffixes, it is worth the effort.

Vowel Suffixes Used in Forming Names

-a: This suffix is extremely common with feminine names, obviously. But in Old Polish, masculine names derived from short forms of dithematic names—such as *Stan* from *Stanisław*—could end with consonants *-a* and *-o*. The suffix *-a* on masculine names was often hypocoristic. It could be added to the first root in a dithematic name, e.g. *Bliza* (*Bliz* + *-a*), *Przyba* (*Przyb* + *-a*); or it could be added to a shortened form of a root with a suffix, e.g., *Święcha* (< *Świę* + *-ch-* + *-a*), and *Bogusza* (< *Bog-* + *-usz-* + *-a*). Names formed from verbs is another category of surname with the suffix *-a*. Rymut gives as exampes *Biega* (< *biegać*, "to run"), *Smaga* (< *smagać*, "to whip"), *Wałęsa* (< *wałęsać się*, "to loaf, loiter, wander"). A third category of surname ending in *-a* is from a genitive formation, e.g., *Anioła* (as in *syn Anioła*, literally "Angel's son") or *Macieja* (understood as coming from *syn Macieja*, "Maciej's son").

-ę: In the Middle Ages, personal names ending with *-ę* often were used for young people—compare the way this ending forms common nouns designating young animals, e.g., *cielę*, "calf," *jagnię*, "lamb," and *orlę*, "eaglet." Not surprisingly, surnames ending in *-ę* could be patronymic. They were rare in historical sources, and were most often seen in the Sanok region. Also seen, though rarely, are surnames with the extended suffixes *-ęta/-ąt*, such as *Borzęta, Borzęt, Borząt*. They were not uncommon in the 15th century in central Poland and Mazovia; but not many have survived.

-i or *-y:* These are variants of the same basic vowel, distinguished by the hard or soft quality of the preceding consonant. If the preceding consonant

is palatalized, the ending is –*i*; otherwise, it is -*y*. Sometimes the ending was used adjectivally, as in *Dęby* (< *Dąb,* from the word for "oak"), *Rybi* (< *Ryba*, from the word for "fish"). Sometimes it came from an expression of possessive relation: *Magdy* ("of Magda" < *Magdalena*), *Kapusty* ("of Kapusta," from the word for "cabbage").

-*o:* This ending gave names a hypocoristic flavor. In the Middle Ages, -*o* could be added to shortened names from the first root of a dithematic name, e.g., *Boro* (< *Bor-* + -*o*), *Przybo* (< *Przyb-* + -*o*), and sometimes from name elements with added suffix, e.g., *Zdzicho* (< *Zdzi-* + -*ch-* + -*o*), *Zbyszo* (< *Zby-* + -*sz-* + -*o*). Polish names ending with –*o* persist to this day. Names ending in –*ko, -enko,* and –*eńko* generally came into Polish from Ukrainian; but it may be more accurate to classify them under suffixes formed with the consonant -*k-,* discussed on page 34.

-*u:* In Old Polish, there were no forms ending with –*u.* In more recent times, names have developed from vocative forms such as *Aleksiu, Janku, Marku.* They can be regarded as diminutive.

Consonant-Based Suffixes Using in Forming Names
Suffixes formed from consonants were especially likely to be ***hypocoristic*** (referring to a "pet" or affectionate form of a name, compare English *Johnny*), ***diminutive*** (compare English *Little John*), or ***augmentative*** (compare English *Big John*). They could seem pejorative, but not necessarily. Consider that an English nickname such as *Johnny* may be perceived as a insult, if you insist on belittling a grown man by calling him that when he clearly resents it; but it can also be used by friends and family without giving offense. Sometimes, names with suffixes formed consonants expressed a relationship between the persons so named. Thus, in the Middle Ages, -*owic* meant "son of," e.g., *Janowic,* "son of Jan." Later, this function came to be filled more often by the suffixes -*k, -ek, -ak,* and -*czak,* which I generally refer to as "-*k-* suffixes."

Virtually all consonants could be used as suffixes to form names in the Slavic languages. But they were not all equally popular: there are many names formed with –*k-* suffixes, very few with –*b-* or –*p-*. Names based on the addition of suffixes with –*k-* can be grouped with those where the -*k-* sound was modified to –*c-* or -*cz-*; similarly, the guttural -*ch-* often modified to –*sz-*. Somewhat less common are names based on suffixes with –*l-, -n-,* and –*t-*. Names formed with suffixes based on –*g-, -j-, -m-, -r-,* and –*w-* are even less common. Names formed with suffixes based on –*b-, -f-, –h-, -p-,* and -*z-* are downright rare.

Suffices formed from consonants may be preceded or followed by vowels. So a given consonant sound could produce a large number of suffixes. For instance, the "sh" sound Poles spell *sz* could show up as -*sz, -sza, -szo, -asza, -aszo, -esz, -esza, -eszo, -isz, -isza, -iszo, -usz, -usza, -uszo, -ysz, -ysza,* or –*yszo*. The nasal vowels show up less often in this capacity. There are no forms ending with -*ęsz* or -*ąsz*, for instance; but there are personal names ending with -*ąd, -ęda,* and -*ęta.*

Suffixes formed from consonants could be added to Slavic and Christian given names, names from common names, and short forms consisting of the first root in a dithematic name. They could also be added to name elements from common nouns. In other words, practically any name root could generate surnames by adding any of a wide variety of suffixes.

Suffixes formed from –ch-: These suffixes tended to be hypocoristic, and could be added to name roots from dithematic names, Christian names, and personal names from appellatives (a common noun or adjective). Rymut gives the following examples: *Goch* (< *Godzi-*, *Gości-*, compare *Godzisław*, *Gościsław*), *Jach* (< *Jaro-* or *Jan*), *Lucha* (< *Luto-*), *Stacho* (< *Stani-*), *Wojch* (< *Woj-*), *Bolech* (< *Bole-*), *Stanich* (< *Stani-*), *Blizoch* (< *Bliz-*), *Boguch* (< *Bogu-*); *Bieniech* (< *Benedykt*), *Fabich* (< *Fabian*), *Jambroch* (< *Ambroży*), *Maciach* (< *Maciej*), *Pietrucha* (< *Piotr*); *Biedacha* (< *bieda*, "poverty, need"), *Golech* (< *goły*, "bare, naked"), *Babich* (< *baba*, "woman"), *Sadlocha* (< *sadlo*, "fat, lard"), *Deptuch* (< *deptać,* "to tread on").

Suffixes formed from –sz-: Up to the 15th century, *sz* was regarded as a "soft" consonant sound, and suffixes formed from "soft" consonants were generally used to form hypocoristic names. Toward the end of the Middle Ages, *sz*, *cz*, *c*, *dz*, and *ż* came to be regarded as "hard" consonant sounds. At that point, we begin seeing the use of *–ś-* instead of *–sz-* for hypocoristic names. Also, *sz* was sometimes replaced by *s*, especially in the regions of Lesser Poland and Mazovia, due to the influence of *mazurzenie*. So in effect, names created by adding *–sz-* suffixes might end up with three different forms. For example, in addition to the oldest form, *Jasz*, we also see *Jaś* and *Jas*; add the *–ek-* diminutive suffix and you get *Jaszek*, *Jasiek*, and *Jasek*. Rymut cites the following examples: *Gosz* (< *Godzi-*, *Gości-*), *Stasza* (< *Stani-*), *Zbyszo* (< *Zby-*), *Bogsza* (< *Bogu-*), *Bogdasz* (< *Bogdan*), *Bolesz* (< *Bolesław*), *Brodzisz* (< *Brodzisław*), *Jarosz* (< *Jaro-*), *Niegusz* (< *Niego-*), *Jaksza* (< *Jakub*), *Bieniasz* (< *Benedykt*), *Maciesza* (< *Maciej*), *Fabisz* (< *Fabian*), *Antosz* (< *Antoni*), *Jakusz* (< *Jakub*); *Gołasz*, *Golesz* (< *goły*, "bare, naked"), *Babisz* (< *baba*, "woman"), *Turosz* (< *tur*, "aurochs"), *Nagusz* (< *nagi*, "naked"), *Czarnysz* (< *czarny*, "black, dark"); *Staś* (< *Stani-*), *Pakaś* (< *Pako-*), *Sobiś* (< *Sobie-*), *Godoś* (< *Godzi-*), *Boguś* (< *Bogu-*), *Urbaś* (< *Urban*), *Grześ* (< *Grzegorz*), *Fabiś* (< *Fabian*), *Mikoś* (< *Mikołaj*), *Urbuś* (< *Urban*); *Chudaś* (< *chudy*, "thin"), *Bieleś* (< *biały*, "white"), *Gębiś* (< *gęba*, "mouth"), *Chleboś* (< *chleb*, "bread"), *Bladuś* (< *blady*m "pale"); *Sobas* (< *Sobie-*), *Dobies* (< *Dobie-*), *Sobis* (< *Sobie-*), *Pakos* (< *Pako-*), *Adas* (< *Adam*), *Antes* (< *Antoni*), *Fabis* (< *Fabian*), *Mikos* (< *Mikołaj*), *Jakus* (< *Jakub*); *Bubas* (< *buba*, "something scary," also "an idiot"), *Wójcis* (< *wójt*, a kind of district official), *Chlebos* (< *chleb*, "bread"), *Gajdus* (< *gajda*, "bagpipes, one who plays bagpipes"), *Mędrys* (< *mądry*, "wise").

Suffixes formed with –k-: This group of suffixes, including *–ek*, *-ka*, *-ko*, *-ik*, and *–ak*, was originally diminutive, indicating youth or smallness. After the Middle Ages, however, its function broadened and *–k-* suffixes could indicate descendants. So in the Middle Ages, *Stanik* meant "young Stan" or "little Stan"; but after the 16th century, it could also mean "son of Stan." These suffixes have been very productive from the earliest times to today. Rymut cites these examples: *Czak* (< *Cza-*), *Dobak* (< *Dobie-*), *Chwałek* and *Chwałko* (< *Chwalimir*), *Stanka*, (< *Stani-*), *Kubak* and *Kubiak* (< *Jakub*), *Janek*, *Pietrzyk* and *Pietryka* (< *Piotr*), *Chudak* (< *chudy*, "thin"), *Ratajek* (< *rataj*, "farmer"), *Golik* (< *goły*, "bare, naked").

Note, too, that the ending *–uk*, also appearing as *–czuk*, is typical of East Slavic languages and has been very common in the areas near the Polish-Belarus and Polish-Ukraine borders since the 15th century. Surnames ending in *-uk* are especially common in the regions of Podlasie and Red Ruthenia; they also show up often in eastern Poland.

As a base for name suffixes, the "ch" sound spelled *-cz-* by Poles developed from softening of the consonant *-k-*. It is not terribly common in its own right, although names ending with *–acz* do appear, based on the use of that suffix to form nouns such as *kopacz*, "digger," and *głowacz*, "one with a big head."

Names based on suffixes with the consonant *c* (pronounced like *ts*, remember), can come from *–k-*, although they can also come from *–t-*. Names with *–c-* suffixes tended to be diminutive, indicating young or small persons. The most common *–c-* suffixes were *–ec, -ca,* and *–ica*, which have been fairly productive. Rymut cites these examples: *Radziec* (< *Rado-*), *Adamiec* (< *Adam*), *Chudziec* (< *chudy*, "thin"); *Jarca* (< *Jaro-*), *Janca* (< *Jan*), *Bielca* (< *biały*, "white"); *Sławica* (< *Sławo-*), *Pawlica* (< *Paweł*), *Gębica* (< *gęba*, "mouth").

Note that forms with *–icz* and *–owicz* are a category unto themselves, and have produced a great many surnames. The original forms in Polish were *–ic* and *–owic*; but under East Slavic influence, they were modified to their current form, which is standard in modern Polish. Some surnames ending in *–ic* survive, however, as do a few with *–owic*. Various historical factors also produced names ending in *–ewic*, and later *–ewicz*. In Greater Poland, Mazovia, and Pomerania, adding the ending *–owic* to roots ending in soft consonants (which, as we said above, at one time included *c, cz, dz, sz*, and *ż*) modified the *–o-* sound to *–e-*, producing names such as *Wojewic* and *Jaszewic*. Another factor in changing the *–o-* to *–e-* was adding the suffix to roots ending with the sounds *-k, -g*, and *-ch*. This happened due to Belarusian influence and occurred later than the change just mentioned. For instance, we see *Jankiewicz* for the first time in documents drawn up in the northeastern regions during the late 15th-century. But this change was not comprehensive; we see today *Jankiewicz* and *Jankowicz, Markiewicz* and *Markowicz*. After the 15th century, the *–k-* suffixes *–ik, -ek*, and *–czak* came to be used more often as patronymics.

Suffixes formed with *–l-*: There are many names with this element, which shows up as *l* or *ł*, depending on whether the final sounds of the root were/are hard or soft. At one time, these *–l-* suffixes were hypocoristic and diminutive in nature; but as time passed, they came to have no particular significance. The ending *–ała* has been very productive, and *X-ała* often means "the X guy, the one always doing X, the one of whom X is the most prominent characteristic." Rymut cited these examples: *Bogal* (< *Bogu-*), *Dobala* (< *Dobie-*), *Bogiel* (< *Bogu-*), *Godla* (< *Godzi-*), *Boglo* (< *Bogu-*), *Tomil* (< *Tomi-*), *Stanul* (< *Stani-*), *Godula* (< *Godzi-*), *Godyl* (< *Godzi-*), *Stanił* (< *Stani-*), *Borzyło* (< *Borzy-*), *Stanioł* (< *Stani-*), *Gostoła* (< *Gości-*), *Wojtyła* (< *Wojciech*), *Przybyło* (< *Przyby-*); *Andral* (< *Andrzej*), *Urbala* (< *Urban*), *Franiel* (< *Franciszek*), *Jakiela* (< *Jakub*), *Macioł, Macioła* (< *Maciej*), *Janula, Januła* (< *Jan*), *Matyla* (< *Maciej*), *Szawała* (< *Szaweł*), *Mikło* (< *Mikołaj*); *Biedal* (< *bieda*, "poverty, need"), *Grubala* (< *gruby*, "thick, coarse"), *Kurzela* (*kura*, "chicken"), *Pędzioł* (< *pędzić*, "to drive, chase"), *Rogula* (< *róg*, "horn, angle, corner"), *Kucala* (< *kucać*, "to squat"), *Brzuchało* (< *brzuch*, "belly"), and *Oziębło* (< *oziębię*, "chill").

Suffixes formed with *–n-*: There are a great many personal names formed this way. In recent times, suffixes with *–n-* have been primarily structural in function, that is, they make it possible to create new name forms without any explicit emotional connotation. The suffixes can feature *–n-* or *–ń-*, depending on the hard or soft quality of the sounds preceding them. They are added to derivatives from dithematic names, Christian names, and names formed from appellatives. Rymut cites these examples: *Ciechan* (< *Ciecho-*), *Sobania* (< *Sobie-*), *Chocian* (< *Chocie-*), *Milana* (< *Miło-*), *Toleń* (< *Toli-*), *Borzen* (< *Borzy-*), *Ciechna, Ciechno* (< *Ciecho-*), *Choteń* (< *Chocie-*), *Borzyn* (< *Borzy-*), *Blizina* (*Bliz-*), *Goszczon* (< *Gości-*), *Bratoń* (< *Bratu-*), *Blizonia* (< *Bliz-*), *Borun* (< *Borzy-*), *Boguń* (< *Bogu-*), *Boguna* (< *Bogu-*) *Borzun* (< *Borzy-*), *Godyń* (< *Godzi-*), *Gorynia* (< *Gorzy-*); *Matan* (< *Maciej*), *Kubień* (< *Jakub*), *Mikno* (< *Mikołaj*), *Fabin* (< *Fabian*), *Pietroń, Pietrun* (< *Piotr*); *Biegan, Biegon,* and *Bieguń* (< *biegać*, "to run"), *Rybień* (< *ryba*, "fish"), *Suchno* (< *suchy*, "dry"), *Wdowin* (< *wdowa*, "widow"), *Białoń* (< *biały*, "white"), and *Brdun* (< *brdać*, "to rave, babble").

Suffixes formed with *–t-*: Suffixes containing *–t-* most often end with *–a*, although some occur ending in plain *–t* or with *–o* and preceded by vowels *-ą/ę-, -o-,* and *-u-*. Obviously, this means the number of *-t-* suffixes is limited. These suffixes can be added to personal names derived from roots in dithematic names, from Christian names, and from common nouns. In ancient times, these suffixes often were added to roots to denote abstracts, e.g., *Dobrota* ("kindness," < *dobry*, "good, kind"), *Mądrota* ("wisdom," < *mądry*, "wise"), *Cnota* ("virtue" < *cnota*, "virtue"). In the Middle Ages, names with *–t-* suffixes tended to be diminutives; but in more recent times, they had no particular significance. Rymut cites these examples: *Bolęta* (< *Bole-*), *Godzięta* (< *Godzi-),* *Blizota* (< *Bliz-*), *Miłot* (< *Miło-*), *Boruta, Borut* (< *Borzy-*); *Jakobięta* (< *Jakub*), *Janota, Janot* (< *Jan*), *Mikuta, Mik-t* (< *Mikołaj*); *Prawota* (< *prawy*, "right"), *Bosuta* (< *bosy*, "barefoot").

Suffixes formed with *–st-*: There are not many names with these suffixes. In the Middle Ages, they usually appeared in names derived from dithematic names; in more recent times, they have also been added to name roots from Christian names and from common nouns. Rymut gives these examples: *Bost* (< *Bogu-, Borzy-*), *Rast* (< *Raci-, Rado-*), *Domast* (< *Doma-), Bolest, Bolesta* (< *Bole-*), *Sulist* (< *Suli-*), *Dobrost, Dobrosta* (< *Dobro-*); *Gawlista* (< *Gaweł), Kubista* (< *Jakub*), *Janyst* (< *Jan*); *Gołost, Gołust* (< *goły*, "bare").

Suffixes formed with –j-: There are not a great many names formed with these suffixes; those that do appear primarily have *-j* added to forms from dithematic names and Christian names, and a little more often, names from appellatives. There is also a group of names with *–j-* from imperative forms of verbs, such as *Czekaj*, which means "Wait!" Rymut lists these examples: *Radaj* (< *Rado-*), *Chociąj* (< *Chocie-*), *Dobrzej, Dobroj, Dobruj* (< *Dobro-), Borzuj* (< *Borzy-*), *Sułuja* (< *Suli-*); *Kubaj* (< *Jakub*), *Pietrzej* (< *Piotr*), *Kubuj* (< *Jakub*), *Bielaj* (< *biały*, "white"), *Kurzej* (< *kura*, "chicken"), *Wilkoj* (< *wilk*, "wolf"), *Biegaj* (< *biegać*, "to run"), *Czekaj* (< *czekać*, "to wait"), *Nalej* (< *nalać*, "to pour"), *Smaruj* (< *smarować*, "to rub something in, to grease").

Suffixes formed with –d-: These, too, have not been terribly productive. They typically have been added to short forms from dithematic names, to Christian names, and to names from appellatives. Rymut's examples: *Standa* (< *Stani-*), *Suled, Suledo* (< *Suli-*), *Radzieda* (< *Rado-*), *Gorząd, Gorzęda* (< *Gorzy-*); *Janda* (< *Jan*), *Szymońda, Szymańda, Szymanda* (< *Szymon*), *Bienięda, Binięda* (< *Benedykt*), *Mikoda* (< *Mikołaj*); *Chlebda* (< *chleb*, "bread"), *Gonięda* (< *gonić*, "to pursue, chase, run").

Suffixes formed with –g-: There are not many surnames in this group. These suffixes are added to short forms from dithematic names, Christian names, and names from appellatives. These suffixes are generally augmentative, so that *Januga* or *Janiga* would mean something like "Big John." Rymut's examples: *Daliga* (< *Dale-*), *Suliga* (< *Suli-*); *Wojtyga* (< *Wojciech*), *Tomaga* (< *Tomasz*), *Maciąg, Macięga* (< *Maciej*), *Janiga* (< *Jan*), *Andryga* (< *Andrzej*), *Januga* (< *Jan*); *Białęga* (< *biały*, "white"), *Gołyga* (< *goły*, "bare, naked"), *Smoługa* (< *smoła*, "pitch, tar").

Suffixes formed with –r-: There are not many personal names formed from dithematic names by adding *–r-* suffixes; Rymut cites only a few from the Middle Ages, including *Stanar* (< *Stani-*), *Świętor* (< *Święto-*), *Wojor* (< *Woj-*), *Kazior* (< *Kazi-*), and *Pękora* (< *Pęko-*). There are more derived from Christian names, such as *Kubara* and *Kubor* (< *Jakub*), *Idzior* (< *Idzi*), *Janura* (< *Jan*), *Szczepura* (< *Szczepan*), and *Pietyra* (< *Piotr*). There are some names formed by adding *–r* or *–ra* with an augmentative function, such as *Gębara, Gębura,* and *Gębarz* (meaning more or less "big mouth"). What's more common in recent times, from the 17th century or thereabouts, are names formed by adding *–arz* to Christian names, such as *Magdziarz*, "son of Magda," and *Augustyniarz*, "son of Augustyn." The ending *-arz* is especially common in names denoting activity or profession, such as *Bednarz* (< *bednarz*, "cooper") and *Stolarz* (< *stolarz*, "carpenter"). These can be formed under the influence of German (compare the common German ending *–er*), and, on the borders of

Poland and the Czech Republic, Slovakia, and Ukraine, under the influence of the languages spoken there. Compare Czech *-ař*, Slovak *-ár*, Russian *-ap* or *-apь*, and Ukrainian *-ap*.

Suffixes formed with —*m*-: These forms are rather rare. There are a few from appellatives, such as *Staroma* (< *stary*, "old"), *Kurzyma* (< *kura*, "chicken," or *kurzyć*, "to raise dust"). In the Middle Ages, some developed from shortened forms of the first part of dithematic names; Rymut cites *Uniema* (< *Uniemysł*), *Borzym* (< *Borzymir*), *Myślim* (< *Myślimir*), *Jaroma* (< *Jaromir*).

Suffixes formed with —*w*-: There are two kinds of names formed with these suffixes, those from nouns and those from adjectives. Those from adjectives include names with *-iw-*, such as *Sędziw* (< *Sędzi-*, or perhaps also < *sędziwy*, "gray, aged"), *Mściw* (< *Mściwuj* or *mściwy*, "vengeful"), *Leliwa* (< *Leli-*), *Męciwa* (< *Męci-* or *mącię*); personal names ending with *-awa*, such as *Godawa* (< *Godzi-*), *Lubawa* (< *Lubo-*), *Janawa* (< *Jan*), *Bielawa* (< *biały, biel*, "white"), *Cichawa* (< *cichy*, "quiet"), *Deptawa* (< *deptać*, "to tread on"); and personal names ending with *-wa*, such as *Kałwa* (< *kał*, "excrement"), *Krzykwa* (< *krzyk*, "shout"). We also see names of adjectival origin with the suffixes *-ow* and *-ów* that have been made into nouns; that may explain the existence of many names ending *-ow* instead of *-ów*, which is what you'd expect in Polish. These were at one time patronymics. Rymut illustrates the development of these names thus: *Maćkow* < older (*Jan*) *syn Maćków*, "(John), son of Maciek."

Of course, this list does not exhaust the possibilities. Rymut concentrated on the most common suffixes, and the ones that were as clear as possible. I believe the discussion sheds at least a little light on the whole subject.

Some Common Suffixes Grouped by Usage

Valuable as Rymut's analysis can be, I believe readers can also benefit from taking a different approach, one categorizing suffixes by the way they are used. So let's examine the same basic information from a different angle.

Here is a summary of the more common suffixes added to adjectives, common nouns, given names, verb roots, or place names to form surnames. Most of this information comes from works by Bystroń[4] and Rymut[5]; anyone who can read Polish and would like to know more should definitely study these works, which offer many more details.

You'll notice many of these suffixes appear in more than one category. Most are not locked into one and only one meaning or usage; that's just not something we see very often in European languages. Some of these suffixes may have started out with a fairly specific meaning; but over time, they became more versatile. Poles had no problem with this because context usually made the meaning clear, when clarity was needed. As a result, these listings are not meant to be unambiguous, comprehensive, or definitive. But they should help you make sense of many a surname.

Suffixes Denoting Agents

We often see these suffixes used with a root to create a name that fit persons known for performing that action or exhibiting that quality.

-acz: *Gadacz,* "swaggerer, big talker" (from *gadać*)

-aj: *Czekaj,* literally an imperative form, "Wait!"

-ak: *Bujak,* "adventurer" (from *buj-,* a root having to do with roaming, soaring, reveling, telling lies)

-ała: *Bąkała,* "mutterer" (from *bąkać,* "to mutter"), *Krzykała* (from *krzyczeć/ krzyknąć,* "to shout, cry"), *Pisała* (from *pisać,* "to write")

-arz: *Kucharz,* "cook," *Pisarz,* "clerk, scribe" (from *pisać,* "to write")

-eń: *Smoleń,* "dirty fellow, slob, one who looks like he's covered with pitch, tar" (from *smoła,* "pitch")

-orz: *Piekorz,* "baker" (almost always a Silesian variant of *-arz*)

-uch: *Paduch* (from *padać,* to fall, also from *paduch,* "brigand")

Suffixes Typically Used with Bynames from a Feature or Trait

These suffixes were added to adjectives or nouns or verb roots denoting a person's distinctive feature or characteristic, and thus often yielded bynames or nicknames that eventually "stuck" as surnames.

-acz: *Głowacz,* "guy with a big head" (from *głowa,* "head")

-ak: *Nowak,* "new guy" (from *nowy,* "new"), *Trzeciak* (*trzeci,* "third")

-al, -ala: *Cichala* (from *cichy,* "quiet"), *Mądrala,* "know-it-all" (from *mądry,* "wise"), *Nosal,* "big nose" (from *nos,* "nose")

-as: *Białas,* "Whitey" (from *biały,* "white")

-ec: *Chmielowiec* (from *chmiel,* "hops")

-ek: *Świątek* (from *święty,* "holy"), *Śmialek* (from *śmiały,* "bold")

-isz: *Brudzisz* (from *brud,* "dirt"), *Cierpisz* (from *cierpieć,* "endure")

-och: *Zimnoch* (from *zimny,* "cold"), *Pierdzioch* (from *pierdzieć,* "to fart")

-ok: *Szostok* (from *szósty,* "sixth"), Silesian equivalent of *-ak*

-oń: *Bystroń* (from *bystry,* "quick"), *Cichoń* (from *cichy,* "quiet")

-osz: *Słabosz* (from *słaby,* "weak"), *Miłosz* (from *miły,* "dear")

-uch: *Ciepluch* (from *ciepły,* "warm")

-us: *Wielgus* (from *wielki,* "big, great, large")

Suffixes Showing Association with a Person, Place, or Object

-ak: *Cierniak* (from *cierń,* "thorn"); also used with a place name to mean "native of," e.g., *Bełzak,* "person from Bełz," and *Podolak,* "person from Podolia"; also with surnames derived from first names: *Walczak* ("Walka's son"), *Gierczak* ("Gertruda's son")

-an(in): *Łęczyczan,* "native of Łęczyca," *Krakowian,* "native of Kraków"

-arz: *Solarz*, "salter" (*sól*, "salt"), *Kolarz*, "wheelwright" (*koło*, "wheel")

-as: usually from given names, *Wojtas* (from *Wojciech*), *Wawras* (from *Wawrzyniec*, Lawrence), but also from verb roots, e.g., *Motas* (from *motać*, "to wind on a reel, entangle")

-nik: *Hutnik*, "founder, smelter" (from *huta*, "foundry"), *Skotnik*, "cowherd" (from *skot*, "cattle, livestock")

-oń: *Lasoń* (from *las*, "woods, forest"), *Boroń* (from *bór*, "forest")

-orz: Silesian equivalent of *-arz*, e.g., *Szaforz = Szafarz*, "steward"

-owicz, -ewicz: means "son of"

-uch: *Cepuch* (from *cep*, "flail"), *Łopaciuch* (from *łopata*, "shovel")

Diminutive or Augmentative Suffixes

These suffixes are extremely common in Polish, especially diminutives. The latter are used not only as we use them in English (e.g., *Janek* is like "Johnny"), but also to distinguish a noun-derived name from the noun itself. For instance, a man might get stuck with the name *Kur*, "cock," but in practice the diminutive *Kurek* worked better. Otherwise, when Kur's mother-in-law wanted to make a meal out of an old cock and told her son to go wring his neck, the wrong *kur* might end up in the soup!

-aś, -oś, -uś: *Gradoś* (from *grad*, "hail"); and from names: *Waluś* (from *Walenty*)

-|i|ec: *Marciniec* (from *Marcin*, Martin)

-ek: *Musiałek* (from *musić*, "to have to, be compelled to"); also patronymic, *Jamrozek* (from *Ambroży*), *Marcinek* (from *Marcin*, Martin); also in nicknames, e.g., Pope John Paul II (Karol Wojtyła) was called *"Lolek"* in his youth)[6]

-ica: *Gębica* (from *gęba*, "mouth"), Janica (from *Jan*, John)

-iga, -yga: *Ładyga* (from *ład*, "order, harmony")

-ik, -yk: *Orlik* (from *orzeł*, "eagle"), *Niemczyk* (from *niemiec*, "German"); also used with surnames derived from first names, *Janik* ("little John, son of John"), *Błaszczyk* (from *Błażej*)

-ina: *Chudzina* (from *chudy*, "thin")

-ka: *Babka* (from *baba*, "woman," compare *babka*, "grandmother")

-ura, -ora, -óra: *Badura* (from *badać*, "to examine, investigate"); also from given names, *Stachura* (from *Stach*, a nickname of *Stanisław*)

Suffixes Denoting Hereditary Relationship

These suffixes are typically added to a person or place name to signify a hereditary relationship. This usage can obviously be patronymic, but is not exclusively so.

-|i|ewicz, -owicz: a true patronymic, meaning "son of"; if you've read the preceding pages, you've seen enough examples of this already.

-in, -yn: *Sosin* (from *Socha* or *Zosia*); very common in Polish and Ukrainian, e.g., *Chomyszyn* (a metronymic from *Chomycha*, "Khoma's woman"—*Khoma* is a Ukrainian equivalent of *Tomasz*, Thomas), *Pawliszyn* (from *Paweł*, Paul)

-ów: *Litwinów* (from *Litwin*, Lithuanian), *Maćków* (from *Maciek*, a form of *Maciej*, Matthias), *Janów* (from *Jan*)

-owski: *Walkowski* ("son of Walka") — the *-owski* suffix more often indicates relationship with a place (see below), but can denote connections with people, especially when added to a first name

-ski, -cki: *Wolski* ("from Wola"), *Tarnowski* ("from Tarnów"), also from given names, *Stefański* (son/kin of Stefan)

More on Patronymics and Metronymics

As seen from the above lists, many suffixes in Polish can be added to a father's given name to form a patronymic, or to a mother's given name to form a metronymic. For example, the suffix *-in/-yn*, a kind of generic Slavic suffix showing possession, was cited above in the case of *Chomyszyn*, "son of Choma's woman." The suffixes listed below are used primarily to mean "son of, offspring of." They're typically tacked onto the father's or mother's given name (*Pawelczyk = Paweł + -czyk*), but they can also be added to words denoting occupation or position, e.g., *Kowalczyk = kowal*, smith + *-czyk* = smith's boy (either in the sense of "smith's son" or "smith's young assistant").

-czak: *Szymczak* (from *Szymek*, a diminutive of *Szymon*, Simon)

-czok: a Silesian form of *-czak*; example, *Klimczok* (from *Klemens*)

-czuk: *Iwanczuk*, "son of Iwan," a form common in eastern Poland, Belarus, and Ukraine

-czyk: not exclusively used as a patronymic, but often so; example: *Niemczyk* (from *Niemiec*, German); also appears in such terms as *Lubelczyk*, a native of Lublin

-icz, -ycz: used in Polish, Ukrainian, and Russian; in early Polish, often *-ic* or *-yc*; example, *Pawlicz* (from *Paweł*, Paul)

-[i]ewicz: a variant form of *-owicz*; example, *Stankiewicz* (from *Stanek* or *Stanko*, short forms or nicknames of *Stanisław*)

-in, -yn: as seen above, a common suffix denoting possession, but also added to personal names to form patronymics or metronymics; example, *Sosin* from *Socha* or perhaps *Zosia*.

-owicz: used in Polish, Ukrainian, and Russian (also spelled *-ovich*, *-evich* in English); in early Polish documents often *-owic*; consists of compounded suffixes *-ow-* + *-ic*; example, *Wojciechowicz* (from *Wojciech*), "son of Wojciech"

-[i]uk: a form common in eastern Poland, Belarus, and Ukraine; example, *Martyniuk* (from *Martyn*, Martin, thus "son of Martin")

Foreign Suffixes

Poland's history has been extraordinarily closely tied to that of its neighbors, and that fact is reflected in the many non-Polish surnames one hears among Poles. Often suffixes are what tip you off that these names were not originally Polish. Surnames ending in the suffixes listed below usually began in, or were filtered through, some other linguistic milieu, even if their pronunciation and spelling have been polonized.

-aff: German, but often a German rendering of *-ow* or *-aw*, so frequently it indicates a German version of a Polish or Czech name; example, *Ratzlaff*, a Pomeranian name = *Racław* or *Radosław*.[7]

-au: German, often equivalent to Polish *-ów* or *-ow-*; example, *Krakau* = Kraków; but note that *-au* can also be a native German ending.

-ckyj: Ukrainian adjectival ending *-цький* [*-tśkyi*], equivalent of *cki* in Polish; example, *Khmelnytśkyj*, spelled *Chmielnicki* in Polish.

-chuk: Belarusian and Ukrainian patronymic *-чук*, usually spelled *-chuk* in English, equivalent of *-czuk* in Polish; example, *Ковальчук* [*Koval'chuk*], "smith's son," would be spelled *Kowalczuk* by Poles

-chyk: Ukrainian patronymic *-чик*, usually spelled *-chik* or *-chyk* in English, equivalent of *-czyk* in Polish; example, *Іванчик* [*Ivanchyk*], son of Ivan, would be spelled *Iwanczyk* by Poles

-enko: Ukrainian *-енко* [*-enko*] or *-енько* [*-eńko*]; example, *Василенько* [*Vasileńko*], Polish spelling *Wasileńko*, son of Vasily

-er: German or Jewish; example, *Krakauer* = someone from *Krakau*, the German spelling for Kraków

-evich: Ukrainian or Russian patronymic *-евич*, usually spelled *-evich* in English, equivalent of *-ewicz* in Polish; see **-[i]ewicz** above

-ich: Belarusian, Russian, or Ukrainian patronymic *-ич* or *-ыч*, usually spelled *-ich* or *-ych* in English, equivalent of Polish *-icz*, see **-icz, -ycz** on page 41

-ishyn: Ukrainian; see **-yszyn** below

-iv, -iw: Ukrainian *-ів* (equivalent of *-ów* in Polish and *-ov* in Russian); example, *Іванів* [*Ivaniv*, spelled *Iwaniw* by Poles] = Russ. *Ivanov*, Polish *Janów*

-ke: German, but used often with Germanized names derived from Polish or Lusatian or Czech first names; example, *Raschke* is from *Raszka* or *Raszek*, short forms of *Racław* or *Radosław*[8]

-ko: Ukrainian or Russian *-ко* (but it can also be Polish); example, *Kościuszko/Kostiuszko*, from Kostia (diminutive of *Konstantyn*)

-man[n]: German or Jewish; example, *Ofman* is a Polish form of the German surname *Hoffmann*

-nyi, -nyj: Ukrainian *-ний* [*-nyi*]; example, *Піддубний* [*Piddubnyi*], "one who lived under or near an oak tree"[9]

-off: German spelling of the characteristically Slavic suffix *-ov* (Polish *-ów*); example, *Romanoff*

-ovich: Belarusian, Russian, or Ukrainian patronymic suffix, equivalent to Polish **-owicz**, q.v. on page 41

-sky, -skyj: Czech *-ský,* Russian *-ский* or Ukrainian *-ський* ; correct Polish spelling doesn't allow *y* to follow *k,* so these suffixes tend to be Czech or renderings in Roman letters of names written in Cyrillic— the form *-skyj* is especially likely to be Ukrainian; example, Ukr. *Польський [Pol's'kyi],* Russ. *Польский [Pol'skiy]* = Polish *Polski*

-stayn, -sztajn, -sztayn, -sztejn, -szteyn: German or Jewish, from German *Stein,* "stone"; example, *Zylbersztayn* = German *Silberstein*

-uk: Belarusian and Ukrainian patronymic *-ук,* e.g., *Ткачук [Tkachuk],* "weaver's son"

-ul, -ula, -ulia: can be Polish (*Rogula,* from *róg,* "corner, horn"), but can be Belarusian or even Romanian

-ych: Belarusian, Russian, or Ukrainian equivalent of Polish *-ycz,* usually spelled *-ych* in English, see **-icz, -ycz** on page 41

-yshyn: Ukrainian *–ишин [-yshyn],* spelled *-yszyn* by Poles and *-yshyn* by English-speakers, usually a metronymic (formed from mother's name); example, *Romanyszyn,* from the female name *Romanykha*[10]

A Little More on -owski *and Toponyms (Place Names)*

The suffix *-owski* (and its variant *-ewski*) is especially prominent in surnames. Sometimes it can point right back to a place of origin if you know a little about it.

First of all, let's look at the suffix *-ow-*. It is the Polish version of a common Slavic possessive. In Russian it appears as *-ов* or *–ев,* generally spelled *ov/ev* or *off/eff* in the Roman alphabet. In Ukrainian it is often *–iв,* which tends to be spelled *-iv* or *-iw* when rendered in our alphabet. In Czech it is *-ov.* Polish spells it *-ów* or *-ew* in closed syllables or at the end of a word, and *-ow-* or *-ew-* in open syllables (compare *Janów* and *Janowo*).

This suffix, by itself, does not end all that many Polish surnames—although in Russian, it is so common that any arbitrary list of Russians will be full of names such as *Romanov, Khrushchev, Gorbachev, Ulyanov,* etc. In Polish, where you see it all the time is in combination with other suffixes: *-owiak, -owicki, -owicz,* and *-owski* are especially common. In such cases, the *-ow-* or *-ew-* component can usually be rendered simply as "of (the) —," where the primary component fills in the blank. Thus *Janowicz* could be broken down as *Jan* (name of a person) + *-ow-* (of) + *-icz* (son) = "son of Jan."

A similar logic is behind *-owski/-ewski.* The suffix *-ski* is adjectival, meaning simply "of, from, connected with, related to." Thus a name such as *Kowalewski* breaks down into "of, related to, pertaining to the X of the smith *(kowal)*." The X is something obvious that doesn't need to be spelled out—

usually either "kin" or "place." So *Kowalewski* can mean just "of the kin of the smith." But in a great many cases, it was formed by adding the suffix *-ski* to a toponym (place name) such as *Kowalew* or *Kowalewo.* So *Kowalewski* = "one from Kowalew/Kowalewo" = "one from the place of the smiths."

Knowing this may clarify names that don't seem to make sense. If you had an ancestor named *Grabowski* and you look in a Polish dictionary, you see that *grab* means "the hornbeam tree." You ask yourself, "How did my ancestor manage to get himself named for a tree?" Perhaps he turned over a new leaf, or his bark was worse than his bite.

I should explain that names beginning *Grab-* can also derive from the root in the verb *grabić,* which can mean "to plunder, pillage," and also "to rake"; the noun *grabież* means "plunder, loot," while *grabie* means "rake." The hornbeam connection is what probably applies in most cases, but the other meanings could be relevant in some.

Whatever the origin of the *Grab-* part, *Grabowski* probably did not start out meaning "person of the hornbeam tree/plunder/rake," but rather "one from Grabów or Grabowo." Here's one possible scenario:

1) at some point a village started up near a grove of hornbeams, or possibly a place owned or founded by a man named Grab;
2) people naturally tended to call it *Grabowo*—or perhaps *Grabie, Grabów, Graby,* etc.—"[the place of] hornbeams" or "the place of Grab";
3) when surnames were forming, it seemed natural to call someone from that place *Grabowski,* "one from Grabów/Grabowo/Graby."

Now this is not the only way a name like *Grabowski* could get started— but it is the way such names were most likely to get started. If you have an ancestral name ending in *-owski,* try looking in the general area he came from to see if there's a matching toponym. If you find one, there's no guarantee that's the place the surname referred to, but the odds are pretty good.

Of course, nothing is allowed to be too simple. Take a look in an atlas for places with names beginning in *Grabow-,* and you'll find dozens of places called *Grabowo, Grabów, Grabowa, Grabowiec, Grabówka,* and so on. Well, when the *-ski* suffix is added to a name, any final vowels on that name (and, in older Polish, other suffixes such as *-iec, -ka,* etc.) tend to drop off. So the sad truth is, *Grabowski* could refer to any of those places. A place named *Graby* could also yield the surname *Grabowski,* because *Graby* is a nominative plural form (meaning literally "the hornbeams"); the genitive plural form is *Grabów* ("of the hornbeams"), just add *-ski* and there you are. So tracing an *-owski* name back to the right toponym isn't necessarily a walk in the park.

Also, if you think about it, you'll realize that with so many places around that could yield the surname *Grabowski,* it's a certainty that surname could arise arose in different places at different times. So all the Grabowskis in Poland aren't going to be related! This is why analyzing a family's surname is often little help in tracing the family back to its ancestral home; there are just too many places in Poland the surname could refer to.

Still, I have found that practically speaking, the *-owski* suffix can often be helpful, especially if you have already acquired enough data to know the general area your ancestor came from. We'll look at more on place names in Chapters Five and Six.

How Suffixes Combine

Many times the union of Polish suffix to root is easy and uncomplicated: *Marcin* + *-ek* → *Marcinek*. Often a final vowel or consonant will simply drop off: *kramarz* + *-ski* → *Kramarski; Warszawa* + *-ski* → *Warszawski*.

Occasionally, however, the addition of the suffix causes changes that are obvious to Poles but a little puzzling to non-Poles. Surnames derived from place names are a major source of confusion in this regard, but the mechanics of suffix combination are not too horribly difficult. Here are a few pointers.

> **-ek**: In most cases the *-e-* is a "filler vowel," added to facilitate pronunciation. When a suffix is added, the *-e-* tends to drop out. So *Klimek* + *-owski* → *Klimk-* + *-owski* → *Klimkowski*. When you see a surname with a *-k-* followed by a suffix, remember that cutting off the suffix (to get at the root form) may restore that *-e-* before the *k*.
>
> *vowels* + **-ski**: The *-ski* ending tends to soften any consonants that come before it. When the *-ski* is added to a noun ending in a vowel, the vowel usually tries to drop out. Consider *Wkra,* the name of a river; *Wkra* + *-ski* → *Wkr-*+ *-ski* — but even Poles can't pronounce *Wkrski.* (Although a Czech wouldn't blink; the Czech motto is "We don't need no stinking vowels!") To facilitate pronunciation, Poles insert an *-eń-* and soften the final *r-* of the root to *-rz-*: *Wkr-* + *-en-* + *-ski* → *Wkrz-* + *-eński* → *Wkrzeński.* (Personally, I don't see that *Wkrzeński* is all that much easier to say than *Wkrski*; but then, no one asked for my opinion.) Also common is the interposition of *-iń-* or *-yń-*: *Zegrze* + *-ski* → *Zegrzyński.*
>
> **-n-** + **-ski**: Sometimes *-iński* points back to a name ending in *-no. Brzezieński* or *Brzeziński* is often derived from *Brzeźno* + *-ski, Dębieński* or *Dębiński* from *Dębno,* etc.

While I don't want to confuse the issue too much, I probably should warn you that surnames formed from toponyms can be pretty frustrating. As I mentioned earlier, they tend to come from older forms of the toponym and may drop suffixes before adding *-ski, -cki* or *-zki.* Also, most Polish surnames originated three to four centuries ago, often much earlier. Since then, both the surnames and place names they were formed from may have changed. I remember going nuts before I figured out that the adjective *wizki* comes from the name of the town *Wizna*. Even more confusing is *Nowosądecki*, from *Nowy Sącz* — *Sącz* is a modern form of the name, which used to be *Sądek*.[11] There's no reliable way to formulate rules for such cases; you just have to be on your guard.

Suffixes And A Sample Surname

At this point you may profit from an illustration of how surnames can be generated from one Polish root by adding suffixes. Let's look at *dąb*, "oak," the root of which often becomes *dęb-* when suffixes are added. Based on information from Kazimierz Rymut's book *Nazwiska Polaków*,[12] this illustration follows his methodology by adding one suffix at a time to the root and then showing how further names for each suffix can be generated by adding still more suffixes.

Dąb	**Dębiec** < *dębiec,* young oak
Dąbal → **Dąbalewski**	**Dębin**
Dąbala	**Dębina** < *dębina,* oak wood
Dąbczak < *dąbczak,* oakling	**Dębnek**
Dąbek < *dąbek,* small oak	**Dębniak**
Dąbich	**Dębniczyc**
Dąbik	**Dębnik**
Dąbka → **Dąbkiewicz** and	**Dębny** < *dębny,* oaken
Dąbkowicz	**Dęboń** → **Dębończyk**
Dębak	**Dębor** → **Dęborczyk**
Dębczak	**Dębosz**
Dębczyk	**Dębow** → **Dębowczyk,**
Dębek	**Dębowiak, Dębowic**
Dębianka	**Dębowiec** < *dębowiec,* oak cane
Dębiarz < *dębiarz,* tanner	or stick
Dębicz	**Dębowy** < *dębowy,* oaken

This is a fairly impressive list, but it doesn't exhaust the possibilities. One extremely important suffix is missing: *-ski*. The first edition of Rymut's book did not list a number of *-ski* surnames, for several good reasons. Many of the names shown in this list spawned *-ski* surnames—we might as well include them, too.

Furthermore, Rymut listed separately *dąbrowa*, "oak grove," which yields such names as *Dąbrowicz, Dąbrowo, Dąbrówka*, etc. Since ultimately *dąbrowa* comes from *dąb*, perhaps we may take the liberty of adding them to our list.

In addition, Rymut deals primarily with "correct" spellings (for perfectly good reasons we need not go into here). If we also include non-standard spelling variations—with the *-ǫ-* often appearing as *-a-*, *-am-*, or *-om-*, and the *-ę-* as *-e-* or *-em-* — we can add many more names to the list. Here is a combined list of the surnames given above plus the alternate spellings (signified with the symbol ×), forms from *Dąbrowa,* and *-ski* names.

Dąbal

Dąbała

Dąbalewski

Dąbczak

Dębinski

Dąbek

Dębkowski

Dębny

Dębnek

Dębniak

Dąbich

Dębniczyc

Dąbik

Dębnik

Dąbka

Dęboń → Dębończyk

Dąbkiewicz

Dębor → Dęborczyk

Dąbkowicz

Dębosz

Dąbkowski < Dąbek (or Dąbka)
+ *-owski*

×Dabkowski → Dąbkowski

Dębowiec

Dąbrowiak < Dąbrowa + *-iak*

Dębow → Dębowczyk and Dębo-
wiak and Dębowic

Debowski → Dębowski

Dębowy

×Dabrowiak → Dąbrowiak

Dąbrzalski < Dąbr + *-alski*

×Dabulewicz from Dąbul[a] +
-ewicz

×Dambek → Dąbek

Dębak

×Debciński from Dąbiec (or Dębiec)+ *-iń-* + *-ski*

Dębczak

Dębczyk

Dębczyński

Dębek

Dębianka

Dębiarz

Dębicz

Dębiec

×Debiec → Dębiec

Dębin

Dębina

×Debski → Dębski

×Dembanowicz from Dęb + *-an-* +
-owicz

×Dembczyński → Dębczyński

×Dembek → Dąbek

×Dembiński → Dębiński

×Dembkowski → Dębkowski

×Dembowski → Dębowski

×Dembski from Dąb + *-ski*

×Dempkowski → Dembkowski

×Dombeck → Dąbek

×Dombek → Dąbek

×Dombkowicz → Dąbkowicz

×Dombkowski → Dąbkowski

×Dombrowiak → Dąbrowiak

×Dombrowoski → Dąbrowski

×Dombrowski → Dąbrowski

×Dombrzalski → Dąbrzalski

Even this list does not exhaust all possible surnames from the root *dąb.* But it gives most of the common ones, and it also gives you an idea how productive the combinations of roots and suffixes can be. All these surnames come from one word. Try doing that with an English word!

Of course, not all the surnames listed above necessarily derived straight from the noun *dąb*. A great many come through some intermediate form, especially from place names. There are many, many towns and villages in Poland called *Dęby, Dębno, Dąbrowa, Dąbrówka,* etc. Such places presumably took their names from a local concentration of oaks and oak groves; so a surname beginning *Dąb-* or *Dęb-* undoubtedly had a connection to oaks somewhere along the line. A family named *Dębiński* probably got that name because an ancestor came from a place called *Dębno,* and it in turn presumably got that name because it was near some oaks. As with the *-owski/-ewski* names I discussed earlier, names ending in *-iński/-yński* tend to come from toponyms, and those toponyms generally had a reason for being named what they were. But if you're a Dembinski, you actually find that one *Dębno* your ancestors came from, and you go over to Poland to visit it, don't be surprised if there's not an oak in sight. Things can change a lot over the course of several centuries!

Building a Better Surname

In my idle moments I've sometimes wondered if you couldn't take all the Polish roots—from verbs, adjectives, nouns, names, etc.—and all the Polish suffixes, put them into a computer, write a program, and generate every possible Polish surname? I suppose the mere fact this could occur to me means I have too much free time and ought to get a life.

Anyway, in theory, this is possible. In practice, it would be an enormous undertaking, and not just because there are so many possible roots and suffixes. A complicating factor is the Poles' tendency to add suffixes onto suffixes. From *Jan,* for instance, we don't see just *Janczak, Janek, Janik, Janisz, Janusz,* we see *Janczakowski, Jankowicz, Janikowski, Janiszczak, Januszek, Januszkiewicz, Januszewski,* and on and on. Take a look at how a few of these names were formed by compounding suffixes:

> *Janczakowski < Jan + -czak- + -ow- + ski*
> *Jankowicz < Jan + -(e)k + -ow- + -icz*
> *Januszkiewicz < Jan + -usz- + -(e)k- + -(i)ew- + -icz* [13]

These names illustrate a fundamental difference between the naming patterns of Poles and, for instance, Germans. Many surnames of Germanic origin started out as compounds of two nouns (e.g., *Fuhrmann < Fuhr + mann*), or of a noun and one or at most two suffixes (*Henseler <* the name *Hans +* the diminutive suffix *-el +* the possessive suffix *-er =* "the son of little Hans"). Even in a nightmare, a German would never dream of tacking four suffixes onto a name root. But Poles do that in their sleep! So a computer program designed to generate Polish surnames would have to be told not only to compound suffixes on suffixes, but also when to stop—not a task I'd care to undertake.

Besides, people are funny critters, and there's often no real rhyme or reason as to which of the myriad possible names Poles actually use. Certain suffixes and suffix compounds are almost obligatory: practically any root you select will have generated surnames ending in *-ak, -ek, -ka, -kiewicz* or *-kowicz*, and *-ski*. Certain others will show up if a particular root was really productive, including: *-ała, -alski, -arz, -awa, -awski, -czak, -czek, -czok, -czyk, -ek, -el, -icz, -iec, -ecki, -ik, -in, -inowski, -iński, -kowiak, -kowski, -niak, -nik, -ny, -och, -oń, -osz, -ow, -owiak, -owicz, -owicki, -owik, -owski, -ski, -uch, -ul, -ur, -urski*. Take a look at some of those names in Volume II that come from first names (e.g., *Jan, Piotr, Szczepan*) with special attention to the numbers from the *Słownik nazwisk* indicating how common they are among modern Poles. You will see that certain combinations of suffixes are more likely than others to generate popular surnames.

But the numbers also hold some surprises. Under the root *kid-*, from a verb meaning "to drip, dribble" or "to throw, fling," I was amazed to note that as of 2002, there were 1,696 Poles named *Kida,* 347 named *Kidacka/Kidacki,* 111 named *Kidaj*, 90 named *Kidała,* 675 named *Kidawa,* 117 named *Kidawska/Kidawski,* 160 named *Kidyba,* 114 named *Kidziak,* 145 named *Kidzińska/ Kidziński*—and 1,061 named *Kidoń!* Why so many Kidońs? Where are all the Kidowskis? That name doesn't even appear! Not one Kidek or Kidkiewicz, but 160 Kidybas!? This is not at all what experience with Polish surnames would have led me to expect, and I still don't know how to account for it.[14]

One more example: I looked at the surnames under the root *stolarz,* "joiner, carpenter," that mean specifically "joiner's son." How do we explain 518 Poles named *Stolarczuk,* 8,496 named *Stolarczyk,* and only 146 named *Stolarzewicz*? They all mean the same thing; why would the name with *-czyk* be so much more popular than the one with *-ewicz*?

I can't answer these questions. Only someone with extensive knowledge of Polish linguistics and onomastics, doing detailed research in the areas where these names are concentrated, would be able to come up with a reliable answer. But the basic moral of the story is clear: you never know what people are going to do! A mechanical approach to surnames works fine when you're dealing with the mundane and ordinary, but it fails you whenever you encounter something extraordinary.

But enough of that. I think I've shown you that Polish has more than a sufficiency of suffixes. Does English have these rich resources for generating names from a single root? No. That's why English-speaking people have a lot of trouble getting a grip on suffixes. And that's why I believe this chapter is a necessary prelude to the discussion of surnames themselves.

Endnotes

[1] Kazimierz Rymut, editor, *Dictionary of Surnames in Current Use in Poland at the Beginning of the 21st Century,* Polish Academy of Sciences, Po-

lish Language Institute, and the Polish Genealogical Society of America®, Kraków-Chicago, 2002, pp. 8,523–8,528.

[2] Kazimierz Rymut, *Nazwiska Polaków,* Wydawnictwo Naukowe DWN, Kraków, 2001, Vol. I, p. XLIV.

[3] Ibid., pp. XLV-LII.

[4] Jan Stanisław Bystroń, *Nazwiska Polskie*, 2nd ed., Lwów-Warsawa, Książnica-Atlas, 1936, especially pp. 7–11.

[5] Rymut, *Nazwiska Polaków,* Vol. I, especially pp. XXXIV–LXXV.

[6] Tad Szulc, "Poland: The Hope That Never Dies," *National Geographic*, January 1988, p. 119.

[7] Hans Bahlow, *Deutsches Namenlexikon*, page 409.

[8] Ibid., p. 407.

[9] Jeff Picknicki, "The Origin and Meaning of Ukrainian Surnames," *Polish Genealogical Society Newsletter*, Spring, 1990, page 6.

[10] Ibid., page 6.

[11] Kazimierz Rymut, *Nazwy miast Polski,* 2nd edition, Zakład Narodowy im. Ossolińskich — Wydawnictwo, Wrocław, 1987, p. 228.

[12] Rymut, *Nazwiska Polaków,* Vol. I, p. 128–129.

[13] Ibid., p. 137.

[14] All numbers on surname frequency are from Rymut, *Dictionary of Surnames in Current Use.*

Chapter Five

"...And the First [Names] Shall Be Last..."

We come now to one of the most prolific sources of Polish last names: Polish first names.

This is not surprising. Even English, which seems to be so different from Polish (but does, after all, come ultimately from the same language, Proto-Indo-European), features many surnames derived from personal names: Davidson, Edwards, Christopher, Roberts, the list is a long one.

Have you ever sat with relatives as they talk family or look over old photo albums? Notice how often you hear statements such as "That's Leon, Frank's son" or "Myra's boy joined the Army when the war started." In a relatively small, intimate circle, such an identification is often all that's needed; and when Polish surnames were being established, for a long time they arose in relatively intimate circles—a village or a parish of at most a few hundred souls. So people could easily get used to referring to "Janek's boy," *Jankowicz,* especially if Janek and his wife were good Catholics and there were too many "Janek's boys" to keep track of all their first names! And an expression used that way was only a short step away from becoming a surname.

Names In and Out of Disguise

Many of these names are quite easy to recognize, once you've become familiar with Polish first names. Tracing any surname beginning with, say, *Jan-* or *Piotr-* or *Ignat-* (Ignacy) back to the progenitor's given name is not too tough. And there are a lot of Polish surnames like that.

Other surnames derived from first names are harder to make out because the first name is "in disguise," so to speak. Polish has its dialects and variations, and thus many names have more than one form in common usage: *Andrzej* (Andrew) can also appear as *Jędrzej,* Latin *Stephanus* yielded both *Stefan* and *Szczepan,* and so forth.

What's more, the old Polish-Lithuanian Commonwealth included today's Poland, Lithuania, and much of Belarus and Ukraine. Many names we think of as "Polish" actually started there, and their forms reflect their linguistic background. The Polish name *Jan,* for instance, is equivalent to the Ukrainian name *Іван* [*Iván,* spelled *Iwan* by Poles], so that there one sees Ukrainian names beginning with *Iwan-* or *Wan-* or *Wasz-,* as Poles would spell them, that are functional equivalents of Polish names with *Jan-* and *Jasz-.* Names often change slightly in passing from one language to another, as the speakers of each language, without even being aware of it, modify them to forms that "sound right." The illustration on page 52 demonstrates that those changes, each minor in itself, can add up to some pretty big changes over the course of time.

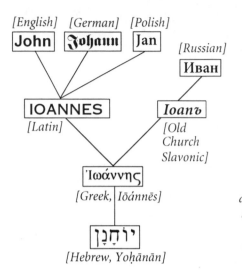

[English] [German] [Polish]

John | **Johann** | **Jan**

[Russian]

Иван

IOANNES
[Latin]

Ioanъ
[Old Church Slavonic]

Ἰωάννης
[Greek, Iōánnēs]

יוֹחָנָן
[Hebrew, Yohānān]

The name "John" began as Hebrew יוֹחָנָן, Yōḥānān. Greek and Latin had no good way to duplicate the guttural h-sound of the letter ח and ignored it, producing Latin Ioannes. That form came into Czech and then Polish, further simplifying to "Jan." The German form, Johann, retained a sound somewhat like the original ח; the spelling "John" suggests English once did so, too, but later dropped it. Meanwhile, from Greek the name came into Eastern Slavic languages with a v-sound instead of the h, to give Russian Иван and Ukrainian Iван.

The Polish scholar Tadeusz Korzon wrote a book on the hero Tadeusz Kościuszko that happens to shed light on several pertinent points. Consider the name *Kościuszko.* The *-uszko* suffix is immediately recognizable as a diminutive ("little so-and-so") typical of East Slavic surnames, common in the eastern territories of the Polish-Lithuanian Commonwealth. But the key is, what does *kości-* mean? Just from a linguistic point of view, it would be entirely reasonable to suppose it comes from the same root as the Polish noun *kość,* "bone"—and in fact some Polish surnames do come from that root. So we triumphantly declare that *Kościuszko* meant "Little Bony."

Not so fast! Korzon traced the Kościuszko family's origins and determined that the first founder of the name was one Konstanty, son of Teodor, as Poles would give his name. A judge and official in the *Камянец* [*Kamianéts*] region of what is now southwestern Belarus, he was mentioned in 1509 and 1546 documents as "pan Kostiuszko Federowicz." [1] This is a Polish spelling of his name in Ruthenian, the East Slavic language from which Belarusian and Ukrainian later developed; in English, we would spell the name *Kosti-ushko Federovich.* His formal given name was *Kostantyn,* derived from the same Greek source as our *Constantine.* But in everyday life at Ruthenian noble courts, the great lords usually called favorite courtiers bearing that name by the diminutives *Kostia* or *Kostiushko,* "little Constantine" (Korzon, p. 3). Polish orthographics turned the latter into *Kościuszko.* That's where the name really came from. So much for thinking the great Tadeusz Kościuszko's ancestor was called "Little Bony"!

And yet, judging just by the roots that survive in modern Polish, "Little Bony" was a logical surmise. Korzon's research shows how vital research into family history may be in establishing the **correct** derivation of a surname! It also tells us that when dealing with Polish surnames, we need to keep in mind the given names used by their neighbors to the east.

Another point Korzon discusses is the question of what languages the family used. He mentions that a later ancestor of Kościuszko went by the name of "Hrehory Kostiushko" (p. 10), a Ruthenian name equivalent to Polish "Grzegorz Kościuszko." Thus Polish *Grzegorz* = Ruthenian *Hrehory* (compare modern Ukrainian *Григорий* [*Hryhóryi*] and *Грыгір* [*Hrýhir*]). These forms demonstrate several Ruthenian tendencies: unlike Poles, Ruthenians preferred simple *r* to *rz, i* to *o,* and *h* to *g* (at least the character г is usually rendered as *h* in the Roman alphabet, when appearing in Ruthenian names; we will discuss this more in Chapter Nine). Depending on context, therefore, the same man might be named *Grzegorz* in Polish documents and *Hrehory, Hrehir,* or even the diminutive *Hurko* in Ruthenian records.

The interesting thing is that Hrehory went by a Ruthenian name and was a faithful follower of the Orthodox Church, not the Roman Catholic; but he raised his children to speak Polish because the ruling culture in the region at the time was Polish. This tells any descendant of "Poles" whose ancestors lived in Belarus and Ukraine that research will at some point probably require familiarity with Ruthenian names as well as Polish. In practice, that means we will need to pay attention to the names of saints popular among adherents of the Orthodox or Greek Catholic Churches, to which most people in Ukraine and Belarus belonged, not just the Roman Catholic Church, which held sway in Poland.

From Person to Place to Person

One last point from Korzon's book bears mentioning. He describes the division of the Kościuszkos' original estate over the years, as one large section of their ancestral land was divided between sons named Iwan and Fedor. These parcels came to be known by the Polish names *Iwanowszczyzna* and *Fedorowszczyzna,* which mean basically "land that belongs to Iwan" and "land that belongs to Fedor" (p. 10). This demonstrates a process seen in Poland as well as in Belarus and Ukraine, the formation of place names from nobles' personal names; and once those place names were established, there's no question that they could impact on surnames of peasants from those areas. A peasant who worked on land in a section called *Janowo* (because it was owned by a Jan) might well come to bear the surname *Janowski*—as if there weren't already enough ways that name might get started!

In Polish, the suffixes used frequently to indicate possession are *-ow-/-ew-* and *-in-/-yn-*. It is no coincidence that these are precisely the suffixes that show up frequently in place names derived from personal names, and that they also are the ones most common in Polish surnames, especially with *-ski* tacked on. True, not all *-owski* and *-iński* surnames were derived from places named for people—but a fair number of them were. (See Chapter Four.)

If you think about it, we do the same thing in English. Consider the child who asks her parents "Can I spend the night at Jenny's?" There the possessive "Jenny's" is being used to designate a place. Or look at the name of Hoffman Estates in Illinois—presumably this place name originated from some connection with an illustrious Hoffman (is there any other kind?). If our ancestors hadn't already had surnames before they came to this country, we might see in America surnames such as "Dallasite" for natives of Dallas (would natives of Paris, Texas, be "Parisites"?).

By the way, these place names derived from personal names were often used only by the locals; many probably never appeared on any map. One of the complications of tracing Polish surnames is dealing with names that were in common usage among the peasants but were never official, and thus may be very hard to find in gazetteers. We will look at this in more detail in the chapter on surnames derived from place name or toponyms.

Name Elements

If you look at the index of name roots in Volume II, you'll see again and again reference to "name elements." They are extremely common in Polish name formation, but they require a bit of explanation. Here's how it works:

Jan → *Ja- [n]* → *Ja-* + a suffix, e.g., *-ch* or *-sz* → *Jach, Jasz*

Poles took a name like *Jan,* extracted the first consonant and vowel *Ja-,* then added suffixes to give name elements such as *Jach-, Jasz-,* etc., which in turn became the basis of surnames. Chapter Four studies the suffixes most often used in creating name elements that could serve as the roots of surnames.

Often someone will ask me, "What the heck does *Jasz* mean?" I answer, "It's a form of *Jan.*" "Oh. But what does *Jach* mean?" "It's also a form of *Jan.*" At this point most people walk off in disgust, determined to go find someone who knows what he's talking about.

Still, the concept of name elements is not so odd. Consider the nickname "Ted." A foreigner might ask, "What on earth does 'Ted' mean?" A person well-versed in the English language, but not so well-versed in onomastics, might step forward and confidently answer, "The word 'ted' is a verb meaning to spread or strew newly-mown grass for drying." (Addicts of crossword puzzles are nodding their heads; they've seen this word before!) In fact, that definition of "ted" is right, but in this context the "expert" is dead wrong: "Ted" used as a name has nothing to do with strewing grass, it's a short form of the standard given name "Theodore."

Now "Theodore" means "gift of God" (from the Greek Θεόδωρος, *Theódōros*), but can you really say "Ted," used as a name, means anything? No, it's just a name element derived from a longer name that did originally have a definable meaning. In the same way, *Jach-* and *Jasz-* and *Stas-* and a jillion other Polish name elements don't really mean much in themselves;

they began as nicknames or shortened forms of longer names that did mean something, but as time went on the elements took on a life of their own. The Poles started tacking on endings to give the names some variety and color. An English-speaker with this Polish trait would never be content with "Ted" and "Teddy," he'd have to make "Teddish" and "Tedly" and "Tedwise" and "Tedman" and Lord knows what else. You didn't just have a *Stanisław,* you had a *Stan* and a *Staś* and a *Stach,* and so on, and they in turn gave rise to a *Stanisz* and a *Staśko* and a *Stachura* and so on. Then, once these varied forms were fairly well established, they often came to be frozen in place as surnames, perhaps after the addition of even more suffixes: *Staniszewski, Staśkiewicz, Stachurowski,* etc. What started as one given name in the 1300s could easily end up spawning a hundred surnames by the 1700s, when surname adoption had spread throughout all levels of Polish society.

So you see, when you ask "What does this name mean?" and I answer "It doesn't really mean much of anything," I'm not being stupid or uncooperative. English does not have the naming resources to reproduce the abundance and variety of Polish suffixes, so there often is only one way to render in English the multitude of surnames that could come from a single Polish root: *Staniszewski* and *Staśkiewicz* and *Stachurowski* may all have to be reduced in English to "Stan's kin" or "one from Stan's place."

The Pagans Live On!

Another factor in Polish naming must also be understood here. Scholars argue about when the original mother Slavic tongue, Proto-Slavic, began to split into recognizably different languages such as Polish, Czech, Russian, and so on. But they agree that the split occurred quite some time after Italian and Spanish, for instance, had become distinguishable languages, rather than just varieties of Latin. This comparatively recent separation helps explain why the Slavic languages retain a surprising degree of similarity to each other. It also explains why Polish retained a large store of name roots common to most of the Slavic languages, so that Polish and Czech, for instance, have many similar names. These old Slavic names are important to surnames.

The original pagan Slavs retained the Indo-European custom of forming many names by combining two separate roots, as a way to give children favorably prophetic names. An ancient German might hope to help a child live in peace *(fridu)* through victory *(sigu)* by naming him *Sigifrith* (modern form *Siegfried*). Similarly, Poles would combine, for instance, the root for "defend," *broni-,* with the root for "glory, fame," *sław-,* to give the name *Bronisław,* "renowned defender." The same tendency that perplexes students of English literature with names like *Beowulf* and *Hrothgar* also gave Poles hundreds of so-called **dithematic** names from two roots: *Wojciech, Władysław, Bogumił, Bolesław, Dalibor, Litomir, Mirosław, Sławomir, Borzysław, Sławobor,* the list goes on and on. It was literally a case of "mix and match."

The scholar Jan Stanisław Bystroń traced the path these old Slavic names followed to become surnames as well, and that path was usually by way of name elements. For example, *Bolesław → Bolko* and *Bolesz; Chwalisław* or *Falisław → Chwalisz, Walisz, Faliszek; Dobiesław → Dobek; Domamir → Domasz; Częstomir → Częstoch; Jarosław → Jarosz; Przybysław → Przybek; Zdziesław → Zdziech.* Then from those names would come patronymics, e.g., *Chwalewicz, Falkiewicz, Jaroszewicz, Bohuszewicz, Zdzichowicz.* But usually only *szlachta* took surnames based on old Slavic surnames; by the time the lower classes were taking surnames, Christianity had already suppressed the old pagan Slav names.[2]

The Church suppressed the pagan names by emphasizing the value of christening children with saints' names. In his patron saint the child had a worthy role model to emulate, as well as an advocate who might intercede with God for him (in these more secular days we have to be content with lawyers). So the custom of naming children for saints caught on, to the point that traditionally (though less so, these days), Poles have celebrated name-days rather than birthdays. One result, however, was the narrowing of the list of potential names from which parents could choose, down from the pagans' thousands and thousands of "mix-and-match" root combinations to the Church's few hundred set names. Another result was the introduction of Biblical names—of Latin, Greek, and Hebrew origin—into Polish life.

The old pagan names were not completely eclipsed, however, and in fact some received proper sanction because they were borne by Poles who were canonized: St. Stanisław Kostka, for instance, bears one of those old pagan first names (from *stań-*, become, + *sław-*, fame, glory). So we still see Poles baptized today as *Kazimierz, Stanisław, Bolesław, Władysław, Mieczysław, Włodzimierz,* and so on. This rose from an attempt by devout Poles to hold onto some elements of their past, even though it was a pagan past!

Even more of those old names found a foothold in Christian society by the back door, as name elements. As mentioned earlier, the names had been around long enough that parts of them had been chopped off and had suffixes added, so alongside *Bogusław* and *Bolesław* we have *Bosz-*, from *Wojciech* and *Wolimir* we have *Woch-*, and so on. The inevitable suffixes came swarming, and soon surnames such as *Boszkiewicz* and *Boszko* and *Wochelski* and *Wochniak* were in the books. The pagan names live on, albeit in disguise.

A Sampling of Polish First Names and Name Elements

You may benefit from a chance to look at some common first names and name elements, just to get a feel for how it all works. The surname root index in Volume II provides a lot of instructive material, but so many different kinds of surnames are given there that it's hard to concentrate on any one category. So I've excerpted some (but by no means all!) of the roots derived from given names and presented them in a different form which will, I hope, make the phenomenon easier to grasp. If you'd like to get a notion just how many surnames can be generated by adding suffixes to the root forms of popular given names, just take a look at then entries for *Jan* and *Szymon* in Volume II!

Two kinds of surname sources are given here. Common first names are given complete (e.g., *Jakób*), whereas name elements or Slavic roots are hyphenated (*Broch-, Bor-*). The division is rather oversimplified in some cases —*Kub-* names are given under *Jakób,* although one could make an argument for presenting *Kub-* as a name element in its own right—but I think the format illustrates the point in a way you can understand without having to first get a Ph.D. in Slavic linguistics.

I should point out that this list deals with surnames formed from first names or name elements, but that overlapping of categories is plentiful. In other words, surnames starting in *Mat-* may have been formed from the first name *Mateusz,* but they may also have derived from the noun *matka,* mother, or the verb root seen in *matać,* to swindle—and it is often impossible to say for sure which derivation applies in a given family's case. The surnames listed under each name or element are some I think likely to have derived from that source, but you should keep an open mind on alternatives.

Here are examples of how to look at these entries. An example of a given name and some of the surnames that derive directly from it is **Jakub:**

> **Jakub** (given name = English *Jacob*): Jakóbczak, Jakóbczyk, Jakóbik, Jakowczyk, Jakubas, Jakubaszek, Jakubczyk, Jakubek, Jakubiak, Jakubiec, Jakubik, Jakubiszyn, Jakubowicz; Kuba, Kubala, Kubat, Kubera, Kubiak, Kubica, Kubicz, Kubik, Kubiszyn

When an English equivalent of a name exists but may not be obvious, I've given it in parentheses. Next come a few examples of surnames formed by adding suffixes. Only a very few derived surnames are given because it seems pointless to repeat here the more extensive lists in Volume II. A semi-colon separates names directly from *Jakób* and those from its derived form, *Kub.*

Now for a sample name element:

> **Bron-** (< ancient dithematic names such as *Bronisław, Bronisąd* with the root *bron-,* "defend, weapon"): Broniarczyk, Broniec, Bronisz, Bronk

The information in parentheses gives a brief note on the origin or meaning of the name element or root; in this case, **Bron-** derives from the first part of names such as *Bronisław* and *Bronisąd,* with no suffix added. A sampling of relevant surnames follows.[3]

*　　　　*　　　　*

Abraham: Abram, Abramczyk, Abramowicz, Abramski

Adam: Adamczak; Adaś, Adaszkiewicz; Hadam, Hadamik, Hadaś

Adrian: Adryan, Adryjanek, Adrych, Andryjan, Hadrian

Agata (= English *Agatha*): Agaciński, Agacki, Jagaciak

Albin (first name *Albin,* from Latin *albus,* white): Albiniak, Albiński

Albrecht (= English *Albert*): Albert, Olbert, Olbrych, Olbryk, Olbryś

Aleksander (= English *Alexander*), Aleksandrowicz, Jaksender, Lachendro, Laksender, Olak, Olczak Olech, Oleś, Oleszczuk, Olko, Sander

Aleksy (= English *Alexis*): Aleksiejuk, Holeksa, Laksa, Leks, Oleksiak, Oleksza

Ambroży (= English *Ambrose*): Ambrożewicz, Amrozik, Zbrożek, Zimroz

Andrzej (= English *Andrew*): Anders, Andruchów, Andrusiewicz, Andrysiak, Andrzejczak, Andrzejuk

Antoni (= English *Anthony*): Antas, Antczak, Antkowiak, Antonczyk, Antosik, Antosz, Antowski, Jantas, Jantos

Arnold, Arndt: Arend, Arendt, Arndt

Aron (= English *Aaron*): Aranowski, Aronowicz, Aranowski

Atanazy (= Latin *Athanasius*): Apanasewicz, Panas, Tanaś

August, Augustyn: Augustin, Augustyniak, Augustynowicz, Jaguścik

Baltazar: Balcarczyk, Balcerak, Balcerek, Balcerkiewicz, Balcerzak

Bartłomiej (= English *Bartholomew*): Bartłomiejczyk, Bartłomowicz

Basz- (*Ba-* < *Sebastian* or *Bartłomiej,* among others + suffix *-sz*): Baśkiewicz, Baszczyński, Baszkiewicz

Bazyli (= English *Basil*): Bazela, Bazydło, Bazyliński

Benedykt (= English *Benedict*): 1. *Bien-* (can also come < *Beniamin*)*:* Benisz, Bień, Bienek, Bienias, Bieniek, Bieńko; 2. *Bin-* (can also come < *Beniamin*) Bińczyk, Binek, Biniak, Biniek, Binko; 3. Bandyk

Bernhard (= English *Bernard*): Behrendt, Berendt, Bernaciak, Bernaś, Bernat, Berndt, Biernacik, Biernath

Błażej (= English *Blase* or *Blaise*) — 1. (element *Bła-* as < *Błażej* + suffix *-ch*): Błachut, Błahut, 2. *Blaschke* (German): Blaschke; 3. *Błasz-:* Błaś, Błaszczyk, Błaszkiewicz, Błaszko, Błaszyk; 4. *Błaż-:* Błażejczyk, Błażek, Błażewicz, Błaźniak, Błażyca

Błoch- (element *Bło-* < *Błażej, Błogota* + suffix *-ch*): Bloch, Błochowiak

Boch- (element *Bo-* as < *Bogusław* + *-ch*): Bochaczyk, Bochan, Bochra

Bog- (< ancient Slavic given names such as *Boguchwał, Bogusław* with the root *bog-,* "god"): Bogdał, Bogdanowicz, Bogumił; Bożek, Bożych

Bol- (< ancient names such as *Bolesław* with the root **bol'e,* "more, better," or, less often, < *ból, "*pain"): Bolek, Bolesta, Boligłowa

Bor- (< dithematic names, e.g., *Borzysław, Bolebor* with the root *bor-,* "fight," but also sometimes < *bór,* "forest"): Borek, Bork, Borowicz, Boruta, Borzyczka, Borzych, Borzym

Brat- (< root *brat,* "brother," in names such as *Bratumił*): Bracichowicz, Bratek, Bratko, Bratuś)

Bron- (< ancient dithematic names such as *Bronisław, Bronisąd* with the root *bron-,* "defend, weapon"): Broniarczyk, Broniec, Bronisz, Bronk

Brykcy (< Latin name *Brictius*): Brychcy, Brzykcy, Brzyszcz

Bud- (< dithematic names with the root *bud-,* originally meaning "to waken," or < *buda,* "shed, stall"): Budzeń, Budzik, Budzisz, Budzyn, Budzyń

Bus- (element *Bu-* from given names such as *Budzisław* + suffix -*s* or -*sz*): Buś, Buśko, Busz, Buszta

Choma (< *Khoma,* East Slavic form of *Thomas*): Chomicz, Chomiuk, Homa

Chwal- (dithematic names with the root *chwal-,* "praise")> Chwała, Chwalisz, Fałek, Faliszek, Kwolek

Chwed- (< East Slavic forms of *Theodore*): Chwedczuk, Chwedoruk

Cibor (< ancient dithematic names with roots *czci-,* "worship, revere" + *bor-,* "battle"): Ciborek, Ścibior, Ściebura

Ciech- (ancient dithematic names with the root *ciech-,* "joy, consolation"): Ciechanowicz, Ciechna, Ciechoński

Ciesz- (ancient dithematic names with the root *ciesz-,* "joy"): Cięszczyk, Cieszko

Cyprian (given name *Cyprian*): Cupriak, Cupryjak, Cupryś, Kaproń, Kupracz, Kuprewicz, Kupryjaniuk

Cyryl (= English *Cyril*): Ciuryło, Curyło, Curzydło, Kiryluk, Kuryło

Czach- (< element *Cza-* as < dithematic names *Czabor, Czasław* + suffix -*ch*): Cachro, Czachara, Czachor, Czachura

Czesz- (< element *Cze-* from dithematic names such as *Czesław* + suffix -*sz*): Czeszak, Czeszejko, Czeszyk

Dacz- (< element *Da-* from names such as *Daniel* + suffix -*cz*): Dacz, Daczkowski, Daczyszyn

Dak- (< element *Da-* from names such as *Daniel* + suffix -*k*): Dakiniewicz, Dakowicz

Dal- (< element *Dal-* from root *dal-,* "far, distant"): Dałek, Dalkiewicz

Dam- (< element *Dam-* from names such as *Adam, Damazy, Damian*): Damasiewicz, Damek, Damętka

Damian (< given name *Damian*): Demian, Demianiuk, Doman, Domian, Dumana, Dziemian, Dziemiński

Dan- (< names such as *Bogdan* or *Daniel*): Dańczak, Danecki, Danek, Daniec, Danikowski, Danisz, Dankiewicz, Dańko

Daniel (<given name *Daniel*): Danielak, Danielczak, Danielewicz, Danilczuk, Daniłowicz

Das- (element *Da-* from names such as *Daniel, Dawid* + suffix -*s*): Dasiewicz, Daśko, Daszek, Daszkiewicz, Daszuta

Dawid (< given name = English *David*): Dawicki, Dawidczyk, Dawidowicz

Dem- (< element *Dem-* from names such as *Demitr, Demian,* and *Nikodem*): Demczuk, Demko, Demucha

Demid- (< given name *Demid*, mainly Orthodox): Demidowicz, Dziemidowicz, Dzimidowicz

Detlaf (< Germ. dithematic name *Dethloff*): Detlaf, Dettlaff, Dytłow

Detmer (< Germ. dithematic name *Dettmer*): Detmer, Ditmar

Dietrich (< Germ. dithematic name *Dietrich*): Ditrich, Dittrich, Dytrych; Wytrykowski

Dionizy (< Greek name *Dionysos* = English *Dennis*): Denisiuk, Denkiewicz, Denys, Dynak, Dyoniziak, Dzienis, Dzienisz

Dob- (< dithematic names with the reconstructed Proto-Slavic root *dobъ, "resourceful, brave"): Dobaj, Dobak, Dobek, Dobiesz, Dobosiewicz

Dom- (< dithematic names with the root *dom,* "home, house"): Domachowski, Domasik, Domek, Domko, Domowicz, Domski

Dominik (< given name *Dominik*): Domin, Domińczak, Dominiak, Dominik, Domiński; Dumin

Don- (< given name *Donat*): Doniek, Donocik; Dunat

Dor- (< element from given names *Dorota, Teodor, Izydor,* etc.): Dorak, Dorka, Doroch, Dorosz, Doruch

Dorot- (< given name *Dorot, Doroteusz, Dorota*): Dorociak, Dorota

Dosz- (< element *Do-* from given names + suffix *-sz*): Doś, Dosz, Doszko

Dymitr (< Ukr. given name *Dmytro* from Greek *Demetrios*): Dmitruk, Dmytryszyn, Domitrz, Dymitruk; Gmiter, Gmitrzak; Mitrus; Zmitrowicz

Eliasz (= English *Elias*): Eljasz, Heliasz; Ilasz, Ilczuk, Ilków, Ilski; Ułasiewicz, Uliasz, Uljasz

Elżbieciak (< given name *Elżbieta* = English *Elizabeth*)

Emilian (< given name *Emilian*): Milian; Omelańczuk, Omilian

Erazmus (< given name *Erasmus*): Erazmus; Rasmus, Rozmus

Ernst (< Germ. given name *Ernst*): Ernest, Ernst

Eustach- (< given name *Eustachy* = English *Eustace*): Astapczyk; Eustachewicz; Ostach, Ostafin, Ostapczuk, Ostas, Ostasz, Ostaszewski

Ew- (< given name *Ewa* = English *Eve*): Ewiak; Hewak; Jewiak; Jewuła

Fabian (< Latin name *Fabianus*): Fabczak, Fabianowicz, Fabich, Fabijański, Fabiniak, Fabisiak, Fabiszewski; Pabian, Pabich, Pabis, Pabjan

Faltyn (< Germ. pers. name *Faltin* < Latin *Valentinus*): Faltyn, Folcik, Fołta, Foltyński

Fed- (< East Slavic *Fiodor, Fedir* = English *Theodore*): Fedak, Fedczyszyn, Federowicz, Fedorczuk, Fedorowicz, Fedyna, Fidor, Fiedor, Fiedorczuk, Fiodorowicz

Fel- (< given names *Feliks, Felicjan*): Feliga, Feliniak, Felisiak, Felka, Felski, Feluś

Feliks (< given name *Feliks* = English *Felix*): Feliks, Feliksiak, Feliksik

Ferdyn- (< given name *Ferdynand* = English *Ferdinand*): Ferdyn, Ferdzyn

Fid- (element < given names beginning *Fid-*): Fidala, Fido, Fidos, Fidyk

Filimon (< East Slavic given name *Fylymon* or *Filimon*): Filimon, Filimoniuk; Chalimoniuk, Chilimoniuk

Filip (given name *Filip* = English *Philip*): Filipczak, Filipek, Filipiak, Filipiuk, Filipski; Pilipczuk

Flor- (< given name *Florian*): Florczak, Florczyk, Florek, Florkiewicz, Florkowski, Floryn, Florysiak

Franciszek (< given name *Franciszek* = English *Francis*) — 1. *Frąc-:* Frąckiewicz, Frąckowiak, Frączek, Frączkowski; 2. *Franc-:* Franc, Franczak, Franecki, Franek, Franik, Frencel; 3. *Frank-:* Frank, Frankiewicz, Franków; 4. *Fronc-:* Fronckowiak, Fronczak, Fronczyk; 5. *Ferenc-* (from Hungarian): Feręc, Ferenc, Ferenczak, Ferens, Perenc

Frydr- (< given name *Frydrych* = English *Frederick,* German *Friedrich*): Fidrysiak, Freda, Friedrich, Fryc, Fryda, Frydrych, Frydrysiak, Fydrych

Gabr- (< given name *Gabriel*): Gaber, Gabor, Gabriel, Gabrych, Gabryś, Gabryszewski, Gawrych, Gawryś; Habrych, Habryło, Hawrylak, Hawryłkiewicz, Hawryś, Hawryszko

Gal- (Latin name *Gallus* as well as other roots): Gałek, Galica, Galoch, Galon, Galus, Gawlak, Gawlikowski, Gawłowski

Gas- (element *Ga-* < given names *Gardomir, Gabryjel, Gaweł,* etc. + suffix *-s* or *-sz*): Gasek, Gasik, Gasz, Gaszka

Gaw- (< given name *Gaweł* from Latin *Gaulus*): Gaweł, Gawełda, Gawlak, Gawlas, Gawlik, Gawlita, Gawłowicz, Hawełka

Gied- (< given name *Gedeon* = English *Gideon*): Gieda, Giedyk, Giedziun

Gier- (< Germanic dithematic names with the root *Ger-* such as *Gertruda, Gerald, Gerhard,* as well as other roots): Gera, Gerus, Giera, Gierach, Gierej, Gierałt, Gierczyk, Gierek, Gierula, Gierut

Gierlach (< Germ. pers. name *Gerlach*): Gierlach, Gierlak, Gierlotka

Ginter (< Germ. pers. n. *Gunther*): Gindera, Ginter, Günther

Gleb (< East Slavic given name *Gleb* or *Hlib*): Gleba, Glib, Hlebowicz

Goc- (< Germ. names beginning *Gotz-* or Slavic dithematic names such as *Godzisław*): Goc, Gocek, Goclik, Goclon, Gocyk

Goch- (element *Go-* < *Gościmir, Godzisław,* etc. + suffix *-ch*): Goch, Gochna, Gochnio

God- (< dithematic names such as *Godzimir*): Godawa, Godel, Godoń, Godos, Goduła, Godyń, Godzik, Godzisz

Gortat (< Germanic pers. name *Gothard*): Gortat, Gurtat

Gost- (< dithematic names such as *Gościmir* with the root *gost-,* "guest"): Gościak, Gościej, Gostek, Gostkiewicz, Goszcz, Hościło

Gosz- (element *Go-* < *Gościmir, Godzisław,* etc. + suffix *-s* or *-ś* or *-sz*): Gos, Goś, Gosek, Gosik, Gosk, Goska, Gosz, Goszka, Hoszek

Gotfryd (< Germanic pers. name *Gottfried*): Gotfryd, Gottfried

Grzegorz (< given name *Grzegorz* = English *Gregory*) — 1. *Grzec-* (*Grze-* + suffix *-c*): Grzeca, Grzeczka; 2. *Grzeg-, Grig-:* Grega, Greger, Gregor, Gregorczyk, Gregorek, Greguła, Gryga, Grygiel, Grygierczyk, Gryglewski, Grygo, Grygorczuk, Grzegorczyk, Grzegorzek, Gzegorzewicz; 3. *Grzel-* (*Grze-* < *Grze-* + suffix *-l*): Grela, Greloch, Grzela, Grzelak, Grzelczak, Grzelec, Grzelka; 4. *Grzes-* (*Grze-* + suffix *-s*)*:* Greś, Greszta, Grześ, Grzesiak, Grześkiewicz, Grześkowiak, Grzeszczak, Grzeszczuk; 5. *Grys-:* Grys, Gryś, Gryszka, Gryszko, Grzyś; 6. *Hreh-, Hryc-, Hryn-, Hrys-* (from East Slavic derivatives): Hrehorowicz, Hryc, Hryciuk, Hryń, Hryniewicz, Hrynkiewicz, Hryszko, Ryć

Gust- (< given names *Gustaw, August*, etc.): Guściora, Gusta, Guśtak, Gustaw, Guszczak

Han or **Hanc** (< Germ. *Han(s)* = Polish *Jan,* English *John*): Anusik; Han, Hanas, Haniżewski, Hankiewicz, Hanusz, Hanysz

Harasym (Blrs./Ukr. given name, no equivalent in English): Arasimowicz; Garas, Geras, Gieras, Gierasimiuk; Harasim, Harasimiuk, Harasimowicz, Haraszczuk, Harazim, Harazin

Heinrich (German form of Polish *Henryk,* English *Henry*): Hajnrych, Heinrich, Hendrych, Hendrysiak; (from Germ. *Heinz, Hintz,* nicknames for *Heinrich*): Henc, Hinc, Hinca, Hintz, Hintzke, Hinz

Hel- (< given name *Helena*): Helak, Heleniak, Heliński, Helon, Heluszka

Hen- (< Polish *Henryk* = English *Henry*, or perhaps short form of *Johannes*): Henek, Henke, Hennek

Herman (< Germ. pers. n. *Hermann*): Armański; Hermaniuk, Hermanowicz, Hermanowski, Hermański, Hermasz, Herrmann; Jarzmik

Hryc-, Hryn-, Hrys- (name elements < *Hryhoriy,* Eastern Slavic form of *Gregory*): Hryciuk, Hryń, Hryniuk, Hrynko, Hryszko

Hur- (< Orthodox given name *Huriy*): Hura, Huras, Hurek, Huryń, Hurysz

Ic- (< Biblical name *Izak,* Isaac): Iciek, Izak

Id- (< given name *Idzi* = English *Giles*!): Idasiak, Idczak, Idec, Idzi, Idziak, Idzik, Idzior

Ignacy (given name *Ignacy* < Latin *Ignatius*): Gnacik, Gnaciński, Gnaś; Hnat, Hnatiuk, Hnatyszyn; Ignac, Ignaczak, Ignaciuk, Ignacy, Ignaczak, Ignarski, Ignasiak, Ignaszak, Ignatiuk, Ignatowicz, Ihnatowicz

Iwan (Ukrainian *Іван* [*Iván*]*,* Russian *Иван* [*Iván*] = Polish *Jan*): Iwan, Iwanek, Iwaniec, Iwankiewicz, Iwaszkiewicz, Iwicki; Wańczyk, Waniek, Wańkowicz

Izydor (< given name *Izydor*, of Greek origin): Izydorczyk, Izydorek; Sidor, Sidorczuk, Sidorowicz, Sydor; Zydorczyk, Zydroń

Jach- (element *Ja-* < *Jan, Jakub*, etc. + suffix *-ch*): Jach, Jachna, Jachowicz

Jack- (< given name *Jacek* < *Jacenty* = *Hyacinth*): Jacek, Jackiewicz, Jackowiak, Jackowicz

Jacz- (element *Ja-* < *Jan, Jakub,* etc. + suffix *-cz*): Jacak, Jacewicz, Jaciuk, Jacoń, Jacyna, Jacyszyn, Jaczun

Jadw- (< fem. given name *Jadwiga*): Jadwidzic, Jadwiszczyak, Jadwiszczok

Jag- (element < given names such as *Agata, Agnieszka, Jadwiga*): Jagas, Jagosz, Jaguś, Jagusiak, Jagusz

Jak- (< given names such as *Jakub, Jakim*): Jakiel, Jakiela, Jakoniuk, Jaksina, Jakus, Jakuszko, Jeka, Jekiel, Jekiełek, Jokiel, Joks

Jakub (given name = English *Jacob*): Jakóbczak, Jakóbczyk, Jakóbik, Jakowczyk, Jakubas, Jakubaszek, Jakubczyk, Jakubek, Jakubiak, Jakubiec, Jakubik, Jakubiszyn, Jakubowicz; Kuba, Kubala, Kubat, Kubera, Kubiak, Kubica, Kubicz, Kubik, Kubiszyn

Jamr- (< given names *Ambroży* or *Emeryk*): Jamro, Jamrocha, Jamróg, Jamróz, Jamrozik, Jamroży

Jan (given name = English *John*): Janaczek, Janas, Janasik, Janaszek, Janczak, Janczura, Janda, Janeczek, Janiak, Janiec, Janiga, Janik, Janisz, Jankiewicz, Janocha, Janosz, Janota, Janowiak, Janta, Janus, Janusz

Jar- (< dithematic names with the archaic root *jar-*, "sharp, strict"): Jarczak, Jarek, Jaroch, Jaroń, Jarosz, Jarota, Jarych

Jas- (element *Ja-* < *Jan, Jaczemir, Jaromir,* etc. + suffix *-s*): Aszyk; Jasek, Jasiak, Jasica, Jasik, Jasiuk, Jaśkiewicz, Jaśkowiak, Jaszek

Jędr- (< given name *Jędrzej* = English *Andrew*): Jędrak, Jędras, Jędrol, Jędrusiak, Jędrych, Jędryka, Jędrysiak, Jędrzejak, Jędrzejczak

Jerem- (< given name *Jeremijasz* = English *Jeremiah, Jeremy*): Jarema, Jaremko; Werema, Weremczuk, Wieremiejczyk

Jermol- (< Old East Slavic given name *Jermoła*): Jarmoła, Jarmołowicz, Jarmuła, Jermołowicz

Jerom- (< given name *Hieronym* = English *Jerome*): Hieronimek, Jaromin, Jaroń, Jeromin

Jerzy (given name, older forms included *Jura* = English *George*): Jerzak, Jerzyk, Jurak, Jurek, Jurgiel, Jurkiewicz, Juroszek

Joachim (< given name): Jachim, Jachimowicz, Jachymek, Jakimowicz, Joachimiak, Jochemczyk, Jochymek, Onichimiuk

Jop- (< Biblical name *Job,* modern Polish spelling *Hiob*): Job, Jobda, Jop, Jopek, Jowik, Jówko

Josz- (element *Ja-* < *Joachim, Józef* + suffix *-s* or *-sz*): Jośko, Josz, Joszko

Józef (< given name = English *Joseph*): Józefczyk, Józefowicz; Jóźwiak, Jóźwiakowski, Jóźwik, Jóźwin, Juzwa; Osip (from the Ukrainian form), Osipiak, Osipowicz, Osypiuk

Józefat (< given name = English *Jehoshaphat*): Józefaciuk, Józefacki

Jud- (< given names *Juda* and *Judyta* = English *Judah, Jude,* and *Judith*): Juda, Judek, Judycki

Jus- (element *Jus-* < *Justyn, Julian, Józef,* etc.): Juś, Juśkiewicz, Juszkiewicz

Just- (< Latin *Justus*): Just, Juszczak, Juszczuk, Juszczyszyn

Justyn- (< Latin Justinus) Justyna, Juszczyński, Uścinowicz, Ustianowski

Kajetan (given name < Latin *Vaietanus*): Kajetaniak, Kajtaniak, Kajtoch

Kalikst (< Latin *Kallistus* and *Kalixtus,* cmp. English fem. n. *Callista*) Kaliściak, Kalista, Kaliszczak, Kaliszczuk

Karol (given name = English *Charles*): Karalus, Karlik, Karłowicz, Karolczak, Karolczyk, Karolewski, Karolkiewicz

Kas- (element *Ka-* < given names *Katarzyna* or *Kasper* + suffix *-s* or *-sz*): Kasica, Kasiuk, Kaska, Kaśzków, Kaszczyszyn, Kaszyński

Kasper (given name = English *Casper*): Gasperowicz, Kacperczyk, Kacprzak, Kasperczyk, Kasperowicz, Kasprowicz, Kasprzak, Kasprzyk
Katarzyna (given name = English *Catherine*): Katarzyniak, Katryniok
Kaz- (< ancient dithematic names with the root *kaz-*, "to destroy,"e.g., *Kazimierz*, or *kazać*, "to order"): Kazana, Kazek, Kazik, Kazior
Kazimierz (given name = English *Casimir*): Kazimierczak, Kaźmierczak, Kaźmieruk
Kirstein (German pers. name, "Christian," as a Jewish name from *Gershom* or *Gershon*): Kiersztan, Kirstein, Kirsten, Kirsztein
Kilian (given name = English *Killian*): Kielan, Kielian, Kieljan, Kilan, Kilanowski, Kilian, Kiljański, Killian
Klara (given name = English *Clara*): Klara, Klarkowski, Klorek
Klemens (given name = English *Clement*): Klemczak, Klemke, Klima, Klimala, Klimas, Klimaszewski, Klimczak, Klimek, Klimkiewicz
Klich (element *Kli- < Klemens* + suffix *-ch*)
Klis- (element *Kli- < Klemens* + suffix *-s*): Kliś, Klisiewicz, Klisz
Konder (< Germ. given name *Günther*): Kander, Kandora, Kondera, Kondras, Kundera
Kondrat or **Konrad** (may be variants of the same name, may be separate names): Kindrat, Kondraciuk, Kondrat, Kondratowicz, Kunat; Kunc
Konon (< East Slavic given name): Konon, Kononiuk, Kononowicz
Konstanty (< given name = English *Constantine*): Konstantinowicz, Kościuszko, Kostiuk, Kostkiewicz
Kordul- (< fem. given name): Kordula, Kordyl, Kordylas
Kornel (< given name = English *Cornelius*): Korneluk, Korniluk
Kosma (< given name < Greek *Kosmas,* cmp. English *Cosmo*): Kosma, Koźma, Koźmiński, Kuświk, Kuźba, Kuźma, Kuźmin, Kuźmiński
Krych-, Krys-, Kryst-, Krysz- (element *Kry- < given names *Krzysztof, Kryspin, Krystian,* etc. + suffixes): Krych, Kryś, Kryściak, Krysiak, Krysik, Krysiuk, Krystan, Krystek, Kryszak, Krzych, Krzysiak, Krzyszewski, Krzysztoń, Krzysztyniak
Krzysztof (given name = English *Christopher*): Krysztofiak, Krzystowczyk, Krzyszczak, Krzysztof, Krzysztofiak
Kusz- (element < *Jakusz,* as a Jewish name may be from *Yekutiel* or *Yekusiel*): Kusz, Kuszel, Kuszka, Kuszyk
Lambert (< Germanic dithematic name): Lambryczak, Lamprycht, Lempart
Lar- (< short form of given name *Hilary*): Lara, Larek, Larysz
Łasz- (< short forms of given names *Łazarz* and *Łaskarz*): Łaszkiewicz, Łazszcz, Łaszczyk
Lawr- (< given name appearing in several forms — German *Lorenz,* Polish *Wawrzyniec,* Russian *Lavrenty,* English *Lawrence*, etc.): Lawera, Lawrenc, Ławrynowicz, Lentz, Lorek, Lorenc, Lorys (see also **Wawrzyniec**)
Łazarz (given name *Łazarz* = English *Lazarus* or *Eliazar*): Lazar, Łazarewicz, Łazarowicz, Łazarski, Łazarz

Lech (root as in *Lścimir,* perhaps also < *Lach*): Lechowicz, Lechowski, Leszek, Leszkiewicz, Leśko

Leon (given name = English *Leon*): Len, Leończuk, Leoniak, Leoniuk

Leonard (given name = English *Leonard*): Lenarczyk, Lenard, Lenart, Leniart

Lesz- (element *Lesz-* < dithematic name *Lścimir* or < *Leon*): Leśkiewicz, Leszek, Leszko

Lew (< *lew,* "lion," as translation of *Leon,* or < Hebrew name *Lewi*): Lefkowitz, Lew, Lewek, Lewiński, Lewkowicz

Liberda (< Germ. pers. n. *Libert* or *Lubert*): Liberda, Luber, Lubera, Luberda

Łucz-, Łuk- (element < given names *Łucja, Łucjan,* and *Łukasz*): Łuczaj, Łuczak, Łuczka, Łuczyszyn, Łuka, Łukowiak

Lud- (Slavic dithematic names with the root *lud-,* "people"): Luda, Ludkiewicz, Ludyga, Ludynia

Ludwik (given name = English *Louis*): Ludwa, Ludwicki, Ludwiczak, Ludwig, Ludwisiak, Lutz (< German *Ludwig*)

Łukasz (given name = English *Lucas, Luke*): Łukasiewicz, Łukasik, Łukaszczyk, Łukaszek, Lukoszek

Maciej (given name = English *Matthias*): Macek, Maciąg, Maciążek, Maciejak, Macioszek, Maciszewski, Maciulewicz, Maćkiewicz, Macko, Maćkowiak, Maćkowski, Macyszyn; Mateja, Matusiak, Matysek; Matwiejczuk, Matwij

Mach- (element *Ma-* < *Maciej, Marcin,* etc. + suffix *-ch,* or < verb *machać,* to swing, sway): Machaj, Machała, Machniak, Machoń, Machowiak

Mad- (< Latin name *Amadeus,* or < *Magdalena*): Madajczyk, Madeja, Madejczyk, Madejewski

Magdalena (< fem. given name *Magdalena*): Madalski, Madela, Madzia; Magdziak, Magdziarek, Magdziarz

Makar- (< given name *Makary*): Makar, Makara, Makarewicz, Makaruk

Maks- (< given names *Maksym* or *Maksymilian*): Maks, Maksim, Maksym Maksymiuk, Maksymowicz

Mal- (< dithematic names with *mał-,* "little," or directly from that root): Malak, Malczyk, Malec, Malek, Małek, Malesa, Małkiewicz, Małyska

Mar- (< given names *Marcin, Marek, Maria,* or < *mara,* night phantom): Maroszek, Maruszczak, Marut

Marc- (< given names *Marcin* or *Marek* or < *marzec,* "March"): Marcisz, Marczak, Marczuk, Marczyk

Marcin (given name = English *Martin*): Marcinek, Marciniak, Marcinkiewicz, Marczyński, Martyniak, Martyniuk

Mark- (< given name *Marek* or *Markus* = English *Mark*): Marek, Markiewicz, Markowicz, Marks, Markus

Marian (< given name *Marian*): Mariański, Marjański

Mart- (< given name *Marta* = English *Martha,* or < *Marcin*): Mart, Marta, Martowicz, Martyka

Masz- (element *Ma-* < names as *Maciej, Marcin,* etc. + suffix *-sz*): Maś, Maśkiewicz, Maszkiewicz, Maszota

Mat- (< given names *Mateusz,* "Matthew," or *Maciej* or *Matyjasz,* "Matthias," or other roots): Matak, Matela, Matosek, Matuła, Matulewicz, Matyka

Melchior (given name, supposedly the name of one of the Magi): Majcher, Majcherczyk, Majchrowicz, Majchrowski, Majchrzak, Malcher

Mich- (element *Mi-* < *Mirosław, Mikołaj,* etc. + suffix *-ch,* or < *Michał*): Mich, Michna, Michniewicz, Michno, Michoń, Michta

Michał (given name = English *Michael*): Michalak, Michalczyk, Michałek, Michalik, Michałkiewicz, Michaluk, Michel, Michlewski

Mikołaj (given name = English *Nicholas*): Micał, Micek, Mickiewicz, Mika, Mikoda, Mikołajczuk, Mikołajczyk, Mikos, Mikoś, Mikulski

Mil- (< dithematic names such as *Miłosław* with the root *miły,* "dear, beloved," or directly from that root): Mila, Miłek, Milewicz, Miłosz

Misz- (element *Mi-* < *Michał, Mikołaj, Miłosław* + suffix *-sz*): Misz, Miszczuk, Miszka, Miszkiewicz, Miszko, Miszkowicz

Mojżesz (given name = English *Moses,* also seen are derivations < *Moises* [Latin] and < *Mojsiej* in eastern Poland, Russia, etc.): Mojsa, Możejko, Mojzych; Mojsiejenko, Mojsiewicz; Mosiej

Mos- (< *Mo-* as in *Mojsław* + suffix *-s,* or < *Mojżesz*): Moś, Mosak, Mosiewicz, Mosionek, Moskiewicz, Mośko, Moskowicz

Mysz- (< element *My-* as < *Myślibor* + suffix *-sz,* or from *mysz,* "mouse"): Mysiak, Myszak, Myszk, Myszkiewicz, Myszko

Nac- (< short form of dithematic name *Naczęsław,* or < short form of given name *Ignacy*): Nacewicz, Naczk

Natan (given name = English *Nathan*): Natanek, Natoński

Naum (given name, mainly Orthodox < Biblical name): Naumczyk, Naumiuk, Naumowicz

Nazar (given name < Greek): Nazar, Nazarewicz, Nazaruk

Nestor (given name, mainly East Slavic < Greek): Neścior, Nesterowicz, Nesteruk, Nieścior

Nik- (< Latin *Nicolaus* or German *Niklaus* = Polish *Mikołaj,* English *Nicholas*): Klaus, Klauz, Klauza; Nicewicz, Nikiel, Niklas; Nitz; Nycz, Nykiel

Nikifor (given name, mainly East Slavic < Greek): Niczyporuk, Nieczypor, Nikiforuk

Nikodem (given name < Greek): Kodym; Nikodem, Nikodym

Onis- (< short forms of given names beginning *On-* including East Slavic *Onisim, Onysym*): Oniszczuk, Onyszkiewicz, Onyszko

Pac-, Pach-, Pak-, Pasz- (element *Pa-* < such names as *Pakosław* and *Paweł* + suffixes, or < the Lithuanian name *Pacas*): Pac, Pacan, Pacek, Pacewicz, Pachla, Pachura, Pacocha, Pacuła, Pacyga, Pakos, Pakosz, Paś, Paszek, Paszkiewicz, Paszko

Paweł (given name = English *Paul*): Pauliński, Pawełczak, Pawełec, Pawełek, Pawelski, Pawlak, Pawlica, Pawlisz, Pawłowicz, Pawłuszek, Pawula

Pelk- (< ancient dithematic names such as *Przedpełk, Świętopełk* with the root *pelk-,* "military detachment, squad"): Pelka, Pełka, Pełkowski

Picch-, Piesz- (element *Pie-* < *Pietr, Pielgrzym* + suffixes *-ch, -sz*): Piech, Piecha, Piechnik, Piechowiak, Piesik, Pieszak, Piezsko, Pioch

Piotr (given name = English *Peter*): Peterek, Petrus; Pietraszek, Pietrucha, Pietrusiak, Pietryga, Pietryszyn, Pietrzak, Pietrzyk; Piotrkiewicz, Piotrowicz; Pitera; Pyter

Pol- (various roots, including short forms < *Polikarp, Apolonia, Leopold*): Polek, Policha, Poliński

Polit (< given name *Hipolit* < Greek name *Hippólytos*): Polit, Politowicz

Prokop, Prokofiy (given name, mostly East Slavic): Prokofiew, Prokop, Prokopczyk, Prokopiuk, Pokropowicz, Prukop

Rach- (element *Ra-* < *Racibor, Radosław, Rachwał* + suffix *-ch*): Rach, Rachoń, Rachuta, Rechnio, Rechul

Rad- (< dithematic names with the root *rad-,* "satisfied, happy," e.g., *Radosław, Radomir,* or < *radzić,* to advise): Radaszkiewicz, Radek, Radkiewicz, Radko, Radoń, Radosz, Radzewicz, Reda, Redzik

Rafał (given name = English *Raphael*): Rachwał, Rafałko, Rafalski

Rasz- (element *Ra-* as < *Rasław, Radosław* + suffix *-sz*): Raś, Rasz, Raszeja, Raszka, Raszkiewicz, Reszka

Rat- (< short forms of dithematic names such as *Racibor, Racisław*): Ratka, Retkiewicz

Reichardt (< Germ. dithematic name *Rīhhart*): Reichert, Richert, Rychert

Rejmund (< German *Reimond* = English *Raymond*): Rajmund, Rejmont, Rymut

Roch- (< given name *Roch* as well as < root meaning "to grow" or < the word for "rook"): Roch, Rochnowski, Rochoń, Rochowiak, Rochowicz

Roman (given name < Latin): Roman, Romańczuk, Romanek, Romaniuk, Romanowicz; Romaszko, Romejko, Romek

Rost- (< dithematic names with root meaning "to grow," or an archaic word for "rust"): Rost, Tostek, Roszcak, Roszczyk

Rosz- (element *Ro-* < *Rościsław, Roch,* etc. + suffix *-sz*): Roś, Roszak, Roszkiewicz, Roszko, Roszkowiak, Roszyk

Rysz- (< *Ryszard,* "Richard," *rysa,* "crack," or *ryś,* "lynx"): Rysz, Ryszkiewicz, Ryszkowski

Sach- (element *Sa-* < names such as *Sambor* and *Salomon* + suffix *-ch*, or (< Germ. pers. n. *Sach*): Sacha, Sachajko, Sachanowicz, Sachnik

Sąd-, Sęd- (<dithematic names with the root *sąd-, sęd-,* "judge," e.g., *Sędzimir, Sędzisław,* or < root in *sędzia,* "judge"): Sądej, Sądel, Sędek, Sędziak, Sędzik, Sendek

Sam- (< ancient names with the root *sam,* "self, alone," e.g., *Sambor,* or < *Samuel* or *Samson*): Samek, Samoraj, Szamota

Samuel (given name): Samojluk, Samel, Samol, Samul, Samulak; Smul, Smulewicz, Smulski, Szmul, Szmulewicz

Sawa (< given name, mostly East Slavic < Biblical name *Sava, Sabas*): Sawa, Sawala, Sawczuk, Sawicz, Sawko, Szawica

Sebastian (given name): Baścik, Bastek, Sebesta, Sobieszczak, Sobieszczyk

Serafin (given name = English *Seraphim*): Serafin, Serafinowicz, Serafiński; Szarafin, Szarafiński, Szerafin

Serwacy (given name < Latin name *Servatius*): Serwa, Serwach, Serwata, Serwin, Serwiński; Szarwas; Szyrwiński

Seweryn (< Latin *severus,* stern, strict): Sawaryn, Seweryniak, Szawaryn

Siem-, Sien- (< dithematic names such as *Siemomysł, Siemosław* with the Slavic root *siemia,* "family"; in names from eastern Poland also < *Siemion* = English *Simeon*): Semczuk, Semkowicz; Seniuk, Senko, Senyk; Siemaszko, Siemek, Siemiaszko, Siemko; Sienicki, Sieńko; Sionek

Sier- (< dithematic names, e.g., *Sirosław,* with the archaic root *siry,* "devoid, lacking," or other roots): Sieraga, Sierka, Sieroń

Sław- (< dithematic names with the root *sława,* "glory, fame," or directly from that root): Sławek, Sławik, Sławuta

Sob- (< dithematic names, e.g. *Sobiesław,* with *sob-,* "self," or < variant of *Sebastian*): Sobala, Sobania, Sobczak, Sobczyk, Sobieraj, Soboń

Stach- (element *Sta-* < *Stanisław* + suffix *-ch,* or < *Eustachy*): Stach, Stachelek, Stachera, Stachnik, Stachoń, Stachowiak, Stachura, Stachyra

Stan- (short form of dithematic names such as *Stanisław* with the root *stani-,* "become," or < *stanąć,* stand): Stancel; Stańczak, Stańczyk, Stanek, Staniewicz, Stanik, Stanisz, Stankiewicz, Stankowiak, Stanula; Stencel

Stanisław (given name = English *Stanislaus*): Stanisławczyk, Stanisławek

Stas- (element *Sta-* < *Stanisław* + suffix *-s* or *-ś* or *-sz*): Staś, Stasiak, Stasik, Staśkiewicz, Staśko, Staszak, Staszkiewicz

Stec- (element *Ste-* < *Stefan* + suffix *-c*): Stec, Steć, Steciuk, Stecko, Steczko

Stefan (given name = English *Stephen,* see also **Szczepan**): Stefan, Stefańczyk, Stefaniak, Stefaniuk, Stefański; Stepaniuk

Stoch-, Stoj-, Stos- (< dithematic names, e.g., *Stoisław, Stoigniew,* with the root *sto[j]-,* "stand," + suffixes): Stoch, Stój, Stojek, Stojko, Stosek, Stosik, Stosio, Stoszek

Sul- (< dithematic names with the root *sul-,* "promise", e.g., *Sulisław, Sulimir*): Sulak, Sularz, Sulej, Sułek, Suliga, Sulik, Suliński, Sulisz, Sulka; Szul, Szulik, Szulim, Szulist

Suprun (East Slavic given name *Sofron, Sopron,* of Greek origin): Supranowicz, Suproń, Suprun, Supryn

Świech- (element *Świe-* < *Świerad* + suffix *-ch*): Świech, Świechowicz

Świerad (ancient dithematic Slavic name): Świerad, Świrad

Święt- (short form of ancient dithematic names such as *Świętobor, Świętosław* with the root *świąt-, święt-,* † "powerful," or < *święty,* "holy"): Świątczak, Świątek, Świętek, Świętoń

Szczepan (given name = English *Stephen*): Szczepanek, Szczepaniak, Szczepaniec, Szczepanik, Szczepankiewicz

Szymon (given name = English *Simon*): Simon, Szymala, Szymanek, Szymankiewicz; Szymaszek; Szymczak, Szymkowiak, Szymoniak

Tadeusz (given name = English *Thaddeus*): Tadeja, Tadeusiak, Tadeusz, Tadla, Tadych, Tadzik

Taras (East Slavic given name *Taras,* or < *taras,* archaic meaning "prison, dike"): Taras, Tarasek, Tarasiewicz, Tarasiuk, Taraszka, Taraszkiewicz

Tasz- (element *Ta-* < *Tatumir, Tadeusz,* etc. + suffix *-sz*): Tasza, Taszek

Tekla (Polish feminine first name < Greek): Tekielak, Tekliński

Tecław (< form of *Těchoslav,* Polish *Ciechosław*): Teclaf, Tecław, Tetzlaff

Teodor (given name = English *Theodore,* Ukr. *Fedir*): Cader; Chodor; Czader; Hodur; Tadrzak; Teodorczyk, Teodorowicz

Teofil (given name = English *Theophilus*): Teofilak, Tofil, Tofiluk

Teres- (< fem. given name *Teresa*): Tereszczuk, Tereszkiewicz, Tereszko

Tobiasz (given name = English *Tobias*): Tabasz, Tabiś, Tabisz, Tobiasiewicz, Tobiasz, Tobjasz, Tobys

Toch- (element *To-* < *Tolisław, Tomasz* + suffix *-ch*): Tocha, Tochowicz

Tomasz (given name = English *Thomas*): Tomala, Tomanek, Tomas, Tomasiak, Tomasik, Tomaszek, Tomczak, Tomkowiak; Tuman, Tumas

Trochim, Trofim (Orthodox given name from Greek): Trochim, Trochimiuk, Trofimiuk

Truchan (Orthodox given name from Greek): Truchan, Truchel, Tryfon

Tybur- (< given name *Tyburcy* < Latin name *Tiburtius*): Tybor, Tyborczyk, Tybura, Tyburczy, Tyburski, Tybuś

Tyc- (element *Ty-* < names such as *Tyburcy* + suffix *-c*): Tyc, Tyczyński

Tymoteusz (given name = English *Timothy*): Cimała, Cimek, Cimoch; Tyma, Tymek, Tymoczko, Tymosiak, Tymoszuk

Tys- (element *Ty-* as < *Tymoteusz* + suffix *-s* or *-sz*) Tysiak, Tyszka, Tyszkiewicz, Tyszko

Urban (< Latin name *Urbanus*): Urban, Urbańczyk, Urbanek, Urbanowicz, Urbański, Urbaś

Urszula (fem. given name = English *Ursula*): Orszulak, Orszulik; Urszulak

Wach- (element *Wa-* < *Wacław, Wawrzyniec,* etc. + suffix *-ch*): Wach, Wachnik, Wachowiak, Wachowicz, Wachowiec, Wachulec

Wacław (ancient dithematic name, originally *Więcesław,* "more" + "glory," but modified under Czech influence): Wacek, Wacławczyk, Wacławek, Wacławik; Węcławik, Wenc, Wencel; Więcek, Więcław, Wiencek, Wiencław, Wienclewski

Wal- (< *Walenty, Walerian,* or < *walić,* to bring down): Walasek, Walczak, Walczyk, Waliczek, Walkiewicz, Walko, Walkowiak, Waluś

Walenty (given name = English *Valentine*): Falenta; Wałędziak, Walenciak, Walenda, Walendzik, Walentowicz, Walentynowicz, Welenc

Walery (given name < Latin *Valerius*): Waleriańczyk, Walerowicz

Wasyl (East Slavic given name = English *Basil*): Wasil, Wasiluk, Wasylik, Wasyluk

Was[z]- (element *Wa-* < *Wasyl, Wawrzyniec,* or *Wan* = Ivan + suffix *-s[z]*): Waś, Wasiak, Wasiewicz, Wasik, Waszak, Waszkiewicz

Wawrzyniec (given name = English *Lawrence*): Wawer, Wawro, Wawryniuk, Wawrzyńczak, Wawrzyniak, Wawrzynowicz, Wawszczak, Wowra

Wic- (element *Wi-* < *Wit, Wincenty, Wiktor,* etc. + suffix *-c*): Wiciak, Wicik, Wiczkowski

Wiel- (< dithematic names such as *Wielimir, Wielisław* with the archaic root *wiel-,* "order, command," or < root *wiel-,* "much"): Wielądek, Wielanek, Wielek, Wielosik

Wiktor (given name = English *Victor*): Wiktor, Wiktorek, Wiktorowicz

Wil- (< Germanic dithematic name *Wilhelm*): Wilamek, Wilas, Wilhelm, Wiliński, Wilma, Wilusz

Wincenty (given name = English *Vincent*): Wicenciak, Wincek, Wincenciak, Winczewski, Winczura

Wisz (element *Wi-* as < *Wisław, Wiktor,* etc. + suffix *-sz*)

Wit- (< *Wit, Witold,* or *Witosław,* or < *witać,* "to greet"): Wit, Wita, Witak, Witan, Witas, Witaszek, Witczak, Witek, Witos, Witusik

Włod- (< ancient dithematic names, e.g., *Władysław, Włodzimierz,* with the root *wład-,* "rule"): Władyka; Włodarczak, Włodarczyk, Włodarski, Włodek, Włudyka, Wodarczyk, Wołodkiewicz, Wołodźko, Wudarczyk

Włost-, Włosz- (< dithematic names such as *Włościbor* with the archaic root *włost-,* "rule, power"): Włoszczyk, Włoszek

Woch- (element *Wo-* < *Wojciech* or *Wolimir,* etc. + suffix *-ch*): Woch, Wochna, Wochnik

Woj- (< dithematic names, e.g., *Wojciech, Wojsław,* with the root *woj-,* "warrior, battle"): Wojaczek, Wojas, Wojczuk, Wojsa,

Wojc- (< Polish first name *Wojciech,* "joyful warrior," or < *wójt,* village headman): Wójciak, Wojciech, Wojciechowicz, Wojcieszak, Wojcieszek, Wójcik, Wojtak, Wojtal, Wojtan, Wojtas, Wojtczak, Wojtkowiak, Wójtowicz, Wojtyła, Wojtyna, Wojtyś, Wojtysiak, Wujcik

Zachariasz (given name = English *Zachary*): Zachara, Zacharek, Zachariasz, Zacharski

Zdan- (< dithematic names scuh as *Zdamir* or < *żdać,* "to await, wait for): Zdancewicz, Zdaniewicz, Zdanowicz, Żdanuk

Żel- (< dithematic names with the root *żel-,* "desire, wish"): Zelek, Żelek

Zen- (given name *Zenon* < Greek): Zenka, Zenowicz, Zieniewicz, Zieniuk, Zienkiewicz

Zin- (short form < East Slavic names such as *Zenon, Zinoviy, Zinaida*): Ziniewicz, Zinkiewicz, Zinkowski

Zych- (element *Zy-* < names such as *Zygmunt* + suffix *-ch,* or directly < *Zygmunt*): Zych, Zychla, Żychliński, Zychowicz, Żychowicz

Zygm- (given name *Zygmunt* = English *Sigmund*): Siegmund, Zygma, Zygmunt, Zygmuntowicz

*　　　　*　　　　*

Coats of Arms

Polish heraldry is an absolutely fascinating topic to which, alas, we cannot begin to do justice here. There are several aspects of Polish nobility and heraldry that set them apart from similar institutions in western Europe,[4] but most of them are not directly relevant to the subject of Polish surnames. For our purposes, we will focus on the names of coats of arms as a small but significant source of Polish surnames, and touch on those other aspects only in passing.

The names of Polish coats of arms are not really the same thing as the first names discussed in this chapter, but for our purposes they are similar in that both kinds are proper names used to designate persons, and the meaning of the names is not particularly relevant to their usage. *Młynarski* suggests that an ancestor was a miller *(młynarz)*, *Warszawski* suggests origin in Warsaw *(Warszsawa)*; but the original meaning of *Piotr* or *Jan* has nothing to do with why a descendant would be called *Piotrowski* or *Janowicz*. In the same way, the meaning of, say, *Rogala* ("a horned animal") in the Rogala coat of arms, while presumably relevant to the original bearers of those arms, played no real role in the adoption of the surname *Rogalski*.

Actually, coats of arms and their names pre-date surnames by several centuries, and their use in surnames might be viewed by a conservative as a perversion of the arms. The coat of arms *(herb)* was used, not by an individual family, but by a clan *(ród)*, and every member of the clan's individual families had the right to use the arms. The names of the oldest coats of arms reach back to the earliest days of Polish history, and frequently arose from the clan's battle-cry (*Boża Wola*, "God's will"), devices on the coats of arms (*Lis*, "fox," *Topór*, "axe," *Łabędź*, "swan"), the place where the clan's members assembled *(Rawa, Doliwa)*, and so on.[5]

The coat of arms was an integral part of the nobles' identity as warriors who fought in defense of the realm, and the usual occasion for the king's bestowing arms was when an individual distinguished himself in battle with some particularly manful deed or valued service. The device on the arms' shield often had some connection with the deed; the *Roch* arms were supposedly first bestowed by a Mazovian prince on a courtier who diverted him by playing chess after a battle—in this case *Roch* means "rook," the chess piece.[6]

Many coats of arms were private, used by a clan composed of only one family, but some of the most prominent were used by many families. Since the *herb* was used by clans, as surnames developed you had a number of families with different surnames but the same coat of arms; any Polish armorial will list the various families which used a given coat of arms. There were also families with the same surnames but different arms: for instance, the

Bielińskis of Junosza arms and the Bielińskis of Szeliga arms, the Drzewickis of Nałęcz arms and the Drzewickis of Ciołek arms. Since many surnames were borne by more than one family, it often became convenient to use the *herb* name in conjunction with the surname to distinguish this noble family from that; that's where names like "Nowina Sokolnicki" came from.

When surnames began to be established, many nobles used the adjectival form of their estate's name as a surname (*Brzeziński, Lipiński,* etc.). But some had no hereditary estate; for this or some other reason, they might form surnames based on the name of their coat of arms. This is why you see such families as the Bronickis of arms Bronic, the Dołęgowskis of arms Dołęga, the Dąbrowiczes of arms Dąbrowa, and so on.

Once *herb* names began being used as surnames, all hope of confining them to the nobility—the only people authorized to use them—was lost. If *-ski* names were popular among the non-noble because they sounded aristocratic, you can imagine how elegant names from coats of arms sounded! For a time the nobles managed to stem the tide, but eventually the middle-class and peasants were going around using the names formerly reserved for *szlachta*. It didn't help that after the partitioning of Poland, the governments of Russia, Prussia, and Austria assumed the right to determine who was and was not noble, and the criteria they set were less than foolproof. A great many families were recognized as noble who in fact had no justification for that status; and there was no effective way to keep the "lower classes" from using whatever name they liked.

As a result, bearing a name derived from a coat of arms doesn't even begin to mean one is of noble descent. If your name is *Nowiński,* for instance, it's rather exciting to think that this surname may have come from the name of the Nowina coat of arms, so maybe your ancestors were noble. This is entirely understandable, and in some cases may even turn out to be true. But you should realize the odds are very much against it!

Endnotes

[1] Tadeusz Korzon, *Kościuszko: Biografia z dokumentów wysnuta,* 2nd ed., Kraków-Warszawa, Muzeum Narodowy w Rapperswilu, page 1. All citations come from chapter one. As of this writing, the book is available online from the Wielkopolska Digital Library <http://www.wbc.poznan.pl/dlibra/docmetadata?id=3569&from=latest>, and possibly other digital libraries in Poland.

[2] Jan Stanisław Bystroń, *Nazwiska Polskie*, 2nd ed., Lwów-Warsawa, Książnica-Atlas, 1936, p. 23.

[3] The introductory chapters to Kazimierz Rymut's *Nazwiska Polaków,* Wydawnictwo Naukowe DWN, Kraków, 2001, Vol. I, contain more information on Slavic name roots and Polish name elements. However, one

must be fluent in Polish to read those sections, unlike the main body of his book, which any intelligent person can make out with the help of a decent Polish-English dictionary.

[4] For an introduction to this subject, see Felix W. Holewinski, "The Nature of Polish Knighthood and Chivalry from the Thirteenth to the Eighteenth Centuries," originally appearing in *The Augustan,* XX:3, reprinted in the *Polish Genealogical Society Newsletter,* Spring 1989 issue. See also Count Juliusz Nowina Sokolnicki, "The Noble Clans," *Polish Genealogical Society Newsletter,* Fall 1990 issue, beginning on page 1.

[5] Bystroń, *Nazwiska Polskie*, pp. 73–74.

[6] Korzon, *Kościuszko*, p. 4.

Chapter Six

Home Sweet Homeski

We identify people by the place where they live or came from more often than we might realize. I lived for several years in the town of New Milford, Connecticut. I remember one afternoon when our exterminator, a man named Hal, was scheduled to make a service call at my house. A slight change in my schedule meant I needed to leave by three p.m., so I called to let him know he needed to come by before then. His secretary answered the phone, and I gave my message, identifying myself as "Mr. Hoffman." She promptly paged Hal and informed him, in some excitement, that the actor Dustin Hoffman wanted his home serviced before three p.m.! As it happens, one of Dustin Hoffman's houses was in a nearby town (Roxbury, I think), and we used the same exterminator; so the mistake was understandable (except that I sound nothing like Dustin Hoffman). Hal told me about this later and we had a good chuckle over my being confused with a movie star. But Hal had known all his stops that day were in my town, New Milford, not in Roxbury. So he knew the phone call must have come, not from the wealthy Roxbury Hoffman, but from the insignificant New Milford Hoffman!

(Still, considering how quickly that secretary relayed my request, maybe I should have impersonated "cousin Dustin" more often!)

During the period when Polish surnames were being established, there probably wasn't much trouble confusing Polish movie stars with ordinary people. We have already mentioned, however, that the most eminent members of the society, the *szlachta,* found toponyms (place names) could provide handy and prestigious ways to identify themselves. The expression *z* (from, of) plus the name of one's estate in the genitive case, bore the same cachet as *de* in French names such as *de Montfort,* and *von* in German names such as *von Richthofen.* So if a nobleman named *Piotr* owned an estate at Kozłowo, he'd be called *Piotr z Kozlowa.* But another way to say *z Kozłowa* is with the adjective *Kozłowski,* so that *Piotr Kozlowski* was a perfectly good equivalent of *Piotr z Kozlowa.* It's hard to say exactly why the *-ski* form became more popular than the *z* expression, but that's what happened. As these second names gradually turned into surnames, the process of adding *-ski* (or *-cki* or *-zki*) to an estate name, and later to almost any toponym, became one of the most common ways to form a surname.

The Rich Don't Always Get Richer

Students of English literature are familiar with Thomas Hardy's *Tess of the d'Urbervilles,* and personally, I think this book should be required reading for those who hope to trace their lineage back to nobility. The story begins when Jack Durbeyfield, a middle-aged drunken haggler in a rural area of England, is told by a local amateur student of heraldry that he is a lineal descendant of an ancient noble family, the d'Urbervilles. (The -*ville* suffix presumably indicates that the surname came from a toponym—*ville* means "town, city" in French—and thus *d'Urberville* means "of Urberville," the name of the family's ancestral estate.) All manner of misery comes from this as Durbeyfield decides he's too good to muck about doing odd jobs all over the countryside, and he sends his daughter, Tess, off to make the acquaintance of some surviving d'Urbervilles, her supposed relatives. In fact, it becomes clear that these d'Urbervilles are wealthy parvenus who bought the right to use the ancient name from the last recognized descendants. It remains unclear whether the Durbeyfields are really descendants of the noble d'Urbervilles in the first place. The book is full of bitter ironies on the subject of "nobility" (and perhaps also how gullible people can be when it comes to descent from nobility).

Tess is fiction, but Hardy drew inspiration from real instances of English nobility who'd gone to seed. Poland, too, had its share of impoverished nobles; many of the "petty" or "minor" nobility were at least as poor as the peasants around them, yet were forbidden to improve their financial situation by marrying beneath their station.[1] Their impoverishment was due to many reasons, one of which may surprise you: unlike the English and most western Europeans, Poles did not practice primogeniture, the custom of having the first-born son inherit the whole estate. All surviving children inherited their share of whatever the parents owned.[2] It sounds like a great idea; in practice, it meant that within a few generations, even a large estate could have fragmented into parcels too small to support anyone.

Meanwhile, there were members of the middle class who had become rather well-to-do, and craved the social status an alliance with nobility brought. As usually happens when the rules prohibit people from doing things that are mutually beneficial, ways were found around the rules.

All this surely helped blur the line between nobleman and commoner, and weaken the custom that only nobles could have surnames, especially those created by adding -*ski* (or -*cki* or -*zki*) to place names. So the suffix that started out denoting the names of nobles' estates eventually was diluted to the point that it applied to all classes and suggested nothing more than origin in a particular village or area. It was applied to other kinds of surnames as well, so that -*ski* was added to names of professions or to prominent features. But in this chapter, we'll concentrate on names formed from toponyms.

You've Got to Know Where You Came From to Know Where You're Going

This homely little platitude has become a cliché, yet in terms of genealogical research it is absolutely true. If your ancestors were Polish, your only hope of success in tracing them lies in knowing where they lived in Poland before they emigrated. A surname derived from a toponym might seem to offer a lot of help in finding that ancestral home; yet such surnames generally fail to live up to their promise. So many toponyms are too obscure to find, or can refer to a dozen different places, or disappoint you in other ways. If you have managed to locate the general area your ancestors came from, however, a toponym may prove truly useful.

The point is, if you frame your question "My ancestor was named *Ostrowiecki,* where'd he come from in Poland?" you will probably get nowhere. As of the late 19th century, Poland had literally dozens of villages and small communities named *Ostrowiec*; it could take many weary years to comb through all their records in search of a familiar name. But if you say "My ancestors named *Ostrowiecki* hailed from the area west of Bydgoszcz; do we know of any place that might be connected with them?" you no longer have to search all over Poland. You can focus intently on a limited area, and that makes a difference. That focus will probably lead you to discover a little rural community called *Ostrowiec* 13 kilometers southwest of the town of Nakło nad Notecią, just west of Bydgoszcz.[3] There's no guarantee that's the place you want; but it certainly is a good place to start looking!

So toponyms aren't necessarily the buried treasure map some researchers expect. But if you've done your homework, they may turn out to be the X that marks the spot on the map. Clearly, they deserve our attention.

Actually toponyms, like other proper names, are a rather odd phenomenon. They seem to go back to the misty beginnings of time. If you ask a typical native of, say, Brooklyn, "Why do you call this place 'Brooklyn?'" you'll usually get no satisfactory answer. "That's just what we call it" is the standard reply. Occasionally you'll encounter someone who can tell you the whole history of a place and where its name came from; but that person is the exception. A name is a name because everyone uses it to denote a given place, yet most of the people using the name haven't the faintest idea where it came from or what it means. I used to live in Holyrood, Kansas, and I still don't know why a tiny Kansas town settled mainly by Germans and Czechs bears the name of a royal castle in Edinburgh, Scotland!

But all toponyms obviously did mean something when they originated. Consider the town of Biskupiec near Olsztyn. I seriously doubt many of the town's residents give it much thought, but it appears the name comes from *biskup,* "bishop," and in fact it does. It was once part of property belonging to the Bishop of Warmia, and the name reflects that historical fact.[4]

While I'm talking about this, however, I'd better warn against "folk etymologies," traps for the unwary who try to interpret names of places or people. I have heard the name of the city of Częstochowa explained as coming from *często,* "often," and *chować,* "to hide, conceal." The name arose, supposedly, because the lie of the land around the town causes it to be hidden from sight from certain places and angles—it's the town that "often hides." This is a rather charming and plausible story; but checking the name back through the records shows that it's also wrong! The town's name arose by way of the personal name *Częstoch,* a shortened form of one of those old Slavic name roots we discussed in Chapter Five—presumably a man by that name founded it or owned it at some point. It's *Częstoch+owa* "Częstoch's place," not *Często+chowa,* the peek-a-boo town. As the years went by and people forgot where the name came from, they turned to a very reasonable explanation based on what the name sounded like. This sort of mistake is very common and thoroughly understandable, and those of us who care about getting things right have to guard against it constantly![5]

The moral of the story: some toponyms are exactly what they seem to be, but others are quite difficult—often because they derived from words or names that have since become archaic and dropped out of the living language. To puzzle out their meaning, you have to delve back into the oldest records you can find, see if the form of the name has changed over the centuries, and look for other instances where that word was used, which may help you deduce its meaning from context. Sometimes it turns out the name is associated with a person, as with Kraków and the name of its legendary founder, Krak. Very often, the name came from some distinctive feature of the geography, as in *Zagórz,* "beyond the mountains," or the local flora and fauna, as in any of a jillion places named *Dąbrowa,* "oak grove." And sometimes, unfortunately, it proves impossible to establish exactly where the name came from.

In other words, place names are a lot like surnames! And tracing a surname back to a place name can be sort of like begging the question, because then you have to ask, "All right, what does the place name mean?" This leads us to two types of surnames formed from toponyms: those formed from general terms, and those from the names of specific places.

General Names

By "general terms" I mean nouns denoting geographical features that are not unique to any specific part of Poland, but may show up in different areas: *bagno,* "marsh," *brzezina,* "birch grove," *dolina,* "valley," and so on. A person who lived near a birch grove might come to bear the name *Brzeziński,* a person from the valley might be *Doliński,* and so forth.

Of course, it often happened that these general names came to be applied to specific places as well. There are a dozen localities named *Bagno,* and even more called *Brzezina* or *Brzezinki* or *Brzeziny.* This makes it hard to say whether a given family *Brzeziński* was originally called that because they lived near a birch grove or because they came from Brzezina or Brzezinki or Brzeziny. In some ways, the question is moot; after all, a place named *Brzezina* surely got that name because there was a birch grove somewhere in the vicinity. But it does make it that much harder to tell someone named *Brzeziński* where his family came from. The toponym just does not offer much in the way of clues.

This helps explain why it's often impossible to tell from the form of a surname where the people bearing that name came from. There is no shortage of marshes or meadows or birch groves in Poland, so a *Bagiński* or *Łączyński* or *Brzeziński* simply must understand that even the most knowledgeable person has to have more to work with before he/she can suggest what part of Poland those names came from! A person named *Gorski* once demanded that I tell him exactly where the Gorskis came from. He was quite put out when I explained that the name, originally *Górski,* came from the word *góra,* "mountain, hill," and there are rather a lot of mountains and hills in Poland. He found that insufficient, hinting that a real expert would have known from looking at his name precisely which village his ancestors came from. I begged pardon for my lamentable ignorance and, following the example of the immortal scholar Groucho Marx, suggested that he bore a hole in himself and let the sap run out.

Have I Got a Preposition for You!

With many Polish surnames, it is possible to look in a dictionary or atlas and find the root of the name fairly easily: *Mularski* comes from *mularz,* *Krakowski* comes from *Kraków,* and so on. Surnames from general toponyms can throw you a curve, however; they often prefix prepositions to the basic root. If you recognize the preposition, you stand a good chance of breaking the name down into its components and figuring it out.

Actually, the prefixing of prepositions makes perfect sense. Think of expressions in English such as "past the road," "by the shore," "up the creek." If you're designating a place, a preposition is often a necessary part of the description. Polish is no different in this respect.

A quick look through the index of name roots in Volume II suggests that these are the prepositions most commonly used as prefixes in surnames:

na: on, upon, at	*pod:* under, near, at	*z:* from, of
nad: above, over	*przy:* at, by, near	*za:* behind, beyond

As an example, let's take the root of our dear friend Gorski's name, *góra,* "mountain." A look through Volume II reveals that there are indeed names from *na + góra* (on the mountain), *pod + góra* (near, under the mountain), *przy + góra* (by, near the mountain), *z + góra* (from, of the mountain), and *za + góra,* (beyond, past the mountain). As for *nad + góra,* that doesn't appear, which makes sense. I would be very interested in meeting anyone who lived "above, over the mountain"!

I find that discussing topics such as this rapidly reaches a point of diminishing returns; after a while, most people do better if you provide them some real examples and let them find patterns for themselves. So let me give a brief list of general toponym roots from Volume II, what they mean, and a few surnames that come from them.

bagno, "marsh": Bagieński, Bagiński, Bagniewski, Bagniuk

bajor, "puddle, pond": Bajor, Bajorek, Bajura

bór, "forest": Borek, Borkowicz, Boroń, Borowy

brzezina, "birch grove": Brzezinka, Brzeziński, Brzeźniak

bugaj, "bend in a river" (also "cluster of shrubs," or "bull," or "big man"); Bugaj, Bugajny

czarny, "black," used in many place names, e.g., Czarnolas (literally, "black forest"), Czarna Góra (Black Mountain)

dąb, "oak," appears in many place names, e.g. *Dębno:* Dąbek, Dębczak, Dombkowicz

dolina, "valley": Dolina, Doliński, Duliński

dolny, "lower," used in several place names: Dolniak, Dolny, Dulnik

dom, "home, house": Domalewski, Domaszk, Domek, Domowicz

domb- → *dąb-*

dwór, "court, manor, yard": Dworak, Dworek, Dworzak, Dworzański

folwark, "manorial farmstead, grange": Folwarczny, Folwarski

góra, "mountain": Góra, Góral (compare *góral,* "mountain-dweller of southern Poland"), Górek, Górski, Gurak, Hora, Horacek, Horak

gozd, gwozd, (archaic) "forest": Gozdal, Gozdek, Guzdek

granica, "border": Granica, Graniczka, Graniczny

grób, "grave": Grobosz, Grobys

gród, "fortress, citadel, city": Grodek, Gródek, Grodoń, Horodko

grządka, "hen-roost, garden-bed," or *grzęda,* "patch, flower-bed"; Grządka, Grzęda, Grzenda

gumno, "farmyard, barn, threshing floor"; Gumieniak, Gumienny, Gumny

gwozd- → *gozd-*

hor- → *gór-*

jama, "cavern, den": Jama, Jamka, Jamuła

jatka, "primitive hut," also archaic "butcher's shop": Jata, Jatczak, Jatkowski

jezioro, "lake": Jezierny, Jezierski, Jeziorny, Jezioro, Ozioro

kaczma- → *karczma*

kałuża, "pool, puddle": Kałuziak, Kałużka, Kałużniak, Kałużny, Kałużyński

kamień, "rock, stone," very common root in toponyms: Kamieniak, Kamieniec, Kaminiarz, Kamionka

kapla, "chapel": Kapliński, Kaplita, Kapluk

karczma, "inn," especially by way of *karczmarz,* "innkeeper": Kaczmar, Kaczmarczyk, Kaczmarek, Karczmarek, Koczmara

komora, "chamber, room": Komora, Komorniczak, Komorowski

koniec, "end, limit": Koneczny, Konieczko, Konieczny

kraj, "country, end, limit": Krajecki, Krajda, Krajka, Krajnik

kujawa, "sand dune," also "an open, bare place" (cmp. **Kujawy,** p. 84); Kujawiński, Kujawka, Kujawowicz

kuźnia, "smithy, forge": Kuźniak, Kuźniar, Kuźnic, Kuźnicki, Kuźnik

łąka, "meadow": Łąka, Łankiewicz

ławica, "sand-bank," cmp. Ławica, Sieraków gmina: Ławicki
majdan, "open square, clearing": Majdan, Majdanik, Majdanowski
miedza, "balk, boundary strip": Miedziak, Miedzik
mierzeja, "sandbar": Mierzejek
mogiła, "grave, mound," cmp. *Mogiła,* town near Kraków: Mogiła, Mogiłka
murawa, "lawn, greensward": Murawa, Murawiec, Murawko, Murawski
na "on, to" + *dół,* "bottom": Nadolnik, Nadolny, Nadolski
na "on, to" + *góra,* "mountain": Nagórka, Nagórny, Nagórski, Nahorski
niwa, "field": Niwczyk, Niwczyk
obora, "cow-shed, barn": Oborski, Oborzyński
ogród, "garden": Ogrodniczak, Ogrodnik, Ogrodny, Ogrodowicz, Ogrodzki
okraj, "border, edge": Okraj, Okrajek, Okrajni
osada, "settlement": Osada, Osadnik, Osadziński
pieczara, "den": Pieczara, Pieczarka, Pieczora, Pieczur
podgórny, "near/under the mountain," or *podgórze,* "foothills": Podgórczyk,
    Podgórniak, Podgórnik
polny, "of or relating to a field": Polniak, Polnik
polowy, (adj.) "of a field, farm": Polowiec, Polowy
poręba, "clearing (in a forest)": Porąbka, Poręba, Poremba, Porombka
potok, "stream": Potoczak, Potoczek, Potok
przymor-, "littoral, maritime," literally "by the sea"; Przymorski
rżysko, "stubble-field": Rzyski, Rzysko, Rżysko
sioło, archaic "settlement, village"; Sielczak, Sielewicz, Sieluk, Sioła, Siołek
skonieczny, "final, living at the edge": Skonecki, Skoneczny, Skoniecki, Sko-
    niezcka, Skonieczny
staw, "pond": Stawarczyk, Stawarz (*stawarz* = "digger of ponds"), Stawny,
    Stawowy (sttawowy, "pond caretaker")
stodoła, "barn": Stodoła, Stodolak, Stodolny, Stodulski
stok, archaic "stream," now "hillside, slant, flank, slope": Stoczek, Stoko-
    wiec, Stoksik
świat, "world, earth": Światkowski, Światowy, Świeciak
tabor, "military camp, transport": Taberski, Tabor, Taborski, Tobera, Toborek
targ, "market": Targos, Targosz
wądół, "pit, ravine": Wądołowski, Wądolny, Wędołowski
wierzch, "top, peak": Wierzchołek, Wierzchoń
wyrąb, "clearing": Wyrębak, Wyrembek, Wyremblewski
zabłocie < *za błotem,* "beyond, past the muddy place": Zabłocki, Zabłotny,
    Zabłotowicz
zabor < *za* + *bor-,* "beyond the woods" (or < *za* + *bor,* "to the fight"): Zabor,
    Zaborek, Zaborny
zadrożny, < *za* + *droga,* "beyond the road": Zadroga, Zadrożny, Zadrożyński
zagórski < *za,* "beyond, past, behind" + *góra,* "the mountain": Zagóra, Za-
    górny, Zagórowicz
zagroda, "fenced-in place; farm, croft": Zagroda, Zagrodzki

zalas- < *za* + *las,* "beyond the woods" (but *Załęski* or *Załężny* < *za* + *łęg,*
= "beyond the moor," or the place name *Załęg*): Zalas, Zaleś, Zalesko,
Zaleśny

zapolski < *zapole,* "place beyond a field, mow," cmp. the common toponym
Zapole: Zapolnik, Zapolny, Zapolski

zarzec- < *za* + *rzeka,* "beyond the river": Zarzecki, Zarzeczny, Zarzeka, Za-
rzycki, Zarzyczny, Zarzyka

zdrój, "spring, spa": Zdrojek, Zdrojkowski, Zdrojowy

żuława, "river delta, marshland, fen": Żuławiński, Żuławnik, Żuławski

*   *   *

Specific Place Names

I should clarify that by "specific place names" I mean those associated
with specific towns, villages, regions, and the like, such as Kraków, Warszawa, as opposed to more general terms such as *dąbrowa,* "oak grove," and
zdrój, "spring, spa. " The distinction is admittedly arbitrary, since many of
those general names became names of specific towns; but I think it is a useful one for our purposes. You can look up *dąbrowa* in any Polish dictionary
and get its basic meaning; but looking up, say, *Włocławek* will yield at most
the information that that's the name of a Polish city, period. You may or may
not succeed in finding remarks on where a specific place's name came from;
for most surname researchers the link with a specific place is all that matters.

As I explained earlier, surnames derived from specific toponyms will
occasionally lead you straight back to where they originated, but usually
they won't. The fly in this particular ointment is that relatively few names
of Polish towns and villages are unique. If you find one *Krzemień* or *Piaski,*
odds are you'll find two or three more without even trying. In fact a Polish
map website, <http://mapa.szukacz.pl/>, shows some 80 places named *Piaski*
("Sands") or *Piaski* with a second word forming a compound name.[6]

This isn't a plot devised by crafty Slavs to bewilder Americans. It's just
that the circumstances that suggested a particular name for a particular locale
were likely to be duplicated in other parts of Poland; or folks who came from
a given village and moved to settle a new area often named their new home
after the old one. This isn't true only of Poland; Connecticut, for instance,
has a Fairfield and a New Fairfield, a Milford and a New Milford, and so on.
If a name's good enough to be used once, it's good enough to be used again.

Back centuries ago, when place names were becoming established, people thought locally, not globally. If everyone thought the perfect name for
their village near an oak grove was *Dąbrowa,* it didn't bother them that there
was another *Dąbrowa* just a few dozen miles away—any more than it bothers natives of Moscow, Idaho, that there's another city called Moscow. If all
politics are local, as Tip O'Neill said, so are all place names. Ancient Polish

society was rather less mobile than contemporary American society, so referring to a spot as *Łąka,* "meadow," was plenty good enough for the locals, who weren't likely to confuse it with the *Łąka* a week's journey away—that other *Łąka* might as well be on the moon.

You can see this clearly when you look at a map and see a *Sromowce Niżne* ("Lower Sromowce"), a *Sromowce Średnie* ("Middle Sromowce) and a *Sromowce Wyżne* ("Upper Sromowce") in a mountainous area just a few miles from each other, southwest of *Stary Sącz* ("Old Sącz") and *Nowy Sącz* ("New Sącz"). In this case the villages were close enough together that they needed to be distinguished as "Lower," "Middle," and "Upper"—but there was certainly no need to resort to anything as drastic as completely different names. Naming places isn't a contest, where originality counts; it's a practical business, and when most of these names arose, the people doing the naming considered their universe bounded more or less by the horizon. They certainly weren't worried that the names they used would confuse people centuries later on another continent!

Add to this picture the fact that a given Polish locality was generally composed of dozens of tinier subdivisions, each of which had a name. For example, a gazetteer lists four different places called *Sadki,* and proceeds to explain that one of them, located 10 kilometers northwest of Nakło nad Notecią, was a parish seat that included the communities of "Bażantarnia, Bnin, Borek, Jadwiga, Kulaski, Mrozowo, Ostrowiec, Pólko, Popówka, Radzice, Sadki, Samostrzel, Słojek, and Żelazno." The parish church was rebuilt in 1573 by Paweł Samostrzelski, and again in 1749-1755 by Wojciech and Konstanty Bniński (presumably the noble family Samostrzelski owned the area in the 16th century, but later it passed to the Bnińskis).[7] This entry suggests that at least two surnames, Samostrzelski and Bniński, came from names of those small estates or communities. For all we know, any or all of the other names may have produced surnames, especially by the time the peasants got around to adopting surnames—so we may find people in the area named *Borecki* or *Borkowski, Mrozowski, Ostrowiecki, Radzicki,* etc.

Perhaps I've made this subject seem so complex that you despair of ever tracing a surname. Don't give up! The idea is simply to show why you must always see your research as rooted in specific places and try to learn whatever you can about those places. Look at it this way: even if you have reason to think your surname derives from one of those 39 villages named *Piaski,* that's still more of a clue than you get with a surname like *Nowak* or *Kowalski*!

A Small Selection of Toponymic Surnames

In view of all this, it's clearly pointless to try to present a comprehensive list of all Polish surnames derived from toponyms. Such a list would have to be at least as big as the most complete Polish atlas and gazetteer ever written! But a brief list of selected surnames from Volume II and the place names from which they probably derived will give you a feel for the process and make it easier for you to deal with such names when you encounter them. It can also provide illustrations of how adjectival surnames (*-ski, -cki,* and *-zki*) relate to the toponyms from which they were formed.

When looking over this list, please remember two points: 1) the relationship between toponyms and names formed from them is tricky, so I can't promise all of these are right, and 2) even when a surname is shown as derived from a specific place's name, chances are there are other places by that same name, so the surname could have derived from them, too. In fact, in most cases, I guarantee it—did you know there's more than one *Warszawa* in Poland?

Note: all references to "provinces" refer to the 16 województwa *into which Poland was divided as of 1999, not the setup with 49 that was in force from 1975 to 1998. The* powiaty, *abolished in 1975 and restored in 1999, are administrative subdivisions of a province, much as a county is of a state in the United States. The* "powiat *seats" were/are reasonably good-sized and prominent towns.*

Aleksandrowski < numerous places named *Aleksandrów, Aleksandrowice,* etc.

Augustowski < *Augustów,* a *powiat* seat in Podlaskie prov., or other places named *Augustów* or *Augustowo*

Balicki < *Balice,* several villages in Poland

Baligrodzki < village *Baligród,* Podkarpackie province

Baliński < *Balin, Balino,* several villages

Będziński < *Bądzyn,* Mazowieckie prov., or *Będzin,* a *powiat* seat, Śląskie prov.

Belski < toponyms such as *Belsk Duży,* Mazowieckie prov.

Bełzki, Bełzak < *Bełz,* a former *powiat* seat in Galicia, now in Ukraine

Berdychowski < top. *Berdychów, Berdychowo*

Berestecki < toponym such as *Beresteczko*—this is a Russian or Ukrainian form (= Polish root *brzost-*)

Berliner, Berliński < the German city *Berlin* or in some cases the Polish town *Berlińce* in territory east of Poland's current borders

Białostocki < *Białystok,* powiat seat, capital of Podlaskie prov.

Bielski < numerous places with names such as *Biała, Bielsk, Bielsko,* etc.

Bieszczad, Bieszczat < *Bieszczady,* mountain range in southern Poland

Biłgorajski < *Biłgoraj,* a *powiat* seat, Lubelskie prov.

Błoński < *Błonie,* name of a number of places

Bobrzecki < *Bóbrka,* Podkarpackie prov., or several villages named *Bobrek*

Bocheński *or* **Boch eński** < *Bochnia,* powiat seat in Małopolskie prov.

Bolanowski < *Bolanowice,* a village near Mościski in Galicia, now in Ukr.

Bolkowski < *Bolków,* a village in Łódzkie prov.

Map of present-day Poland with rough indications of some of the major regions into which it is divided. The Polish names are given above; in English these regions are usually called as follows: *Kujawy,* Kujavia; *Małopolska:* Little Poland; *Mazowsze:* Mazovia; *Mazury:* Masuria; *Podlasie:* Podlasie; *Pomorze:* Pomerania; *Śląsk:* Silesia; *Warmia:* Warmia, *or* Ermland *(German name); Wielkopolska:* Great Poland.

Borczyński < *Borczyn* near Pińczów, Świętokrzyskie prov.
Brański < various places called *Branice, Branno,* and *Brańsk*
Brodzki < *Bród* and *Brody,* names of a number of localities
Brzeski < a number of places named *Brześć, Brzesko, Brzeg*
Brzozowski < a number of places name *Brzozów, Brzozowa,* etc.
Buczacki < *Buczacz,* a Galician *powiat* seat, now Бучач [*Buchach*], Ukraine
Bukowski < numerous places named *Bukowa, Bukowe, Bukowno,* etc.
Bychowski < a number of places named *Bychów, Bychowo*
Bystrzycki < a number of places named *Bystrzyca*
Chełmiński < several places named *Chełmno,* including a *powiat* seat in Kujawsko-Pomorskie prov.
Chełstowski < villages named *Chełst, Chełstów, Chełsty*
Chojnicki < several villages named *Chojnice* and *Chojnica*

Chojnowski < numerous places *Chojna, Chojnów, Chojnowo,* etc.

Chrzanowski < numerous places *Chrzanów, Chrzanowice, Chrzanowo*

Ciechanowski < *Ciechanów, powiat* seat in Mazowieckie prov.

Cieszyński < places named *Cieszyn* and *Ciesyzna*

Cywiński < villages *Cywiny Wojskie* and *Cywiny-Dynguny,* Mazowieckie prov.

Czerkawski < *Cherkasy,* name of several places in Ukraine, especially the capital of Cherkasy *oblast'*

Czermiński < several villages named *Czermno,* pssibly also *Czermin, Czermna,* etc.

Częstochowski < *Częstochowa,* powiat seat in Śląskie province

Długokęcki < *Długokąty* in Mazowieckie prov., perhaps other places with that name

Długołęcki < a number of places named *Długołęka*

Długopolski < *Długopole,* Małopolskie prov. and other places by that name

Dobrzycki < several places named *Dobrzyca*

Dobrzyń, Dobrzyński < several places named *Dobrzyń*

Dramiński < village *Dramin,* Mazowieckie prov.

Drużkowski < toponym *Drużków,* Małopolskie prov.

Drwęcki < *Drwęcz,* Mazowieckie prov., or *Drwęca,* Warmińsko-Mazurskie prov.

Dunaj, Dunajski < *Dunaj,* Polish name of the Danube river

Elsner < German *Elsner* < Slavic *olesna,* alder, or < dweller on the Els

Falęcki < places named *Falęcice, Falęcin, Falenty* in Mazowieckie prov.

Faściszewski < top. *Faściszowa,* Małopolskie prov.

Faszczewski < top. *Faszcze,* various villages in Mazowiecke and Podlaskie prov.

Frysztak < *Frysztak,* Podkarpackie prov., originally *Frysztat* < German *freie Stadt,* "[tax]-free city," or *Frysztat,* Silesia, now *Fryštát,* part of Karviná

Gadomski < *Gadomiec,* formerly called *Gadom,* Mazowieckie prov.

Garwoliński < *Garwolin, powiat* seat, Mazowieckie prov.

Gdaniec < *gdaniec,* resident of Gdańsk

Giżycki < *Giżycke,* name of several villages

Glinojecki < *Glinojeck,* Mazowieckie prov.

Gliwicki < *Gliwice,* city in Śląskie prov.

Głogowski < several places named *Głogów, Głogowa, Głogowiec*

Głuchowski < places named *Głuchów, Głuchowo, Głóchówek, Głuchowice*

Gorlicki < *Gorlice, powiat* seat in Małopolskie prov.

Górowski < places named *Górowo, Górowa, Gurowo*

Gostyński < top. *Gostyń, Gostynin, Gostynki*

Grabowski < numerous places named *Grabów, Grabowa, Grabówka, Grabowo* from personal name *Grab* or the term *grab,* "hornbeam"[8]

Grajewski < places named *Grajewo* and *Grajów*

Grodecki < numerous places named *Gródek*

Grotkowski < *Grotkowo*, Wielkopolskie prov., or variant of *Grodkowski*

Grunwald < places named *Grunwald*, Warmińsko-Mazurskie prov., or *Grunwald*, now *Grywałd*, Małopolskie prov.

Halicki < *Halicz*, now *Halych* in Ukr., gave its name to *Galicia*, the section of Poland and western Ukraine ruled by Austria after the partitions

Jarociński < *Jarocin, powiat* seat, Wielkopolskie prov., or perhaps other places with similar names

Jarosławski < a number of places named *Jarosław, Jarosławice, Jarosławiec*

Jasielski < *Jasło, powiat* seat in Podkarpackie prov.

Jaworowski < places named *Jaworów, Jaworówka*

Jaworski < places named *Jawor, Jaworze*

Jędrzejowski < places with names such as *Jędrzejewo, Jędrzejów*

Jeżewski, Jeżowski < various places named *Jeżewo, Jeżów*

Jodłowski < a number of places named *Jodłowa, Jodłów, Jodłówka*

Kaczyński < places named *Kaczyn, Kaczyna*, etc.

Kadłubowski < village named *Kadłubowo*, Mazowieckie prov.

Kadow < *Kadow*, Mecklenburg-Vorpommern, Germany

Kalinowski < numerous places named *Kalinów, Kalinowa, Kalinowo*

Kaliński < numerous places named *Kalina* and *Kaleń*

Kałuski < places named *Kałusyzn* in Mazowieckie prov.

Karliński < *Karlin*, Śląskie prov., perhaps also other places named *Karlin* or *Karlino*

Kemnitz < German place name *Kemnitz*

Kępiński < places named *Kępno* and *Kępina*

Kijewski, Kijowski < places named as *Kijewice, Kijów*, which could include the city of *Kijów*, Kiev, now *Київ* [*Kyiv*], Ukr.

Kłodzki < places named *Kłocko* and *Kłoda*

Kobrzyński < *Kobrzyniec*, Kujawsko-Pomorskie prov., perhaps in some cases also < *Kobrzyń*, now *Кобрын* [*Kobryn*], Belarus

Kolberg < German name for the Polish town *Kołobrzeg*, Zachodniepomorskie prov.

Kołomyjski < *Kołomyja*, now *Коломия* [*Kolomyia*] in Ukraine

Konecki < *Końskie, powiat* seat, Świętokrzyskie prov.

Koniński < *Konin*, today called *Kunin*, Świętokrzyskie prov.

Kościański < town *Kościan*, Wielkopolskie prov.

Kowalewski < numerous places named *Kowale, Kowalewo, Kowalów*, etc.

Kownacki < *Kownaty*, Mazowsze, perhaps other places with that name

Kozielski < places named *Koźle* and *Kozielsko*

Koźmiński < *Koźmin*, several places

Kożuchowski < *Kożuchów*, several villages

Krakowczyk, Krakowiak, Krakowski < *Kraków*, Małopolskie prov.

Krotoszyński < *Krotoszyn*, Wielkopolskie prov.

Krzemieniecki < *Krzemieniec*, Eastern Borderlands, presumably referring to what is now *Кременець* [*Kremeneť*], Ternopiľ *oblasť*, Ukr.

Kujawski < *Kujawy*, region of Poland, or individual localities with that name

Kurlanc < *Kurlandia*, Courland, area now in Latvia

Kwidziński < *Kwidzyn*, city in Pomorskie prov.

Lanckoroński < *Lanckorona*, Małopolskie prov.

Łańcucki < *Łańcut*, city in Podkarpackie prov.

Landsberg < *Landsberg*, German name for *Gorzów Wielkopolski*

Langner < German top. *Langen* and *Langenau*

Lauterbach < common German place name *Lauterbach*

Łęczycki < *Łęczyca*, Łódzkie prov.

Łempicki, Łępicki < *Łempice*, Mazowieckie prov.

Leszczyński < places called *Leszczyny* and *Leszczno* (including the town to-day called *Leszno*, Wielkopolskie prov.)

Lewandowski < *Lewandów*, a section of Warsaw, or < *lawenda*, the lavender bush

Lewartowski < *Lewartów*, now called *Lubartów*, Lubelskie prov.

Licbarski, Lidzbarski < *Lidzbark* and *Lidzbark Warmiński*, both in Warmiń-sko-Mazurskie prov.

Limanowski < toponym *Limanowa*, Małopolskie prov.

Lipiński < numerous places called *Lipiny*, *Lipno*, etc.

Litwiński < *Litwa*, "Lithuania"

Lityński < several villages named *Lutynia* in the Wielkopolska region

Łobaczewski < *Łobaczew*, Lubelskie prov., possibly also various places cal-led *Łobacze*, *Łobaczów*, mostly in Lithuania, Belarus and Ukraine

Łomżyński < the city of *Łomża*, powiat seat, Podlaskie prov.

Lubański < several villages named *Lubania*

Lubawski < *Lubawa*, city in Warmińsko-Mazurskie prov.

Lubiński < several places called *Lubień* and *Lubin*

Łucki < places called *Łuka* and *Łucki* in the Eastern Borderlands, presum-ably including the city *Łuck*, now *Луцьк* [*Lutśk*] in Ukraine

Łukowski < various places called *Łuków* and *Łukowa*

Makowski < numerous localities named *Maków* and *Makowo*

Mazowiecki < *Mazowsze*, Mazovia, region of Poland

Męciński < *Męcina*, Małopolskie prov.

Męczyński < *Męczyn*, Mazowieckie prov., and *Mączniki*, several villages in Wielkopolskie prov.

Meissner < German *Meißner*, native of Meißen in eastern Germany, called *Miśnia* in Polish

Metelski < *Metele*, now *Meteliai*, Lithuania (among other sources)

Modzelewski < several villages called *Modzele*

Mogielnicki < villages called *Mogilnica*, *Mogielnica*, *Mogilno*

Mogielski *or* **Mogilski** < *Mogiła*, now part of Kraków, or *Mogilno*

Morawski < several villages called Morawa, Morawce, Morawsko, in some cases possibly < *Morawy*, Polish name for Moravia

Moskal, Moskala < *moskal*, Polish word for "Muscovite"

Moskwa < *Moskwa,* Polish name for Moscow (cmp. Russian *Москва, Moskvá*)

Nakielski < *Nakło nad Notecią,* Kujawsko-Pomorskie prov., or perhaps other places named *Nakło*

Narewski, Narowski < *Narew,* Podlasie prov.

Nidecki < top. *Nidek,* Małopolskie prov.

Niesłuchowski < *Niesłuchów,* Eastern Borderlands, now in Ukraine, perhaps also places named *Niesłuchowo, Niesłuchy* in Mazowieckie prov.

Niewiadomski < *Niewiadom,* part of Rybnik in Śląskie prov. parish, perhaps also *Niewiadoma,* Mazowieckie prov.

Niezabitowski < *Niezabitów,* Lubelski prov.

Nojszewski < *Nojszew,* Mazowieckie prov.

Nowobilski < top. *Nowa Biała,* Małopolskie prov.

Nowodworski < places named *Nowodwór* or *Nowy Dwór*

Nowogórski < a number of villages named *Nowa Góra*

Nowogrodzki < places named *Nowogród, Nowy Gródek,* etc.

Nowosielski < numerous villages named *Nowe Sioło, Nowosielce,* etc.

Nowotarski < *Nowy Targ* (literally "New Market"), Małopolskie prov.

Nowowiejski < any of numerous villages called *Nowa Wieś* (New Village)

Nur < *Nur,* Mazowieckie prov.

Odrowski < *Odry,* Pomorskie prov., or *Odrów*

Ogiński < top. *Ogińce,* Eastern Borderlands, presumably now *Uogintai,* Kaišiadorys *raionas,* Lith.

Ogonowski < villages named *Ogonów, Ogony,* presumably also *Ogonowo*

Olkuski < *Olkusz,* Małopolskie prov.

Olsztyński < *Olsztyn,* Śląskie prov., or perhaps the Polish city of Olsztyn, which the Germans called *Allenstein,* Warmińsko-Mazurskie prov.

Opolski < various places called *Opole*

Orawiec < *Orawa,* name of a town, region, and river in Slovakia

Orchowski < *Orchowo,* Wielkopolskie prov., or *Orchów,* Łódzkie prov.

Orłowski < numerous places named *Orłów, Orlowo, Orły*

Osiecki < places caled *Osiek, Osiecko, Osieczany*

Osowski, Ossowski < places named *Osów, Osowa, Osowie, Osowo, Ossowo*

Ossoliński < *Ossolin* (formerly *Osolin*), Świętokrzyskie prov.

Oświęcimski, Oświeciński < city *Oświęcim* (German *Auschwitz*), Małopolskie prov., or also a village by the same name in Wielkopolskie prov.

Pałucki < *Pałuki,* Mazowieckie prov., possibly also the Pałuki region of Great Poland between the Welna and Noteć rivers

Parczewski < *Parczew* in Wielkopolskie and Łodzkie provinces

Pepliński < *Pelplin,* a town in Pomorskie prov.

Piński < *Пинск* [*Pinsk*], a city near Minsk in Belarus

Podbielski < *Podbiel,* Wielkopolskie prov., also *Podbiele* and *Podbielko,* Mazowieckie prov.

Podlasiak, Podlaszewski < *Podlasie,* region in Poland between Lithuania and Mazovia

Podolak, Podolski < *Podole,* Podolia (region in Ukraine)

Poleski < various places named *Polesie*

Pomierski < *Pomierki,* Warmińsko-Mazurskie prov.

Pomorski < places named *Pomorze* and *Pomorzany*—note that *pomorski* is the adjective meaning "of Pomerania"

Powicki < *Powidz,* Wielkopolskie prov.

Poznański < the major city *Poznań,* capital of Wielkopolskie prov.

Prabucki < *Prabuty,* Pomorskie prov.

Przebindowski < *Przebędowo,* Gdańsk prov., or *Przebendów,* Tarnów prov.

Pułaski < *Pułazie,* Mazowieckie prov., or *Pułazie-Świerze,* Podlaskie prov., seat of Kazimierz Puławski's family

Puławski < *Puławy,* Lubelskie prov.

Radomski < the city *Radom,* Mazowieckie prov.

Rawski < *Rawa Mazowiecka,* Łódzkie prov.

Rzeszowski < city *Rzeszów,* Podlaskie prov., or the village once called *Rzeszów,* now *Rzeszówek,* Świętokrzyskie prov.

Rzymski < *Rzym,* Kujawskie-Pomorskie prov., or *Rzymsko,* Wielkopolskie, prov.—note that *rzymski* means "of Rome"

Sądecki < *Sądecz,* old name, now *Sącz* as in *Nowy Sącz* and *Stary Sącz,* both in Małopolskie prov.

Sanocki < the city *Sanok,* Podkarpackie prov.

Sarzyński < *Szarzyn,* Pomorskie prov., or *Sarzyn,* Mazowieckie prov., or *Sarzyna,* Podkarpackie

Sieracki, Sieradzki < city *Sieradz,* Łódzkie prov.

Skawiński < *Skawina,* Małopolskie prov.

Ślaski < *Ślasy,* Mazowieckie prov., but the noble Slaski family of Grzymała arms, also called Ślaski and Szlaski, came from the area of the village Szlasy, Podlaskie prov.

Śląski *or* **Ślężak** < *Ślązak,* inhabitant of Silesia, or *śląski,* "Silesian"

Stoliński < village *Stolno,* Kujawsko-Pomorskie prov.

Stolpa < *Stolp,* German name for *Słupsk*

Stypułkowski < several villages with two-part names beginning *Stypułki,* all in Podlaskie prov.

Suwalski < the city *Suwałki,* Podlaskie prov.

Sypniewski < several villages named *Sypniewo*

Szamotulski < *Szamotuły,* Wielkopolskie prov.

Szczeciński < city *Szczecin* (German *Stettin*), capital of Zachniopomorskie prov., or villages named *Szczecin* and *Szczecyn*

Tarnowski < localities called *Tarnów* and *Tarnowo,* presumably including the city Tarnów in Małopolskie prov.

Trocki < *Troki,* Polish name of the Lithuanian city of *Trakai*

Urzędowski < *Urzędów,* Lubelskie prov.

Ustarbowski < *Ustarbowo,* Pomorskie prov.

Warszawski < *Warszew,* Wielkopolskie prov., or *Warszow,* today *Warszówek,* Świętokrzyskie prov., in names of more recent origin < *Warszawa,* Warsaw, capital of Poland

Westfal < *Westphal,* the German prov. of Westphalia

Wileński < *Wilno,* Polish name for *Vilnius,* the capital of Lithuania

Wisłocki < *Wisłok Wielki,* Podkarpackie prov.

Wolski < common place name *Wola* < *wola,* term for a colony established with a set period of freedom from tax or corvée for its settlers

Wrocławski < the city *Wrocław,* German name *Breslau,* capital of Dolnośląskie prov.

Zabłocki < common toponym *Zabłocie*

Zakroczymski < *Zakroczym,* Mazowieckie prov.

Zakrzewski < numerous places called *Zakrzew, Zakrzewo, Zakrzów*

Zaleski < extremely common toponym *Zalesie* (more than 100!)

Zamojski < a number of places named *Zamość,* including the city in Lubelskie prov.

Zapolski < a number of places named *Zapole*

Zawiślak < *za Wisłą,* beyond the Wisła (Vistula) River

Zdrojewski < many places named *Zdrój* or *Zdroje,* from *zdrój,* "spring"

Zgórski < *z,* "of, from," + *góra,* "mountain," or < several places named *Zgorze*

Żywicki *or* **Żywiecki** < city *Żywiec,* Śląskie prov.

*　　　　　*　　　　　*

Endnotes

[1] Felix W. Holewinski, Ph.D., O.A.A., K.C.R., "The Nature of Polish Knighthood and Chivalry from the Thirteenth to the Eighteenth Century," *Polish Genealogical Society Newsletter,* Spring 1989, page 6.

[2] Gerald A. Ortell, *Polish Parish Records of the Roman Catholic Church: Their Use and Understanding in Genealogical Research,* Polish Genealogical Society of America®, Chicago, 1996, p. 14.

[3] Filip Sulimierski, Bronisław Chlebowski and Władysław Walewski, *Słownik geograficzny Królestwa Polskiego i innych krajów słowiańskich,* Warszawa: Nakładem Władysława Walewskiego, 1880–1902, vol. 7, p. 719.

[4] Kazimierz Rymut, *Nazwy miast Polski,* Zakład Narodowy im. Ossolińskich — Wydawnictwo, Wrocław, 1987, p. 34.

[5] Ibid., p. 57.

[6] Website <http//:mapa.szukacz.pl> accessed 1 August 2012.

[7] Sulimierski, *Słownik geograficzny,* vol. 10., pp. 197–198.

[8] Rymut, *Nazwy miast Polski,* p. 82.

Chapter Seven:

Professionally Speaking

I've been looking forward to writing this chapter, because it should be the shortest and simplest in the book. It's not at all difficult to comprehend intuitively how an occupation can provide a secondary way of labeling someone. Don't we constantly hear peopled referred as "politician so-and-so, columnist so-and-so, quarterback so-and-so"? Even in an age when people customarily bear three names, citing their occupation is still a useful way of distinguishing and identifying them. Polish terms for occupations are relatively easy to find in dictionaries, present few complications, and should not require extensive explanation.

In fact, I can only think of three points I need to make. They deal with the definition of occupations, the addition of suffixes, and terms that come from German.

Occupations, Positions, etc.

First of all, I should point out that we're not dealing here only with occupations or professions; there are names that clearly fit into this category yet aren't so much occupations as terms of honor, rank, etc. It would sound odd if someone said his job was being a bishop or a landowner or a commander; but we see Polish names derived from *biskup, dziedzic, hetman,* and so on.

The concept of "occupation" or "profession" has changed in Europe over the centuries. No noble had anything so crude as a job; but he might well hold various positions of honor that involved performing certain dutiesfor his liege lord, and he could change those positions frequently over the course of his life. The peasant, on the other hand, didn't *have* a job so much as he *was* a job. His existence was so totally defined by his function—a farmer, a cook, a coachman—that he was probably called by the name of his job as much as by whatever his Christian name happened to be (and very often his job was the same as his father's had been). If you look at certain eastern European vital documents, you see that a person's occupation was often given under the column entitled *Conditio* (in Latin), *Stand* (in German), or *Stan* (Polish), terms that basically meant "standing, status in the community."[1] Social positions were clearly defined; one knew one's place and generally had little choice but to stick to it.[2] So we need to define this category with a little flexibility.

Since we have to keep all this in mind anyway, we might as well remember as well that many of these professions or positions involved distinctions that make no sense in terms of contemporary Western society; so it shouldn't surprise us if some of the terms are hard to translate. There were, for instance, different Polish words for farmers, among them: a *kmieć,* a self-supporting farmer owning nearly 50 acres of land and employing poor peasants to work on it; a *półkmieć,* owning some 25 acres; a *zagrodnik,* owning a small parcel of land (less than 12 acres), a *chałupnik,* owning a house with a garden; a *komornik* owning neither house nor land, etc.[3] There were also several different terms for the steward of an estate, including *włodarz, ekonom, rządca,* etc.; there were even different classifications of *szlachta.* Rather than devote a lot of time to these distinctions, most of us content ourselves with a general translation such as "farmer," "steward." The alternative is to plunge into learned treatises on the social and economic makeup of Polish society over the centuries. I recommend that course of action to those interested in understanding the distinctions; but the subject is beyond the scope of this work.

Suffixes, Suffixes, Suffixes

Occupation-derived surnames do not escape the swarming hordes of suffixes that infest Polish. The most common, of course, is *-ski,* and you'll find some of these words listed in the dictionary: *piekarski* is listed alongside of *piekarz* (baker), and the meaning is given as "baker's, bakers'." In this instance, the word is being used as the adjective it is, coming from *-ski's* basic meaning of "of, from, pertaining to." Originally, that's all a word like *piekarski* was: an adjective describing something associated with a baker. But as surnames spread through Polish society and people admired the elegant sound of those estate-derived *-ski* surnames, they started preferring not the plain old plebian-sounding *Piekarz* but the aristocratic-sounding *Piekarski.* What exactly does *Piekarski* mean? I guess the best way of saying it in English is "the baker's folk, the baker's kin"—although we should note that it can also mean "one from Piekary," that is, "one from [the place of] the bakers."

But *-ski* is not the only suffix to deal with. A particularly useful way of labeling someone was "the miller's son, the innkeeper's son," and so on, so the patronymic suffixes often were added to terms denoting professions. The popular *-owicz/-ewicz* shows up here *(Bondarewicz, Mielcarzewicz),* but also common are *-czyk* and *-[i]ak,* so that the son of a soldier *(żołnierz)* was *Żołnierczyk,* the son of a sexton *(kościelny)* was *Kościelniak,* of an innkeeper *(karczmarz)* was *Karczmarczyk,* and so on. The diminutive suffix *-ek* was also used *(Bednarek, Piekarek, Kaczmarek),* and sometimes after it was added further suffixes latched on *(Piekarkiewicz, Kaczmarkiewicz),* and the same is true of *-ow-* and *-ew- (Kotlowski, Kowalewski).*[4] I think Chapter Four, on suffixes, covers this subject adequately.

What Are All These Germans Doing Here?

Any list of Polish terms for professions—including the one I'm about to give, excerpted from roots found in Volume II—has one feature that may puzzle descendants of Poles: a surprising abundance of words that are obviously German in origin. Since relations between Germans and Poles over the centuries have not always been an uninterrupted flow of mutual love and respect, you might be forgiven for asking, "What are all these Germans doing here?"

I don't want to spend too much space on this—the subject is, after all, discussed in Chapter Nine—but I think a few words here may be justified. There are two reasons for the profusion of Germanic names in Volume II, and in the list below.

The first reason is that one source from which I originally compiled the list of names in Volume II was an index of obituaries in the Chicago-area Polish-language newspaper *Dziennik Chicagoski*. Many of the names were borne by Poles who lived and died in the Chicago area. A great many of the Polish immigrants settling in the Midwest came from the Prussian partition, that is, the western part of Poland (in its current borders). Over the centuries Poles and Germans had mixed and intermarried, and individual areas had gone back and forth between Polish and German control. The upshot is that you have people named *Schmidt* living in Poland and people named *Gutowski* living in Germany; and this ethnic and linguistic confusion lives on in the names of descendants of people who immigrated to America. If I had compiled my index from a list of people living in, say, the northeastern United States, German names would be somewhat less prominent and Lithuanian and Ukrainian names somewhat more so, because the immigrants who settled in that area tended to come more from the eastern regions of Poland.

But I've added many surnames to the index since I drew up that list for the first edition of my book. The last two editions have drawn heavily from databases listing surnames borne by modern Poles—and there are still a lot of occupational surnames originating in German. That's because the Poles learned many skills and occupations from German immigrants. The Polish language lacked native words for them, so it borrowed the German words.

Bearing the name of Hoffman as I do, I want to be very careful what I say here. I do **not** want to suggest that Poles were backward peasants who didn't know enough to pound sand until some brainy Germans came along and taught them. After all, the Poles built and maintained a stable and relatively humane social and political system that lasted for centuries—during which there was no "Germany," just a bewildering hodgepodge of individual cities and states and principalities and whatnot. And once the Germans did finally get together and form a coherent country, the history of that country has been something less than a model of civilized behavior. I think Poles have a right to resent ferociously any implication that they were clueless savages till the Germans came along and civilized them!

But for various reasons, Germans had developed more skill in certain trades and crafts than Poles. It was natural that Poles who wanted to learn those trades and crafts would learn them from Germans and use German terminology, which would then slowly start to be polonized. This borrowing process went on for centuries. In modern times, we see something rather similar happening with English technical terms from England and the United States that have been adopted into languages all over the world.

Furthermore, scholars agree that for various reasons, a sizable native middle class never developed in Poland; the society was divided into the nobles and the peasants, with relatively few occupying a middle ground.[5] As time went on, the need was felt for someone to fill that role. It was filled primarily by Germans and Jews, fleeing miserable living conditions in other countries, who came to Poland and more or less monopolized the niche for craftsmen and tradesmen. The Jews had been expelled from most other countries in Europe and were welcomed by the ruling elite in Poland. Many Germans (and also Dutch) fled economic problems and religious conflicts in their native regions, so they headed east; some were even invited to come and colonize sparsely-settled parts of Poland.[6] Many of the immigrants were skilled craftsmen; Jews, who found themselves shut out of many professions, learned to excel in those that were needed but not occupied by Poles. In effect, Germans as well as Jews who spoke German and Yiddish (which is largely based on a medieval dialect of German) took over the niche where a large native Polish middle class had never quite developed.

All this explains not only why there are quite a few German-derived words in Poland, but also why they are prominent in terms dealing with trades and crafts. It's not that there were no Polish artisans or craftsmen; but various circumstances combined to make German and Jewish artisans and craftsmen common in Poland. Since both the Germans and the Jews spoke varieties of German, German technical terms came to be widely used. And as you might expect, those terms also came to be reflected in occupation-derived surnames.

Where Did All the Germans Go?

Interestingly enough, now that I've explained why there are so many German names here, I have to explain why there aren't as many as one might expect. If one of my main sources of surnames, the *Dziennik Chicagoski* obituaries, had more Germans than one might expect, the others—the *Słownik nazwisk współcześnie w Polsce używanych,* and its 2002 update—have far fewer than one might expect. When I began looking up names in the *Słownik,* I noticed that many German names—names I had good reason to believe were once common in Poland—were much rarer, and had far smaller totals, than I would have predicted. If you looked primarily at the names in that source, you'd have reason to ask "Where did all the Germans go?"

The answer is not hard to discover. Once there were a great many Germans living in Poland; but as World War II was coming to a close and Germany's defeat was just a question of time, more and more Germans began wondering if it was wise to go on living in Poland. In the latter days of the war, it was no secret that the Allies planned not only to restore Poland as an independent country but also to return to it territories long incorporated into Eastern Germany, to which Poles had a historical claim—the so-called *Ziemie Odzyskane* (Recovered Territories). These are basically the western and northern parts of modern-day Poland; they were partly intended to compensate Poland for eastern territories seized by Stalin in Lithuania, Belarus, and western Ukraine, land that had once been under Polish rule and that many had regarded as integral parts of the Polish state even after the partitions wiped that state off the map.

So by 1944, Germans living in Poland, and especially in those western territories, had good reason to consider heading west for their health. It occurred to them that Germans living within the borders of a reinstated Poland just might be held accountable for the incredible atrocities Nazis had committed there during the war. In any case, the Allies would hardly agree to leaving a large German population within Poland—a destablizing element that might give future Hitlers a pretext to invade and take over (as Hitler had done with the Germans in the Sudetenland). So by the end of 1944, about half a million Germans had already left East Prussia, some voluntarily, some not so much.[7]

Once the war was over and the Potsdam Agreement went into effect, the resettlement of Germans shifted into high gear. In the years 1946-1947, according to the data of the Central Statistical Office, 2,170,826 persons were "repatriated" to Germany. Taking into account a rough estimate of the number of voluntary emigrants and resettlers who had gone to the Soviet zone before official resettlement began, "it can be said that in the period from the signing of the Potsdam Agreement up to the end of 1947, approximately 3.2 million Germans had left Poland."[8]

The *Slownik nazwisk,* based on 1990 data, and its 2002 update, based on 2002 data, reflect this historical fact. Post-war Poland had millions fewer German residents than pre-war Poland. Many people of ethnic German descent still live there—generally people who have long since become polonized, even if their names haven't been. But the names and number of bearers given in the 1990 and 2002 surname compilations show far fewer Germans than would have appeared in a similar work compiled from, say, 1939 data. And that's why German surnames are, to some extent, underrepresented in Volume II of this book.

A Sampling of Occupations That Yielded Surnames

Volume II gives a much more comprehensive list of these roots and names —see all the roots marked with *{o}*, for "occupation"—and there's no point repeating all that here. But I thought it would serve as a useful illustration to show you a representative sampling of words denoting occupations and a few of the surnames typically formed from them. My hope is that a look through these will give you a sense and feel for these derivations that will make Volume II easier for you to understand.

Ackermann (German), "farmer, peasant": Ackermann, Akerman, Akierman

arendarz, "leaseholder, publican"; Arendarczyk, Andrendarski, Harendarz

ataman, "commander of the Cossack armies": Ataman, Atamańczuk

baca, "head shepherd, flock-master": Bac, Baca, Bacewicz

Bäcker (German), "baker": Bakiera, Becker, Beker, Bekier

bakalarz, "teacher" (from Latin *baccalareus*): Bakalarczyk, Bakalarski, Bakalarz, Bekalarek

balwierz, "barber; surgeon": Balbierz, Balwierz

bartnik, "beekeeper": Bartniak, Bartniczak, Bartnik, Bartnikowski, Bortnik

Bauer (German), "farmer, peasant": Bauer, Bauerek, Baur

Bauman (German), "farmer": Baumann

bednarz, "cooper": Bednarczyk, Bodnar, Bondar (influenced by Ukrainian бондар [*bóndar*])

Bergman (German), "miner; mountain man": Bergman, Bergmann

Binder (German), "binder, cooper": Binder

biskup, "bishop": Biskup, Biskupek, Biskupiak

blecharz or *blicharz,* "one who bleaches": Blecharczyk, Blicharski, Blicharz

Bohner (German), "bean grower": Bonar, Bonarski, Bunar

Braksator (Latin), "maltster": Braksator

Brauer (German) "brewer": Brajer, Brauer

Browar, "brewer": Browarczyk, Browarek, Browarski

chłop, chłopek, "peasant": Chłopaś, Chłopek, Chłopik

chorąży, "standard-bearer, ensign": Chorążak

cieśla, "carpenter": Cieśla, Ciesielczyk, Cieśliński

cyrulik, "barber, surgeon": Cyrulik

czebotar (< *Russ.* чеботарь [*chebotár'*] < Ukr. чоботар [*chobotár*], "boot-maker, shoemaker": Czebotar

cześnik, "cupbearer": Cześnik

dailidė (Lithuanian), "carpenter": Dojlida, Dojlidko, Dojlido

dekarz (< German *Decker*), "roofer, tiler": Decker, Dekarz, Dekert, Dykier

diak, djak, dyak, "seminarist in a Ukrainian church," also "cantor, church singer": Diak, Diakowicz, Dyjak

dragon, archaic *dragan,* "dragoon": Dragan, Dragon, Dragun

drwal, "woodcutter": Drwal

dziedzic, "heir, squire, landowner": Dziedzic

dziekan, "dean, deacon": Dziekan, Dziekański, Dziekoński

ekonom, "estate steward": Akonom, Ekonomiuk

faber (Latin), "smith, craftsman": Faber, Faberski

fajfer, "piper" (cmp. German *Pfeiffer*): Fajfer, Fejfer

Fiedler (German), "fiddler": Fiedler, Fidler

figula (< Latin *figulus*), "potter": Figuła

Fleischer (German), "butcher": Flajszer, Fleischer, Flejszar, Fleszar

flis, flisak, "raftsman": Flis, Flisek, Flisiak

fornal, "stable-hand, coachman": Fornal, Fornalczyk, Fornalik, Fornol

foryś, "carter's assistant, lord's coachman": Foryś, Forysiak
fularz or *folarz,* "fuller": Fularczyk, Fularski
furman (< Middle High German *vuorman,* modern German *Fuhrmann*) "carter, drayman": Fórmaniak, Fuhrmanm, Furmańczyk, Furmanek
garbarz, "tanner": Galbarczyk, Garbarczyk, Garbarz
garncarz, "potter": Gancarz, Garczarek, Garncarz
gazda, "farmer in the Carpathians": Gazdecki, Kazda
Girtler (< Germ. *Gürtler),* "maker of leather belts": Girtler
Glaser (German *Glaser*), "glazier": Glaser, Glazar, Glazer, Glejzer
górnik, "miner": Górniak, Górnik
gospodarz, "farmer (landowner), steward": Gospodarczyk, Gospodarek
grabarz, "grave-digger, undertaker": Grabarczyk, Grabarek, Grabarz
gracz, "player, gambler": Graczek, Graczkowski, Graczyk
hajduk, "Hungarian infantryman, manoral servant dressed like a *hajduk,* robber": Hajduczek, Hajduk, Hejduk
Hauptmann, (German) "captain, chieftain, commander"
hepner (< German *Heppner, Höppner),* "hops grower or dealer": Hepner
hetman, "leader, commander": Hetman, Hetmańczyk
huzar, "hussar": Husar, Huzar, Usarek, Uzarek
jezuita, "Jesuit": Jezowit, Jezuit
kapela, "choir, band of musicians": Kapela
kapelan, "chaplain, priest performing duties at a chapel": Kapelan, Kapelański
kapitan (< German) "captain": Kapitan
kapłan, "priest": Kapłan, Kapłański
karczmarz, "innkeeper": Kaczmarczyk, Kaczmarek, Karczmarczyk
kasztelan, "castellan": Kasztelan
kat, "executioner": Kaciczak, Kata, Katulski
Kessler (German), "coppersmith, boilermaker": Kesler, Kessler
Kleinschmidt (German), "locksmith, mechanic": Kleinschmidt, Kleinszmidt
kmieć, "peasant": Kmieciak, Kmiecik
knap, knop, "weaver, clothier": Knap, Knapczyk, Knapik, Knop
kolarz, dialect term for "wheelwright": Kolarczyk, Kolarz
koleśnik, dialect term for "cartwright": Koleśnik
kołodziej, "wheelwright": Kołodziejczak, Kołodziejczyk, Kołodziejski
komisarz, "commissary, commissioner": Komisarczyk, Komisarek
koniarz, "herder or seller of horses": Koniarek, Koniarski, Koniarz
konował, "farrier": Konefał, Konowalczyk
kościelny, "sexton": Kościelniak, Koócielnik, Kościelny
kotlarz, "boiler-maker": Kotlarski, Kotlarz
kowal, "smith": Kowacki, Kowal, Kowalczyk
kramarz, "merchant, keeper of a small shop or stall": Kramarczyk, Kramarz
krawiec, "tailor": Krawczak, Krawczyk, Krawiec
Kretschmer, Yiddish or German form of *karczmarz,* q.v.
Krüger, (German) "innkeeper": Krüger, Krugier, Krygier

ksiądz, "priest": Ksiądz

kucharz, "cook": Kucharczyk, Kucharek, Kucharz

kuczer, "driver, coachman": Kucera, Kuczera

kuglarz, "juggler, magician": Kuglarz, Kugler

kupiec, "merchant": Kupczyk, Kupiecki

kuśnierz, "furrier": Kućmierz, Kuśmierek, Kuśmierz, Kuśnierek

kustosz, "custodian, keeper, guardian": Kustos, Kustosz

ławnik, "town councillor, alderman, assessor": Ławniczak, Ławniczek

legat, "ambassador, envoy": Legat

lekarz, "doctor": Lekarczyk

leman (cmp. German *Lehmann*) "vassal": Lehmann, Lemańczyk, Lemański

lokaj or *łokaj,* "lackey, valet, footman": Lokaj, Łokaj

major, "military rank": Majorek, Majorkowski

malarz, "painter": Malarczyk, Malarski, Malarz

masarz, "butcher": Masarczyk, Masiarek, Masierak

marszałek, "administrator of the royal court": Marszałkiewicz

masztalerz, "court master of the horse; stable hand": Mastalerz, Masztalerz

mendyk, "beggar": Mędyk, Mendyk, Mendyka

mielcarz, "maltster, brewer": Melcer, Mielcarek, Mielczarek, Milczarek

misiarz, "animal gelder": Misiarz, Misiorek

młynarz, "miller": Młynarczyk, Młynarz

mnich, "monk, friar": Mnich, Mniszka (*mniszka* = nun)

molenda, (Latin *molendinator*), "miller": Molęda, Molenda

molitor (Latin) "builder, miller": Molitor, Molitorys

Mueller, Müller, (German) "miller," can also appear as *Meller, Miller, Moeller, Moller, Möller*: Meller, Miler, Miller, Mueller, Müller

mularz or *murarz,* "bricklayer, mason": Mularczyk, Mularski, Mularz

myśliwy, "hunter": Myśliwiec, Myśliwy

Neugebauer, (German) "colonist, settler": Najbor, Neubauer, Neugebauer

ogrodnik, "gardener": Ogrodniczak, Ogrodnik

oryl, "raftsman": Oryl, Orylski

owczarz, "shepherd": Owcarz, Owczarczyk, Owczarz

pachołek, "servant, soldier": Pacholik, Pacholski

pagac, dialect for *pajac,* "jester, acrobat": Pagacz

papież, "Pope": Papierz, Papież

parobek, "servant, young man; farmhand": Parobczy, Parobiec

pasterz, "shepherd, herdsman": Pasterczyk, Pasterski, Pastor

pastuch, "shepherd, tender of a flock": Pastucha, Pastusiak, Pastuszak, Pastuszka

Pfeiffer, (German) "piper, one who plays the pipes": Pfajfer, Pfeifer

piekarz, "baker": Piekarczyk, Piekarek, Piekarz, Piekorz

piwowar, "brewer": Piwowarczyk, Piwowarski

pleban, "pastor": Kleban, Plebanek

płóciennik, "dealer in linen or cloth": Płóciennik, Płuciennik *poborca,* "tax collector": Poborca, Poborczyk

podsędek, "assistant judge, subaltern judge": Posędek

pop, "clergyman of the Eastern church," also in older Polish "a Roman Catholic priest": Popa, Popczyk, Popek, Popko, Popowicz

porucznik, "lieutenant": Porucznik

posel, "envoy, delegate": Poselski

pracz, "one who launders clothes, especially linen": Pracz, Praczyk

prałat, "prelate, high-ranking churchman": Prałat

prasoł or *prasuł,* archaic term for "salt merchant": Prasał, Prasoł, Prasuła

proboszcz, "pastor": Proboszcz

prochownik, "manufacturer of gunpowder": Prochownik

prugar, "toll collector on a bridge": Prugar

prymas, "primate (church official)": Prymas

przeor, "prior, head of a monastery": Przeor, Przeorek

pulkownik, "colonel": Pukownik, Pułkownik

rabin, "rabbi": Rabinowicz

radca or *rajca,* "advisor, councillor; member of a town council": Rajca, Rajczyk, Rejczak

rajtar, "mounted soldier" (from German *Reiter*): Rajta, Rajter, Reiter

rataj, "hired hand on a manorial farmstead, farmhand": Rataj, Ratajczyk

retman, rotman, rytman, "senior raftsman; guide": Retman, Retmańczyk

Riemer (German), "maker of leather reins or similar items": Riemer, Rymer

rolnik, "farmer": Rolnik

rybak or *rybarz,* "fisherman": Rybaczuk, Rybak, Rybarczyk

rychtarz, archaic, "official presiding over a court under German law," cmp. German *Richter*): Richter, Rychtarczyk, Rychter

rymarz, "craftsman who makes leather goods," cmp. *Riemer*: Rymar, Rymarczyk, Rymarz

rządca, "manager, steward of an estate": Rządca, Rzońca

rzeźnik, "butcher": Rzeźniczak, Rzeźnik

Schneider (German), "tailor" (= Polish *krawiec*): Schneider, Sznajder

Schreiber (German), "clerk, scribe" (= Polish *pisarz*): Schreiber, Szrajber

Schroeder, Schröder (German) "tailor" (= Polish *krawiec*): Schröder, Schroeder, Szreder

Schubert (German), "shoemaker (= Polish *szewc*)": Schubert, Szubert

Schuetz or *Schütz* (German), "marksman, shot" (= Polish *strzelec*): Schuetz, Szyc

Schultz (< German *Schultheiß*) "village headman, mayor": Schultz, Schulz, Szolc, Szulc, Szulczyński—cmp. *sołtys*

Schumacher (German) "shoemaker" (= Polish *szewc*): Schumacher, Szumacher

Schumann (German), "shoemaker" (= Polish *szewc*): Schumann, Szuman

sędzia, "judge": Sędziak, Sędzik, Sendziak

sergiel, "house caretaker, farmhand": Sergiel

siedlak, "peasant, farmer": Sedłak, Siedlaczek, Siedlok
Singer, (German) "singer": Singer, Szyngiera
sługa, "servant": Sluga, Służałek
ślusarz, "metal-worker": Slósarczyk, Ślusarczyk, Ślusarz
sołtys, "village administrator": Sołtys, Sołtysiak, Sołtysik, Szołtysek
stangret, liveried coachman, driver": Stangreciak, Stangret
starosta, "administrator of a *powiat,* or leaseholder of royal esates":
     Starościak, Starosta, Starostka
stelmach (from German *Stellmach*), "cartwright, coach-builder": Stalmach,
     Starmach, Stelmach, Stelmaszczyk, Stelmaszyk
stolarz, "joiner, carpenter": Stolarczyk, Stolarek, Stolarski, Stolarz
straż, "guard, sentry": Straż, Strażnik
stróż, "caretaker, watchman": Stróż, Strózik, Stróżyk
sutor (Latin), "shoemaker" (cmp. Polish *szewc*): Sutor
szafarz, "court or estate manager," cmp. German *Schaffer*: Szafarczyk, Sza-
     farz
szambelan, "court chamberlain": Szembelan
szarmach (< German *Scharmacher*), "maker of plows": Scharmach, Szarmach
szefler (< German *Scheffler*), "cooper," or from a term meaning "steward,
     bailiff": Scheffler, Szefler
szenk (< German *Schenk*) "innkeeper": Schenk, Szenk
szewc, "shoemaker": Szewc, Szewczyk, Szwec
szmid (< German *Schmied* = Polish *kowal*), "smith": Schmidt, Śmidowicz,
     Szmidt, Szmit, Szmyd, Szmyt
szuster (< German *Schuster*), "shoemaker" (= Polish *szewc*): Szuster
szyfer (< German *Schiffer*) "skipper, seaman": Schiffer, Szyfer
szyndlar (cmp. German *Schindler*), "shingle-maker, roofer": Schindler,
     Szendzielorz, Szyndler
szynkarz, "innkeeper": Szynkarczuk, Szynkaruk
szyper, "owner of a fishing boat, skipper": Szyper, Szyperski
tambor, "drummer (military)": Tambor, Tamborski
Tepper (German), "publican," or a variant of *Töpfer*, "potter": Teper, Tepper
tkacz, "weaver": Tkacz, Tkaczuk, Tkocz
tokarz, "turner, lathe operator": Tokar, Tokarczyk, Tokarz
tracz, "sawyer": Tracz, Traczyk
tragarz, "porter, carrier": Tragarz, Trygar
Wagner, (German) "wagon-maker, wainright (other common forms are *Wa-
     jnert, Wegner, Weiner[t],* but as a Jewish name *Weiner* often means "wine
     dealer"): Wagner, Wegner
wajda, "leader, commander," or "Gypsy leader": Wajda, Wajdzik
Weber (German), "weaver" (= Polish *tkacz*): Weber
węglarz, "coal merchant": Węglarski, Węglarz
wikary, "curate": Wichary, Wikarek
włodarz, "steward of an estate": Włodarczyk, Włodarski, Włodarz

wódz, "army commander": Wódz
wojewoda, "voivode": Wojewoda, Wojewódzki
wójt, "village headman": Wojtkiewicz, Wojtkowiak
woźnica, "driver, coachman": Woźnica
woźny, "court crier, beadle; janitor, caretaker": Woźniak, Woźny
wrotny, archaic, "doorman, gatekeeper": Wrotniak, Wrótniak, Wrotny
wyrobek, archaic, "workman, day-laborer": Wyrobek
zdun, "potter, maker of tile-stoves": Zduńczyk, Zdunek
żeglarz, "seaman": Żeglarski
Zimmermann (German), "carpenter": Cymerman, Zimmermann
żolnierz, "soldier": Żołnierczyk, Żołnierek

* * *

Endnotes

[1] Jonathan D. Shea and William F. Hoffman, *Following the Paper Trail: A Multilingual Translation Guide,* Avotaynu, Inc., Teaneck, NJ, 1994, pp. 10–14, 104–107, 172.

[2] Gerald A. Ortell, *Polish Parish Records of the Roman Catholic Church,* Polish Genealogical Society of America®, Chicago, Illinois, 1996, pp. 12–13.

[3] Rafał T. Prinke, "Beyond Names and Dates," *Polish Genealogical Society Newsletter,* Fall, 1987, p. 24.

[4] Jan Stanisław Bystroń, *Nazwiska Polskie,* 2nd ed., Lwów-Warsawa, Książnica-Atlas, 1936, p. 26.

[5] For instance, Jan Stanisław Bystroń wrote, "Poland was perhaps the one country of the time in which the middle class was even numerically weaker than the nobility" (Chapter 7, "Chłopi," *Dzieje obyczajów w dawnej Polsce, w. XVI-XVII,* vol. 1, Państwowy Instytut Wydawniczy, 1960; a partial English translation appeared in the *Polish Genealogical Society Newsletter,* Spring 1991).

[6] Zdzisław Pentek, "The Relationships of the So-Called 'Dutch Populace' in Greater Poland," from *Gens,* the publication of the Towarzystwo Genealogiczno-Heraldyczne, Poznań, translated and reprinted in the Polish Genealogical Society *Bulletin,* Summer, 1991.

[7] Piotr Lippóczy, Tadeusz Walichnowski, *Przesiedlenie ludności niemieckiej z Polski po drugiej wojnie światowej w świetle dokumentów* [Resettlement of the German Population from Poland after World War II in the Light of Documents], Państwowe Wydawnictwo Naukowe, Warszawa—Łódź 1982, ISBN 83-01-01858-5 (in German, Russian, Polish, and English), p. 20.

[8] Ibid., pp. 25–26.

Chapter Eight

"Why Is a Raven Like a Writing-Desk?"

Fans of Lewis Carroll will recognize this as the riddle the Mad Hatter asked Alice at the Tea Party. They will feel it is entirely in keeping with the spirit of the Tea Party that I'm asking a riddle that not only has no answer but also has nothing to do with surnames. And yet, it is pertinent: when you begin dealing with Polish surnames derived from names of food, animals, and the like, you find yourself asking such questions. For instance, why is a man like a bark beetle? If your ancestors bore the surname *Kornik,* the answer to that question is quite relevant, because *kornik* means "bark-beetle"! And you may be a bit ticked if, like the Mad Hatter, I answer, "I haven't the slightest idea."

But consider a moderately common Polish surname, *Myszka.* The dictionary says that *myszka* means "little mouse" or "birthmark." That's clear enough. But exactly how does that apply to you if your surname is *Myszka*? Was this a nickname applied to a mousy ancestor? Did he catch mice? Did he live in an shack overrun by mice? Did he live near a local landmark that looked a little like a mouse and get his name from it? Or did he have nothing to do with mice, but rather had a large birthmark? We'll ignore the possibility that in a specific case the name may have nothing to do with *myszka.* It could conceivably be a variant spelling of *Miszka,* a surname dating from circa 1256 and derived from a diminutive for *Michał,* "Michael," or a variant of *miśko,* a diminutive of *miś,* "bear."[1] You get the idea.

At this distance from the establishment of surnames, it is probably too much to expect that we could establish exactly how every surname got started. What we can do is suggest possible—and plausible—connections.

The surnames we will discuss in this chapter come from many different kinds of words: names for persons or objects, verb roots that describe a particular kind of action, the names of animals, plants, trees, food, or sounds. What they all have in common is that these words somehow became associated with individuals or groups of people, in the form of surnames, because they seemed to fit or be typical of those people.

My Ancestor Was a Thill?

The question I'm asked most is "What does my ancestor's Polish name mean?" Running a close second is the usual follow-up: "How on earth did someone get a name like that?" For instance, someone asks "What does my great-grandfather's name, Grządziel, mean?" I answer, "According to Professor Rymut, it comes from the noun *grądziel, grządziel,* thill of a plow, one of the long poles to which an draft animal is fastened." I hold my breath, because I know what's coming next: "That makes no sense! How does a person get himself named for the thill of a plow?" It's either that or "How the hell do you pronounce *grządziel?*" to which I reply by saying my wife's calling me and I have to go.

In all fairness, it is an excellent question, and I often can't offer a really convincing answer. Perhaps a person came to be called *Grządziel* because he was so thin and tall he reminded people of a thill (compare our English expression "beanpole"). Maybe he made thills, or repaired them. None of these explanations satisfy me fully; but as of 2002, there were 1,250 Poles named *Grądziel* and 1,633 named *Grządziel*—so the name is real, is moderately common, and came from something. I can't find any other name or root that seems to fit any better. And the sheer number of names in Polish that seem to come from such homely and unlikely terms is so overwhelming that we have to accept that at least some of them generated surnames, even if we don't see any plausible connection.

I think there's something here we need to remember: it doesn't matter whether these names make sense to us, as long as they made sense to Poles hundreds of years ago. And it can be pretty hard for us to put ourselves in their shoes; you have to make allowances for how different their society was from ours. To agrarian people whose lives depended on whether or not a cart or plow was in good enough shape to use, a "thill" was not a remote, unfamiliar object, but an integral part of their lives. That most of us have no idea what the word means doesn't matter a hill of beans (with or without beanpoles).

Consider another name, *Trzepacz,* borne by 412 Poles as of 2002. It presumably comes from the term *trzepacz,* which the dictionary defines as "a scutching tool, or an itinerant scutching specialist." Fine. How do you scutch, and is it something you want to admit doing? Well, to scutch is to separate the useful fibers of flax or hemp from the useless wooden parts by beating. Again, this means nothing to people who buy their clothes at a mall—but in rural Poland, *Trzepacz* might have seemed a fine name for a good scutcher.

Sometimes, too, a bewildering surname comes from a root, but as time has passed the language has changed, and the name and the root have gone different directions, to the point that the connection is no longer obvious. For instance, *Byczyński* probably comes from the place name *Byczyna,* of which there are several in Poland. *Byczyna* means "bull's meat" in modern Polish, and you might wonder why on earth a person would have a name meaning "of bulls' meat." But in older Polish, *byczyna* also meant "a place for keeping or feeding cattle."[2] Suddenly things become clearer. Your ancestor *Byczyński* wasn't being kidded about being bull-headed; nor were his friends presciently predicting that he could have played for the Chicago Bulls if he hadn't fouled up and gotten born in the wrong time and place. No, he came from a place noted for its cattle pens and feeding lots. Nothing could be more sensible; yet at first glance, you might well have said, "Bull's meat? That's ridiculous! That can't be right."

In the search for sensible interpretations of odd names, I also think we must not underestimate the importance of nicknames. Take English nicknames: some, such as "Scarface," "Stinky," "Tiny," present no mysteries. But I have personally known people who went by the nicknames "Skip," "Stretch," "Budge," "Weasel," and "Tammy the Viking." The names fit these people perfectly if you know them, but may seem a trifle odd if you don't. I think "Skip" got the name from a childhood bout with polio that left one leg underdeveloped, so that he walked with a skipping gait. "Stretch" was well over six ft. tall and so thin he might have just climbed off a medieval rack. "Weasel" is explained on page 111—I guarantee you won't guess where that one came from! And "Budge" was... well, he was just "Budge." He's one of my brothers; we haven't called him that since we were kids, and I don't remember any more how the name got started. I do know it wasn't that he was too big to budge, or that he reminded us of a budgie; the sound of the name just fit him. He was "Budge."

As for "Tammy the Viking," well, we'd all been drinking that night. Tammy has forgotten how he got that name, and I bet he wishes the rest of us would, too!

If you stop to think about, you almost certainly can think of at least one person you've known who had an interesting and unusual nickname. We humans sometimes display considerable ingenuity in the names we give each other. Give 17th-century Polish peasants credit for their fair share of ingenuity! Don't be surprised if some of the nicknames they came up with, which came to stick as surnames, are not immediately obvious.

Persons

These names arose because they designated certain very special and particular people. For instance, quite a large group of Polish surnames came from words denoting indigenous or foreign ethnic groups who lived in specific regions of Poland.

We tend to think of Poland's populace as being homogeneous, consisting solely of ethnic Poles, all of whom are Catholics. But even if this is largely true these days, historically, the geopolitical entity associated with the name *Polska* has been the home of many different ethnic groups. A recent book of essays on the history of different peoples who lived "under the common sky" of the Commonwealth of Two Nations, Poland and Lithuania, had chapters on Lithuanians, Belarusians, Ukrainians, Germans, Jews, Armenians, Tatars, Karaites, Gypsies/Romani, Italians, Scots, and Mennonites.[3] The events of World War II—the mass murder of millions the Nazis considered "subhuman," the westward shift of Poland's historical borders, and forced relocations of huge numbers after the war to suit the communist governments' purposes—changed contemporary Poland to a state and population from what had gone before. Surnames, which are, after all, rooted in the Poland of centuries ago, derived from terms for ethnic and religious groups once prominent in Poland that have virtually disappeared.

Besides the general term *Polak*, "Pole," surnames from terms describing natives of Poland and surrounding regions include:

Bojko, an ethnic group living in the eastern Carpathians (this name can have other origins)

Góral, mountain man of southern Poland; Góralczyk, Góralski

Kaszub, native of the Kashubia region in Pomerania; Kaszub, Kaszubski

Kujawiak, native of the Kujawy region, between the Wisła and Noteć rivers and lake Gopło; Kujawa, Kujawiak

Lach, a term for Poles used by eastern Slavs; Lach, Lachowicz

Mazur, one from northern Mazowsze; Mazur, Mazurek

Orawiec, from *Orawa,* an area of northern Slovakia

Podlasiak, from *Podlasie,* region in eastern Poland

Podolak, from Podolia in Ukraine

Ślęzak, Silesian

Wołyniec, from Volhynia [in Polish, *Wołyń*] in Ukraine).[4]

In addition, Poles have had frequent contact—and not always friendly contact!—with many different nationalities, and they all left their mark on the population. Among the surnames bearing witness to this are:

Bem, "Bohemian, Czech": Bemka

Cygan, "Gypsy:" Cyganek

Czech, "Czech": Czechowicz

Duniec, "Dane": Doniec, Duniec

Kozak, "Cossack": Kozakiewicz

Litwin, "Lithuanian": Litwiniuk

Łotysz, "Lett, Latvian"

Madziar, "Hungarian, Magyar"

Moskal, a term for a Muscovite, or for Russians in general, not a word generally spoken with a great deal of love and respect: Moskal, Moskała

Niemiec, "German," also often pronounced with clenched teeth; Niemczuk, Niemczyk, Niemiec

Olęder, from German *Holländer,* a Polish term used for German and Dutch colonists who came to settle in Poland; Olenderczyk, Olenderek

Ormianin, "Armenian": Orman, Ormianiec

Prus, "Prussian": Prusak, Prusik

Rusin, "Ruthenian, Ukrainian": Rusinek, Rusiniak, Rusinowicz

Sas, "Saxon," also the name of a coat of arms; Sasak, Sasin

Serb, "Serb or Lusatian": Serba, Sorbian

Szot, "Scot, peddler": Szot, Szott

Szwed, "Swede"—Sweden invaded Poland in the 1600s: Szweda

Tatar, one of the Mongolian tribes that attacked Europe for many centuries; Tatara, Tatarek

Turek, "Turk," Turks also attacked Europe until Jan III Sobieski settled their hash in 1683 at Vienna: Turkiewicz, Turko

Węgrzyn, "Hungarian, Magyar": Węgier, Węgrzynowicz

Żyd, "Jew"—there were millions of Jews in Poland and its eastern neighbors before World War II: Żydek, Żydziak

Some other surnames come from roots that recognize a person's special status (see also Chapter Seven). Among those names are:

Bojar, "Lithuanian or Ruthenian noble": Bojarczuk, Bojarski
Burmistrz, "mayor": Burmistrzak
Car, "Tsar": Carewicz, Caruk
Cesarz, emperor < *Caesar* (like "Tsar" and German *Kaiser*): Cesarek, Cesarczyk, Cesarz
Dragon, "dragoon": Dragan
Drost, (Germ.) "lord high steward"
Junker, "Prussian country squire": Junkier, Junkiert
Król, "king": Korol, Korolczuk, Królak, Królczyk, Królewicz

Książę, "duke, prince"
Meister, (Germ.) "master": Majstrak
Pan, "man, master, bridegroom": Panek, Panicz
Prorok, "prophet"
Rajca, "advisor, councillor": Rajczyk, Rejczak
Rycerz, "knight," cmp. German *Ritter:* Ritter, Rycerz, Ryter
Sułtan, "sultan": Sołtan, Szołtun
Szlachta, "nobles": Szlachcic, Szlachetka
Ziomek, "fellow-countryman"

Some names indicate family relationships († means "archaic"):

Dziad, "grandfather, old man": Dziadek, Dziadkiewicz
Dziewierz, † "brother-in-law": Dziewior, Dziwura
Kawaler, "bachelor": Kawalerski
Kum, † "godfather, chum": Kumala
Mater, (Latin) "mother": Matera, Materek
Mąż, "man, husband": Mężyk
Nieć, † "nephew": Niećko
Ojciec, "father": Ojczenasz, Ojczyk
Patek, dial. "godfather": Patka
Pater, (Latin) "father": Paterek, Paterka

Sierota, "orphan": Sierociuk
Stryj, "paternal uncle": Stryjek
Swach, † "sister's husband": Swacha, Szwoch
Syn, "son": Synak, Synal, Syniec
Tata, "father, dad": Taciak, Tatko, Tatkowski, Tatuś
Wdowa, "widow": Wdowiak
Witwer, (German) "widower"
Wnuk, "grandson": Wnęk, Wnuczek, Wnukowski
Wuj, "maternal uncle": Wujek
Zięć, "son-in-law": Zięcina, Zientak, Zientara, Ziętara, Ziętek

Harder to categorize, but still clearly indicative of facts about a given person, are such names as:

Baba, "woman": Babiak, Babiarz, Babicz, Babiuch, Babula
Dwojak, "twin": Dwojacki
Gość, "guest": Gościej, Gościk
Gromada, "flock, community"
Mamcarz, † "wet-nurse's son"
Osoba, "person, individual"
Pachoł, † "boy, lad": Pacholczyk

Parafianin, "parishioner"; Parafiniuk, Parafinowicz
Przechrzta, "Jewish convert to Christianity"
Swat, "matchmaker": Swaciak, Swatek, Swatko, Szwat
Szmajda, "left-handed person": Smajdor, Szmaj, Szmejda

Tułacz, "wanderer, exile"
Wyrostek, "teenager, youth": Wy-
    rostkiewicz
Żak, "student, pupil": Zaczek,
    Żaczek, Zok

Zapaśnik, "athlete, wrestler"
Żegleń, "baby, or a bore": *Żegliń,*
    Żegliński
Znajda, "abandoned child, found-
    ling": Znajdek

There are also many Polish name roots that express opinions about the persons involved:

anioł, "angel": Angielczyk, Anioła,
    Aniołowski
Bachor, † "brat, illegitimate child"
Bies, "devil"; Biesek, Bis
Buba, "fright, idiot"; Bubak, Bubka
Bugaj, dialect term for "bull, strong-
    man"
Cham, "boor, yokel": Chamczyk
Czart, "devil": Czarciński, Czartek
Drab, "mercenary, uncouth fellow":
    Drabczyk, Drabik
Hołota, "rabble, pauper"

Hołysz, "tatterdemalion, starveling"
Kaduk, † "devil": Kadłuczka
Kiep, † "dunce": Kiepura
Mazgaj, "cry-baby"
Szatan, "evil spirit, devil"
Waligóra, "fairy-tale giant": Walgó-
    ra, Waligórski
Zawłoka, "tramp, vagabond"
Żołdak, contemptuous term for "sol-
    dier"
Zuch, "brave fellow": Zuchniak
Żulik, "rogue, swindler"

#$*&^%

Before I leave the category of surnames from words describing different kinds of people, there's one more sub-category I have to mention: insulting names. I'm not talking about the mild insults conveyed by some of the words above. I'm talking about the kind of name that, if you call someone by it, you just might get your teeth kicked in.

Ever since I started studying Polish surnames, I've been struck by how many of them come from pretty rude words, some of which can only be translated in English with four-letter words. I hope you won't be offended, but I'm not going to be squeamish here. If a name comes from a word that means "shit," pure and simple, there's no point pretending it means "excrement."

I've had to tell quite a few people over the years that their ancestral names meant something pretty insulting. Most take it well, laughing and saying, "Well, just because my ancestor was a (bleep) doesn't mean I have to be a (bleep)." But some get upset, and I can't really blame them. I figure my best course, however, is to level with you, and then let you choose how you want to proceed.

For instance, I once had a father write to me, saying his fourth-grade daughter had been given a school assignment to find out what her name meant. The name was *Bzdawka.* I answered as follows:

In Polish this name is pronounced roughly "B'ZDOFF-kah." Polish name expert Prof. Kazimierz Rymut mentions it in his book *Nazwiska Polaków* [The Surnames of Poles] ... He says that names beginning *Bzd-* come from the archaic and dialect term *bzdzieć*, which means "to fart; to talk nonsense." The ending *-ka* is a diminutive and means "little," so that *Bzdawka* would mean more or less "little fart." The good news [?] is that you could also interpret it "little one who talks nonsense." But the basic meaning would have to do with farting; the sense of "talking nonsense" probably started out as a way of saying someone's words were no more worth listening to, and made no more sense than, a fart.

As of 1990, according to the best data available (the *Słownik nazwisk współcześnie w Polsce używanych*, "Dictionary of Surnames in Current Use in Poland," which covers about 94% of the population of Poland), there were 183 Polish citizens named *Bzdawka*. The largest numbers lived in the following provinces: Bydgoszcz 94, Piła 23, and Toruń 20; the rest were scattered in much smaller numbers all over. Unfortunately I don't have access to further details such as first names or addresses, so I can't tell you how to find that info.

That's all I can tell you, and it may be more than you wanted to know, actually. Still, the best I can do is tell people the information I have available. How they use it is up to them. If you want to quote the surname frequency and distribution data I gave above, and skip the part about the meaning, that's your decision.

I debated long and hard over whether I should even tell him the whole truth. I've had daughters in the fourth grade, and I can't imagine having them stand in front of a class and say "My name means little fart." For that matter, writing this book may end up embarrassing someone. I hope not, but I guess it's possible. But I believe knowing is better than not knowing. If your name means something rude, you'll probably hear about it sooner or later. Maybe I can at least help you know it and prepare how to deal with it.

In Volume II, I used the abbreviation *{x}* to indicate names that, in my opinion, have to be regarded as rude, insulting, or downright obscene. Let me give you a list of some of them, just to show you I'm not making all this up. You have to wonder how the hell people got stuck with some of these names?

Bacior < *baciarz, baciar*, "scoundrel, tramp"

Bagłaj < Ukr. dial. *баглаï* [*bahlayí*], "laziness" and Russian *баглай* [*baglái*], "lazy good-for-nothing"

Bajtała < *bajtała*, "oaf"

Bizon or *Bizoń* < *bizoń*, "a large, awkward fellow, a great lout" (from *bizon*, "bison")

Chołuj < dial. *chołoj, chołój*, "dirty, stupid fellow"

Ciemięga < *ciemięga*, "oaf, lout"

Ciupa < *ciupa*, "worthless fellow"

Ciura < *ciura*, "flunkey, oaf"

Cymbała < *cymbał, cembał*, "dulcimer; dolt"

Cyra < *cyra*, "dirty, lazy girl"

Deja < *deja*, "heavyset, awkward fellow"

Dejnak < *dejnak*, "good-for-nothing"

Depta < *depta*, "dawdler"

Dubiel < *dubiel*, "fool, simpleton"—but more and more scholars feel the name came from a word for a kind of fish, so it was not necessarily meant as an insult

Duchna < † *duchna*, "pillow," also "woman of loose morals"

Dupa < *dupa*, "ass, butt"

Durak < *durak*, "fool"

Dziama < dialect *dziama*, "good for-nothing, sluggard"

Dziuda < *dziudzia*, "sleepy, heavy-set fellow"

Fafuła < dialect *fafuła*, "booby, good for nothing"

Fagas < *fagas*, "flunkey, snoop"

Fajdek < *fajdać*, "to foul, to shit" (though there are other possible derivations)[5]

Fujarski < *fujara*, "pipe, also twerp," dial. *fujarski*, "dunce, dope, ninny"

Fuławka < dial. *fuła*, "fool, a rather stupid or clumsy person"

Gabzdyl < Cieszyn dial. *gabzda* < *ga-*, a prefix indicating diminution or contempt + *bzda-*, "fart"

Gajda < *gajda*, "bagpipes; player of bagpipes; bad leg, coarse or clumsy person"

Gałgan < *gałgan*, "good-for-nothing, scoundrel; rag"

Gamoń < *gamoń*, "bumpkin, numbskull"

Gaza < Proto-Slavic root **gaziti*, "to wade, flounder," also "to disgust, make repulsive"

Gidek < *gid, gizda*, "something horrible; a repulsive person": Gidaszewski, Gidelski, Gidziela, Gidziński, Gizdoń

Gługla < dialect *gługla*, "stupid woman, strumpet"

Gmerek < dialect *gmerek*, "one who fumbles around; fool, idiot": Gmyrek

Gnes < dialect *gnes, gnyś*, "penis": Gnyż, Gnyzska

Gniotek < dialect *gniotek*, "lazy fellow"

Gnojek < *gnój*, "manure, dung, muck," *gnojek*, "turd; slob"

Grochal < *grochal*, "simpleton, yokel"

Halama < † *halama*, "uncouth fellow, simpleton, yokel"

Hujek < *chuj*, "cock, dick, prick"

Kałabun < dialect *kałabania, kałabunia*, "obese person"

Kałęba < dialect *kałęba*, "old, thin cow; obese woman"

Karwala < † *karw*, "an ox, especially an old, lazy one," also used in the meaning "lazy fellow": Karwan, Karwasz

Kiep < † *kiep*, "dunce, dumbbell," in medieval Polish also "woman's genitals"

Koim < dialect *kojma*, contemptuous term for "fellow, peasant"

Kozdrój cmp. *kozdrój*, "disheveled fellow, good-for-nothing"

Kuciapa < *kuciapa*, "female genitals"

Kuczma < † *kuczma*, "a kind of fur cap," can also mean "woman's genitals"

Kulfan < dialect *kulfan*, "deformed person, simpleton"

Kunda < dialect *kunda, konda*, "scoundrel, womanizer," or < fem. given name *Kunegunda*: Kondak, Kondej

Kurdziel < *kurdziel*, "abscess on a horse's tongue"

Kuś < † *kuś*, "boy serving an apprenticeship with a baker; penis," cmp. modern Polish *kuśka*, "penis": Kuśka

Kutas < *kutas*, "tassel on a cap or headwear," also "penis"

Łajda < *łajda*, "scoundrel, rascal"

Legieć < dialect *legieć, lęgeć,* "idler, lazybones": Legęć, Legięć

Łępa < *łęp*, "oaf, twerp," or *łępać,* "to hit, pound"

Mamaj < † *mamaj*, "blockhead"

Mamzer < † *mamzer*, "bastard"

Muża < dialect *muża*, "lout, simpleton"

Myga < dialect *myga*, "mosquito," also "harlot"

Nicpoń < *nicpoń*, "good-for-nothing"

Nieroba < *nieroba*, "lazybones, tramp"

Nyga < *nyga*, "lout, twerp"

Pec, cmp. *pec, peć*, "penis," or < short form of *Peter*

Pierdzioch < *pierdzieć, pirdzieć,* dialect *pardać*, "to fart"

Pinda < *pinda*, "contemptuous term for a woman; slut, bitch"

Pitek, cmp. dialect *pitek*, "penis" and dialect *pita*, "vulva"

Pituła < *pituła*, "pudenda," also dialect "fodder for livestock"

Piziak < root *piż-*, cmp. *pizia,* "vulva," *piż*, "musk"

Pizda < *pizda*, "vulva, cunt"

Poparda < *pardać*, "to fart"

Purtak < *purtak*, "one who farts or craps his pants"

Sałaga < *sałaga*, "vagrant, good-for-nothing"

Sarga < *szargać*, "to soil, to destroy," also < † *sarga*, "trollop"

Sik < *sikać*, "to trickle, spurt; to piss," *sik*, "enema, one who pees in bed"

Siuber < dialect *siuber*, "bastard"

Siurek < *siurek*, "person or thing emitting water in a thin, steady stream; small boy; male organ"

Sral < root seen in *srać*, "to shit," *sracz*, "crapper, restroom," *sral*, "one who talks a lot of crap, clumsy or sluggish fellow," *sraka*, "buttocks"

Szalewicz < East Slavic *shalava, shelava*, "tramp, vagrant," *shalavyi*, "stupid fellow," cmp. Ukr. шалава [*shaláva*], "gaping fool"

Szuda < dial. *szuda*, "excrement"

Wrodarczyk < *wroda*, "ugly fellow, repulsive person"

Wyłupek < *wyłupek*, "good-for-nothing, oaf; circumcised Jew"

Zagłoba < † *zagłoba*, "obstruction; care, trouble; good-for-nothing"

Zalupski < *załupa*, "dolt, buffoon"

Zbęk < *zbęk*, "fellow who stinks"

Zebzda, cmp. *zebździć, zebździeć,* "to make a stink, fart"

Żminda < *zminda*, "bumbler, oaf, lout"

Żmuda < † *zmuda, żmuda,* "waste of time; one who wastes time, dawdler; a bore"

Quite a list, isn't it? And I did not include the many names from words meaning "devil, satan, evil spirit"—although in a country as religious as Poland, perhaps those were even worse insults than the ones listed above.

Admittedly, some of these names are less insulting than others. But it would tick me off if you called me by any of them!

"He's Such an Animal!"

The concept of people coming to have names based on animals' names is not difficult to grasp. What parent hasn't tritely warned kids not to act like pigs or hogs? "Cock of the walk," "chicken," "bitch," there are more than a few examples of comparing people to animals, and sometimes the names stick. One of my college friends was called "Weasel"—with his full approval! —not because he reminded us of a weasel (well, maybe partly because he reminded us of a weasel) but largely as a reference to his favorite album, Frank Zappa and the Mothers of Invention's *Weasels Ripped My Flesh*.

Fortunately, relatively few Polish surnames derive from references to Frank Zappa albums. But nicknames and bynames often came from names of animals—Bystroń mentions a few, including *Skowroniak* from the word for "lark," and *Lisak* from the word for "fox"—and at the right time and the right place, those names could be handed down to descendants and become surnames.[6] Another source for such names, not so obvious, is from the names of inns; a man who ran an inn named for, say, a hart or stag, *jeleń,* could very easily be referred to *Jelenik,* as a kind of verbal shorthand—"hart," that is, "you know, the guy who runs the inn at the sign of the hart." This suggestion is worth keeping in mind, because it may explain a great many names for which a possible connection to a person seems improbable.[7]

Birds were enormously popular as a source for names. A partial listing of surnames derived from names for birds would include the following:

bąk, "bittern, gadfly" (among other roots): Bączek, Bączkiewicz

bałaban, (Ukrainian or Belarusian) "kind of hawk or falcon"

bocian, "stork": Bocek, Bociąga, Bocian, Bociek

ćwik, † "game bird, sparrow hawk": Ćwik, Ćwikowski

cyran, cyranka, "garganey": Ceran, Cyroń

czajka, "lapwing": Czaja, Czajor

czapla, "heron": Czaplak, Czaplik

czeczotka, "redpoll": Cecot, Czeczot

czermak, †, "redstart": Czermak

czyż, czyżyk, "green finch, siskin": Czyż, Czyżak, Czyżo, Czyżyk

derkacz, "corncrake": Derkacz

drop, "bustard": Drop, Dropiński

drozd, "thrush": Droszcz, Drozd, Drozdek, Drozdowicz, Dróżdż

dudek, "hoopoe": Dudka, Dudka

dzięcioł, "woodpecker": Dzięcioł, Dziędziel, Dziendziel

gapa, "crow": Gapiński

gąsior, "gander": Gąsiorek

gawron, "rook": Gawron, Gawronek

gęga, "goose": Gągała, Gągol

gęś, "goose:" Gąska, Gęsiak

gil, "bullfinch, red finch": Giel, Gil, Gilas, Gill, Gilski

gogol, "a kind of wild duck": Gogół, Gogola, Gogolin

gołąb, "pigeon": Gołąb

indyk, "turkey": Indyk, Indyka

jarząbek, "hazel grouse": Jarząbek, Jarzębak, Jarzombek

jaskółka, "swallow": Jaskółka, Jaskuła, Jaskulak

jastrząb, "goshawk": Jastrząb, Jastrząbek

kaczka, "duck": Kaczka

kaczor, "drake": Kaczor, Kaczorek

kania, "kite": Kania, Kanik

kanarek, "canary": Kanarek

kawka, "jackdaw": Kafka, Kawka

kiełp, "swan": Kiełpikowski, Kołpa

kobuz, kobus, "hobby": Kobus

kogut, "cock": Koguciuk, Kogut

kokot, "rooster": Kokot, Kokott

kos, "blackbird": Kos, Koss

krak, "crow": Kraczek, Krak

krogulec, "sparrow hawk": Krogulec

kruk, "raven": Kruk, Krukiewicz

kukułka, "cuckoo": Kukuła, Kukułka

kulik, "curlew": Kuliga, Kulik

kura, "hen": Kurak, Kuras

kuropatwa, "partridge": Kuropatwa

łabędź, "swan": Łabędź, Lebiedź

orzeł, "eagle": Orlicki, Orlik, Orzeł

papuga, "parrot": Papuga

paszkot, "mistle thrush": Paszkot

paw, "peacock": Paw, Pawiński

pelikan, "pelican": Pelikan

piegża, "hedge-sparrow": Piegza

piekut, † "snipe, cock"; Piekut

pinka, "chaffinch": Pinkawa, Pinkiewicz

pisklę, "nestling": Pisklak, Pyskło

pliszka, "wagtail": Pliszka

przepiórka, "quail": Piepiórka, Przepióra, Przepiórka

ptak, "bird": Ptach, Ptaszek

puchacz, "eagle owl": Puchacz

pustułka, "kestrel": Pustuła, Pustuła

pyka, "finch": Pyka

raróg, "saker (falcon)": Raróg

sęp, "vulture": Semp, Sępek

sikora, "titmouse": Sikora

skowronek, "lark": Skowron, Skowronek, Skowroński

ślepowron, "night heron": Ślepowroński

słowik, "nightingale": Słowik

sójka, "jay": Sojka, Sójka

sokół, "falcon": Sokół, Sokolik

sołowiej, "nightingale" (East Slavic): Sołowiej

sowa, "owl": Sowa, Sowała, Sówka

sroka, "magpie": Soroka, Sroka, Stroka

struś, "ostrich": Struszczyk

strzyż, strzeż, strzyżyk, "wren": Stryż, Stryżykowski

szczygieł, "goldfinch": Szczygieł

szpak, "starling": Szpak

trznadel, "yellow-hammer"; Sternal, Trznadel

wilga, "golden oriole": Wilga, Wilgos, Wilgosz

wróbel, "sparrow": Wróbel

wrona, "crow": Woronko, Wrona, Wronka, Wronkowski

zazula, "cuckoo": Zazula, Zezula

zięba, "chaffinch": Dziemba, Zięba

żołna, † meaning "woodpecker": Żołna, Żołnowski, Żołyniak

żuraw, "crane": Żuraw, Żurawik

Also popular as a source of names were terms for fish:

brzana, "barbel": Brzana

dorsz, "cod": Dorsz

dubiel, "a cross of kinds of carp (Carpio collari)": Dubiel

fiut, dialect "bleak," also an exclamation for something going by very fast: Fiut, Fiuta

flądro, "flounder": Flądro

jaszcz, "ruff," names beginning
Jaszcz- can also come from
Jan: Jaszczak, Jaszczyk
jazgarz, "pope, ruff": Jazgar
jesiotr, "sturgeon": Jesiotr
karaś, "crucian carp": Karaś, Kara-
sek, Karasiewicz
karp, "carp": Karp, Karpowicz
kiełb, "gudgeon": Kieln,
Kiełbowicz
kurpierz, "a kind of fish": Kurpierz
leszcz, "bream": Leszcz, Leszczyk
łosoś, "salmon": Łosoś
miętus, "burbot": Miętus
okoń, okuń, "perch": Okoń, Okonek
piskorz, "loach": Piskorek, Piskorz
płocica, "roach": Płocica

pstrąg, "trout": Pstrąg, Pstrong
rak, "crab" (I know, it's not a fish):
Rak, Rakowicz, Rek
ryba, "fish": Ryba, Rybka, Rybus
sielawa, "European whitefish":
Sielawa
śledź, "herring": Śledź, Śledzik
śliz, "stone loach": Śliz
som, † for a kind of catfish: Somin-
ka, Szoma
sum, "European catfish, *Silurus
glanis*": Sum, Sumka
szczubiel, "pike": Szczubełek,
Szczubiał
szczuka, † term for pike: Szczuka
szczupak, "pike": Szczupak
ukleja, "bleak": Ukleja

I don't think anyone will be surprised that in an agrarian society such as Poland's was during the period of surname formation, pets and farm animals provided names as well:

baran, "ram": Baran, Baraniak,
Barański
baranek, "lamb": Baranek, Baran-
kiewicz
byczek, "bullock": Byczek, Byczko
byk, "bull": Byk, Bykowski
cap, "he-goat, ram": Cap, Capała
cielę, "calf": Cielas, Cieleń, Cie-
loch, Cieluch, Ciołek, Telus
cipa, "hen" (in modern Polish can
be a vulgar word for the female
genitals): Cipa, Czypionka
kalęba, "a thin old cow; an obese
woman": Halemba, Kalemba
karw, "an ox, especially an old,
lazy one": Karwala, Karwan
kicia, "pussycat": Kiciak
klacz, "mare": Klaczak, Klaczyński
kobyla, "mare": Kobylak, Kobyłka
kocur, "tomcat": Kocur, Koczor,
Koczur
koń, "horse": Koń, Konik, Konior

kot, "cat": Kocik, Kot, Kotala
koza, "nanny goat": Kozek, Koźka
kozioł, "he-goat": Kozieł, Kozioł
krowa, "cow": Krowiak, Krówka
kuc, "pony": Kuc
kwoka, "brood hen": Kwoka
maciora, "sow," † "mother": Ma-
ciorowski
muł, "mule": Muła, Mulica
myrcha, † "mare": Myrcha
nasiadka, "brood hen": Nasiadka
ogar, "bloodhound": Ogar
opas, "a fattened animal (calf, pig,
etc.)": Opasek
osesek, "suckling": Osesek, Osysko
osioł, "ass, donkey": Osieł, Oślak
owca, "sheep": Owca
ozimek, "young animal born before
winter": Ozimek, Ozimkiewicz
pies, "dog": Piesik, Psiuk
pszczoła, "bee": Pszczoła,
Pszczółka

rap, rapa, "dark-colored horse": Rapa

skop, "wether": Skop

skot, "horned cattle": Skotak

sobaka, "dog": Sabak, Sobacki

świnia, "hog, swine, pig": Świniański, Świniuch

wieprz, "gelded male pig": Wieprzkowicz

wół, "ox": Wołowicz, Wołowski

wyżlica, "female pointer (dog)": Wyżlic

źrebię, "colt": Żerebiec, Źrebiec

And, of course, the less domesticated members of the animal kingdom are represented. Some animal names, such as *Miś* (bear) or *Lis* (fox), one might be pleased to bear; others—*Czerw* (grub, maggot), *Gad* (reptile, wretch), *Ślimak* (snail, slug) come immediately to mind—probably aroused little or no pleasure on the part of people hearing themselves addressed by them. But the simple fact that these names survive suggests that at some point there must have been some reason for applying them. If one of your ancestors bore such a name, make the best of it and assume it was meant affectionately, or perhaps ironically, the way we sometimes call a tall fellow "Shorty."

bawół, "buffalo": Bawoł, Bawół

bóbr, "beaver": Bober, Bobryk

chrabąszcz, "cockchafer, Maybug": Chrąbaszcz

czerw, "grub": Czerw, Czerwik

gacek, "bat": Gacka, Gackowski

gad, "reptile": Gad, Gadzina

jaźwiec, "badger": Jaźwiecki

jeleń, "deer,stag": Jeleń, Jelonek

jeż, "hedgehog": Jeż, Jeżak

kapłon, "capon": Kapłon

klępa, "female elk," also "old woman": Klempka, Klępka

koczkodon, † "monkey, ugly person": Koczkodaj, Koczkodon

komar, "mosquito, gnat, midge": Komar, Komor, Kumor

kornik, "bark beetle, borer": Kornik

łabaj, "big dog": Łabaj

łania, "hind, doe": Łaniewicz

łasica, "weasel": Łasica

lew, "lion": Lew, Lewiński

lis, "fox": Lis, Lisak, Lisek

łoś, "elk": Łoś, Łosiak, Łosiewicz, Łosik

miś, "bear": Miś, Misiak

mól, "moth": Mól

motyl, "butterfly": Motyl, Motyliński

mrówka, "ant": Mrówca, Mrówczyński, Mrowiec

mszyca, "aphid": Mszyca

mucha, "housefly": Mucha, Muchła

mysz, "mouse": Myszak, Myszka

niedźwiedź, "bear": Medwid, Niedźwiedź

pająk, "spider": Pająk, Pajęcki

pluskwa, "bedbug": Pluskwa

reczek, "small mole-like mouse": Rećko, Reczek

religa, "old hourse, nag": Religa

robak, "worm, grub, maggot": Chrobak, Chrobok, Robak

ryś, "lynx": Ryś

salamandra, "salamander": Salamandra

samiec, "male animal": Samiec

sarna, "roe-deer": Sarna, Sarniak

ślimak, "snail, slug": Ślimak

smok, "dragon": Smoczyk, Smok

sobol, "sable": Sobol, Soból, Sobolak

sorek, "shrew mouse": Sorek
suseł, "gopher": Suseł, Suślik,
   Susło
świerszcz, "cricket": Świerc,
   Świercz, Świerczek
szczur, "rat": Szczur, Szczurek
szerszeń, "hornet": Sierszeń, Sier-
   szyński, Szerszeń, Szyrszeń
trąd, "male bee, drone": Tręda,
   Trędowicz, Trendak
trzmiel, "bumblebee": Ćmiel,
   Czmiel, Trzmiel
tur, "aurochs": Turoń
wąż, "snake": Wąż, Wężyk
węgorz, "eel": Węgorek
weszka, diminutive, "louse":
   Weszka

wielbłąd, "camel": Wielbłąd
wiewiórka, "squirrel": Wewiorski,
   Wiewióra
wilk, "wolf": Wilczak, Wilczek,
   Wilk, Wilkosz, Wołczyk, Wołk
wszoł, "louse": Wsół, Wszołek
wydra, "otter": Wydra, Wydrych
żaba, "frog": Żaba, Żabka
zając, "hare": Zając, Zajko
żbik, "wildcat": Zbiciak, Żbik
zdeb, "wildcat": Zdeb, Zdebski
żmija, "viper": Żmija
żubr, "bison": Żuberek
żuk, "dung beetle": Żuczek, Żukowski
zwierz, "beast": Zwierz, Zwierzyk,
   Zwierzyna

Food and Drink

This category of surnames may be enough to make you downright hungry, and also downright confused; why would anyone be named for food and drink? I suspect no one simple answer will suffice. Was a person named *Kiełbasa* because he made wonderful sausage, or because he constantly ate sausage, or because he was shaped like one? If nicknames and bynames could become surnames—and we know from previous reading that they could—then there are several possible ways such a name might arise. In most cases, I doubt there is any certain way to determine what about a person seemed so obviously connected with food or drink; perhaps it is enough for us to know that such a connection existed.

arak, "arrack": Arak
bałuk, "smoked fish": Bałuk
barszcz, "borscht," also a genus of
   plants, *Heracleum*: Barszcz,
   Barszczak, Borszcz
bigos, "meat dish": Bigos, Bigus
blin, "a kind of thin pancake": Blin
bób, "bean": Bobek, Bobik, Bobko
bochen, "loaf of bread": Bochenek
braja, breja, bryja, "thick mash,
   pulp": Brej, Brejnak, Bryja
brambor, dialect "potato": Brambor
brukiew, "rutabaga": Brukwicki

bryndza, "cheese from ewe's milk":
   Bryndza
buchta, "large piece of bread, bun":
   Buchta
cebula, "onion": Cebulski, Cybula
chleb, "bread": Chlebek, Chlebosz
chrzan, "horse radish": Chrzan,
   Krzan, Krzon
ciasto, "dough": Ciastek, Ciastoń
cukier, "sugar": Cukier, Cukierski
ćwikla, "beet, beet root": red beet
   salad": Ćwikła, Ćwiklik
cytryna, "lemon": Cytryniak

czosnek, "garlic": Czosnek, Czosnyka

dynia, "pumpkin": Dynia, Dyniak

faruga, "curds, cottage cheese": Faruga

faryna, "flour, meal": Faryna

figa, "fig tree": Figa

gduła, "kind of pear": Gdula

gleń, "piece of bread": Gielnik, Gleń

gogłosa, "beverage brewed from barley": Gogłoza, Ogłoza

golonka, "knuckle of pork": Golonka

groch, "pea": Groch, Grochowicz

groszek, "green pea": Groszek

gruszka, "pear": Gruszka

gryka, "buckwheat": Gryka, Gryko

grzanka, "toast": Grzanka

grzyb, "fungus, mushroom": Grzyboś, Grzybek

hałwa, chałwa, "kind of confection": Hałwa

harbuz, "pumpkin": Harbuz

imbir, "ginger": Imbierowicz, Jambor

jabłko, "apple": Jabcoń, Jabłecki

jagła, "millet groats": Jagieła, Jagła

jagoda, "berry": Jagoda

jajo, "egg": Jaje, Jajko

jarmuż, "collard, cale": Jarmusz, Jarmuż

jarzyna, "vegetables, spring corn": Jarzyna, Jarzyński

jęczmień, "barley": Jęczmięń, Jęczmyk

kapusta, "cabbage": Kapuścik, Kapuściński, Kapuśniak

karma, "food, nourishment": Karmowski

karpiel, "rutabaga": Karpiel, Korpal

kasza, "cereal, kasha": Kasza

kawa, "coffee": Kawa

kawon, "watermelon": Kawończyk

kiełbasa, "sausage": Kiełbasa, Kiołbasa

Kirsche, (German) "cherry": Kirsz

kisić, "to pickle": Kisiel (kind of fruit jelly), Kiszel

kiszka, "bowel; cured meat;" dial. "sour milk": Kiszczak, Kiszka

kłos, "ear of corn": Kłos, Kłosek

klucha, "dumpling": Kluch

kluska, "kind of noodle or dumpling

kmin, "cumin": Kminikowski

kołacz, "cake": Kołacz, Kołaczek, Kołaczyk

kolender, "coriander": Kolender

koper, "dill": Koper, Kopera, Koperek, Kopyra

krupa, "groats": Krupa, Krupka

kuch, † "a kind of cake": Kuch

kukurydza, "corn, maize": Kukurenda, Kukorowski

kułaga, East Slavic, "groats with cheese": Kułaga

lędzian, "kind of pea": Ledzion, Lendzion

mąka, "flour, meal": Mączka, Mąka

malaga, "malaga, kind of sweet Spanish wine": Malaga

malaj, Ukr., "cake made of corn flour": Malajka

marchew, "carrot": Marchewka, Marchwiak, Marekwica

masło, "butter": Maślana, Maślany

mast-, "oil, grease, fat, gravy": Masny, Mastej

mięso, "meat": Miąsik, Miąsko

mięta, "mint": Miętek, Minta

migdał, "almond": Migdał, Migdalski

miód, "honey": Miodek, Miodoński, Mioduski, Mioduszewski

mleko, "milk": Mleczko, Mleko
nabiał, "dairy products": Nabiałczyk, Nabiałek, Nabielec
obarzanek, "round cracknel": Obarzanek
obrzód, "dried fruit": Obrzud
ocet, "vinegar": Ocetek
ogórek, "cucumber": Ogórek, Ogurek
okrasa, "lard, butter, condiment": Okrasa, Okraska
oliwa, "olive oil": Oliwa, Oliwiak
orkisz, "spelt; kind of barley": Orkisz, Orkiszewski
orzech, "nut": Orzech, Orzeszek
osiory, "bran from groats": Osyra
oskwarek, "crackling": Oskwarek
ostręga, "blackberry": Ostręga
osuch, "a dry piece of bread, a cracker": Osuch, Osuszek
otręba, "husks, bran": Otręba, Otrębski, Otremba
owies, "oat": Owsianik, Owsiany
owoc, "fruit": Owoc, Owocki
owsianka, "oatmeal, porridge": Owsianka
pajda, "piece of bread": Pajda, Pajdo, Pajdzik
pampuch, "kind of *pączki* or pancake": Pampuch
pasternak, "parsnip": Pasternak
perec, "pepper": Perec
pica, † "nourishment": Picz
pieprz, "pepper": Pieprzak, Pieprzyca
piernik, "honey-cake, gingerbread": Piernicki, Piernik
pieróg, singular of *pierogi:* Pieróg, Piróg
piwo, "beer": Piwek, Piwko
poleć, "large slice of meat": Poleć, Poletek
polewka, "a kind of soup": Polewka, Poliwka

półgęsek, "smoked half of a goose": Półgęsek
potrawa, "dish, course": Potrawiak
powidło, "plum confection": Powideł
prażmo, † "a kind of food prepared from roasted grain": Prażmo
przasnek, "unleavened bread": Przasnek
pszenica, "wheat": Psonka, Pszeniczkny, Pszon
pujany, dialect, "potato dumplings": Pujanek
racuch, "a kind of fried cake": Reczuch
Rindfleisch, (German) "beef": Rentflejsz
rodzynek, "currant, raisin": Rozenek, Rozynek
rosół, "broth, consommé": Rosół, Rosołowski
rozmaryn, "rosemary": Rozmarynowicz
rydz, "edible fungus": Rydz
rżanny, † "of rye": Rzanny, Rzany
rzepa, "turnip": Repeć, Rzepa
rzodkiew, "radish": Rzodkiewicz
sałamacha, "grain dish cooked in lard": Sałamacha, Szałamacha
sałata, "lettuce": Sałaciński, Sałata, Szałata
schab, "pork loin, pork chine": Schab, Schabowicz
semel, from German *Semmel*, "bread roll": Semla
ser, "cheese": Serek, Serowik, Serzysko, Syrek
serwatka, "whey": Serwatka
skrok, "cracklings": Skrok
słonina, "pork fat, bacon": Słonina
smalec, "lard": Smalec, Smolec, Szmalc, Szmalec
smardz, smarz, "morel (mushroom)": Smardz, Smarz

śmietana, "cream": Śmietana, Śmietanka

soczewica, "lentil": Soczewka, Soczówka

sól, "salt": Solak, Soluch

sołoducha, "sweet bread, sweet soup": Sołoducha

sperka, spyrka, "back-fat, pork fat": Sperka, Spyrka, Szpyrka

stypa, "funeral banquet": Stypa, Stypka

szafran, "saffron": Szafran, Szafranek, Szafrański

szczypior, "leaves of the onion plant": Szczypior, Szczypiór

szkiłądź, dialect, cmp. Lith. *Skiłándis*, "pig or sheep's stomach stuffed with miced meat": Szkiłądź

szołdra, "ham, pork fat": Szołdra

szparaga, "asparagus": Szparaga

szponder, "beef from the spine": Szponder

sztokfisz, "dried fish": Stokfisz, Stokwisz

twaróg, "fresh cheese, cottage cheese": Twaróg, Tawrogowski

urda, "whey from cheese from sheep's milk": Urda

warmuz, "kind of soup": Warmus, Warmuz

wątroba, "liver": Wątroba

więdłocha, "kind of turnip": Więdłocha

wruk, "rutabaga": Wruk

żemła, "wheat roll": Zemła, Żymełka

ziarno, in dialect *ziarko*, "grain, seed": Ziarek, Ziarko

żur, "a kind of sour soup": Żur, Żurek

żyto, "rye": Żytkiewicz, Żyto

Trees and Other Growing Things

I don't want to wax too mystical here, but I often get the feeling that something in the Slavic soul has a particular love of growing things, and especially trees. Among Poles, Russians, Ukrainians, and so on, there seems to be a deep attachment to the beauty of the birch, the linden, the oak, the rowan. I suspect it's not entirely an accident that the only surviving piece of the primeval forest that once covered most of northern Europe is in Poland and Belarus (at Białowieża); and trees figure too prominently in the names of Polish people and places for it to be mere happenstance. We could speculate that some element of the forest-dwelling pagans lives on in their thoroughly Catholicized descendants.

Whether that is nonsense or not, there's no denying that an awful lot of Polish surnames come from the names of trees. Presumably they arose most often by way of a place designation—one who lived by the oak grove, near the big birch, and so on. It is also likely that some got such names because they worked with or dealt in lumber of a particular kind of tree. However they arose, here is a partial list of tree-derived surnames.

bereza, (East Slavic) "birch tree": Berezewski, Bereźniak

brzost, "Scotch elm": Brzostek, Brzostko, Brzostowski

brzoza, "birch tree": Brzóski, Brzózka, Brzozowski, Brzuska

Buchholz, "(German) beechwood": Bucholc, Bucholz

buk, "beech": Bukowski

choja, choina, "fir, spruce": Chojak, Chojna, Chojnacki, Hojka

cis, "yew-tree": Cis

czeremcha, "bird cherry": Czeremcha

dąb, "oak": Dąbek, Dębek, Dębiec

dąbr, dąbrowa, "oak grove": Dąbroś, Dąbrowa, Dąbrówka

dereń, "dogwood": Dereń

drzewo, "tree"

dub, East Slavic, "oak," cmp. Polish *dąb*: Dubicki, Dubowski

Eich, (German) "oak" (= Polish *dąb*, Russian *dub*): Eichel

fikus, "kind of fig tree": Fikus

grab, "hornbeam": Grabowy (= adj. "of hornbeam")

grusza, "pear-tree": Gruszczyk, Gruszka

jabłonka, "(small) apple tree": Jabłonka

jałowiec, "juniper"

jarząb, "rowan, sorb": Jarząb, Jarzątek, Jarzębak, Jarzombek

jawor, "sycamore": Jaworek, Jaworowicz

jedlina, "fir tree": Jedliński

jesion, "ash tree": Jasieniecki, Jesionowski

jodła, "fir tree": Jedłowski, Jodłowski

kasztan, "chestnut-tree"

klon, "maple tree": Klonek, Klonowski

las, "forest, woods": Lasek, Lasiewicki, Lasiewicz

Linde, (German) "linden": Lindemann, Linden

lipa, "linden": Lipa, Lipecki, Lipek, Lipiński

modrzew, "larch": Modrzyński

olsza, olcha, "alder": Olszak, Olszewicz, Olszyna, Wolszak

osika, osina, "asp, aspen (tree)": Osikowicz, Osina

rokita, "kind of willow": Rokicki

śliwa, "plum-tree, sloe": Śliwicki, Śliwiński, Śliwka

smerek, smrek, dialect, "spruce": Smereka, Smreczak

sosna, "pine": Sośniak, Sosnowski

świdwa, "red dogwood": Świdecki, Świdowski

świerk, "spruce": Świerkowski

szachor, "maple tree": Szacherski

topola, "poplar": Topolewski, Topoliński, Topolski

trześnia, "(black) cherry-tree": Trześniak

wierzba, "willow": Wierzbicki, Wierzbowski

wiśnia, "cherry-tree": Wiśniewski

But trees are not the only plants that yielded many surnames. Here are a few terms for bushes, flowers, and the like that you'll see appearing in any phone book, census, collection of vital records, or family "tree."

barwinek, "periwinkle, myrtle": Barwinek

Baum, (German) "tree": Baum

best, "lilac, elderberry": Bestwina, Biestek

bez, "lilac, elder": Bzówka, Bzowy

Blum, (German) "flower": Blum, Bluma

bluszcz, "ivy": Blus, Bluszcz

Busch, (German) "bush": Busch

chebda, "elderberry": Hebda

chmiel, "hops": Chmiel, Chmielak

chwast, "weed, tassel": Chwastek, Chwaszcz, Faszcza, Kwast

cierń, "thorn": Cierniak, Cierzniak

cwalina, "hemlock": Cwalina

dzięgiel, "angelica": Dzięgiel

fiołek, "violet": Fijołek, Fiołek

firleta, "kind of plant," cmp. firletka, "campion, lychnis": Firlit

gałąź, "branch, twig": Gałązka, Gałęza

głąb, "stalk, e.g., of cabbage": Głąb, Głąbik, Glomb, Głomb

głóg, "hawthorn": Głogiewicz

jaskier, "buttercup, crowfoot": Jaskiernia, Jaskierski

jaster, "aster": Jaster, Jastrowicz

jemioła, "mistletoe": Imiołek, Jamioła, Jemioła

jeżyna, "blackberry, bramble": Jeżyna

kaczan, "cabbage stump, corn cob": Kaczan, Kocan, Koczan

kąkol, "corn cockle": Kąkol, Konkol

kalina, "Viburnum, cranberry tree (shrub)": Kalina

karda, "thistle": Karda, Kardacz

kępa, "cluster of trees; holm": Kempa, Kempka, Kępa, Kępka

kierz, archaic, "bush; laurel tree": Kierzek

kiper, archaic, "fireweed": Kiper

kniat, knieć, "Caltha, marsh marigold, cowslip": Kneć, Knet, Kniat

kocierba, "bird cherry, hagberry": Kocerba, Kotarba, Koterba

kokorz, kokornak, "birthwort": Kokora, Kokorniak

kolec, "thorn, spike": Kolczyk

konopie, "hemp": Konopa, Konopka, Konopko

korzeń, "root": Korzeń, Korzeniak, Korzon, Korzun

kostrzewa, "fescue": Kostrzewa

koszcz, koszczka, "horsetail": Koszczuk

krzak, "bush": Krzaczek, Krzak

krzew, "shrub": Krzewina

kwiat, "flower": Kwiatek, Kwiatoń, Kwiotek

łabuz, "weed, bush": Łabuz, Łobaza

lawenda, "lavender": Lewandowski, Lewański

lebioda, "pigweed": Lebioda, Łoboda

len, "flax": Len, Leniec, Lenik

łęt, "potato stalk": Łęt, Łętocha

liana, "liana": Liana

łodyga, "stalk, stem, haulm": Łodyga

łopian, łopuch, "burdock": Łopion, Łopuch

łoza, "grey willow": Łoza, Łoziak

łub, "tree bark": Łuba, Łubik

mak, "poppy": Mak, Makoś, Makowiec

malina, "raspberry bush": Malina, Malinka

majeran, archaic, "marjoram": Majeran

mech, "moss, down": Mech

mirt, "myrtle": Myrta

Mistel, (German) "mistletoe": Miśtal, Misztal, Misztela

obara, "felled pine tree": Obara, Obarski

oczeret, "water plant, rush": Oczeretko

oset, "thistle": Ościk, Oset, Osetek

otawa, "new grass grown in a meadow after mowing": Otawa

ozimina, "crop sown in fall": Ozimina, Oźmina

palma, "palm tree": Palma

perz, pyrz, "a kind of weed, couchgrass": Perz, Perzan, Pyż

pień, "tree trunk, stem": Pieniak, Pieniek, Pieńkos
pigła, archaic, "quince": Pigiel, Pigla, Pigła
piwonia, "peony": Piwoń, Piwoni
płonka, "ungrafted tree": Płonka
pniak, "tree trunk, stump": Pniak, Pniok
podbiał, "coltsfoot": Podbioł
pokrzywa, "nettle": Pokrzywa
poziomka, "wild strawberry": Poziemski, Poziomek
prymula, "*Primula*, primrose": Prymula
rdest, "plants of the *Polygonum* family": Rdest
rogoża, "reed-mace, cat's tail": Rogoz, Rogoż, Rogóż
rokita, "kind of willow": Rokita, Rokitka
rosocha, "forked tree trunk": Rosocha
rozpłoch, "kind of fern": Rozpłoch
róża, "rose": Różek, Różewicz, Różyło
rozsada, "seedling": Rosada, Rosadziński
ruta, "rue": Ruta, Rutka, Rutkiewicz, Rutowicz
rzęsa, "*Lemna*, duckweed": Rzęsa
rzerzucha, rzeżucha, † *żerzucha,* "cuckoo-flower, lady's smock (*Cardamine*)": Rzeżuchowski
saladera, dialect, "plant used for fodder": Saladra
sawina, "savin": Sawina
siano, "hay": Sianko, Sienniak
sierżęga, "sharp grass": Sierżęga
skrzyp, "horsetail (plant)": Skrzyp

ślaz, "mallow": Ślaz, Szlas
smołd, "broad leaved sermountain, *Laserpitium latifolium*": Szmołda
stokłosa, "brome grass": Stokłos, Stokłosa
suwar, szuwar, "bushes, bullrushes": Suwara, Szuwara
szalej, "cowbane": Salej, Szalej
szałwia, "*Salvia*, sage": Szałwiński
szczoczarz, † "blue cornflower": Szczoczarz
szypuła, szypułka, "pedicel": Szypuła, Szypulski
szyszka, "cone": Szyszka, Szyszko
tabaka, "tobacco": Tabaczyński, Tabaka
tlałka, "rotting tree": Tlałka
trawa, "grass": Trawa, Trawka
trybuła, trebula, trzebula, "cow-parslip, wild chevril": Trbała, Trybuła, Trybulski
trzcina, "reed": Trzcina, Trzcinka, Trzcionka
tytoń, "tobacco": Tytoń
wisz, "thicket": Wiszowaty
wrzos, "heather": Wrzos, Wrzosek, Wrzoskiewicz
wyka, "vetch": Wyka, Wykowski
wykrot, "uprooted tree": Wykrota
zagaj, "copse, shrubbery": Zagaja
źdźbło, ździebło, "stalk of grassy plants and grains": Zdziebko, Zdziebło
zioło, "herb": Ziółko, Zioło
ziomber, dial. "kind of plant": Dziambor, Dziębor, Ziąber, Ziomber
żywica, "resin": Żywica

A Feature Attraction

In a world where popular public figures have gone by or been known by names such as "Carrot Top," "the Big Mouth" (Martha Raye), "the Schnozz"

(Jimmy Durante), and "Leo the Lip" (Leo Durocher), and "the Beard" (Fidel Castro), it is quite easy to see how some prominent feature of a person's body or personality could evoke a nickname. In Polish, you take that one step further and imagine those nicknames turning into surnames. There is an enormous number of such names, and I see no point in repeating here all or even most of them, especially since Volume II shows so many. But I will mention a few, just by way of illustration.

A fine, thick beard can set a man apart, so it's not suprising that a number of Polish surnames derive from *broda,* including *Broda, Brodacki, Brodala, Bródka, Brodowy*, and so on. We also see compounds such as *Białobrodec,* from *biały* "white," meaning "white-beard." But already I have to stop and add a note of caution: in a Polish armorial, a section on the Brodzic coat of arms states that the name "Brodzic" could come from *broda* but might also come from the name of estates at Brody; the coat of arms was granted in 1038, but there's no sure way to give the derivation of its name![8] And Rymut's book on surnames points out that names beginning *Brod-* can also come from the words *bród*, "ford, place to cross a river," and the verb *brodzić*, "to wade across, ford." [9]

So while many surnames beginning *Brod-* do come from the obvious root, *broda*, "beard," you can't assume they all do. This is a good lesson to learn, because Polish, like English, has a number of words or word roots that can mean more than one thing. When trying to establish the derivation of a surname, always keep your eyes open for possibilities besides the obvious ones.

More examples of names from prominent bodily features are *brzuch*, "belly, paunch" (*Brzuchacz*, compare *brzuchacz*, "fellow with a big belly", and *Brzuszek*, "little paunch"); *garb*, "hump" (*Garbaciak*, from *garbaty*, "humpbacked," *Garbacz* and *Garbaczyk*, from *garbacz*, "humpback"); and *głowa*, "head" (compare *Głowa, Głowacz* from *głowacz*, "fellow with big head," and *Główka*, from *główka*, "little head, knob"). A *Kudełka* was a mop-top, because *kudeł* is a mop of hair. A *Krzywonogi* was bow-legged, and a *Krzywonos* had a crooked nose (*krzywonos* is also a term for the grosbeak, a kind of finch). Names from such roots as *długi,* long, *łysy,* bald, *mały,* small, and *wielki,* large, are equally obvious.

But parts of the body weren't the only features that could occasion names. A *Dziki* probably was pretty wild and savage, because that's what *dziki* means. It's worth noting, by the way, that once a surname became hereditary, there was no guarantee it would remain appropriate: *Dzikiewicz*, the son of a guy named *Dziki*, may have been a real pussycat; but he was stuck with the name unless he was willing to undertake the task of getting people to quit calling him that! As for names from *młody,* "young," they have built-in obsolescence. Or what about a spry young fellow stuck with the moniker *Sędziwy,* "elderly"?

A *Bystroń* must have gotten that name because he was quick or made quick movements, because the connection with the adjective *bystry,* swift, rapid, is pretty firm. Anyone with a name starting with *dur-* must surely have resisted getting stuck with it, because it means "foolish, stupid"—and that root shows up in Polish, Belarusian, Russian, and Ukrainian, so a *Duraj* or *Durak* or *Duran* was branded just about anywhere he went.

It's funny how some attributes show up in a number of different names. For instance, *Bodura, Gniotek, Kujan, Legieć, Leń, Leżuch, Munia, Nieroba,* and *Susfał* all come from words that mean "lazy-bones, loafer." *Biba, Kaleja, Oblój, Ochlasta, Pijak,* and *Szalaban* all come from words that mean "drunkard." In view of the nobles' constant complaints about the peasants' drunkenness, the competition for a name like *Pijak* must have been fierce! More than one Pole has also noted how fractious Poles can be—it's almost proverbial that where you have three Poles you'll have four opinions on any subject!— and perhaps that's why we find names such as *Niezgoda,* "dissension," and *Warchol,* a "trouble-maker, squabbler, sower of discord." Fortunately, there's always a *Mądrala* around (from *mądry,* wise, but *mądrala* means "smart guy, know-it-all") to keep the Niezgodas and the Warchols from getting too obstreperous.

Objects, Verb Roots, Days and Time, and Miscellany

It's unfortunate that the features that produce the most names—objects and verb roots—are the ones to which I have to devote the least space. But because virtually any word denoting an object or an action can produce (and probably has produced) at least a couple of surnames, a listing of these roots and names from them would be at least the size of a good Polish dictionary! The sheer volume of them demands that I content myself to citing a few examples. Fortunately, in many cases it is quite easy to visualize how such names originated.

A quotation from a popular book written in the 1600s, Walerian Nekanda Trepka's *Liber chamorum,* gives a splendid example of how these surnames could originate, one that dates from the time when surnames were being established: "Dudecki, or sometimes Dudkowski ... was a servant of lord Maniowski in Sieradz district; he was the son of a peasant, but made himself out to be a nobleman. His father played the pipes and that's why the lord called him that."[10] The word *duda* means "bag-pipe," and although in modern Polish *dudek* means "hoopoe" (a kind of bird) or "nincompoop," obviously at that time it could be used to mean one who played the pipes; I suspect that *dudek* may already have started to signify an idiot who went around making a lot of empty noise, and that was part of the humor in the lord's name for this fellow.

Now we shouldn't take this story for Gospel truth; a prime expert in Polish genealogy, Włodzimierz Dworzaczek, criticized *Liber chamorum* for relying too much on oral sources that could not be verified,[11] so it is possible that this story is apocryphal. Nonetheless, Dworzaczek admitted that the book is a valuable source for understanding Polish culture and many customs of the time, and this story demonstrates the point: any association of a person with a particular item or action could be enough to produce a surname, or a nickname that would evolve into a surname.

Many surnames derived from objects or from verb roots can be interesting studies in their own right. One I find cute is *Niedośpiał,* for which the dictionary definition is "lazybones, sluggard"; it comes from *nie,* not, plus *dospać [się],* "to sleep one's fill, to get enough sleep"—so *Niedośpiał* was a person who never got his fill of sleeping! I like the word "lazybones," but *Niedośpiał* somehow strikes me as a more imaginative way to say pretty much the same thing.

Some verb-derived names puzzle because they must have arisen due to a propensity to perform the action of the verb. But it's difficult to imagine someone earning the name *Rygała,* for instance—*rygać* means "to vomit, belch out," and the *-ała* suffix implies continual repetition of the verb's action. So *Rygała* was someone who was known for continual vomiting? How did this person live long enough to acquire a surname? What woman stayed around him long enough to call him by name—let alone cooperate in carrying on the family name?

Some objects also yield interesting names. The noun *błona,* for instance, means "membrane, film," and is used much the same way as the English word "membrane." Rymut's book on Polish surnames mentions *Błoniarz,* and he explains that it derives from an archaic term *błoniarz* that meant "maker of windows from animal membranes." I'm sure there are grosser jobs, but I for one would rather not hear about them!

Names from expressions indicating time or date are not too hard to understand, although sometimes they require a little reflection. For instance, why would a person be named *Sobota,* Saturday, or *Styczeń,* January? The most reasonable explanation I've seen is that such names commemorate a day or month or season significant in an ancestor's life. It is fairly well established that *neoficy,* Jews who converted to Christianity, often assumed names of this sort: *Styczyński, Lutyński,* (and on through the rest of the months), as well as *Niedzielski,* "of Sunday."[11] I don't know whether something similar is at work in the old sayings about "Monday's child is fair of face, Tuesday's child is full of grace…" but it is an interesting cultural parallel.

I suppose a similar explanation accounts for some of the names that come from weather features: *Chmura* (cloud), *Mróz* (frost), *Wiatr* (wind). Perhaps a name like *Wiatr* or *Wietrzyński* got started because the bearer was born on an unusually windy day, so he or she got the nickname "Windy" and it caught on. (Readers the same age as I am are probably irresistibly reminded of the words to that song, "Everyone knows it's Wietrzyńska").

Summary

It is difficult to conclude a discussion of these surnames because anything less than a few hundred pages simply can't do justice to them. You can open a Polish dictionary to any page and find plenty of words that produced surnames fitting the categories examined in this chapter. The mere scope and volume of this subject require more space than I can afford to devote to it. I realize that some readers may want to learn everything possible about a given name or group of names, and this chapter may fall short of satisfying their curiosity.

Fortunately, many Polish scholars have used their talents to uncover and illuminate the origins of these names. In Chapter Twelve I provide information that will lead you to their work and, with any luck, to more details on the names of interest to you, if you want more.

In the meantime, however, I hope that this chapter has given you not only some facts to work with but also a sense of the fascination this subject can evoke. Deciphering the origins and meanings of these names is no picnic, but the attempt to do so can provide a lot of mental stimulation and pleasure —much like a whole series of frustrating but potentially rewarding riddles. And unlike the Mad Hatter's riddle, these do, in most cases, have answers!

Endnotes

[1] Kazimierz Rymut, *Nazwiska Polaków,* Wydawnictwo Naukowe DWN, Kraków, 2001, Volume II, pp. 105–106.

[2] Kazimierz Rymut, *Nazwy miast Polski,* Zakład Narodowy im. Ossolińskich—Wydawnictwo, Wrocław, 1987, pp. 470–471.

[3] *Pod wspólnym niebem: Narody dawnej Rzeczypospolitej,* ed. Michał Kopczyński and Wojciech Tygielski, Museum of Polish History in Warsaw and Bellona SA, Warszawa, 2010. ISBN 978-83-11-11724-2. A translation in English by yours truly is due to be published in 2013 or 2014. The title means "Under a Common Sky: The Nations of the Former Commonwealth."

[4] Jan Stanisław Bystroń, *Nazwiska Polskie*, 2nd ed., Lwów-Warsawa, Książnica-Atlas, 1936, p. 12.

[5] In order to check on the contemporary meanings of some of these terms, I referred often to Stanisław Kielbasa's *Dictionary of Polish Obscenities*, 3rd, revised edition, Scythian Books, 1994, ISBN 0-933884-93-1. He notes that *fagas* can mean "prick, dick; lecher; flunkey," and *fajdać* is best translated as "to shit." Among the many words he defines as meaning "cock, prick" are *fujara* (also meaning "fool, ass"), *gmyrek, kuś, kuśka, kutas,* and *siurek*. He gives as vulgar synonyms for the female genitals *kuciapa, kuczma, pinda* (which can also mean "whore, bitch"), *pitula,* and *pizda*. He says *gnojek* can mean "youngster, kid, little stink-

er"; *kiep* is "asshole, idiot"; *pierdzioch* is "farter"; and *zebździć* is "to fart." Of course, even if you take everything he says as true, a word's modern meaning doesn't necessarily reflect what it meant centuries ago, when surnames were forming. But this information does tend to substantiate what my other sources say about the words these names came from. I think it's valid for us to be curious about these, if only so that we won't be surprised if someone takes offense when these words are mentioned.

[6] Bystroń, *Nazwiska Polskie*, p. 26.

[7] Mirosław Zbichorski, "The Polish Inn in History," *Polish Genealogical Society Newsletter,* Spring, 1992, p. 19.

[8] From Kasper Niesiecki's *Herbarz polski* (quoted in the *Polish Genealogical Society Newsletter,* Spring 92, page 13).

[9] Rymut, *Nazwiska Polaków*, Vol. I, p. 53.

[9] Quoted in Bystroń, *Nazwiska Polskie,* p. 169.

[10] Włodzimierz Dworzaczek, *Genealogia,* Państwowe Wydawnictwo Naukowe, Warsaw, 1959. Chapter Three, the source of this citation, appeared in translation in the *Polish Genealogical Society Newsletter,* starting with the Fall 1985 issue, pp. 23ff. As of this writing, my updated translation of Chapter Three (revised in 2004) is available as a PDF that can be downloaded from the website of the Polish Genealogical Society of America®: <http://www.pgsa.org/PDFs/DworzaczekIII.pdf>.

[11] Bystroń, *Nazwiska Polskie,* pp. 254ff.

Chapter Nine

"Gente Rutheni, Natione Poloni"

In talking with people about the origins of Polish surnames, I have noticed that much confusion arises from the concept they have of what "Poland" means. If I tell them their name comes from a German or Ukrainian or Lithuanian root, they often answer, "No, that can't be, my ancestors were from Poland." It is, of course, quite natural to assume that Poles lived in Poland, Germans lived in Germany, Lithuanians lived in Lithuania, and so on. I am sorry to say that this view is not only simplistic, it absolutely has to be smashed to smithereens before you can hope to understand Polish surnames (or history or culture, for that matter).

The Latin quotation heading this chapter means literally "as a people Ruthenians, as a nation Poles," although it is smoother to translate it as "Ruthenians of the Polish nation." It appears in old records as formula used by Ruthenians who maintained their ethnic identity but also gloried in their citizenship in the Polish state.[1] I quote it here to illustrate that over the centuries, the borders of central and eastern Europe have been in constant flux; and for a long time, the Polish-Lithuanian Commonwealth was a major power that included regions populated largely by non-Poles. At various times, the political entity called "Poland" has ruled most of Prussia, much of Silesia, Ukraine, Byelorussia (now Belarus), and much of Lithuania; its borders expanded and contracted, and from the late 18th century till 1919, Poland disappeared from the map entirely. The result is that in the last few centuries, there have been Poles living in Germany and Germans living in Poland, Czechs living in Poland and Poles living in Czechoslovakia, Poles living in Ukraine, Lithuania and Belarus, and Ukrainians, Lithuanians, and Belarusians living in Poland—and Jews living throughout the whole area.

It would be superfluous for me to turn this into a treatise on eastern European history, since there are plenty of works that do the job at length and in detail. I will give a horrendously oversimplified summary of the centuries in a few words, however, and trust you to deepen your knowledge of the subject if necessary by turning to those other works.

The essential points are these. We first begin to speak of a Poland when King Mieszko I of the Piast dynasty, ruler of most areas where ethnic Poles were living, accepted Latin-rite Catholicism in 966. For the next few centuries, Poland went through a period of division into principalities and reunion, while it had frequent problems with its neighbors: the Prussians to the north and west, the Bohemians to the south, and the Lithuanians (who gradually came to control most of Belarus and western Ukraine) to the north and east. Poland eventually settled with Bohemia, yielding part of Silesia, and managed to hold off the Prussians to the west. There were so many enemies to the

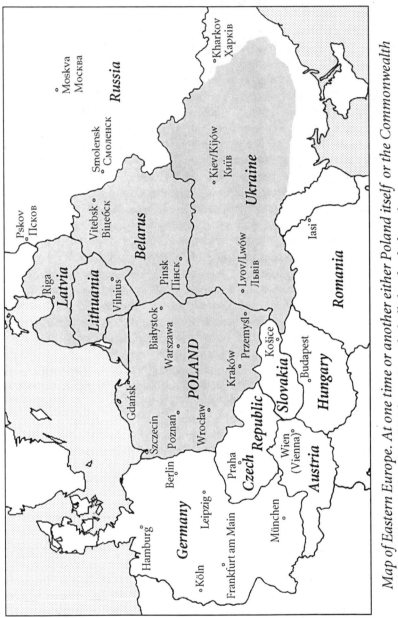

Map of Eastern Europe. At one time or another either Poland itself or the Commonwealth of Two States, Poland and Lithuania, ruled all the shaded territory.

east—Lithuanians, Muscovites, Mongols, Cossacks, Ruthenians—that some way of co-existing had to be found; the solution began with the personal union of Queen Jadwiga and the Lithuanian prince Jogaila (called Jagiełło by Poles) in 1385. With this union began a slow process whereby the Kingdom of Poland and the Grand Duchy of Lithuania, which initially ruled most of what are now Belarus and western Ukraine, merged into one geopolitical entity with two equal components under a single ruler. Victory over the Teutonic Knights at Grunwald in 1410 helped solidify the western border, while the union with Lithuania made the eastern border a little more secure; and for several generations, the Polish-Lithuanian Commonwealth was a comparatively peaceful place. By the middle of the 17th century, however, the Commonwealth was under serious attack, especially during a Cossack uprising under Bohdan Khmelnytsky and repeated invasions by Sweden. By the end of the 18th century, its weakening situation *vis-à-vis* the growing strength of the German, Russian, and Austrian empires led to the partitioning of the Commonwealth and its eventual disappearance from the map. An independent Poland reappeared after World War I, after the defeat of the German and Austro-Hungarian empires and the collapse of the Tsar's government in Russia. Poland lost some of its eastern territory in Ukraine and Belarus to the Soviets in the Polish-Soviet War of 1919–1921; but many historians emphasize that in that war, Poland checked the westward expansion of Soviet power. In 1939, the Nazis' and Soviets' invasion brought new agony to Poland. After World War II, Poland was "liberated" by the Soviets and established as an "independent" nation, but with its borders permanently shifted westward, so that Lithuania, Belarus, and Ukraine remained under Soviet control. Poland was compensated for the lost territory by being ceded much of eastern Germany, regions to which Poland had a historical claim. Poland remained under Soviet control until it finally broke free of the Soviet bloc in 1989.[2]

This summary is so inadequate that it makes me blush. But if you're not familiar with Poland's history, it may serve its purpose: to explain why your Polish ancestors could come from many areas no longer part of the nation of Poland. In Lithuania, Belarus, and western Ukraine, Poles were the upper class for centuries. The Poles probably thought they exerted a benevolent and progressive influence; the nationalists in those countries thought otherwise. Many Poles settled there, and Polish language and culture came to be more or less dominant. Many natives of the regions identified themselves as Polish in nationality, even as they retained their separate ethnic identities.

In the west, meanwhile, the passage of such regions as Pomerania, eastern Prussia, and Silesia back and forth between German and Polish control had caused considerable mixing of ethnic elements. Also—as mentioned in Chapter Eight—Poles invited or allowed many Germans, tired of religious and economic problems in their homeland, to settle in Poland, even to colonize underpopulated areas. German craftsmen put down roots and supplemented the rather small, native-Polish middle class.

A great many Jews also migrated to Poland after being expelled from other European countries. There often was considerable tension between Poles and Jews, to the extent that many Jews whose ancestors lived in Poland vehemently refuse to be identified as "Polish." But I think it is fair to say that on the whole, they found a comparatively hospitable welcome. Great centers of Jewish life developed all over the region, not just in Poland proper but also in Lithuania, Belarus, and Ukraine. Many of these centers were located in areas that came under rule of the Russian Empire after the partitions, so that Jews who lived there are often referred to as "Russian Jews." But the large Jewish communities of western Ukraine were in Galicia, ruled by Austria-Hungary. And of course, there were many Jews who found themselves under Prussian rule. Over the centuries, the inhabitants of those regions had grown used to considering themselves part of Poland; so even after the partitions they might still think of themselves, or be regarded by others, as "Polish." This causes a lot of confusion, and to a large extent, national identity depended on what historical perspective one used. If you regard the inhabitants of these regions only in the context of the 19th century, they were "Russian" or "Austrian" ("Galician") or "Prussian." But if you take a longer view that encompasses, say, 1600-1900, they might reasonably be regarded as "Polish."

For many readers all of this is old news, and I apologize for wasting their time. But if you're just starting to research family history in eastern Europe, it can save much frustration to *be flexible about nationalities and boundaries!* If your ancestors said they were Poles but you find they came from a town in Ukraine; or if they said they were Poles but the records say they came from a town in Prussia; or if they said they were Czechs but you find they came from, say, Kraków—in all these cases, the facts don't necessarily conflict. Dig a little more, consult a historical atlas of the region, and you may find the apparent contradictions all disappear.

Now let us take a quick look at some of the non-Polish ethnic and linguistic elements that have contributed to the stockpile of Polish surnames.

Czech Names

The Czech influence on Polish surnames is less conspicuous than that of, say, German or Ukrainian. This is partly because many Czech and Polish words are similar, and it can be hard to tell whether a particular name started out as Czech or as Polish. For instance, the name *Novotný,* spelled with the accent, is clearly Czech. But in America, *Novotny* might be the Czech *Novotný* without the diacritical mark, or it might be Polish *Nowotny* spelled *Novotny* by English phonetics. You might say, "Polish doesn't use the letter *v* and Czech doesn't use the letter *w,* so *Novotny* has to be Czech." But is that *v* there because the name is Czech, or is it there because an American spelled Polish *w* the way it sounded to him, like a *v*? You can see the danger of jumping to conclusions.

The confusion is compounded in the United States because, to many Americans, there was no discernible difference between Czechs and Poles; they were all just foreigners from some far-off corner of Europe where people talked funny! Polish immigrants to this country often went to Czech churches until their communities grew large enough to found their own parishes, as happened in Baltimore, for instance.[3] The creation of "Slavic communities" in American cities helped blur the distinction between Czech and Pole in the eyes of Americans, although no Pole or Czech would confuse the two. The listing of Polish names among Czech parish and cemetery records adds to the confusion.

Another reason the Czech influence on Polish names does not appear strong is that in Poland, that influence, significant in the Middle Ages, lessened with time. Bohemia was the bridge whereby Christianity came to Poland, so one sees Polish Christian names modified by Czech influence: original Polish *Włodzisław* became *Władysław,* Polish *Więcesław* or *Więcław* became *Wacław,* etc. But by the time surnames were being adopted by most Poles, their own culture and language had grown so strong that they were less likely to follow Czech examples. Czech influence on Polish surnames didn't grow again until the partitions, when southern Poles found themselves in the Austrian partition with the Czechs and Slovaks.[4]

There are quite a few names that are quite similar in Polish and Czech if you take into account linguistic tendencies. I've already mentioned *v* vs. *w* *(Novotný* vs. *Nowotny),* but you should also look out for:

> Czech *a, u* vs. Polish *ą, ę: huba* vs. *gęba* (mouth), *holub* vs. *gołąb* (pigeon, dove)
> Czech *č* vs. Polish *cz: Pavliček* vs. *Pawliczek* (< *Pavel* vs. *Paweł*)
> Czech *h* vs. Polish *g: hlava* vs. *głowa* (head)
> Czech *ou* vs. Polish *u: dlouhý* vs. *długi* (long)
> Czech *ř* vs. Polish *rz* or *ż: hospodář* vs. *gospodarz* (farmer)
> Czech *š* vs. Polish *sz: šrám* vs. *szrama* (scar)

There are a few surnames appearing in Volume II that clearly came from or were influenced by Czech, and I list some of them here. I don't doubt for a second that a far longer list could be compiled, but these should be enough to give you a notion how the names compare.

Bem < *Bem,* "Czech, Bohemian": Bejma, Bem, Bemke, Bemowski, Boehm
Cerny < *černý,* "black" (cmp. Polish *czarny*)
Cerven < *červen,* "June," also *červený* is "red" (cmp. Polish *czerwiec,* "June," *czerwony,* "red"): Cervenka, Cerveny
Czech < *Czech,* Czech, "Bohemian" (or can be a name element *Cze-* < *Czesław* + suffix *-ch-*): Czech, Czechański, Czechowicz, Czechowski
Czermak < Czech *čermák,* "redstart," common European songbird, in archaic Polish *czermak,* "a red-winged bird": Czermak

Dlouhy < Czech *dlouhý*, "long" = Polish *długi:* Dlouchy, Dlouhy

Dvořák, Czech equivalent of Polish *Dworzak* < *dworak*, "courtier, aristocrat"

Havel < given name *Havel* < Latin name *Gallus* = Polish *Gaweł:* Havlíček, Hawel, Hawełka, Hawliczek

Holak < Czech *holak*, "ragamuffin, scruffy fellow"

Holub < Czech *holub* = Polish *gołąb*, "dove": Hałub, Holub, Holubek

Hor- < Czech *hora*, "mountain," *horký*, "hot," *horši*, "worse," *hořet*, "to burn," *hořký*, "bitter," cmp. Polish root *gor-*: Horak, Horczak, Horka

Hubacz < Silesian form, cmp. Czech *hubač*, "big-mouth, bawler, barker": Hubacz

Hulak, cmp. Czech *hulák*, "loudmouth": Hulak

Hus < Czech *hus*, "goose," or a follower of Jan Hus: Hus, Husak

Kalus < Czech pers. n. *Kalus* < *kalous*, "the long-eared owl": Kalus, Kałus

Kmita, name of a prominent Polish family < Czech *kmit*, "flash, sparkle," *kmitati*, "flash, flicker" (said of a light), or perhaps < the Proto-Slavic root *kъmy*, "clan, tribe"

Krejci- < Czech *krejčí*, "tailor": Krejci, Krejczy

Mraz, cmp. Czech *mráz*, "frost": Mraz

Nawratil < Czech *Navrátil*, "convert": Nawratil

Prochas- < Czech personal name *Procházka*, "walk, stroll; talkative fellow": Prochasek, Prochaska, Prohaska

Sedlak < Czech *sedlák*, "farmer, peasant," and its diminutive form *sedláček*: Sedlaczek, Sedlak

Stastny < Czech *šťastný*, "happy": Stastny

Tetzlaff < German version of Czech first name *Těchoslav*, *Těslav*, Polish equivalents *Ciechosław*, *Ciesław*: Teclaf, Tecław, Tetzlaff

Tesar < Czech *tesař*, "carpenter," cmp. Polish *cieśla*: Tesarczyk, Tesarski, Tessar, Tysarczyk, Tyszer

Tesmer < Germanic version of Polish *Cieszymir* or Czech *Těšimir*: Tesmar, Tesmer, Tessmer

Zajiček < Czech *zajíc*, "hare," cmp. Polish *zając*: Zajic, Zajiczek

Zlatkin < Czech *zlato*, "gold," which in Jewish names = *Golda, Golde*

German

At one point, I had intended to list here all the names from Volume II that were of German origin, but I had to abandon the idea because the list ran more than 20 pages!

As I discussed in Chapter Seven, in the section on occupation-derived names, there are several reasons for all these German surnames. The source of some of the surnames in Volume II was an index compiled in the Chicago area, and in that area a particularly large number of Poles came from the Prussian partition, the populace of which included many originally of German ethnic origin. But Germans could be found all over Poland, because they were invited, as so-called "colonists," to settle in underpopulated areas and contribute their skills. So not only were Germans significantly represented in the population of Poland, German terms related to some skills and crafts made their way into the language and could become the source of surnames.

Bystroń points out that Germans in Poland—at least for the first generation or two—felt that they were a breed apart, tended to concentrate in their own communities, and kept their German surnames intact. Sometimes the names remained completely unchanged; but as time went on, many came to be spelled out more in agreement with Polish phonetic values. Thus, *Schumann* gradually came to be spelled *Szuman, Brückner* modified to *Brykner, Ziegelstreich* became *Cygielsztrejch*. This involved no essential change to the names themselves, you understand, but simply a tendency to spell the name by Polish phonetic values; a Pole hearing a German say *"Ziegelstreich"* would naturally write down *Cygielsztrajch* or *Cygielsztrejch* (depending on German dialect differences). An interesting sidelight is that when the Prussians partitioned Poland with the Russians and Austrians, they forbade such changes in their section—but in the Russian section, where names were transcribed in Cyrillic, spelling changes became more and more common.[5] Still, a great many German surnames survived essentially unchanged, either in original spelling or in a form easier for Poles to pronounce.

A factor that complicates tracing the origins of surnames in Poland is that the German names often became confused with Polish words that sounded similar, even though they meant something entirely different. Bystroń cites such examples as German *Rolle* (something rolled up, as an official list or proclamation) → *Rola* (in Polish, "soil, field"), German *Ruck* ("back") → *Róg* (in Polish, "horn, corner"). There are many such words that sound alike but mean different things in each language; and often the only way to determine for certain whether a surname was originally German or Polish is to trace it back in the records. Since middle-class and peasant records, as a rule, don't go as far back as *szlachta* records, if your family wasn't noble, there are often no documents to let you find out for sure.[6] As I was working on Volume II, I often had to ask myself whether a particular name came from the German or the Polish word pronounced that way. When I could not be sure, I tried to indicate both possibilities, and I regret to say there was often no way to be sure—undoubtedly, some families named *Rola* derived their name from Polish *rola* and some from German *Rolle*.

The process of polonizing also meant that some German names were translated into names that meant the same thing in Polish as the old one had in German, so that a *Schmidt* ("smith") might be called *Schmidt* by Germans, *Kowal* by Poles, and show up as *Faber* in Latin-language church records! Other examples of the same process are: a *Schwarz* might be called *Szwarc* (with the name written according to Polish phonetic values) or *Czarny* (translated, as German *schwarz* = Polish *czarny* = English *black*). More examples:[7]

Gutteter ↔ *Dobroszyński* (*gut* = Polish *dobry,* English "good")
Roterman ↔ *Czerwieński* (*rot* = *czerwony,* English "red")
Schultz ↔ *Sołtysiak* (both names come ultimately from an old
      German word for a local headman or administrator)
Hoffman or *Ofman* ↔ *Dworzański* (*Hof* = *dwór,* English "court,
      manor, yard, plot of land")
Lang ↔ *Dłużyński* (*lang* = *długi,* English "long")
Wilderman ↔ *Dzikomęski* (*wild, man* = *dziki* + *męski,* English
      "wild man")
Moller ↔ *Młyński (Möller* = *młynarz,* English "miller")

If I may bore you with more details on a name that interests me (but that also illustrates some of these points nicely), the book *Liber chamorum* mentions a middle-class family named *Hoffman*: "the middle-class Offmans of Kraków, sons of the Kraków hatter Hoffman, called themselves *Nowodworski*, and their cousin Offmanek in Olkusz called himself *Dworzański,* in a word, none of them called themselves *Offman.*"[8] Notice the translation of German *Hof* with Polish *dwór,* which means approximately the same thing. I suspect examples of this sort are not all that common, but the point is that there are existing records that prove this kind of thing happened—and if one of your ancestral surnames stems from polonized German, being aware of this little trick can keep your research from grinding to a halt.

Sometimes a pair of decent dictionaries, one German and one Polish, is enough to let you match names up: *Neumann* ↔ *Nowak* ("new"); *Hahn* ↔ *Koguciński* ("cock"); *Rot* ↔ *Czerwiński* ("red"); *Blum* ↔ *Kwiatkowski* ("flower"); *Nachtigall* ↔ *Słowiński* ("nightingale"); *Krebs* ↔ *Rakowski* ("crab"); *Hoppe* ↔ *Chmielewski* ("hops"); *Wild* ↔ *Dzikowski* ("wild"); *Erdman* ↔ *Ziemęcki* ("earth, land"); *Gänsler* ↔ *Gąsiorowski* ("goose"). By the way, notice that the Germans who let their names be polonized also went for *-ski* suffixes in a big way, although it's questionable how many of them were noble. In this case it may not have been pretensions that motivated them, but rather the feeling that *-ski* names were "more Polish" than any other kind.

Bystroń even quotes a 1741 source from Wrocław where the same people are given with different names in separate Polish and German lists; each name is a translation—sometimes accurate, sometimes loose—of its counterpart in the other language:[9]

Wojciech Wilkołek ↔ *Albrecht Bärwolf*
Jakób Maślanka ↔ *Jakob Buttermilch*
Tomasz Złotomęski ↔ *Thomas Goldmann*
Jan Tarnowski ↔ *Johann Tarnau*
Jerzy Samotya ↔ *Georg Selbstfett*
Jakób Wierzbicki ↔ *Jakob Weidner*

I'm pleased to say that after the first edition of this book was published, I heard online from a lady who found her ancestor Elizabeth Niedzielski listed on the 1880 census as "Lizzie Sonntag"! She recognized the name partly because she had read these pages and realized that German *Sonntag* and Polish *niedziela* both mean "Sunday."

It's a little unsettling for Americans to realize that people might change ethnic identity so easily, but success in research can depend on familiarity with this fact. I've heard from people who'll say something like, "My great-grandfather's name was Johann Lech, he came from Danzig, he was Protestant, and he spoke German and Polish. He always said he was German, but Danzig is Gdańsk, in Poland. What was he?" It can be very difficult trying to sort something like this out without a lot more facts because you can make a case either way. Danzig was part of Germany, and there was no Poland at the time; but *Lech* is a Slavic name in origin. Sometimes you can go mainly by what sort of first names the family used. If they called each other "Georg" and "Johann," it's safe to bet they were Germans; if they called each other "Jerzy" and "Jan," they were probably Poles. Just remember, the names they bore on official documents are less reliable, because the ruling government often dictated what names were to be used, in compliance with their ethnic policies.

There's another subject I should discuss briefly, because its importance in dealing with surnames of is enormous: **dithematic names**. I talked about them in Chapter Five, but it may do no harm to review the subject. Dithematic names are formed by taking two *(di-)* basic roots *(themes)* in a language and combining them. Most of the peoples who speak languages descending from Proto-Indo-European used, and still use, such names. I, for instance, bear the names *William* and *Frederick*, both of which are English versions of ancient Germanic names meaning "will-helm" and "peace-ruler," respectively. The same names are used in German in the forms *Wilhelm* and *Friedrich*.

The idea behind them is not hard to understand. After all, if you call your son "that miserable little bugger we ought to feed to the pigs," he will probably not turn out to be the apple of your eye. But if you call the him "man of the people" or "savior of his kin" or "wise giver of counsel," the name may well prove to be a self-fulfilling prophecy. For myself, I am somewhat strong-willed, and I rule my household in peace (as long as the females let me). So there may be something to the whole idea. Then again, maybe not...

Most of these names originated in ancient times, long before pagans were converted to Christianity. Many are still used. Consider *Alexander*, from Greek roots *aléxō*, "to protect" + *anēr*, "man," thus "defender of men." Or there's *Adalbert*, in English generally used in the form *Albert*, from Germanic roots *adal*, "noble," and *beraht*, "shining, splendid"—"one of splendid nobility." Polish *Wojciech* comes from the Slavic roots *voi-*, "warrior" + *těch-*, "joy, comfort" = "joyful warrior." There were many, many such two-part names meant to augur well for the child given them.

They can represent a real challenge to the student of names—especially the Germanic ones, because their forms are far more changeable those of, say, Lithuanian or Polish. The root that took the form *walt-* in Old High German shows up in such given names as *Arnold, Bertold, Edwald, Ewald, Gerald, Gwalbert, Oswald, Rajnold, Walburga, Waldemar, Walter,* and *Witold.* You can see that breaking Germanic dithematic names down into their roots can prove difficult and frustrating.

Still, certain roots tend to appear again and again, and I'd like to give you a list may help you make sense of them when you encounter them. I based this list on information from Volker and Rosa Kohlheim's *Duden Familiennamen.* Note, incidentally, that most of these names are so ancient that in some cases, the original meanings of the names and even the roots have never been established with certainty. So you will see them interpreted inconsistently, and not always with great confidence.

A few symbols need explanation. The asterisk * before a root means it is reconstructed; that is, no surviving sources document this root, but linguists feel certain it, or something very like it, must have existed. The tilde ~ before a root means it was apparently not used in the ancient names, but only in more modern creations. Thus, *~Traugott,* "trust-God," expresses a very nice sentiment, but not one Germanic pagans used as a name. In some cases, experts differ on which of two similar roots appears in a name. Some authors say the first part of *Emeryk* comes from the root *amal-,* while others say it's from *amar-. Emeryk* is listed here under both, but the notation [?] is meant to warn you that there is disagreement on this point.

Each root is given in bold italic print, followed by an English rendering of its basic meaning in Roman type and quotation marks. A colon follows, and then, a selection of given names with that root that appear often in Volume II. The spelling of some is more Polish than German (e. g., *Gotfryd* vs. *Gottfried*), but the idea is to present the names in forms you can recognize.

adal-, adel-: "noble [clan]": Adelajda, Adelgunda, Adolf, Albert, Alfons, Alwin, Edelgarda, Edeltrauda, Edelweis
agi- → *eck-, ekka*
al-: "all": Alfons, Alodia, Alojzy, Elwira
alb-, alp-: "elf": Albin
amal-: perhaps "brave, valiant" or "hard-working": Amelia, Emeryk [?]
amar-: "ardent, zealous": Emeryk [?]
ans-: "one of the Ansen" (Germanic demi-gods): Anzelm, Oskar [?], Osman, Oswald
arn-: "eagle": Arnold, Arnolf
aud- → *ôd-, ōt-*
bald-: "bold, brave": Baldwin, Leopold, Teobald
bert-, beraht-: "bright, shining, brilliant": Albert, Bertold, Bertram, Engelbert, Gilbert, Herbert, Hubert, Lambert, Norbert, Robert, Zygbert
berg-: "protect": Burghard, Ingeborga, Walburga

bero-: "bear" (the animal): Bernard

brunja-: "armor": Brunhilda

dag-: "day": Dagobert

dank-: "think" (or "thank"): Dankwart

diet-: "people, folk": Detlef, Dieter, Dietmar, Dietrich, Teobald, Teodoryk

eber-: "wild boar": Eberhard

eck-, ekka-: "sword": Eckhard, Egbert

ed-, eād-: "inherited wealth, property" (old English, cmp. *ôd-*): Edgar, Edmund, Edwald, Edward, Edwin, Edyta

edel- → *adal-*

eg- → *eck-, ekka*

engel-: "Angle, angel": Engelbert

êr-, ehr-: "honor": Ehrenfried, Ehrentraud, Erhard [?], Erwin [?]

erman-: "great, all-encompassing whole," or *Ermin,* byname of the deity Tiu: Irmgarda, Irmtrauda

ēve-: "law, order": Ewald

frid-, fried-: "peace": Ehrenfried, Ferdynand, Friedel, Friedrich/Fryderyk, Gottfried/Gotfryd, Manfred, Wilfried, Winfried, Siegfried/Zygfryd

funs-: "quick, eager": Alfons, Ildefons

gang-: "go, walk": Wolfgang

gard-: "defend, guard": Edelgard, Edgar, Hildegarda (or < *gard,* "enclosure"), Irmgarda, Ludgard

geb-: "give": Gebhard

gēr-: "spear, spear warrior": Gerald, Gerard, Gertruda, Oskar [?], Roger

gisel-: "offspring," or "hostage, pledge": Gilbert, Giselher, Gizeltrauda

got-: "god": Gottfried/Gotfryd, Gothard, Gotlib, Traugott

grîm-: "mask, helmet": Krimhilda

gund-: "battle": Adelgunda, Ginter, Hildegunda, Kunegunda

gyth-: "strife" (old English): Edyta, Gudrun

hadu-: "battle": Jadwiga

haim-: "home": Heinrich/Henryk

hard-: "strong": Bernard, Burghard, Eberhard, Eckhard, Erhard, Gebhard, Gerard, Gothard, Hartmunt, Hartmut, Hartwig, Herta, Leonard, Medard, Meinhard, Rajnard, Ryszard

heil-: "health, salvation": Helman, Helmut

heit-: "person, condition, kind": Adelajda

helm-: "helmet": Anzelm, Wilhelm

her-: "people, army" (or *heri-,* "lord, master"): Dieter, Erhard, Erwin, Ginter, Giselher, Herbert, Herman, Lotar, Rajner, Volker, Walter, Warner

hild-: "battle": Brunhila, Hilda, Hildegarda, Hildegunda, Hiltruda, Ildefons, Klotylda, Krimhilda, Matylda

hlūt-: "famous": Klotylda, Lotar, Ludwik

hraben-, ram-: "raven": Bertram, Wolfram

hrōd-: "glory, victory": Robert, Roderyk, Roger, Roland, Rozwita, Rudolf

hrōm-, hruom-: "fame, glory": Romuald
hŭgu-: "mind, thinking spirit": Hubert
ing-: Ingi, name of a Germanic deity: Ingeborga, Ingrid
kunni-: "clan," or **cunja,* "well-born, noble": Kunegunda
kuoni-: "bold, valiant, battle-tested": Konrad
*landa-: "land": Lambert, Roland
lef-: "offspring": Detlef
lewo-: "lion": Leonard
˜līb, lieb-: "dear, beloved": Gotlib, Lipman
lind-: "shield" (made of linden wood): Gerlinda, Zyglinda
liut-: "people, folk": Leopold, Ludgard, Ludgier, Ludwina
magin-: "strength": Manfred [?], Meinhard
mahal-: "court, justice": Malwina
maht-: "power, might": Matylda, Medard [?]
man-: "man": Helman, Lipman, Manfred [?], Osman
mār-: "famous, renowned": Dietmar, Otmar, Waldemar
mēta-: "wage, pay": Medard [?]
mund-: "protector": Edmund, Hartmunt, Rajmund, Zygmunt
muot-: "spirit": Hartmut, Helmut
nand-: "bravery": Ferdynand
nord-: "north": Norbert
ôd-, ōt-: "inheritance, estate, property": Alodia, Otmar, Ottokar
ort-: "point of a sword or spear": Ortwin
os- → ans-
rad- → rāt-
ragin-: "counsel, council": Rajmund, Rajnard, Rajner, Rajnold
ram- see hraben
rāt-: "counsel, advise": Konrad, Ralf
rich-, rīhhi-: "rule": Dietrich, Emeryk [?], Fryderyk, Henryk, Roderyk, Ryszard, Ulrich
rid-: "rider": Zygryda
rūn-: "secret" (old English): Gudrun
sigŭ-: "victory": Zygbert, Zygfryd, Zyglinda, Zygmunt, Zygryd, Zygward
swinths-: "strong, powerful": Rozwita
theu[d]- → diet-
˜trau-: "trust": Traugott
trud-: "strength": Adeltrauda, Edeltrauda, Ehrentraud, Gertruda, Gizeltrauda, Hiltruda, Irmtrauda, Waltrauda
uodal-: "inheritance, property" (cmp. *ôd-, ōt-*): Ulrich
volk-: "people, folk": Volker
wakar-: "alert, vigilant": Ottokar
wal-: "battle": Waltrauda
walt-: "rule, govern": Arnold, Bertold, Edwald, Ewald, Gerald, Gwalbert, Oswald, Rajnold, Walburga, Waldemar, Walter, Witold

war-, wer-: "true": Elwira [?]
ward-, wart-: "guard, keep, protect": Dankwart, Edward, Zygward
warj-: "guard, protect": Werner [?]
warn-: "warn": Werner [?]
widu-, witu-: "forest": Gwidon, Witold
wīg-, wīk-: "battle": Hartwig, Jadwiga, Ludwik
wilja-: "will, desire": Wilfried, Wilhelm, Wilibald
wini-:, "friend": Albin, Alwin, Baldwin, Edwin, Erwin, Gerwin, Ludwina,
    Malwina, Ortwin, Winfried
wisi-: "wise, knowing": Alojzy
wīz-: "white": Edelweis
wolf-: "wolf": Adolf, Arnulf, Detlef (? or *lef-*), Ralf, Rudolf, Wolfgang, Wol-
    fram

The subject of German names vs. Polish names could fill a thick book
by itself. I hope this brief overview will help explain why there can be Poles
named "Jakob Schmidt" and Germans named "Stefan Jaworski." For better
and for worse, Germans and Poles have had to deal with each other for centuries, and their names reflect this simple, but sometimes confusing, truth.

Hungarian

A look at a current map of Europe could lead one to think there was very
little contact between Poles and Hungarians. If this chapter accomplishes
nothing else, I hope it suggests the danger of that kind of regional thinking.
Over the centuries, Poles and Hungarians did have contact; one need only
read about King Stefan Batory to recognize that. At least a few surnames used
in Poland stem from Hungarian. Some date from the period of the partitions,
when southern Poland was part of the Austrian Empire. Rymut cites these
surnames from the Pogórze region as examples: *Batia, Bafija, Bator, Bekiesz,
Butur, Cider, Haza, Kisz, Szyposz,* amd *Ujwary.* He adds that sometimes polo-
nization has proceeded to the point that Polish suffixes are tacked onto those
names, e.g., *Batorzek* and *Batorczyk.*[10]
The index in Volume II does not include a large number of Hungarian
names, but a few obvious ones do appear:

Bafia < Hungarian personal name *Abaffy:* Bafia
Bal < Hungarian personal name *Bal*, although there are many other possible
    derivations for names beginning *Bal-*: Bal
Bałazy < Hungarian personal name *Balász*, the Hungarian equivalent of
    Poish *Błażej* and English *Blaise*: Bałaziński, Bałazy, Bołoz
Bator < Hungarian *bátor,* "courageous, bold": Bator, Batory, Batura, Batyra
Bekiesz < *bekiesz*, "a long fur with strings, of Hungarian cut" < Hung. *bekes,*
    "fur": Bekiesz, Bekisz

Bołdyzer, presumably < Hungarian given name *Baldizsár*, equivalent to *Baltazar*: Bołdyzer

Ferenc < Hungarian given name *Ferenc*, equivalent to Polish *Franciszek* and English *Francis*: Feręc, Ferenc, Fereniec, Ferens, Ferenz, Perenc

Gabor < Hungarian *Gabor*, equivalent to *Gabriel*: Gabor, Gaborski

Hajduk *{p}* < Hung. *hajdúk,* "mercenary foot soldiers recruited from the Carpathian mountain dwellers and robbers, used mainly to defend the borders against the Turks," a term that came into Polish meaning "armed retainer of a nobleman," and in the 16th-century Polish army it signified a Hungarian foot soldier: Ajdukiewicz, Chajduk, Hajduczek, Hajduk, Hajdukiewicz, Hejduk[11]

Kuruc < *kuruc*, "Hungarian soldier of Rákóczi": Kuruc

Listwan < *Istwán*, Hungarian form of *Stefan*: Listwan, Lisztwan

Madziar < *madziar,* "Hungarian" < Hungarian *Magyar*, "Hungarian": Madziar, Madziara, Madziarz

Nagy < Hungarian *nagy*, "big": Nagy

Rakoczy < Hungarian personal name *Rákóczi*, the name of a noble Magyar family, most prominent in Slovakia and northern Hungary: Rakoca, Rakociński, Rakocki, Rakocy, Rakoczy, Rokocz

Sabal- < Hungarian *szabó* or Slovak *sabol*, both meaning "tailor": Sabala, Sabała. Sabo, Szabała, Szabo

Seged- < Hungarian personal name *Szegedi* < top. *Szeged*: Seget, Segieda, Segiet, Segieta, Siegieda

Tekiel < Hungarian personal name *Tekely*: Tekiel, Tekiela, Tekielak, Tekieli, Tekielski

Tokaj < *tokaj,* "kind of wine originally produced near the town of Tokaj, Hungary": Tokaj, Tokajuk

Uram < Hungarian nickname for one who often said *Uram*, "My Lord!": Uram, Uramowski

Wojd- < Hungarian *vaida*, "voivode," although names beginning *Wojd-* can also come from old Polish names with the root *woj-*, "war": Wojda

Jewish Names

I would be less than candid if I didn't admit that the thought of tackling Jewish names intimidates me! This is a people whose culture and traditions go back not centuries but millenia, and involve many places and languages. But Jews were such an important part of life in Poland that it would be an injustice to overlook them in any discussion of Polish surnames. So while I'm no expert on this subject, I will venture to make a few remarks. Fortunately, there are some outstanding English-language works on the surnames of Ashkenazic Jews, especially the books of Alexander Beider. Anyone who would like to study the subject in greater depth than I have room for here can find those works listed in Chapter Twelve and learn much more from them.

My main focus in this book is names of Polish or Slavic origin, and a great many Jewish names are rooted in Hebrew, Yiddish, or other languages from countries in which Jews had lived before they came to Poland. I will briefly discuss the non-Slavic Jewish names—in this chapter, particularly, that is appropriate—but my main focus is on those that came from Slavic roots, most of which were not used all that differently by Jews and Christians.

As we've seen, many Polish surnames derive from given names, and given names of Jewish origin are actually quite prominent in Poland, coming from two sources: Biblical personal names dating from before the time of Christ (often many centuries before), some of which Christians also used, and the more contemporary names borne by Jews who came to live in Poland. To some extent the names overlap; *Abram, Daniel,* and *Rafal* are examples of names a Christian or Jew might bear. But it was important to Jews to maintain their identity and sense of separateness as the Chosen People. So it was not unnatural for them to avoid using names, even names of Hebrew origin, that were closely associated with Christian saints. They either chose names distinct from those used by Christians—e.g., *Berko, Herszko, Jankiel, Moszko*—or, when using names common among Christians, preferred distinctively Jewish forms, closer to the original Hebrew versions that Gentiles had, to some extent, mangled: *Szmul* instead of *Samuel, Miriam* instead of *Maria, Szlomo* instead of *Salomon.* Anyone familiar with Jewish names can tell from even a brief list whether it deals with Christians or Jews.

Still, there is plenty of room for error. For instance, anyone who noticed a family in northeastern Poland with the name *Jogiel* would certainly expect it to come from the name of the great Lithuanian leader Jogaila, called Jagiełło by Poles; and most of the time that connection would prove right. But Alexander Beider's book on the surnames of Jews from the Kingdom of Poland mentions that the Jewish families named *Jogiel* in the Suwałki and Władysławów areas probably traced their surname from the Biblical name *Jogli,* the father of Bocci, a supervisor of land allotment from the tribe of Dan (Numbers 34:22). The name's accidental similarity to Jogaila/Jagiełło could mislead even a vaunted "expert" such as yours truly. In any case, once you're on the right track with the name's derivation, you realize it is unlikely many Christians ever bore this Biblical name; but a Jew who felt (with or without justification in fact) that he descended from the tribe of Dan might consider it a splendid name.

First names are of enormous significance for surnames of Polish Jews because, as I mentioned in Chapter One, the surname process for Jews living in the lands of the Polish-Lithuanian Commonwealth—Poland, Lithuania, Belarus, and western Ukraine—was somewhat different from that of non-Jews. As a rule, the Jews of the Commonwealth did not use surnames until Poland and Lithuania were overcome and partitioned by Prussia, Russia, and Austria. From the late 1700s until the mid-1800s, the partitioning powers concentrated on requiring Jews to take surnames, in order to facilitate administration of taxes, conscription, and the like. Before then, the most common way for Jews to form a second name was to use a patronymic, so that a man named Lejb whose father was Lewko would be called *Lejb Lewkowicz*—the Slavic equivalent of the Hebrew expression *ben,* e.g., *Leib ben Levko*—and Lejb's son Mośko would be *Mośko Lejbowicz,* and so on. To the imperial authorities, such names were not adequate because they changed with each generation. Jews were ordered to take hereditary, unchanging surnames.

It is likely that most Jews viewed these orders as an unwarranted intrusion in their lives. The orders generally came as part of an entire package of rules and regulations dictating how they should live. It's not surprising Jews got around the orders when they could; and when they couldn't, they chose names with no great enthusiasm. To them, these weren't real names, names with religious and familial and traditional significance; so what difference did it make what Gentile bureaucrats called them? The result is that many different families ended up going by the same common surnames. All the Weisses and Kleins and Jungs were not necessarily related, and may not have been all that "white" or "small" or "young."

Of course, there were some Jews who had preferences as to what name they would bear; but the question was often, did they have any choice in the matter? The rules requiring surnames were handed down in three different empires and enforced by many different local authorities. The procedure followed in one area was not necessarily the same as that followed in another. In some places, Jews were allowed to take whatever name they liked, and in those places, the resulting names might be somehow appropriate or fine-sounding. In other places, the names were imposed by officials, many of whom did not like Jews in the first place; so the names could be silly or vulgar. There are tales (perhaps apocryphal, perhaps not) of officials charging Jews for nice-sounding names and tagging the non-cooperative ones with offensive names. These factors contribute to the variety in the names borne by the Jews of central and eastern Europe.

Incidentally, it's worth noting that surnames of Polish Jews originated in the 19th century, as a rule, which is two or more centuries after those of Polish Christians. As a result, Jewish surnames can be easier to trace back, because you don't have to trace them as far. Also, they can often be interpreted in terms of modern Polish, German, Russian, or Ukrainian, whereas many surnames of Christians came from archaic terms that have since died out in the living language.

We also see a mix of languages in Jewish surnames, which really should not surprise anyone. Surnames were drawn not only from ancient Hebrew and Aramaic names, but also from Yiddish words, or terms from the language of the area in which the families lived—in some cases, German (those fun-loving Prussians had an endearing habit of insisting on this), in other cases, Polish, Ukrainian, Belarusian, Russian, etc. If a disproportionate number of Jewish names seem Germanic, that is partly due to the influence of Yiddish, which derives from a medieval dialect of German and thus has many words virtually identical in sound and meaning to German ones.

A great many Jews simply took patronymic surnames. Since such names were already common in their culture, although not as surnames, it was a fairly painless option. Many Jews took names ending in the Slavic suffix *-ovich* (Polish spelling *-owicz*) or the German suffix *-sohn* ("son," compare *Mendelssohn*, "Mendel's son"). At least such a name had a link with family tradition. As I said earlier, Jews generally did not use the same first names as Christians; why on earth would Jewish parents want to name their children after Christian saints? So Jewish patronymics can be readily distinguished from those of Polish Christians. Instead of *Piotrowicz* and *Jankiewicz*, we see *Berkowicz, Lewkowicz, Herszkowicz, Jankielewicz, Moskowicz,* and so on.

Toponyms were also useful and productive sources of Jewish names, but here one must be careful: they would come from places important in Jewish life, and it's easy to jump to the wrong conclusion. For instance, *Poznański* usually means "from Poznań," and in most cases that probably will prove to be the right derivation. Beider, however, points out that for a family from the town of Balta, in Podolia, the name surely came instead from a local village, Poznanka. Similarly, the Ukrainian name *Kirilenko* derives from the personal name *Kiril* (Cyril, a Christian saint); but the Jewish surname *Kirilenko* comes from the name of the village *Kirileny,* which in turn was based on the Christian given name, presumably because of an connection at some point in the past with a locally prominent Kiril.[12]

This brings up a point of great importance to those who care about getting the right answer: Jewish surnames that appear identical to Christian surnames did not always arise from the same sources. Consider *Fischman:* it has to mean "fish-man" or "fisherman," right? Well, not necessarily, at least not when it is a surname borne by Jews. Kaganoff cites a study by Dr. Y. Gumpertz tracing the name *Feivus* (in Yiddish *Fayvel*) back to French *Vives, Vifs, Vis,* which were French equivalents for *Yehiel, Hayyim,* and *Chai,* all from roots meaning "life." This name came into German and was mangled into various forms, including the first syllable of *Fischman.* So if this research is correct, for some Jewish families, the surname *Fischman* has nothing to do with fish but ultimately comes from the Hebrew word for "life"![13] Of course, on the other hand, Rabbi Shmuel Gorr said that Dr. Gumpertz was a fine man but wrong on this point.[14] I remember reading (but forgot to note down where) another Jewish scholar who opined that the good rabbi was a fine man but wrong about Gumpertz being wrong on this point. For what it's worth, Alexander Beider, the scholar whose expertise I find most reliable, refuses to swallow the bait: in all three of his books on Jewish surnames, he analyzes Fischmann/Fiszman/Fishman as coming from the obvious roots "fish" and "man."

I don't bring this up to intimidate you into despairing of tracing the true derivation of Jewish surnames, but simply to suggest you keep in mind that all is not necessarily as it seems. If you really want the right answer, you may have to do a lot of digging!

A great many Jews chose, or had imposed on them, Polish-language surnames not much different from those borne by Polish Christians. Names derived from a feature could apply just as well to Jews as to Christians, and we see a great many such names: *Gołąb* (often spelled *Golomb* in English) from the Polish word for "dove," *Zając* (often spelled *Zaiontz* or *Zaentz* in English) from the Polish word for "hare," *Garbaczewski* (from the same root that gave *Gorbachev* in Russian, a word meaning "hump-back"), and so on. Occupations yielded many surnames, and some occupations were open to Jews as well as Christians. At the same time, we must recognize that certain occupations were far more likely to be filled by Jews than others—the *karczmarz*, "innkeeper," was very often Jewish, as was a *szkolnik* when used in the meaning "sexton" or "synagogue attendant."

Two other kinds of Jewish surnames are fascinating because they are unique to Jewish onomastics: rabbinical surnames and names formed from acronyms.

There are not that many rabbinical surnames, but they recur constantly as leading figures in the community or as scholars. They derive from place names or from Hebrew expressions. Beider lists those from toponyms as: *Auerbach, Bach(a)rach, Bloch, Brojde, Epsztajn, Etynger, Frenkiel, Gincburg, Gordon, Halbersztadt, Halborn, Horowic, Kacenelenbogien, Landau, Lipsczyc, Luria, Minc, Murawczyk, Rapoport, Szpira,* and *Trywasz.* The ones from the Hebrew lexicon are: *Aszkinazi, Chejfec, Jofe, Margolis, Szor, Teumin,* and *Zak.*[15] I believe anyone who has ever paid the slightest attention to surnames will immediately recognize many of these (and variant forms more familiar in this country, such as *Ginsburg, Shapiro,* and *Margolis*) as having been borne by illustrious people known to Jews and non-Jews alike.

Surnames from acronyms and abbreviations were derived from the initials of the first name and patronymic, from descriptive phrases or titles, or from places of origin. They include some fairly common names. For example: *Schatz,* as a German name, means "treasure"; but as a Jewish name, it can come from the Hebrew words צִיבּוּר שְׁלִיחַ [sho*liyaḥ* tzī*bbūr*], "messenger of the community," a term for one who leads prayer in the synagogue. *Segal*—which is not the same as German *Siegel,* "seal"—comes from the Hebrew expression סְגַן לְוִיָּה [sgan l*e*viyyāh], "member of the Levites." As a Jewish name, *Katz,* "cat" in German, is more likely to come from כֹּהֵן־צֶדֶק [kō*hēn* tsĕdĕq], "righteous priest."[16]

One more class of names that must be touched on—although it cannot be a pleasant subject for Jews—consists of surnames borne by Jews who converted to Christianity, voluntarily or otherwise. Such names often make a great display of piety—*Wiernicki* (from *wierny,* "loyal, faithful"), *Krzyżanowski* (from *krzyż,* "cross"), *Chwalibowski* (from *chwała,* "praise," and *Bóg,* "God"), *Bogusławski* (from *Bogu,* "to God," and *sława,* "glory").

By the way, *Bogdański, Bogusławski* and *Chwalibóg* are ancient *szlachta* dithematic names; I suspect there were some nobles who were outraged to see these names being used by Jewish converts. Other converts took names referring to the fact of changing or converting—*Nawrocki* (from *nawrót,* "return, conversion"), *Nowakowski* (from *nowy,* "new"), *Przechrzta* ("conversion"). Some names stress the nature of the conversion, as in *Dobrowolski,* from *dobra wola,* "free will, good will." Interesting are those that mark the month or day of conversion: *Niedzielski,* "of Sunday," *Grudziński,* "of December," and so on.[17] It is essential to realize that none of these names were exclusively used by Jewish converts. But when one sees them, it is a good idea to keep in mind the possibility—not a certainty, but a possibilty—that Jewish converts to Christianity may be involved.

For those of you deeply interested in Jewish names, this brief discussion has probably done little more than whet your appetite; that's why I encourage you to get hold of the sources mentioned in Chapter Twelve and read more on the subject. Inasmuch as this book is primarily devoted to names originating from Polish-language roots, however, I feel this discussion is adequate, so long as I supplement it by listing some names from Volume II which I noted as being typically Jewish. Please notice that most of the names listed here are not Polish in origin, because most Jewish names derived from Polish roots are not exclusively Jewish and do not differ from the same names borne by Christians in any essential respect. I suggest only that you remember that differences in customs and/or geographical origins may affect the way a name like *Rzeźnik* (for Gentiles a butcher, for Jews a ritual slaughterer) or *Poznański* came to be used by Polish Jews as opposed to Polish Christians.

I should also mention that in the first edition of this book I relied primarily on material in Benzion Kaganoff's *A Dictionary of Jewish Names and Their History*; but then I learned that a number of experts found errors in the book and considered it "a disappointment."[18] Alexander Beider's books on Jewish surnames from the Russian Empire, the Kingdom of Poland, and Galicia seem far more reliable to me; so I have attempted to change anything Kaganoff said that Beider did not agree with. Incidentally, I was amazed at how often Beider gives the derivations of Jewish names as differing from those for Polish Christians with the same names; there are just so many more influences that might affect Jewish names. Even though Jewish surnames are of comparatively recent vintage, they may be connected with roots and concepts going back centuries, even millenia.

A brief listing follows of some names in Volume II that are, or can be, of Jewish origin.

Aszkinazi, rabbinical surname < Hebrew אַשְׁכְּנָזִי [*'aškᵉnazī*], "German Jew": Aszkenazy, Aszkienazy
Auerbach, rabbinical surname < toponym *Auerbach,* Hessen, Germany
Bachrach, rabbinical surname < toponym *Bacharach,* Rheinland, Germany

Bałaban < Ukr. or Blrs. *балабан* [*balabán*], "a kind of hawk or falcon," as a Jewish name also "duffer, oaf, lout"

Baruch {*j,n*} < Hebrew בָּרוּךְ [*Bārūkh*], a Biblical name meaning "blessed one": Baruch, Barucha, Baruk

Berk- < the first name *Berko* < *Ber,* Yiddish for "bear": Berk, Berka, Berkowicz, Berkowski

Bernstein < German *Bernstein,* "amber," a common toponym in Germany and Austria, but as a Jewish name, it is likely to be connected with < *Berko,* see preceding entry: Bernstein, Bernsztajn

Birn- < German *Birne,* "pear": Birnbach, Birnbaum

Bloch, rabbinical surname, can come < a Polish term for a Jew who immigrated to Poland in the late Middle Ages, cmp. Polish *włoch,* which meant originally "foreigner" (it now means "Italian"): Bloch, Błoch

Brojde, rabbinical surname < the toponym *Ungarish Brod,* Moravia: Broda

Bronsteyn < German *Braunstein,* "brown stone": Braunstein, Bronsztejn

Chaim < Jewish given name Chaim < Hebrew חַיִּים [*hayyīm*], "life": Chaim

Chejfec, rabbinical surname < Hebrew הֵפֶץ [*hēfets*], "desirable thing": Chejfec, Heifetz

Epsztajn, rabbinical surname < toponym *Eppstein,* Germany: Epstein, Epsztajn, Epsztein, Epsztejn

Etyngier, rabbinical surname < toponym *Öttingen,* Germany: Ettinger, Etyngier

Frenkiel, rabbinical surname < dim. of *Frank,* Franconian: Fraenkel, Fränkl, Frenkiel

Gelbart < German *gelb,* "yellow," + *Bart,* "beard": Gelbart

Gierszon < Biblical names גֵּרְשׁוֹן [*Gērshōn*] or גֵּרְשֹׁם [*Gērshom*]

Gincburg, rabbinical surname < toponym *Günzburg,* Bavaria: Gincburg, Ginsberg, Guenzburg

Gold- < German *Gold,* "gold": often refers to kin of a woman named "Golda": Golda, Goldberg, Golden, Gołdyga, Gołdyn

Golomb < Polish *gołąb,* "dove," translation of Hebrew יוֹנָה [*Yōnāh*]

Gordon, as a Jewish name, a rabbinical surname < toponym *Grodno*

Halbersztadt, rabbinical surname < toponym *Halberstadt,* Germany

Halborn, rabbinical surname < toponym *Heilbronn,* Germany: Halborn, Heilbronn, Heilpern, Heilprin

Hecht < German *Hecht,* "pike," a fish

Hein, sometimes used by Jews because of it sounds like the name *Chaim,* see above: Heina, Heine, Heinen, Hejna

Herszkowicz < Jewish patronymic from *Herszko*

Hirsz < as a Jewish name < Yiddish הירש [*hīrsh*], "deer," compare German *Hirsch* with the same meaning; often used in Jewish names because the deer was the symbol of the tribe of Naphthali: Hirsch, Hirsh, Hirsz

Hoffman < German *Hofmann,* "courtier," or "peasant attached to a particular manor," or < *Hoffmann,* "estate steward"; may have been adopted by some Jews because German *hoff-* means "hope" and they interpreted *Hoffman* as "man of hope": Hoffman, Hoffmann, Hofman, Hofmann, Hofmański, Offman, Ofman, Ofmański

Horowicz, rabbinical surname < the Bohemian town of *Horoviče*: Horowic, Horowicz, Horowitz

Huber < German *Huber,* owner of 60 *morgas* of land, also Yiddish for "oats": Huber

Ic- < first name *Icek, Izak,* Isaac< Biblical name יִצְחָק [*Yitzḥāq*], "laughed, rejoiced": Icek, Iciek, Ickowicz, Icyk, Iczkowski, Isak, Issakiewicz, Izak

Jankielewicz < patronymic from the Jewish first name *Jankiel*

Jofe, rabbinical surname < Hebrew יָפֶה [*yofeh*], "beautiful": Jaffe, Joffe

Kabala < *kabala,* "the Cabala, fortune-telling, predicament": Kabala, Kabela

Kac < Hebrew כֹּהֵן [*kōhēn*], "priest" + צֶדֶק [*tsĕdĕq*], "righteousness," so it means "priest of righteousness" = "righteous priest": Kac, Katz

Kacenelenbogien, rabbinical surname < toponym *Katzenelnbogen* (Hessen-Nassau province, Germany): Katzenellenbogen

Kafka < as a Jewish name can come from *Yaakov* (Jacob): see also the entry **Kawa** in Volume II: Kafka, Kawka

Kagan, in Jewish names < Hebrew כֹּהֵן [*kōhēn*], "priest": Kagan, Kaganiec

Kaufman < as a German name < *Kaufmann,* "merchant," but as a Jewish name can be < *Yaakov* (Jacob) → Yakofman → Kofman → Kaufman

Kierstan, as a Christian name < a form of the given name *Christian,* but as a Jewish name *Kirschstein* or *Kirschenstein,* "cherry stone", or < *Kersten* because of its similarity to the Jewish given name *Gerson*: Kierstan, Kierstein, Kiersztyn, Kirstein, Kirsztztajn, Kirsztein

Klein < German *klein,* "small, young": Klajn, Klein, Kleinfelt, Klejna

Kochan, as a Jewish name < Hebrew כֹּהֵן [*kōhēn*], "priest": Kochan

Koenig < German *König,* "king," usually referred to a king's servant or retainer, or one who was somehow like a king, or one who farmed land belonging to royal estates; as a Jewish name, often a translation of Hebrew מֶלֶךְ [*melekh*], "king": Kenig, Kienig, Kienik, Koenig, König

Kolman, as a Jewish name *Kalman* < Greek *Klonimus,* "beautiful name": Kalman, Kalamon, Kollmann, Kolman

Kopel, as a Jewish name < the given name *Jakub*: Kopel, Koppel

Korach, as a Jewish name < Hebrew כּוֹרַח [*kōraḥ*], "bookbinder": Korach

Kreczmer < Yiddish for *karczmarz,* "innkeeper": Kratchmer, Kreczmar, Kretschmer

Kusz-, Jewish names with *Kus[z]-* may be derived from the Hebrew name יְקוּתִיאֵל [*Yekuthiel* or *Yekusiel*] which produced the Yiddish short form *Kushl*: Kisiel, Kusch, Kuszel

Landau, rabbinical surname < toponym *Landau,* Germany

Lejb < Jewish given name *Lejb,* Yiddish *Leib,* used as a kinnui (vernacular equivalent) of *Judah*: Lejb, Lejba, Lejbowicz

Leman, as a Jewish surname can come < *Lehmann,* "vassal," or < a given name, *Leman*, used by German Jews < *leo*, "lion" + *mann*, "man": Lehman, Lehmann, Leman, Lemanowicz, Lemański

Lew < *lew*, "lion," as Slavic equivalent of the given name *Leon*, or from Hebrew *Levi*: Lefkowitz, Lew, Lewek, Lewko, Lewkowicz

Lipman < Jewish given name *Libman* < German *Liebmann*, "dear man, beloved man," also seen is the variant *Litman*: Libman, Lipman, Litman

Lipszyc, rabbinical surname < the toponyms *Liebeschitz* (Libšice, Bohemia) or *Leobschütz*, Silesia, now *Głubczyce*, Poland: Lipschütz, Lipszyc

Luria, rabbinical surname, ? < toponym *Loria*, Italy: Lurie, Lurje

Majer < German *Meier, Meyer*, "steward of an estate, dairy-farmer," but as a Jewish name usually < Hebrew מֵאִיר [*mē'īr*] from a root meaning "light, illumination": Maier, Majer, Majerczak, Majerczyk, Majerowicz, Majerowski, Mayer, Meier, Mejer, Meyer, Meyers

Mamet, as a Jewish name < a distortion of *Melamed* < Hebrew מְלַמֵּד [*melammed*], "teacher in a Jewish school": Mamet

Manes, as a Jewish name < given name *Manes* or *Mannes* < Biblical name מְנַשֶּׁה [*Menasseh*]: Manes

Manis- < Yiddish *man*, "man": Maniszewicz, Maniszewski

Mankowski, as a Jewish name, often from the place name *Mankówce*

Margol- < Hebrew מַרְגָּלִיוֹת [*margolīōth*], "pearl": Margol, Margolin, Margula

Mendel < *Mendel*, popular first name, as a Jewish name < *Man* → **Manis-**: Mendel, Mendelewski, Mendelski

Minc < the rabbinical family Mintz/Minc < the town of *Mainz*, Hessen, Germany: Minc, Mincewicz, Mintz, Mync

Model, as a Jewish name < Hebrew name מָרְדְּכַי [*Mordechai*]: Model

Mojżesz < the Hebrew name מֹשֶׁה [*Mosheh*], in English *Moses*, in Polish *Mojżesz*, names are also derived from *Moises* (Latin) and *Mojsiej* (eastern Poland, Russia, etc.): Mojsa, Mojsiej, Mojsiejenko, Mojsiejuk, Mojsiewicz, Mojżeszewicz, Mojżuk, Mojżych, Moszej, Możejko

Morel, as a Jewish name < *morela*, "apricot": Morel

Moryc, used by Jews because its sound reminded them of *Mordechai*: Moric, Moritz, Moryc

Mos- for Jewish names most often < the name the Hebrew name מֹשֶׁה [*Mosheh*], Moses; *Mosko* is a common Polish name for *Moses*, so *Moskowicz* or *Moskiewicz* are Jewish names meaning "son of Mosko (Moses)": Mosak, Mosiek, Mosiewicz, Moska, Moskiewicz, Mośko, Moskowicz, Moszyński

Nachman < Jewish first name < Hebrew נַחְמָן [*naḥmon*], "consoler"

Orl- < Polish *orzeł*, "eagle": Orlik (can come from *Aaron*), Orlikowski, Orliński (or < the town of *Orla*), Orlof, Orloff, Orłowski, Urlik

Pałgan < Hebrew פַּלְגָּן [*palgon*], "schismatist, heretic": Pałgan

Perl- in Jewish names often indicates a link with a woman named *Perel, Perl*, "Pearl": Perlak, Perlik, Perliński, Perlmann, Perlmutter (< German

Perlmutter, "mother of pearl"), Perłowski

Pinkos < Hebrew name פִּינְחָס [*Pīneḥās*] (1 Samuel 1:3): Pinkos, Pinkus

Rabin < *rabin,* "rabbi": Rabin, Rabinek, Rabiński

Rapoport, rabbinical surname, exact origin uncertain: Rapaport, Rappaport

Redel, as a Jewish name < Yiddish *redel* or *redler,* "little wheel" (for perforating unleavened bread, or one who uses it): Redel, Redler

Rubin < Jewish first name רְאוּבֵן [*Rᵉ 'ūvēn*]: Rubin, Rubinek, Rubinkiewicz

Ryfka < Jewish feminine name *Rivke* < Hebrew רִבְקָה [*Rivqāh*], the Biblical figure called Rebecca in English: Ryfka, Ryfkin, Rywkin

Rzezak, as a Jewish name, *rzezak* means "kosher butcher, circumciser": Rzezak, Rzeźnik

Sabat < Hebrew שַׁבָּת [*shavvath*], "Sabbath": Sabat, Szabat

Sachar, as a Jewish name ? < Biblical name יִשָּׂשכָר [*Issākhār*]: Sachar

Salam- or **Salom-** < the Hebrew name שְׁלֹמֹה [*Šᵉlōmōh*], in English *Solomon*: Sala, Salach, Salamowicz, Salomon, Solomon

Samuel < the Biblical name שְׁמוּאֵל [*Šᵉmū'ēl*], *Samuel;* Samoiła, Samul, Samulski, Smul, Smulewicz, Smulski, Szmul

Segal < Hebrew סְגַן לְוִיָּה [*sgan lᵉviyyāh*], "member of the Levites": Segal

Surman, as a Jewish name, "son of Sora": Surman

Szac, typically < Hebrew שָׁלִיחַ צִיבּוּר [*sholiyaḥ tzībbūr*], "synagogue prayer leader": Szac

Szach, in Jewish names an abbreviation of שִׂפְתֵי כֹהֵן [*šiftey kōhēn*], "lips of the priest," the pen name of a prominent Vilnius rabbi

Szkolnik, as a Jewish name, "sexton at a synagogue, or director of the Jewish community": Szkolnik

Szlama, as a Jewish name < the Hebrew name שְׁלֹמֹה [*Šᵉlōmōh*], in English *Solomon*: Szlama

Szor, rabbinical surname < Hebrew שׁוֹר [*šōr*], "ox, bull": Schorr, Szor

Szpiro, rabbinical surname < toponym *Speyer,* Bavaria: Spira, Szapiro

Szulman < Yiddish שׁול [*shul*], "synagogue, shul" + *man*, "man": Szulman

Szyjer, as a Jewish surname < *Szyja*, short form of Hebrew יְהוֹשֻׁעַ [*Yᵉhoshua' *], commonly rendered as *Joshua* in English: Szyjer

Taratuta, as a Jewish surname < a nickname meaning "chatterer": Taratuta

Teumin, rabbinical surname < Hebrew תְּאוֹמִים [*t'ōmīm*], "twins": Teomim

Trywasz, rabbinical surname < toponyms *Trier,* Germany or *Troyes,* France: Treves, Trywasz

Wajner, as a Jewish name < Yiddish ווײַנער [*vayner*], "wine merchant, one with a wine shop": Wajner, Weiner, Wejner

Wallach < German *Welsch,* "foreign," there is also possible confusion with **Wałach** and **Wołoch-**, q. v.

Zak < *Zak,* rabbinical name < זֶרַע קֹדֶשׁ [*Zera' Qōdeš*], "holy seed": Saks, Zak

Zarach < variant of the Biblical name זֶרַח [*Zoraḥ*] , a son of Judah by Tamar: Zarach, Zarachowicz

Zemler, as a Jewish name < Yiddish זעמל [*zeml*], "roll, small white loaf," or < the Biblical name usually rendered as *Solomon* in English: Zemler

Zlatkin < Czech *zlato*, "gold," which in Jewish names = *Golda, Golde*

Żyd {j,p} < *żyd*, "Jew": Żydak, Żydek, Żydowicz, Żydowski, Żydziak, Żydzik

Zylbersztejn < German *Silberstein*, literally "silver stone," a name typically applied to a jeweler, most often Jewish

Lithuanian Names

Lithuanian-derived Polish surnames present a bit of a problem, because this particular linguistic stream tended to flow one way: that is, Polish influenced Lithuanian names far more than Lithuanian influenced Polish names. Surviving records such as the *Metryka Litewska* document this trend. Before the 1400s, there was little onomastic contact between Lithuania and Poland; Poles and Lithuanians were too busy fighting each other to compare notes on names. After Jogaila/Jagiełło married Jadwiga to begin forming the Jagiellonian dynasty and a union between Poland and Lithuania, Polish gradually came to be regarded as the dominant cultural language in Lithuania, replacing Old White Ruthenian (the ancestor of modern Belarusian) as the official language in legal documents. There were relatively few Lithuanian nobles who even spoke Lithuanian every day, and even they tended to opt for more prestigious Polish-sounding names, changing their native names into ones with Polish suffixes or translating them into Polish equivalents.

As an example, Bystroń cites princes of the Gedraitis clan who took bynames and shows how those names developed into Polish-sounding surnames: *Bortko (Bortkowicz), Dowmont, Gogul, Jagajło, Juraha (Jurażyc), Juszko (Juszkowicz), Kozłowicz, Mack (Mackowicz), Micko (Mickowicz), Paszko (Paszkowicz), Pukieść (Pukelewicz), Stanko (Stankowicz), Szerejko (Szerejkowicz), Wojn, Zdan (Zdanowicz)*. Please note, these names are spelled as Bystroń gave them, by Polish, not Lithuanian, phonetic values. Other Lithuanian nobles added Polish suffixes to their names (often after dropping the distinctive Lithuanian suffixes), and changed the spelling and pronunciation slightly to reflect Polish phonetic values: *Gedrajtis → Gedrojć, Daugirdis → Dowgird, Daukantas → Dowkont; Poszka → Paszkowski* or *Paszkiewicz, Valanczius → Wołonczewski, Juszka → Juszkiewicz, Ruszkys → Ruszkiewicz, Baronas → Baranowski, Matulajtys → Matulewicz*.[19]

Eventually, Lithuanian peasants began taking surnames. While it was the peasants who kept the Lithuanian language alive, even some of them took names that sounded Polish, modified their native names to sound more Polish, or even translated them outright—and they often added the *-ski* suffix while they were are it, so that Lithuanian peasants sounded like Polish nobles. Some examples of the latter process are: *Strazdelis (< Lith. strazdas, "thrush") → Drozdowski, Vabalas ("beetle") → Żukowski, Žvirblis ("sparrow") → Wróblewski, Ožys ("billy-goat") → Kozłowski*.[20]

Lithuanian surnames that maintained their native form need not be considered too frightful, even though sources on the Lithuanian language are not always easy to come by in this country. Suffixes often give a clue. If a name ends in *-aitis, -unas, -onis, -enas,* or *-ynas,* it is probably a patronymic; thus, *Jonaitis* means "son of Jonas," the Lithuanian version of *John,* and *Matulionis* is "son of Matulis," from *Matas,* a nickname or short form of the given names we know as *Matthew* and *Matthias.* The odds alone suggest that many names you encounter will be patronymics: by the 18th century, 60% of registered Lithuanian surnames for men, and 90% of those for women, were patronymic in origin. The endings *-elis* and *-utis* are diminutives. On the other hand, if the name ends in *-auskas, -inskas,* or *-ickas,* you are probably dealing with Lithuanian adaptations of Polish names ending in *-owski, -iński,* or *-icki,* or their Belarusian equivalents. The only difficulty may lie in making allowances for the difference in phonetic values. For instance, *Kazlauskas* is an extremely common name in Lithuania today, and it comes from the Polish name *Kozłowski* (which we just saw in the last paragraph).[21]

As an example of the interesting mix of names one finds among Polish and/or Lithuanian immigrants to the United States, here is a selection of patronymic surnames appearing in a list compiled by David Zincavage from residents of Carbon and Schuylkill Counties in Pennsylvania, an area with a high concentration of Lithuanians. This is raw data which David is analyzing to produce insights on Lithuanian surnames, but it is also grist for our mill, and I have added my interpretation of the names' origin.[22]

> [*p = patronymic; m = metronymic; L = Lithuanian; P = Polish; † = Anglicized spelling of a Polish name*]

Abram-: Abramaitis [*Lp*], Abramavage [*† Abramowicz Pp*], Abramowicz [*Pp*], Abrasonis [*?Lp*], Abromitis [*Lp*]

Adam-: Adamaitis [*Lp*], Adamavage [*† Adamowicz, Pp*], Adamchik [*† Adamczyk, Pp*], Adomaitis [*Lp*]

Andr- *(< Polish Andrzej, etc.)*: Andershonis [*? Lp*], Andescavage [*† Andeśkiewicz, Pp*], Andrauskas [*Lp = Polish Androwski*], Andrejewski [*† Andrzejewski, Pp*], Andrescavage [*† Andreśkiewicz Pp*], Andrewcavage [*† Andrzejkiewicz Pp*], Androkitis [*Lp*], Androsavitch [*† Androsiewicz Pp*], Androshick [*† Androsik Pp*], Andrukanis [*Lp*], Andrukitis [*Lp*], Andruscavage [*† Andruskiewicz Pp*], Andruskiewicz [*Pp*], Andrusyshyn [*Um*], Andulevich [*† Andulewicz Pp*], Andulonis [*Lp*]

Anel-, Anil- *(probably < Polish anioł, "angel")*: Anelauskas [*L = Polish Aniołowski*], Anilosky [*† Aniołowski*]

I wish we had room to list many more of these names, because they provide fascinating insights into the way different languages and phonetic values are interwoven in American surnames; but these few samples give you an idea of what's involved. Notice that in this area settled primarily by Lithuanians we find Polish names with spelling essentially unchanged [*Abramowicz, Andruskiewicz*], Lithuanian names essentially unchanged [*Abramaitis, Andrukanis, Andulonis*], Anglicized spelling of Polish surnames [*Abramavage, Andruscavage*], Lithuanian-influenced spelling of Polish surnames [*Andrauskas, Anelauskas*], even a Ukrainian metronymic [*Andrusyshyn*]. To me this data suggests that Lithuanian names, and Polish names modified due to Lithuanian influence, are less hard to recognize than some Anglicized Polish surnames! It takes a close look to recognize that *Abramavage* and *Andruscavage* are not some bizarre, hitherto unencountered kind of name—they're just Polish patronymics with our old friend *-wicz* in disguise!

David suggested a few other points I could mention that might save researchers a bit of trouble. One is to remember that *a* and *o* are similar sounds in Lithuanian and are often switched (the same is true in Polish, for that matter). Lithuanians use the letter *v* where Poles use *w;* and *č, š,* and *ž* match up consistently with Polish *cz, sz,* and *ż.* Also, as in Polish, *i, j,* and *y* have been used interchangeably in the past, so that you should always be ready to recognize *-aitis* and *-ajtys,* for instance, as different Polish spellings of the same Lithuanian suffix. Since we often see Lithuanian surnames affected first by Polish phonetics and then, in this country, by English phonetics, you need to absorb these points so that you'll recognize *Kalwajtys* and *Kalwejt* as variations of *Kalvaitis,* a name meaning "son of the smith."

Another point deals with endings added to female names. Much as Poles add *-owa, -ówna,* etc. (as we saw in Chapter Two), Lithuanians customarily add to the surnames of married women the suffix *-ienė,* so that a Lithuanian instantly recognizes *Petraitienė* as the name of the wife of Mr. Petraitis. For unmarried females, the rules are a bit more complex. If the surname ends in *-us,* the suffix is *-utė,* e.g., *Martinkutė* is "Miss Martinkus"; if the name ends in *-is* or *-ys,* the suffix is *-ytė* (*Jonaitytė* is "Miss Jonaitis"); if the name ends in *-a* or *-as,* the suffix is *-aitė* (as in *Kazlauskaitė,* "Miss Kazlauskas").[23] Also seen in older documents are the suffixes *-učia* (added to *-us* names), *-yčia* (added to *-is* and *-ys* names), and *-aičia* (added to *-a* and *-as* names).[24] Familiarity with this feature of the language can save you a lot of confusion.

Also worth remembering is that the native Lithuanian patronymic suffixes *-aitis, -unas, -onis, -enas,* and *-ynas* are functionally equivalent to the Polish suffixes *-owicz, -czyk,* etc. A hybrid is *-evičius,* a Lithuanian version of Polish *-owicz/-ewicz*—which, in turn, came originally from Old White Ruthenian, the ancestor of modern Belarusian and the language of record for the Grand Duchy of Lithuania, so in some cases the Lithuanians may have adopted it directly rather than from the Poles. Since all these suffixes mean the same thing, and since at one time Lithuanians tended to polonize their names, and then later tended to go back to native forms, one cannot assume a *Janaitis,* for instance, was always *Janaitis*—at one point he might have gone by *Janowicz* or *Janiewicz.*

Diminutives are popular in Lithuanian, and one often sees them added to surnames; a "goodman" is not just a *Geras,* he is a *Gerulas,* or even a *Gerulaitis.* As that last name shows, Lithuanians enjoy compounding suffixes, so that a son of a man named "Thomas" may have ended up with any of the following names: *Tomkus, Tomka, Tomkievičius, Tomaitis, Tomalaitis, Tomasas, Tomasaitas, Tomkunas, Tomeliunas, Tomašiunas,* and so on.

The Lithuanians shared with all other Indo-Europeans a pagan past during which they often gave their children **dithematic** names, that is, names formed by combining two native roots to express a wish or hope for the child's future. Some of these roots appear again and again in surnames. Here is a list I compiled from *Lieutvių vardų kilmės žodynas* [Etymological Dictionary of Lithuanian Names] of roots seen in Lithuanian dithematic names, each followed by a few examples, when I could find them:

al-: root as in Lith. *aliai vienas* = "each, every"—cmp. Greek *allos,* "other," Gothic *alja,* "other": Algirdas, Alvydas
alg-: "reward, recompense": Algimantas
alk-: "sacred grove, sacrificial site": Alkmena
ar-, ari-: "too, also, similarly": Arbutas, Arminas Arvydas (but note that in names such as *Arūnas,* the root is *aras,* "eagle")
aš-: prefix from *až, už,* "beyond, at": Ašmantas, Ašvilas
au-: Prussian *au,* "from, without, away, off"; cmp. Lith. *au-monėm,* "without consciousness": Aurimas
aug-: "grow, advance": Augmantas, Augvilas, Augvydas
bar-, bart-: "to contend with, fight": Bargailas
ber-: root in *bernas,* "lad, fellow": Birmantas
bil-: "talkative": Bilmantas
bu- → but-
bud-: "wake, waken, stand watch": Budvilas
bug-: "frighten, scare": Bugailas, Bugvilas
bui-: "existence, way of life": Buivydas
bur-, burt-: "to conjure, charm": in Burgailas
but-: *būti,* "to be" or *butas,* "lodging": Arbutas, Butrimas
by-: "fear, dread": Bygailas, Bytautas
dar-: "to make, do": Darvydas
darg-: "dear, expensive, costly": Dargvainas
dau-, daug-: "much, very, many": Daugantas, Daugirdas, Daukantas, Daumantas, Mindaugas
dei-: "god": Deimantas
ding-: "think, know, have a presentiment of": Dingailas
dir-: root seen in *dirbti,* "work": *dirva,* "soil": Dirmantas
do-: "give": Dovainė, Dovaldas, Dovilė
draud-: "forbid, prohibit": Draudvilas
dro-: "shy, diffident": Dromantas

džiug-: "glad, happy": Džiugintas
ei-, eis-: "go, walk": Eigilas, Eigirdas, Eisvaldas, Eivyda
eid-: "swift-footed, nimble": Eidvilė
erd-: "land": Erdvilas
gai-: "life, vivifying": Gaivilas
gail-: "strong, mighty": Bargailas, Jogaila, Rimgailas, Skirgaila
gal-: "ability, power": Galigantas
gant- → *gin-, gint-*
gard-: "convey news, be famous": Daugardas
gaud-: "catch, get": Milgaudas, Rimgaudas, Vygaudas
ged-: "long for, grieve for": Gedvydas, Gediminas
geid-: "crave, wish for": Geidbutas
geis-: "long for, crave": Geistautas
gel-: "ache, hurt": Daugėlas, Gelminas
gend-: "miss, feel the absence of": Gendvilas
ger-: "good": Gervydas
ges-: "miss, feel the absence of": Geskantas
gil-: "pain, heartache": Eigilas, Jogilė, Norgilas
gin-, gint-: "protect, preserve, stand up for": Daugantas, Gintaras, Gintautas
gir-: cmp. *girti,* "praise": *giria,* "woods": Girmantas
gird-: root as in *girdėti,* "to hear": *girdas,* "hearsay": Algirdas, Daugirdas
girs-: "hear": Girstautas
gland-: "comfort": Koglandas
go-: "go, walk": Gomantas
god- → *got-*
gos-: root in *gostis,* "regain consciousness": Gostartas
got-: "forbid": Gotartas
graud-: "violent, wrathful"
graž-: "beauty": Gražvilė
gund-: "kindle fire, incite": Nirgundas
gyd-: "crave, attain": Eigydas
imt-: "take": Gedimtas
ir-: "also, too": Irdangas
jau-: "young, already": Jaugedas
jaut-: "ask about, inquire": Pajauta
jo-, jos-, jot-: "ride (on horseback)": Jogaila (Polish version Jagiełło), Jogilė, Jogirdas, Josvydas
kal-: "sound, resound, read": Kalmantas
kan-, kant-: "patient," as in *kantrus,* "patient": Daukantas, Geskantas, Kant-vydas
kar-: "war, army": Kargaudas
kas-: "who, whom": Kastautas
ker-: "conjure": Kergailas
kęs-: "suffer, endure": Kęstautas (Polish version: Kiejstut)

kil-: "rise, be descended from": Kilmintas

kint-: "bear, suffer, endure": Vykintas

kir-: "move, stir": Kirbutas

klaus-: "hear, listen, obey": Klausgailas

ko-: "who": Kovydas

lab-: "good": Labgaudas

laisv-: "free": Laisvydas

lei-: "let": as in "Let this be, let it be done": Leikantas

liau-: "finish, end, stop": Liaubaras

liaud-: "people, folk, throng": Liaudbaras

lin-, ling-, link-: "have an inclination for, gift for": Lingailas

liu- → liau-

ly-, lyg-: "flat, even, level": Lygmantas, Lybartas

main-: "change, make different": Normainas

man-: "think, thought": Almanas, Mangirdas

mant-: as in *mantùs,* "clever, intelligent," or *mantà,* "rich": Algimantas, Daumantas, Skirmantas

maž-: "small, little": Mažrimas

med-: "forest, woods, the hunt": Medginas

men-: "remember, recall": Alkmena

mil-: as in *pamilti,* "come to love, grow fond of": Almilas, Daumilė, Milgaudas

min-, mint-: root as in *minèti,* "mention," *miñti,* "remember": Arminas, Butmina, Gediminas (Polish version: Gedymin), Mindaugas

nam-: "inhabited place, farmstead": Namgailas

nar- → nor-

nart-: "persistent, stubborn": Einartas

nau-: "new": Naubartas

naud-: "wealth": Jonaudas

ner-, nir-: "anger, rage": Nerdingas

no-: "on, upon, from": Nodravas

nor-: "wish, want": Daunoras, Narimantas, Norgilas, Norvydas (Polish version: Norwid)

pa- → po-

per-: "through, over, too": Pervainas

po-: hard to translate, much like *po-* in the Slavic languages; it can be a preposition meaning "in, under, after": or it can be a prefix giving a verb a perfective meaning (i.e., "done once and over with") as opposed to imperfective ("done repeatedly, not finished"): Pajauta

prei-, prie-: "at, by, with": Preibutas (apparently meaning "at home, at a settlement")

put-: "swell, blow up": Putaviras

rad-: "find": Radmantas

ram-: "calm, quiet, tranquil": Ramantas

rim-, rin-: "quiet, serious": Butrimas, Rimgailas, Rimgaudas, Rimtautas

sam-, san-: "with": Sambartas

sar-: "wander, ravage": Sargautas

sau-: "one's own": Saudargas

sin-: "think": Singailas

sir-: "surround, cover, embrace, attack": Sirgaudas

skaud-: "grave, stern, severe": Joskaudas

skir-: "allot, determine, decide": Skirgaila, Skirmantas

sko-, skot-: "take care of, strive": Skomantas

sprung-: "run, take off": Dausprungas

steig-, steng-: "strive": Steigintas

su-: "with": Subartas

svai-: cmp. roots in Prussian *swais,* "one's own," and Lith. *svainis,* "brother-in-law": Svaidargas

svir-: "serious, heavy, important": Svirgailas

švitr-: "quick, nimble, brisk": Švitrigaila

tan-: "prone to swell, stiff, self-important": Tanbutas

tar-: "voice, utter, pronounce": Gintaras, Gotartas

taut-: "people, folk": Gintautas, Kęstautas (Polish version: Kiejstut), Tautvilas, Tautvydas, Vytautas (Polish version Witold)

tol-: "from far off": Toldravas

tul-: "a lot, frequent": Tulgaudas

tur-: "have, hold, keep": Daugturas

tvir-: "strong, firm": Tvirbutas

vai-: "drive, march": Vaidaugas

vaid-: "apparition": Dovaidas

vain-: "fault, excuse, reason, guilt": Dargvainas, Dovainė

vaiš-: "village, farmstead": Gaudvaišas

vait-: "discuss": Vaitkantas

val-, vali-: "be able": Valimantas

vald-: "govern, own": Dovaldas, Eisvaldas, Visvaldas

vard-: "throw, cast lots, conjure, word, name": Daugvardas

vart-: "turn over": Govartas

vid- → *vyd-, vyst-*

vien-: "one": "unite": Vientautas

vieš-: "village, farmstead": Vieštautas

vil-: "hope": Budvilas, Butvilas, Dovilė, Erdvilas, Gražvilė, Tautvilas

vin-: "guilt, fault" (cmp. *vain-*) Vingailė

vir- → *vyr-*

vird-: the root seen in Prussian as *wirds* and in Latvian as *vārds,* "word": Butvirdas

vis-: "all, entire": Visvaldas

vy-: "drive, chase away, lead": Vygaudas, Vykintas, Vytautas (Polish version: Witold)

vyd-, vyst-: cmp. Pruss. *widdai,* "sees," Lith. *išvýdo, išvysti,* "see," *pavida-las,* "form, semblance" (thus having to do with appearance, the way something is seen): Alvydas, Arvidas, Josvydas, Norvydas (Norwid), Vidmantas, Vytautas (Polish version Witold)

vyr-: as in *vyrauti,* "rule, dominate" or *vyras,* "man": Putaviras

vyst- → *vyd-*

vyt- → *vyd-, vyst-*

žad-: "intend, speak, promise": Geržadas

žut-: "kill, torment: " Žutartas

žy-, žyg-: "march, advance": Žybantas

Many of these roots produced very few names. But a limited number of them produced a great variety of dithematic names, some of which you can see in Volume II, either in their original Lithuanian spellings or in polonized forms.

Note that those are mostly ancient names used by pagans. As in Poland, Lithuanians eventually accepted Christianity, only to find that the priests urged them to take the names of Christian saints. But it is interesting to see that the Lithuanians were slow to abandon the old dithematic pagan names; we frequently see them in records used along with Christian names, often hyphenated, e.g., *Joseph-Tautvila, Vladislav-Jogaila.*[25]

Here is a selection of names from Volume II that appear likely to be of Lithuanian origin.

Aszkiełowicz < Lith. pers. name *Aškelovičius,* cmp. Belarusian pers. n. *Ашкяловіч* [*Ashkialovich*], perhaps < Lith. *Ožkelis*

Atraszkiewicz < Lith. pers. n. *Atraška* < Belarusian pers. name *Атрошка* [*Atroshka*] < given name *Trofim*

Awiżeń, perhaps < Lith. surname *Avižienis* < *aviža,* "oat"

Balczun ? < polonized form of the Lith. pers. name *Balčiunas* < Lith. *baltas,* "white": Balczun, Balczunas

Balnis ? < Lith. adj. *balnas,* "white," or *balnius,* "saddle-maker"

Bitowt < polonized form of the Lithuanian dithematic name *Bytautas*

Bojar < Lith. *bajoras,* "Ukrainian or Lithuanian noble": Bojar, Bojarczuk, Bojarowski, Bojarski

Boltr- ? < Lith. *Baltramiejus,* hypocoristic form *Baltras* < the given name we know as *Bartholomew*: Bałtrukiewicz, Boltromiuk, Bołtruczuk, Boltru-kanis, Bołtryk

Borejsza, polonized form of the Lith. pers. name *Bareiša* < the Lith. root *bar-,* "contend with, fight": Borejsza, Borejszo

Budr- ? < Lith. *budrus,* "alert, vigilant" — in Polish, a term for "a Lithu-anian": Budrewicz, Budrys

Bujwid < polonized form of the Lith. dithematic name *Bùivydas* < *būti,* "to be" + *vyd-* as in *išvysti,* "to see": Bujwid, Bujwidz

Butkus, normally of Lith. origin < short form of dithematic names with the root *but-*, "being, existence"

Butry- < Lith. dithematic name *Bùtrymas* < *būti,* "to be" + *rim-,* "quiet, serious": Butrym, Butrymowicz, Butryn, Butryński

Ciunajtis < Lith. *ciunaitis,* "son of the *tijūnas,*" the administrator of a *gmina* or estate: Ciunajcis, Ciunajtis

Czepulonis < Lith. *Čepulionis,* "son of Čepulis," which may have developed < *Czepan,* cmp. the Polish given name *Szczepan*

Dauksza < Lith. name *Daukša,* from the root *daug-,* "much": Dauksz, Dauksza, Daukszewicz

Dereng- < *Deręgowski,* Lith. noble family: Derengowski, Deringowski

Dojlid- < polonized form of Lith. *dailidė,* "carpenter": Dajlidis, Dojlida, Dojlidko, Dojlido

Dowejko < polonized form of Lith. pers. name *Doveika,* possibly < Lith. *dovis,* "portion, part"

Dowgiałło < polonized form of Lith. dithematic name *Daugėla* < *daug-,* "very, much" + *gėl-,* "great pain": Dawgiałło, Dowgiałło, Dowgielewicz

Dowgird < polonized form of Lith. dithematic name *Daugirdas,* from *daug-,* "much, a lot," and *gird-,* a verb root meaning "to hear," meaning perhaps "all-hearing" or "famous, much heard of" [26]

Dowiat < polonized form of Lith. dithematic name *Daujotas* < *dau-,* "much, a lot" + *jóti,* "to ride a horse" [R]: Dowiat, Dowjat

Dowkontt < polonized form of Lith. dithematic name *Daukantas* < *daug-,* "much, a lot" + *kant-,* "patient"

Dowmont < polonized form of Lith. dithematic name *Daumantas* < *dau-,* "much, very" + *mant,* "intelligent, sensible"

Downar < polonized form of Lith. dithematic name *Daunoras* < roots *daug,* "much" + *norėti,* "to want," perhaps meaning one who was much wanted or who wanted a lot: Downar, Downarowicz

Ejsmont < Lith. dithematic name *Eismantas* < *eis-,* "go, walk" + *mant-,* "clever, intelligent," or < Germanic dithematic name *Eismund* < *Eis(en),* "iron" + *munt,* "protection, defense": Ejsmont, Ejsymont, Eysymontt

Giedraitis, also polonized forms *Gedrojć* or *Giedrojć* < Lith. root *giedras,* "clear, serene": Gedrojć, Gedroyć, Giedrojć; *from the same basic root:* Gedris, Giedrys, Giedryś

Gerul- < Lithuanian *gerulis,* "good-natured person, good soul": Gerula, Gerulis, Gierula, Gierulski

Giełaż- < polonized version of Lith. names < *geležius,* "smith, iron-worker" < *geležis,* "iron": Giełażyn, Giełażys

Gintowt < polonized form of Lith. dithematic name *Gintautus* < roots *gìnti,* "to defend" + *tauta,* "the people"

Giruć < polonized version of the Lith. pers. name *Girutis* [LPZ]

Gryguć < Lith. pers. name *Grigutis* < short form of *Grigalis* = *Gregorius*

Jogaila < Lith. pers. name *Jogaila,* polonized as *Jagiełło,* name of royal family of Poland and Lithuania, although some forms may come from Polish *jagły*, "millet groats": Jagieło, Jagielski, Jokiel

Jozaitis < polonized form of Lith. *Juozaitis*, "son of Juozas," from a short form of the Lith. version of *Joseph*: Jozajtis, Jusajtus

Jundziłł < polonized form of Lith. name *Jundzila* < *juñdilas*, "restless person, scapegrace, mischievous child"

Juraha < Lith. byname, probably related to *Jurgis*, "George"

Kalwajtys < polonized spelling of Lith. *kalvaitis*, patronymic from Lith. *kalvis*, "smith": Kalwajtys, Kalwejt

Kaszkiel ? < polonized version of the Lith. pers. n. *Kaškelis*, origin unclear, perhaps < *kaškis*, "itch, scab"

Kazlauskas < Lithuanian version of Polish *Kozłowski* or Belarusian *Казлоўскі* [*Kazloŭski*], which are essentially the same name

Kiszkiel < Lith. pers. n. *Kiškelis* < Lith. *kiškis*, "hare"

Korejwo < polonized form of Lith. *kareiva*, "warrior": Karejwo, KOrejwo, Korewo

Korybut < Lith. pers. n. *Kaributas* < Lit. *karias*, "army," *karas, karys*, "warrior, soldier" + *butas* < *būti*, "to be": Korbut, Korybski, Korybut

Mażejko < polonized form of the Lith. pers. name *Mažeika* < *mažas*, "small, little"

Mingajło < Lith. dithematic name *Mingaila* < roots *min-*, "remember" + *gail-*, "strong" or *gailus*, "bitter, tart," or *gailas*, "sorrow": Mingajło, Mingałło

Misiukanis, presumably < dim. form of *Misiukas* < *Misius* < Slavic short forms of *Michal/Mikhail* such as Blrs. *Мicь* [*Miś*]

Miszkiel ? < Lith. surname *Miškelis* < *Miškys*, origin unclear, possibly a variant of *Meškys*, possibly < *miškas*, "forest," or possibly < Slavic names as discussed under **Misz-**

Miszkin- ? < Lith. *miškinis*, "living in the forest," or ? < Polish *miszkinie*, kind of mushroom < Lith. *meškinis*, of or relating to a bear—both *Miszkinie* and *Miszkinis* are Polish names of several places in Lithuania: Miszkin, Miszkinis, Miszkiniuk

Mitrus < Lith. *mitrus*, "quick, swift" (or from the first name *Dmitri*)

Montwiłł < polonized form of Lith. dithematic name *Mantvilas* < roots *mant-*, "wise, clever" + *vil-*, "hope": Montwiłł, Montwiłło

Monwid < polonized form of Lith. dithematic name *Manvydas* < *man-*, "think, thought" + *vyd-*, "see, sight," surname of a noble Lith. family

Narbut, Norbut < Lith. compound name *Narbutas* or *Norbutas,* from roots *nor-*, "to want," + *būti*, "to be": Narbut, Narbutowicz, Narbutt

Narel ? < Lith. pers. name *Narelis, Norelis*

Narkun < Lith. pers. name *Narkūnas*

Naruszewicz < Lith. pers. name *Narušas*, in some cases < Polish *naruszyć*, "to violate, infringe"

Narwojsz *{l,n}* < polonized verison of Lith. dithematic name *Norvaišas* <

nor-, "desire" + *vaiš-*, "treat, show hospitality," † "homestead, village"

Niewulis < polonized form of the Lith. pers. n. *Nevulis*, origin unclear but may be connected with *Navulis*, thought to come < *naujas*, "new" + the ending *-ulis*

Norkiewicz < Lith. first names *Norkus, Narkus*, origins unclear

Ogiński, name of a noble Lith. family, < top. *Ogińce*, Eastern Borderlands, presumably now *Uogintai*, Kaišiadorys *raionas,* Lith.

Oksztulski < Lith. pers. name *Aukštulis* < Lith. *aukštas*, "high"

Oszkinis ? < Lith. pers. n. *Ožkinis* < Lith. *ožka*, "goat, she-goat"

Ożys < Lith. *ožys*, "billy-goat"

Parszuto < Lith. pers. name *Paršuta* < Blrs. *Паршута* [*Parshuta*] < East Slavic given names *Parfeniy* or *Paramon*

Paukszt- < Lith. pers. name *Paukšta* < *paukštis*, "bird": Pauksztełо, Paukszto

Pawtel < reconstructed Lith. pers. n. *Pautelis < *pautas*, "egg"

Perwejnis < Lith. pers. name *Pervenis, Perveinis*, origin unclear: Perwejnis, Perwenis

Piłsudski < Lith. toponym *Pilsūdai* near Girdiškė and Skaudvilė, west of Raseiniai, Lith.

Poczobut < Lith. pers. n. *Počobutas, Počebutis, Pačebutas*, cmp. Blrs. *Пачабут* [*Pachabut*]

Pryzmont ? < Lith. pers. name, perhaps *Prišmantas*

Pujszo < Polish *puja*, "she-cat," or < Lith. pers. name *Puiša*, possibly < *puišis*, "someone always dirty," or < *puižė*, "cat"

Pukszta < Lith. pers. name *Pukšta, Pukštas*

Purwin < Lith. pers. name *Purvinis* < *purvas*, "mud, filth"

Radziwiłł < Lith. princely family *Rádvilas,* possibly < Lith. *radvilas*, "foundling," or from a dithematic name < *rad-*, "to find" + *vil-*, "hope, expectation": Radziwiłko, Radziwiłł, Radziwiłłowicz, Radziwiłowicz

Ragauskas < Lith. form of Polish *Rogowski*

Ramanauskis < Lith. version of Polish *Romanowski*

Raud- < Lith. pers. name *Rauda* < Lith. *ráuda*, "weeping, lamentation," or *raudà*, "red dye": Raudzis, Rawdanowicz

Rawinis ? < Lith. surname *Ravinis*

Rekść ? < Lith. pers. n. *Rekščis* < *Rekštys*, possibly from Lith. *rekštis* < "net, woven bag " or < Lith. *rėkšti*, "to pluck, cut, clear away"

Ruks < Lith. pers. name *Rukša* [R]: Ruks, Ruksza

Rukść < Lith. pers. name *Rukšta*

Ruszkauskas < *Ruškauskas,* a Lith. version of the Polish surname *Ruszkowski*

Rutkauskas < Lith. version of Polish *Rutkowski* or Russian *Рутковский* [*Rutkovskiy*]

Rymsz- < polonized version of Lith. pers. n. *Rimša* < *rimša*, "calm, quiet one": Rymsza, Rymszewicz

Rzekęć < Lith. pers. n. *Reketýs*

Sałapat < Lith. pers. name *Salapeta*: Sałapat, Sałapata, Sałapatek

Sienkiel < Lith. pers. name *Sinkelė*

Skinder < Lith. pers. name *Skindōris*: Skinder, Skinderowicz, Skindzier

Skipor < Lith. pers. name *Skìparis*

Skrabut < Lith. pers. n. *Skrabùtis*

Smilgin < Lith. pers. name *Smilginis*: Smilgin, Śmilgin

Strazdelis < Lith. *strazdas*, "thrush"

Stulgis < Lith. *stulgys*, "green sandpiper *(Tringa ochropus)*; crybaby," *stulgus*, "oval; haughty, conceited"

Sudenis < Lith. pers. n. *Sudenis* < the Slavic roots discussed under **Sud-**

Surkont ? < Lith. pers. n. *Surkontas* < roots *sur-*, "about, around" + *kant-*, "patient"

Surwiło < Lith. dithematic name *Survila* < *sur-*, "about, around" + *vil-*, "hope": Surwiłło, Surwiło

Surynt ? < Lith. pers. name *Surintas*, origin unclear

Świrbut < Lith. pers. name *Svirbutas*: Świerbutowicz, Świrbutowicz

Szeksztełło < Lith. pers. name *Šekštelė, Šiekštelė*

Szerejko < Lith. byname, cmp. Lith. *Šereika* < Lith. pers. n. *Šerys* < *šerys*, "bristle, thick hair"

Szerenos < Lith. pers name *Šerėnas, Šaronas*

Szkiłądź < *szkiłądź*, Polish dialect, undoubtedly from Lith. *skilándis*, "pig or sheep's stomach stuffed with miced meat"

Szlaużys ? < polonized form of the Lith. pers. name *Šliaužys*, cmp. *šliaužti*, "to crawl, go on all fours"

Szlejter ? < Lith. pers. name *Šleiteris*, cmp. Germ. *Schleider*

Szuksztul < Lith. pers. name *Šukšta*, perhaps < the root in Lith. *šiukštas*, "one quick to anger," or *šiukštus*, "sharp, rough; angry"

Tanona < Lith. pers. name *Tananas*

Tarwid < Lith. pers. name *Tarvidas, Tarvydas*

Terelak < Lith. pers. n. *Tėrelis*

Trocki < top. *Troki*, the Polish name of Trakai, Lith.

Trypuc- < Lith. pers name *Trypuckas*: Trypuć, Trypucki, Trypuz

Wabalis < polonized form of the Lith. *vabalas*, "beetle"

Wanago < polonized form of Lith. *Vanagas*, "hawk"

Wiesztort < Lith. pers. name *Vieštartas* < Lith. roots *vieš-*, "village, farmstead" + *tar-*, "voice, utter"

Wiln- < top. *Wilno*, Polish name of the Lithuanian capital of Vilnius: Wileński, Willner, Wilner

Wojsznis < polonized form of Lith. *Vaišnys* < *vaišnus*, "hospitable"

Wojszwiłło < polonized form of the Lith. pers. name *Vaišvila* < roots *vaiš-* as in *vaišės*, "treat, entertainment, feast," *vaišinti*, to treat to," or *vieš-* as in *viešės*, "visit," *viešėti*, "to stay with, be on a visit to" + *vil-* "hope"

Wołejko < polonized form of the Lith. pers. name *Voleika, Valeika*, possibly < Lith. *valia*, "will," more likely < Latin *Valentinus*

Wolejszo < polonized form of the Lith. pers. name *Voleiša, Valéiša*

Wolonc- < polonized form of the Lith. pers. *Valančius,* in turn a Lith. version of Polish *Walenty* < Latin *Valentinus;* Wołoncewicz, Wołonciej

Zasztowt ? < polonized form of the Lith. pers. name *Žostautas* < Lith. *žosti,* "to say, to utter; to scold, call names" + *tautas,* "people"

Żejmo < polonized form of the Lith. pers. name *Žeima, Žeimýs*

Żemaitis, Żemoj- < Lith. *žemaitis,* native of *Žemaitija* (Latin and English *Samogitia*), the lowlands of Lithuania—in Polish this name became *Żemojty,* later *Żmójdź, Żmujdź,* and finally *Żmudź*: Zemajtis, Żemajtis, Żemajtys, Żemojcin, Żemojdzin, Żemojtel, Żmojda, Żmójdzin, Żmudzin, Żmudziński, Żmujdzin

Żwirblis < Lith. *žvirblis,* "sparrow": Żwirbla, Zwirbulis, Zwyrblis

Ukrainian (& Belarusian & Russian)

Dealing with names originating among Poland's Slavic neighbors to the east is tricky, because there's a kind of blending of linguistic gradations from Poland to Belarus and Ukraine to Russia that can make it hard to tell exactly which language a name came from. Both Belarusian and Ukrainian were rather similar to Polish to start with, and over the centuries, both have borrowed a lot of words from Polish (and Polish from them). The result is that often, the only way to tell whether a given name comes from Polish, Belarusian, or Ukraine is to look for telltale spelling peculiarities. Even they may not help much, however, given how readily some names change form to fit into whichever language is prevalent in the area. In a given case, is *Hospodar* from the Ukrainian word *господар* [*hospodár*], "host, master of the house," or is it from Czech *hospodář* minus the diacritical marks, or is it Polish *gospodarz* spelled that way because the locals automatically adjusted the slightly foreign-sounding word to fit their own linguistic predilections? You may see the name spelled *Hospodar* in one record, *Gospodarz* in the next!

Before discussing this further, let me deal with a couple of "mechanical" problems. First, the alphabet. Belarusian and Ukrainian are written with the Cyrillic alphabet, and the only really accurate way to explain some aspects of those languages is to use Cyrillic spellings. The one minor drawback is that I feel certain most of you don't happen to read that alphabet! So while I will give most words in their Cyrillic forms, for the sake of accuracy, I will also give a transliteration by English phonetic values, for the sake of convenience. I'm sure you will find *Mykhailevych*, for instance, easier to read rather than *Михайлевич*. However, if your research leads you to the lands east of Poland's current borders, do yourself a favor and start getting used to the Cyrillic alphabet now—you'll need it!

By the way, here and in Volume II, East Slavic words and names are given in the "italic" version of Cyrillic, as opposed to the standard print form. The differences are not major—except for a few letters, such as print г vs.

italic *г*, print д vs. italic *д*, print и vs. italic *u,* print т vs. italic *m.* I think the italic forms may be slightly more helpful to you because they look like the script forms you'll usually see in documents. In records, personal names and data are often written in by hand; so if you encounter the name *Matviy* in your research, it will probably look more like *Матвій* than Матвій.

Secondly, the *g/h* problem. All three of the East Slavic languages (Belarusian, Russian, and Ukrainian) have minor peculiarities in regard to the sound represented by *h* in English. Russian doesn't have the sound at all. Until recent decades, Russians routinely substituted for it the letter г (italic form *г*, which corresponds to the hard "g" sound in "goat"—most of the time, anyway). When I took Russian classes in college, my teachers called me G*offman.* They called the German poet Heinrich Heine G*enrikh* G*eine*; Hitler was G*itler,* and so on. I should add, however, that in recent decades, Russians seem to have realized the Cyrillic letter **x** is closer, phonetically, to our *h,* and so they have taken to rendering our *h* as **x**. Change is slow, however; a check of the Russian Wikipedia (as of 10 August 2012) showed that Hitler was still *Гитлер* [*Gitler*] and Heine was still *Гейне*—but Hemingway was *Хемингуэй* [*Kheminguei*], and George Harrison was *Харрисон, Джордж* [*Kharrison, Dzhordzh*].

As for Belarusian and Ukrainian, they use that same Cyrillic letter г for a sound that is kind of a cross between an *h* and a *g* (the technical term is a "glottal fricative"). Poles and others who use the Roman alphabet have hesitated when hearing that sound, unsure how to write it. Thus one of the major cities of Belarus is usually called G*rodno* by Poles; but these days, most English-language references give the name as H*rodna.* If you know the Cyrillic alphabet and look on a Belarusian map, you'll see the name is given as *Гродна*, which transliterates as *Grodna* or *Hrodna,* depending on how you render the first letter. In this book, I have rendered Belarusian and Ukrainian г as *h,* because it sounds closer to *h* than *g* in our ears. But Russian/Soviet domination over recent centuries has often caused that г to be transliterated the way it sounds in Russian, as a hard *g.*

This *g/h* confusion is not a major problem as long as you know about it in advance. In names of Polish origin, a *g* is a *g;* but Poles writing Belarusian or Ukrainian names tend to spell them with *h* rather than *g.* In fact sometimes this tendency gives you a useful clue. A place Poles call *Borowa Hora,* as opposed to *Borowa Góra,* will almost certainly be found in or near Belarus or Ukraine, simply because the Polish form of the name, with *Gó-,* would have prevailed if the inhabitants had been mainly Poles.

Some Historical and Linguistic Considerations

As a practical matter, we can concentrate primarily on the distinctions to be drawn between Polish and Ukrainian names. Russian has not had much influence on Polish surnames, mainly because the Poles wouldn't allow it! I still shake my head when I read in the paper of a "Russian" named *Stanislav*

Jablonsky. Scratch a Russian with a name like that and you'll find a Pole who's gotten stuck in the wrong country! As for Belarusian, I won't make many friends in Minsk or Hrodna/Grodna/Grodno by saying this—but for our purposes, it can be regarded as essentially the same as Ukrainian. Rymut says, "In view of the similarity of structure of both the Ukrainian and Belarusian languages, it is difficult to conclude from the form of a contemporary surname whether it is Ukrainian or Belarusian."[27] He was not trying to outrage Belarusians (or Ukrainians, for that matter). It's just that back when surnames were developing, the older forms of these languages differed less than they do now. The distinctions between the two were far less striking than the distinctions between them and Polish, or them and Russian.

When the Kingdom of Poland and the Grand Duchy of Lithuania began to team up and slowly move toward forming the Commonwealth of Two Nations (a process beginning in the late 14th century and culminating in 1569 with the Union of Lublin), Belarus and much of western Ukraine were part of the deal because the Grand Duchy of Lithuania had been gaining more and more control over them since the collapse of the Kyivan state in 1241. Polish nobles welcomed the nobles of the eastern countries, accepting them as full equals and inviting them to share coats of arms. Part of the reason for this was that the languages and customs of their new Slavic partners didn't feel all that foreign to Poles. (Lithuanian was a different story, but the advantages of the merger were great enough that Poles overlooked this.) As the union grew closer and Polish influence over the *Kresy Wschodnie* or "Eastern Borderlands" expanded, this feeling of familiarity and kinship did, too. Writing in 1936, Bystroń makes the comment "we feel that *Horodyski, Hołowiński,* and *Tretiak* are just as good Polish names as *Grodziski, Głowiński,* and *Trzeciak* ... Only in the last few decades, in connection with the growth of national separatism among Ukrainians, do we see a tendency toward the separation of Polish and Ukrainian surnames."[28] At that, when you transliterate the Ukrainian names from their Cyrillic forms, you find many of the names vary only slightly from their Polish counterparts—so slightly that you almost wonder what all the fuss was about.

To show what I mean, compare the Ukrainian versions of these surnames with their Polish counterparts, generally with the same meanings:

Ukrainian	*Polish*
Дід [*Did*]	*Dziad,* "grandfather, old man"
Галицький [*Halytśkyi*]	*Halicki,* "one from Halych"
Горбатюк [*Horbatiuk*]	*Garbaciak,* "humpback"
Коваль [*Koval'*]	*Kowal,* "smith"
Крамар [*Kramar*]	*Kramarz,* "shopkeeper"
Колодій [*Kolodiy*]	*Kołodziej,* "cartwright"
Кравець [*Kraveś*]	*Krawiec,* "tailor"
Кривоніс [*Kryvonis*]	*Krzywonos,* "crooked nose"

Михайлевич [*Mykhaylevych*]	*Michałowicz*, "Michael's son"	
Муляр [*Mulyar*]	*Mularz*, "mason, bricklayer"	
Ткач [*Tkach*]	*Tkacz*, "weaver"	
Заболотний [*Zabolotnyi*]	*Zabłocki*, "one living beyond the marsh"	

If you take into account phonetic values instead of just spelling—transliteration of the Cyrillic forms of the Ukrainian names is never totally accurate anyway—you'll realize that most of these names are pronounced almost identically. There are, of course, some differences: Ukrainian prefers a plain *r* where Polish likes *rz*, Ukrainian *l* does not have the "w"-sound of Polish *ł*, there's always the *g/h* question I mentioned above, and so on. But the *ch* sound in *Tkach* is essentially the same as the *cz* in Polish *Tkacz;* the *v* in *Koval* is no different from the *w* in *Kowal;* the *-ts* in *Kravets'* differs only slightly from the *c* in *Krawiec,* and so on. The point is that the differences between the names are quite minor, and this is true of many Ukrainian and Polish surnames.

First Names and Suffixes (Does This Sound Familiar?)

First names show a little more difference, however, as is evident from the following list of the more common ones. In this list, blanks indicate there is no really common equivalent in Polish or English; asterisks by Polish "equivalents" mark names Poles have more or less adopted from Ukrainian:

Ukrainian	*Polish*	*English*
Аврам [*Avram*]	*Abram*	*Abraham*
Агафія [*Ahafiya*]	*Agata*	*Agatha*
Адріан [*Adrian*]	*Adrian*	*Adrian*
Анастасія [*Anastasiya*]	*Anastazja*	*Anastasia*
Андрій [*Andriy*]	*Andrzej*	*Andrew*
Антін [*Antin*]	*Antoni*	*Anthony*
Арсеній [*Arseniy*]	**Arseniusz*	*Arsenio*
Артемій [*Artemiy*]	**Artemiusz*	*Artemis*
Богдан [*Bohdan*]	*Bogdan/*Bohdan*	—
Борис [*Borys*]	**Borys*	*Boris*
Вадим [*Vadym*]	**Wadim*	*Vadim*
Валерій [*Valeriy*]	*Walery*	—
Варвара [*Varvara*]	*Barbara*	*Barbara*
Василь [*Vasyl'*]	*Bazyli*	*Basil*
Вікентій [*Vikentiy*]	*Wincenty*	*Vincent*
Віктор [*Viktor*]	*Wiktor*	*Victor*
Вікторія [*Viktoriya*]	*Wiktoria*	*Victoria*
Віталій [*Vitaliy*]	*Witalis*	*Vitaly*
Володимир [*Volodymyr*]	*Włodzimierz*	*Vladimir*

Гаврило [*Havrylo*]	*Gabriel*	*Gabriel*
Галина [*Halyna*]	*Halina, Helena*	*Helen*
Ганна [*Hanna*]	*Hanna, Anna*	*Hannah, Anna*
Гарасим [*Harasym*]	*—*	*—*
Геннадій [*Hennadiy*]	*—*	*—*
Григорій, Григір [*Hryhoriy, Hryhir*]	*Grzegorz*	*Gregory*
Данило [*Danylo*]	*Daniel*	*Daniel*
Дарина [*Daryna*]	*Daria*	*—*
Дем'ян [*Demyan*]	*Damian*	*Damien*
Дмитро [*Dmytro*]	**Dymitr*	*Dmitri*
Єва [*Yeva*]	*Ewa*	*Eve*
Євгеній [*Yevheniy*]	*Eugeniusz*	*Eugene*
Євдокія [*Yevdokiya*]	**Ewdokia*	*—*
Єлизавета [*Yelyzaveta*]	*Elżbieta*	*Elizabeth'*
Єфросинія [*Yefrosyniya*]	**Eufrozyna*	*—*
Захар [*Zakhar*]	*Zachariasz*	*Zachary*
Іван [*Ivan*]	*Jan*	*John*
Ілля [*Illia*]	*Eliasz*	*Ilya, Elias*
Ірина [*Iryna*]	*Irena*	*Irene*
Йосип [*Iosyp*]	*Józef*	*Joseph*
Катерина [*Kateryna*]	*Katarzyna*	*Catherine*
Кирило [*Kyrylo*]	*Cyryl*	*Cyril*
Клим [*Klym*]	*Klement*	*Clement*
Костянтин [*Kostiantyn*]	*Konstanty*	*Constantine*
Ксаверій [*Ksaveriy*]	*Ksawery*	*Xavier*
Кузьма [*Kuźma*]	*Kosma, Kuźma*	*Cosmo*
Купріян [*Kupriyan*]	*Cyprian*	*Cyprian*
Лаврентій [*Lavrentiy*]	*Wawrzyniec*	*Lawrence*
Лавро [*Lavro*]	*—*	*—*
Лариса [*Larysa*]	*—*	*Larissa*
Лука [*Luka*]	*Łukasz*	*Luke, Lucas*
Людмила [*Liudmyla*]	**Ludmiła*	*Ludmilla*
Максим [*Maksym*]	*Maksym*	*Max*
Марія [*Mariya*]	*Maria*	*Mary*
Марко [*Marko*]	*Marek*	*Mark*
Матвій [*Matviy*]	*Maciej, Mateusz*	*Matthew, Matthias*
Микита [*Mykyta*]	*—*	*Nikita*
Микола [*Mykola*]	*Mikołaj*	*Nicholas*
Михайло [*Mykhailo*]	*Michał*	*Michael*
Мойсей [*Moisei*]	*Mojżesz*	*Moses*
Надія [*Nadiya*]	*Nadzieja*	*Hope*
Наталія [*Nataliya*]	*Natalia*	*Natalie*
Оксана [*Oksana*]	*—*	*—*

Олександр [Oleksandr]	Aleksander	Alexander
Олексій [Oleksiy]	Aleksy	Alexis
Олена [Olena]	Helena	Helen
Ольга [Ol'ha]	*Olga	Olga
Омелян [Omelian]	Emilian	Emil
Остап [Ostap]	Eustachy	Eustace
Павло [Pavlo]	Paweł	Paul
Панас [Panas]	Atanazy	—
Петро [Petro]	Piotr	Peter
Пилип [Pylyp]	Filip	Phillip
Прокіп [Prokip]	*Prokop	—
Роман [Roman]	Roman	Roman
Сава [Sava]	*Sawa	—
Самійло [Samiylo]	Samuel, Szmul	Samuel
Семен [Semen]	Szymon	Simon
Степан [Stepan]	Szczepan, Stefan	Stephen
Софія [Sofiya]	Zofia	Sophie
Тарас [Taras]	—	—
Тимофій [Tymofiy]	Tymoteusz	Timothy
Фадей [Fadei]	Tadeusz	Thaddeus
Феодосія [Feodosiya]	Teodozja	—
Федір [Fedir]	Teodor	Theodore
Фома [Foma]	Tomasz	Thomas
Харитон [Kharyton]	—	—
Хома [Khoma]	Tomasz	Thomas
Юрій [Yuriy]	Jerzy	George
Яків [Yakiv]	Jakób	Jacob

These Ukrainian first names—including several for which Polish and/
or English have no real native equivalents, and excluding feminine names
formed directly from masculine names, such as *Oleksandra* vs. *Oleksandr* —
are among the most common, and they are worth studying because they are
the basis for numerous patronymics and metronymics.[29] Familiarity with the
Ukrainian forms will often help you recognize a patronymic "in disguise,"
one very similar to a Polish patronymic with which you may already be familiar. (Remember *Grzegorz Kościuszko/Hrehor Kostiushko* in Chapter Five?)

The allusion to Polish patronymics may suggest to you that Ukrainian
forms patronymics the same way as Polish: by the addition of suffixes. And
that's absolutely right! The suffixes involved were mentioned in Chapter
Four: the main ones are *-ko, -enko, -[i]uk, -chuk, -chak, -ych, -ovych* and
-evych. The last three are Ukrainian equivalents of Polish *-icz, -owicz* and
-ewicz, while *-chak* and *-chuk* are the same as Polish *-czak* and *-czuk*. The
suffixes *-uk* and *-ko* are not exclusively Ukrainian, but they are most common
in that language. The suffix *-enko* is most closely identified with Ukrainian;

when you see a name ending that way, you can be fairly sure you're dealing with someone who traced his ancestry to Ukraine, one way or another.

Also typically Ukrainian are names ending in the suffix *-ишин*; we usually spell it *-yshyn*, Poles spell it *-yszyn*. These were formed from women's names; the wife of a *Petro* could be called *Petrykha* ("Peter's woman") and *Roman's* wife would be *Romanykha*. The addition of the suffix *yn* modifies the *kh* sound to *sh*—Poles would spell it *ch* → *sz*—giving the metronymics *Romanyshyn* and *Petryshyn*, literally "son of Roman's woman" and "son of Peter's woman."[30] ... My study of massive lists of surnames from Poland gave me a distinct impression that surnames formed from women's names are much more common in Ukrainian than in Polish. I'm not sure if this is due to a skew in the data I've used or if there is a real cultural difference; but that is how it seemed to me. The names with *-yshyn* are the easiest to spot, but by no means the only examples. I realize this is hardly glorious news for feminists—after all, a name meaning "son of Peter's woman" is not exactly an expression of profound admiration for the strength and wisdom of the woman involved—but it is an interesting phenomenon, and one I hope to learn more about as my study of surnames continues.

After viewing these suffixes, one can decipher a great many Ukrainian names. *Jurko* is the name *Jurij* (Polish spelling for *Юрій, Yuriy,* George) + *-ko; Savchuk* (Polish spelling *Sawczuk*) is the name *Sava* + *-chuk, Maksym-chak* is the name *Maksym* + *chak,* and so on. Factor in other suffixes similar to their Polish counterparts, such as *-skyj, -ckyj,* and *-zkyj* (much like *-ski, -cki,* and *-zki* in Polish), and *-iv-* (the Ukrainian equivalent of Polish *-ow-*), and names such as *Ivanivskyj* and *Fedorivskyj* are not as unlike Polish as they might seem at first.

I just mentioned that *-iv-* is the Ukrainian equivalent of Polish *-ow-,* and this is worth emphasizing. Where Polish (and Russian, for that matter) tend to use the vowel *-o-,* Ukrainian often likes *-i-.* (There's even a term for this, *ікавізм* [*ikavizm*] in Ukrainian, *ikawizm* in Polish.) Thus the city called *Lwów* in Polish and *L'vov (Львов)* in Russian is *L'viv (Львів)* in Ukrainian. The Polish prefix *pod-* ("near, under") is *pid-* in Ukrainian. The surname *Pidhirnyj* is not hard to decipher if you see that *pid-* = Polish *pod,* and *hir-* = Polish *gor-* ("mountain, hill") — so a *Pidhirnyj* lived near or beside a hill.

-SKI vs. -SKY?

I have to say a word on this, as it summarizes one of the questions most often asked about names from eastern Europe. People notice that one surname ends in *-ski* but another ends in *-sky,* and wonder if this has any significance. The rule of thumb is: **if it's *-ski,* chances are it's Polish; if it's *-sky,* it's more likely to be Czech, Russian, or Ukrainian.** There are many, many, many exceptions, but this is true more often than not.

Why? I think it's because Poles arrived in this country with a name already written in our alphabet; so the endings, at least, didn't really need to be changed. Proper Polish spelling says **always -ski, never -sky.** So Polish names were correctly spelled *-ski,* and they tended to stay that way. Czech names also are written in Roman letters, and the standard adjectival ending in Czech is *-ský;* drop the accent and you have a name spelled in a way Americans can read.

Russian, Belarusian, and Ukrainian names, however, had to be transliterated from the Cyrillic alphabet. In Russian the suffix is *-ский,* in Ukrainian it is *-ський,* and there's no one really adequate way of rendering those sounds in our letters, at least not in a way people can grasp intuitively. I've seen Russian names rendered *"-ski, -sky, -skij, -skiy"*; Ukrainian names are often given with *"-skyj, -škyj, -śkyj, -sky."* More often than not, they ended up as *-sky* in English. Belarusian names end with the suffix *-скі,* which can be rendered as *-ski* just fine, and probably was so rendered sometimes, especially by Poles. But due to Russian influence, it probably ended up as *-sky* more often than not.

I repeat, there are jillions of exceptions, and I've seen plenty of undoubtedly Polish names spelled *"-sky."* But in my experience, a *-ski* is usually Polish, and a *-sky* tends to be Czech, Belarusian, Russian, or Ukrainian.

I did not find as many name roots in Volume II that I could characterize as uniquely Ukrainian or Belarusian as I would have expected, other than those deriving from first names far more common among eastern Slavs than Poles. I think one reason for this is that the Polish onomastic experts on whom I relied the most tend to regard those roots as "versions used in eastern Poland" rather than as roots from different languages. Ukrainian and Belarusian nationalists would no doubt find this most offensive; but I think most of my readers are looking for the simplest adequate explanations possible, not linguistic subtleties. So I'll confine myself to listing some of the more prominent examples of surname roots that are clearly Eastern Slavic in origin.

Anikiej < Ukr. given name *Аникій/Оникій* [*Anikiy/Onikiy*]: Anikiej, Onik

Anis- < Blrs. *Аніська* [*Aniśka*], *Анішка* [*Anishka*], cmp. Russ. *Онисий* [*Onisiy*]: Anisiewicz, Aniśkiewicz, Aniśko, Aniszkiewicz

Antyp- < given name *Antip*, used in the Orthodox Church, cmp. Ukr. given name *Антип* [*Antýp*]: Ancuta, Antypiuk

Apan- Ukr. name *Афанасій* [*Afanasiy*], in Polish *Atanazy*: Afanasjew, Apanasewicz, Apanasowicz, Apanowicz, Panas, Panaś, Panasiuk, Tanaś

Arseniuk < East Slavic given name, cmp. Ukr. *Арсеній* [*Arséniy*]

Artem- < East Slavic given name *Artemi*, cmp. Ukr. *Артемій* [*Artémiy*]: Arcimowicz, Arciuch, Artemiuk, Artych, Artymiak, Artymiuk, Artymowicz, Artysiewicz, Artyszuk, Orciuch

Bałaban < Ukr. or Blrs. *балабан* [*balabán*], "kind of hawk or falcon"

Bałabuch ? < Ukr. *балабух* [*balábuch*], "a kind of bun or pastry"

Bałanda, in some cases ? < Ukr. *баланда* [*balánda*], "uncouth or clumsy person"

Berenda < Ukr. given name *Бериндій* [*Beryndiy*], of Turkish origin

Berez- < Russ. *берёза* [*berióza*], Ukr. *береза* [*beréza*], Blrs. *бяроза* [*biaróza*], all meaning "birch tree," or toponyms from this root in Ukraine, Belarus, and Russia, cmp. Polish root **Brzez-**: Bereza, Bereziński, Bereźnicki, Berezowski

Bil- < Czech adj. *bilý* and Ukr. adj. *білий* [*bilyi*], "white" (cmp. Polish *biał-, biel-*): Bil, Bilewicz, Bilicki, Bilik, Biłka, Biłyk

Bondar- < Ukr. *бондар* [*bóndar*], "cooper," cmp. Polish *bednarz:* Bondar, Bondarenko, Bondaruk, Bondyra

Borod- < Ukr. *борода* [*borodá*], "beard," cmp. Polish names with *brod-*: Borodacz, Borodeńko, Borodzicz, Borodziuk

Botwin- < *boćwina, botwina,* cmp. Blrs. *бацьвіна* [*batśvina*], Ukr. *ботвина* [*botvýna*]: Boćwiński, Botwina

Burian ? < Ukr. *бур'ян* [*bur'ián*], "weed": Burian, Buriański

Chadaj < Ukr. *Хадай, Хадей* [*Khadai, Khadei*], East Slavic versions of the given name we know as "Thaddeus": Chadaj

Charyt- < Ukr. given name *Харитон* [*Kharytón*]: Charytanowicz, Charyton, Charytoniuk

Chom- < Ukr. first name *Хома/Фома* [*Khoma/Foma*] = Polish *Tomasz,* English *Thomas*: Choma, Chomczyk, Chomiak, Chomicz, Chomiuk, Chomko, Chomski, Chomyszyn, Homa, Homik

Chwed- < East Slavic given name, cmp. Blrs. *Хведар* [*Khvedar*] and Old Ukr. *Хведор* [*Khvedor*] = English *Theodore*: Chwedczuk, Chwedorowicz, Chwedoruk, Chwesiuk, Chwiećko, Chwieduk

Czebotar < Russ. *чеботарь* [*chebotár'*] < Ukr. *чоботар* [*chobotár*], "boot-maker, shoemaker"

Demid- < Ukr. given name *Демид* [*Demýd*]: Demidowicz, Dziemidowicz

Derez- ? < Ukr. *дереза* [*dereza*] = Polish *dzieraza,* a plant, *lycopodium clavatum*: Dereziński, Dereżyński

Diak < *diak,* † *dyjak,* "seminarist in a Ukrainian church," or "cantor, church singer," cmp. Ukr. *дяк* [*diak*]: Diak, Dyjak

Dmitr- < Ukr. first name *Дмитро* [*Dmytró*]: Dmitruk, Dmitrzak, Dmytryszyn, Domitrz, Dymitruk, Gmitruk, Gmitrzuk, Mitrus, Zmitrowicz

Droni < East Slavic given name *Andronik,* cmp. Ukr. *Андроник* [*Andronýk*]: Droń, Dronia, Dronka

Dub- < *dub,* Czech, Russ., Blrs., and Ukr. for "oak" (Polish *dąb*): Dub, Dubaj, Dubel, Dubik, Dubiński, Dubowski, Dubrawski

Fed- < eastern Polish given name *Feodor,* Ukr. *Федір* [*Fédir*], Russian *Фёдор* [*Fiódor*] = English *Theodore:* Fedak, Federowicz, Fedor, Fedorowicz, Fiedorczuk, Fiedorowicz

Filimon < Ukr. given name *Филимон* [*Fylymón*]: Chalimoniuk, Chilimoniuk, Filimoniuk

Filon < Ukr. given name *Філон* [*Filon*]: Filon, Fiłończuk, Fiłonowicz

Froń, in some cases < Ukr. name *Єфросинія* [*Yefrosynia*] = Polish *Eufrozyna*

Hajdam- < *hajdamach, hajdamak, hajdamak,* "Cossack, Ukrainian peasant who took part in battles in Ukraine in the 17th century," cmp. Ukr. *гайдамака* [*haidamáka*]: Gajdamowicz, Hajdamowicz

Hap- < Ukr. given name *Агафон, Агапон* [*Ahafón, Ahapón*] and the short form *Гапон* [*Hapón*]: Aponowicz, Hapon, Haponiuk

Haras- < Ukr. given name *Гарасим* [*Harasým*]: Arasimowicz, Araszkiewicz, Garasimowicz, Gierasimiuk, Harasimiuk, Harasymowicz, Haraszczuk

Hawryl- < Ukr. given name *Гаврило* [*Havrýlo*]: Habryło, Hawrylak, Hawryluk, Hawryło, Hawryszko

Hlib < East Slavic given name, cmp. Russ. *Глеб* [*Gleb*], Ukr. *Гліб* [*Hlib*]: Gleb, Gleba, Glib, Glibowski, Hlebowicz

Hnat < Ukr. given name *Гнат* [*Gnat/Hnat*] < Latin *Ignatius*: Hnat, Hnatiuk, Hnatów, Hnatyszyn

Hołod- < East Slavic root meaning "cold," cmp. Ukr. *холод* [*khólod*] = Polish root *chłod,* possibly also connected with Ukr. *голод* [*hólod*], "famine, hunger": Hołod, Hołodniak, Hołody

Hołow- < Ukr. *голова* [*holová*] = Polish *głowa,* "head": Hołowacz, Hołowaty, Hołowienko, Hołowiński, Hołówka, Hołownia

Holub < Czech *holub,* Ukr. and Blrs. *голуб* [*hólub*] = Polish *gołąb,* "dove": Hałubiec, Hołub, Hołubiec, Hołubowicz

Hord- < *horda,* "Tatar horde, crowd, gang," in some cases also < Ukr. *гордий* [*hórdyi*], "domestic," can also mean "proud, haughty," possibly also relevant in some cases is the Ukrainian given name *Гордій* [*Hordiy*]: Hordejuk, Hordyj

Horosz- < Ukr. *хороший* [*khoróshiy*], "handsome, beautiful, fine," or < Ukr. *горох* [*horókh*], "pea," cmp. Polish names under **Groch**: Horosz, Horoszczak, Horoszkiewicz, Horoszko

Hreh-, Hren-, Hreś- < element *Hre-* from East Slavic forms of the given name we know as *Gregory,* cmp. Ukr. *Григорій/Григір,* forms that have been rendered in Roman letters many different ways, including *Grygoriy/Grygir, Hryhory/Hryhir, Hrehory/Hrehir* etc.: Hrehorowicz, Hrehoruk, Hreniak, Hreśka

Hryc-, Hryn-, Hryw- < element *Hry-* from Ukr. *Григорій* [*Hryhoriy*] + suffixes *-c-, -g-, -h-, -n-,* or *-s-*: Hryc, Hryciuk, Hrycyszyn, Hryń, Hryniewicz, Hrynkiewicz, Hryszko

Hur- < Ukr. name *Гурій* [*Huriy*] or < short form of Ukr. *Григорій* [*Hryhoriy*] = English *Gregory*: Huras, Hurek, Huryn

Huszcza < *huszcza,* "multitude, crowd," cmp. Ukr. *гуща* [*húshcha*], "sediment, thickness": Huszcza, Huszczo

Iwan < Ukr. *Іван* and Russ. *Иван (Iván)* = Polish *Jan*: Iwan, Iwanek, Iwankiewicz, Iwanów, Iwaszkiewicz, Iwon, Wańczyk, Waniek, Wańkowicz

Jefim- < East Slavic given name, cmp. Russ. *Ефим* [*Yefim*] and Ukr. *Єфим* [*Yefým*]: Jefimiuk, Jefimow, Jefimowicz

Jegorow < Ukr. name *Єгор* [*Yehór*], a form of the name we know as *George*

Jermol- < Old East Slavic given name *Yermoła*, used in the Orthodox Church, cmp. Ukr. *Єрмолай* [*Yermolái*] and *Ярмолай* [*Yarmolái*]: Jarmoła, Jarmolik, Jarmołowicz, Jarmoluk, Jarmuł

Jewdokimow < Ukr. given name *Євдоким* [*Yevdokým*]

Jewtuch < East Slavic given name *Yevtukhiy*, cmp. Ukr. *Євтихій* [*Yevtýkhiy*], short form *Євтух* [*Yevtúkh*]

Juchim- < given name used in the Orthodox Church, cmp. Ukr. *Юхим* [*Yukhým*]: Juchimiuk, Juchimowicz

Jur- < Russ. *Юрий* or Ukr. *Юрій* [*Yuriy*], equivalents of Polish *Jerzy*, English *George*: Jura, Juras, Jurczak, Jurczyszyn, Jurek, Jurkiewicz

Kiryk < given name *Kiryk*, used in the Orthodox Church, cmp. Ukr. *Кирик* [*Kýryk*]: Kieryk, Kiryczuk, Kiryk

Kiryl- < Ukr. given name *Кирило* [*Kyrýlo*]: Kiryło, Kiryluk, Kuryło

Kniaz- < *kniaź*, "headman of a village settled under Wallachian law, prince" (esp. Lith. or Ruthenian), cmp. Russ./Blrs./Ukr. *князь*; Kniaź, Kniaziuk

Konon < Ukr. given name *Конон* [*Kónon*]: Konon, Konończuk, Kononowicz

Korol- < Ukr. *король* [*koról'*], "king," cmp. Polish *król*: Korol, Korolczuk

Kośc-, Kost- < Polish *kość*, "bone," but in East Slavic names mainly < a form of the name we know as *Constantine*, cmp. Ukr. forms *Костянтин, Кость* [*Kostiantýn, Kost'*]: Kość, Kośćiuk, Kościuszko, Kost, Kostek

Kupr- < *Купріян* [*Kupriyán*], Ukr. form of first name *Cyprian*: Kuprewicz, Kuprianowicz, Kupryjańczyk, Kupryjanowicz, Kupryś

Kurian < given name *Kirian*, used in the Orthodox Church, cmp. Russ. *Кириан* [*Kirián*]: Kurian, Kurianowicz, Kuriański, Kurjan

Kuźm- < *Кузьма* [*Kuźma*], Ukr. form of first name *Kosma*: Kuźma, Kuźmiak, Kuźmicz, Kuźmin, Kuźmiuk

Łob- < Blrs. and Ukr. *лоб*, "forehead, brow": Łobacz, Łobaczewski (or < top. such as *Łobacze, Łobaczów*, mostly in Lith., Belarus and Ukr.), Łobejko

Ludian ? < Ukr. *людяний* [*liúdianyi*], "polite, kind"

Lwowski < major city of *Lwów*, Ukr. name *Львів*

Majdan < Ukr. *майдан* [*maidán*], "public square, common grass lot"

Makar- < Ukr. name *Макар* [*Makár*], Polish *Makary* or *Mękarz:* Makar, Makara, Makarewicz, Makarski, Makaruk

Malajka < Ukr. *малай* [*malái*], "maize bread, bread made of corn flour"

Malat- < Ukr. *малата* [*maláta*], "dish from corn flour": Malaca, Malatyński

Matwiej- < East Slavic given name, cmp. Russ. *Матвей* [*Matvéi*] and Ukr. *Матвій* [*Matvíy*] = Polish *Maciej*: Matwiej, Matwiejczuk, Matwiejuk, Matwij

Melan- < fem. given name *Melania*, Ukr. *Меланія* [*Melániya*]: Mełańczuk, Melaniuk, Melanowicz

Mikita < East Slavic given name used in the Orthodox Church, cmp. Ukr. *Микита* [*Mykýta*], Russ. *Никита* [*Nikíta*]: Mikiciuk, Mikita, Mikitiuk

Miron < Ukr. name *Мирон* [*Miron*]: Miron, Mirończuk, Mironiuk

Miron <East Slavic given name *Miron*, e.g., Russ. *Мирон* [*Mirón*], Ukr.

Мирон [*Myrón*]: Miron, Mirończuk, Mironiuk, Mironowicz

Moroz < Ukr. and Russ. *мороз* [*moróz*], "frost," cmp. Polish *mróz*

Mudr- < Ukr. *мудрий* [*múdryi*] = Polish *mądry*, "wise": Mudrak, Mudry

Naum < Ukr. given name *Наум* [*Naúm*]: Naumczyk, Naumiuk, Naumowicz

Nikifor < Ukr. given name *Никифор* [*Nykýfor*], also seen as *Ничипір* [*Nichýpir*]: Niczyporuk, Nieczypor, Nikiforuk, Nitychoruk

Nikon < Orthodox given name *Nikon*, cmp. Ukr. *Никін/Никон* [*Nýkin/Nýkon*]: Nikończuk, Nikoniuk, Nikonowicz

Ochrym- < Orthodox given name, cmp. Ukr. *Окрім/Ефрем* [Okrím/Efrém]: Ochrymiuk, Ochrymowicz, Ochryniuk

Oks- < Orthodox given names, cmp. Ukr. masc. name *Оксен/Овксен* [*Oksén, Ovksén*] and fem. *Оксана/Оксенія* [*Oksána/Okséniya*]: Okseniuk, Oksentowicz, Oksiejuk, Oksiuta

Olen- < element *Ol-* < short forms of given names such as *Oleksander* or *Oleksy* + *-en*, or < *Olena*, cmp. Ukr. *Олена* [*Oléna*], "Helen," or < East Slavic *oleń*, cmp. Ukr. *олень* [*óleń*], "deer, hart": Oleńczuk, Oleniacz, Oleniak, Olenkiewicz, Olenkowicz, Oleński

Olichwier < given name used in the Orthodox Church, cmp. Ukr. *Олефір* [*Olefír*]: Olichwer, Olichwier, Oliferuk

Omiel- < Ukr. given name *Омелян* [*Omelián*]: Omelańczuk, Omelczuk, Omeljaniuk, Omielan, Omilian

Onis- < East Slavic given name, cmp. Ukr. *Онисим* [*Onýsym*], dim. *Онисько* [*Onýśko*]: Anisimowicz, Onisk, Oniszczuk, Oniszk, Onoszko, Onyśko, Onyszczuk, Onyszkiewicz, Onyszko

Onufr- < Ukr. given name *Онопрій, Онуфрій* [*Onópriy, Onúfriy*] = Polish *Onufry:* Onufrowicz, Onufrejuk, Onufruk, Onufrzak

Osip < East Slavic given name, equivalent to Polish *Józef* and English *Joseph*, seen in Ukr. as *Йосип, Осип* [*Iósyf, Ósyp*]: Osip, Osipiuk, Osipowicz, Osypiuk, Osypowicz

Ost- < given name, cmp. Ukr. *Євстахій* [*Yevstákhiy*], *Євстафій* [*Yevstáfiy*], and *Остап* [*Ostáp*] = Polish *Eustachy:* Ostach, Ostafin, Ostapczuk, Ostapiuk, Ostasz, Stafiej, Sztafiński

Ower- < East Slavic given name, cmp. Russ. *Аверкий* [*Avérkiy*] and Ukr. *Оверкій* [*Ovérkiy*] and *Оверко* [*Ovérko*]: Owerczuk, Owerko

Owsiej- < Ukr. given name *Овсій, Євсей* [*Ovsíy, Yevséi*]: Owsiejczuk, Owsiejko

Panfil < from given name *Pamfil*, used in the Orthodox Church, cmp. Ukr. given name *Памфіл, Панфіл* [*Pamfíl, Panfíl*]: Pamfil, Panfil

Pant- < given name *Pantelemon*, used in the Orthodox Church, cmp. Ukr. *Пантелеймон* [*Panteleimón*]: Pańta, Pańtak, Pantoł, Poncyliusz

Paraniak < given name *Paramon* used in the Orthodox Church, cmp. Ukr. given name *Парамон* [*Paramón*]

Parfien- < East Slavic given name, cmp. Ukr. *Пархом* [*Parkhóm*], *Пархім* [*Parkhím*], *Парфен* [*Parfén*], Russ. *Парфён* [*Parfíon*] and *Парфений*

[*Parféniy*]: Parchem, Parcheniak, Parchimowicz, Parchomiuk, Parfiano-wicz, Parfieńczyk, Parfieniuk

Pilip < Ukr. first name *Пилип* [*Pylýp*] = Polish *Filip*, English *Philip;* Pilip, Pilipczuk, Pilipiec, Pilipiuk, Pyłypyszyn

Podhorodecki < toponym *Podhorodce,* now *Підгородці* [*Pidhorodtsi*] near Stryi, Ukr.

Ponahaj- < Ukr. *panahaibo,* "God help us!", cmp. Ukr. *помагай бог* [*poma-hai boh*], "God help [us]!": Ponachajba, Ponahajba

Potap- < given name *Potap* or *Potapiy,* used in the Orthodox Church, cmp. Russ. *Потап* [*Potáp*], *Потапий* [*Potápiy*], and Ukr. *Потап* [*Potáp*]: Potapczuk, Potapowicz, Potapski

Prokop < Polish given name *Prokop,* cmp. Ukr. *Прокіп* [*Prokíp*] *Прокопій* [*Prokópiy*]: Prokop, Prokopczuk, Prokopczyk, Prokopek, Prokopiak, Prokopiuk, Prokopowicz

Prokorym < given name used in the Orthodox Church, cmp. Ukr. *Прохор* [*Prókhor*]

Radziwon < Ukr. given name *Радивон/Родіон* [*Radyvón/Rodión*], but names beginning *Radziwon-* can also come from the root **Rad-**

Rosłan < given name *Rosłan,* undoubtedly from the given name that appears in Ruthenia as *Руслан* [*Ruslán*] < Turkish *arslan,* "lion": Rosłan, Rosłaniec, Rosłon, Rosłoń, Rosłonek, Rosłoniec, Rosłoński

Rusin < *Rusin,* "Ruthenian": Rusin, Rusinek, Rusiniak, Rusinowicz, Rusiński

Ryń < Ukr. pers. name *Гринь* [*Hryń*] from a nickname for the Ukr. version of the given name we know as *Gregory*: Ryń, Ryniewicz

Sałamacha < *sałamacha, szałamacha,* "oat or barley grains cooked in lard," cmp. Ukr. *саламаха* [*salamákha*], "dish of rye flour and water; confusion, disorder," and *соломаха* [*solomákha*], "food of buckwheat flour": Sałamacha, Szałamacha

Sapieha < Blrs. *Сапега* [*Sapeha*] < East Slavic *sopeť,* "to wheeze, breathe heavily": Sapiecha, Sapieha, Sapierzyński, Sapieszko, Sapieżko

Saw- < Biblical name *Sawa,* in Ukr. *Сава* [*Sáva*]: Sawa, Sawczuk, Sawczyszyn, Sawka, Sawko

Sem- < given names *Semen, Siemion* if roots in the Eastern Borderlands are involved: Semczuk, Semczyszyn, Semik, Semkiw, Semków

Sered- < East Slavic root *sered-,* cmp. Russ. *середина* [*seredína*], "middle, midst," Ukr. *середина* [*serédyna*], "center, middle," Polish **Środ-**: Sereda, Serediuk, Seredziuk, Seredyka, Seredyn

Siemion < Eastern Slavic given names *Semen* or *Semion,* cmp. Ukr. *Семен* [*Siemién*] and Russian *Семён* [*Siemión*] = the name used in the form *Szymon* in Polish, *Simeon/Simon* in English: Semen, Semeniuk, Semeno-wicz, Siemieńczuk, Siemieniak, Siemieniec, Siemieniuk, Siemion

Siergiej < given name *Sergei* used in the Orthodox Church, Ukr. *Сергій* [*Serhiy*], Russ. *Сергей* [*Sergei*]: Sergiej, Siergiej, Siergiejuk, Sierhej

Sołoducha < *sołoducha,* "sweet bread," or a kind of sweet soup < Ukr.

солодкий [*solódkyi*], "sweet," cmp. Polish *słodki*

Sołowiej < East Slavic *solovei*, "nightingale," cmp. Russ. and Ukr. соловей [*solovéi*], "nightingale," and Polish *słowik*: Sołowiej, Sołowij

Sołowiej < Ukr. соловей [*solovej*], "nightingale" (cmp. Polish *słowik*): Sołowij

Sozon < Orthodox given name *Sozon*, cmp. Ukr. Созон, Созонт [*Sozón, Sozónt*]: Sazon, Sozoniuk

Spiryd- < Orthodox given name *Spirydon*, cmp. Ukr. Свирид, Спиридон [*Svyrýd, Spyrydón*]: Spirydowicz, Świrydowicz, Świrydziuk

Supron- < Orthodox given name *Sofron, Sofroniy, Sopron*, cmp. Ukr. Софрон, Сопрон, Супрун [*Sofrón, Soprón, Suprún*]: Soprych, Supranowicz, Suproń, Suproniuk, Suprun, Supruniuk, Supryn

Szeremet < East Slavic personal name < Ottoman *sheremet*, "prone to anger, rude": Seremet, Szerement, Szeremet, Szeremeta, Szerment

Tałałaj < Ukr. талалай [*talalái*], "chatterer, idle talker," cmp. Russ. талала [*talalá*], "pronouncing words gutturally; tongue-tied," and талалы [*talalý*], "jabber, twaddle"

Taras < given name *Taras*, used in Ruthenia, cmp. Ukr. Тарас [*Tarás*]: Taras, Tarasek, Tarasewicz, Tarasiewicz, Tarasiuk, Taraska, Taraszkiewicz

Teleg- < *telega*, also in the Eastern Borderlands (from Russ.) *telaga, telęga, talaga, teliga,* "plain farm cart": Talaga, Talaśka, Telążka, Telega, Telenga, Teliga

Trofim < Orthodox given name *Trofim*, cmp. Ukr. version of the name, Трохим [*Trokhým*]: Trachimowicz, Trochim, Trochimczuk, Trochimiak, Trochimiuk, Trochimowicz, Trofimiuk

Truchan < Orthodox given name *Trukhon, Trukhan*, cmp. Ukr. forms Трухан, Трухон, Трифон [*Trukhan, Trukhon, Tryfon*], or < Ukr. трухан [*trukhán*], "turkey": Truchan, Truchel, Tryfon

Tych- < East Slavic given name, cmp. Ukr. Тихін, Тихон [*Týkhin, Týkhon*], or < Ukr. тихий [*týkhyi*] = Polish *cichy*, "quiet": Tichoniuk, Tychoniuk

Tymon < Orthodox given name *Tymon*, cmp. Ukr. Тимон [*Tymón*]

Uścin- < Ukr. name Устим/Устин [*Ustým/Ustýn*] = the name we know as *Justin:;* Uścinowicz, Uściński, Ustianowski, Ustymowicz

Wakul- < East Slavic given name, cmp. Ukr. Вакула [*Vakúla*]: Wakuła, Wakulak, Wakuluk

Wasyl- < Ukr. given name Василь [*Vasyl'*], cmp. Polish *Bazyli*: Wasiela, Wasil, Wasilewicz, Wasiluk, Wasyl, Wasyluk

Werem- < Ukr. Ярема [*Yaréma*], Веремій [*Veremíy*], and Єремія [*Yeremíya*] = English *Jeremiah*: Werema, Weremczuk, Weremko, Wieremczuk, Wieremiejczyk, Wieremiejuk, Wieromiej

Worosz < Ukr. ворошити [*voroshýty*], "to search, rummage, poke around," cmp. Polish dial. *woroszyć*, "destroy, ruin": Worosz, Woroszyło

Wowk < Ukr. вовк [*vovk*], Blrs. воўк [*vouk*], "wolf," cmp. Polish *wilk*: Wowczuk, Wowk

Zasim- < Orthodox fem. given n. *Zosim,* cmp. Ukr. *Зосим* [*Zósym*]: Zasim, Zasina, Zaśko

Zin- < East Slavic pers. n. *Zin* < given names such as Ukr. *Зенон* [*Zenón*], *Зіновій* [*Zinóviy*], *Зінаїда* [*Zinaïda*], possibly also *Семен* [*Semyén*]: Zin, Zińczuk, Ziniewicz, Zinkiewicz, Zinko, Zinówko

Zub < Czech *zub,* Blrs., Russ., and Ukr. *зуб* [*zub*], all meaning "tooth," cmp. Polish *ząb;* Zub, Zuba, Zubek, Zubik, Zubko, Zubowicz

I said earlier that Russian had relatively little influence on Polish surnames, and I stand by that statement. There is one way, however, in which Russian has affected Polish names. After Russia grabbed much of central and eastern Poland and all of Lithuania during the partitions of 1772, 1793, and 1795, there came a point where the Russian authorities imposed use of the Russian language in official records. As I said on page 163, Russian lacks the *h* sound. So when Russians recorded the documents required of Polish nobles to prove their nobility, they routinely wrote names such as *Horodelski* and *Hodyński* as *Gorodelski* and *Godyński.* When the documents and proclamations recognizing nobility were changed back into Polish, the *g* could be retained by error; even proclamations of the Polish department of heraldry contributed to this mistake. This error was not confined to nobles' names, but it is easiest to find evidence of it in their cases. So when dealing with Polish names from the eastern part of the country, always be aware that *h* and *g* may have been switched somewhere along the line.[31]

Since I've given a list of Germanic and Lithuanian **dithematic name** roots, I probably should include on for Slavic names, as well. Given that this is a book on Polish surnames, I have given preference to the Polish spellings of these roots. There is considerable similarity between the roots as they appear in names of the various Slavic languages. So while Polish forms get the most attention here, those seen in other Slavic tongues, especially Czech and Ukrainian, are also noted whenever possible. Usually, these are simply cross-referenced to the Polish forms, which readers can compare for themselves.

Note, by the way, that not all names can be interpreted in a straightforward manner. Unquestionably, some were meant ironically, and others were meant to mislead evil spirits. For example, parents might have feared they would "jinx" their child if they named him *Dobiesław,* "may he be famed for his bravery." So instead, they called him *Chudosław,* "may his fame be ill." Or maybe these parents just hated their children! However we interpret them, there are among these names those that defy simple explanation.

Each root is printed in ***bold italic*** type, followed by a brief English rendering, "in quotation marks," of its basic meaning. A sampling of names formed with that root follows. Roots preceded by a tilde ˜ were not used in ancient times, but are seen in names of more recent coinage. In this context "recently" can mean "in the Middle Ages," or "in the last few centuries." That may not seem so recent, but the authentic pagan names are at least a thousand years old, some much older—on that scale a mere century or two ago qualifies as "recent."

Finally, let me add that these derivations are based on material in Kazimierz Rymut's book *Nazwiska Polaków* and his article on dithematic names in issue XXXVIII of *Onomastica* (see the Bibliography). If you credit Professor Rymut for those analyzed correctly, and blame me for all errors and misinterpretations, justice will be served!

będ-: "be, become": Będzisław
bel-, biel-: "white, bright": (Czech) Bělboh
bez-, biez-: "without": *Biezdziad*
bliz-: "near, close": Blizbor
bog-, boh-: "god, divinity": Bogdan, Boguchwał, Bogumił, Bogusław, Chwalibóg
bole-: "more, greater": Bolesław
bor-: "battle, fight": Borysław, Borzymierz, Czcibor, Lutobor, Mścibor, Myślibor, Racibor, Sambor, Wszebor
boż-: "divine, of god": Bożydar, Bożymir
brani-: Czech → broni-
brat-, bratr-: "brother": Bratumił, Bratysław, Miłobrat
břěti-: Czech → brzęcz-
brodzi-: "make one's way, pass": Brodzisław
broni-: "defend, protect": Bronimir, Bronisław
brzęcz-: "resound, ring out": Brzęczysław, (Czech) Břetislav
budzi-: "feel, sense": Budzimierz, Budzisław
by-: "be": Bygost
-čaj: Czech → -czaj
često-: Czech → często-
chleb-: "bread": Chleburad
choci-: "desire, want": Chociesław, (*Czech*) Chotibor
chud-: "poor, evil": Chudosław
chwali-: "praise": Chwalibóg, Boguchwał, Chwalimir, Chwalisław
cicho-: "quiet, peaceful": Cichosław, (*Czech*) Tichomir
ciech-: "comfort, joy," Ciechosław, Siciech, Tecław, Wojciech, (Czech) Těchobud
cieci-: "aunt": Ciecierad
ciesz-: "comfort, joy": Cieszysław, Cieszymir
čsti-: Czech → czci-
cza-: "lie in wait for, await": Czasław
-czaj: "wait," used only as a second element: Boleczaj
czarn-: "black": Czarosław
czci-: "honor, worship": Cźcibor, Czcibor, Czcisław
cze-: "honor, worship": Czesław
często-: "numerous": Częstobor

dadz-: "give": Dadzbog
dale-: "farther": Dalebor
dan-: "given": Bogdan, Danisław, [? Donisław]
dar-: "gift": Bożydar, Daromiła, Darosław
děd-: *Czech → dziad-*
divi-: *Czech → dziwi-*
dług-, dluh-: "long": Długomir (*Czech* Dlúhomir), Długosław
dob-: "brave, resourceful": Dobiegniew, Dobiesław (*Czech* Doběslav)
dobr-: "good, kind": Dobrogost, Dobromił, Dobromir, Dobromysł, Dobroniega, Dobrosław
dom-: "house, home": Domarad, Domasław, Domisław
drag-, drog-: "dear, precious": Dragomir, Drogomiła, Drogosław, Drogowit
duch-: "soul, spirit": *(Czech)* Duchoslav
dzi-, dzie-: "put, place": Dzisław
dziad-: "grandfather": Dziadumiła
-dziej: "do," used only as a second element: Dobrodziej
dzierży-: "hold, keep": Dzierżykraj, Dzierżymir, Dzierżysław
dziwi-: "be amazed at": Dziwisław, *(Czech)* Divislav
gard-: "proud, high": Gardomir, *(Czech)* Hrdobor
gniew-: "anger": Dobiegniew, Gniewomir (*Czech* Hněvomir), Gniewosław, Gniewosz, Jarogniew, Lutogniew, Przybygniew, Zbigniew
godzi-: "join, unite, reconcile": Godzimir, Godzisław
gorzy-: "burn, blaze": Gorzysław, *(Czech)* Hořělut
gości-, gost-: "guest": Dobrogost, Gościsław, Miłogost, Radogost
grodzi-: "build": Grodzisław
grom-: "thunder, defeat, rout": Gromosław
~grze-: apparently from the first name *Grzegorz:* Grzesław ("may Greg be famous" [?!])
~grzym-: apparently from the first name *Pielgrzym:* Grzymisław ("may Grzym be famous" [?!])
hněv-: *Czech → gniew-*
hořě-: *Czech → gorzy-*
hrdo-: *Czech → gard-*
imi-: "catch, grasp": Imisław
iz-: "from, take": Izasław
jacz-: "illustrious, mighty": Jacław, *(Czech)* Jačěmir
~jag-: perhaps from first names *Agata* or *Agnieszka:* Jagusława ("[may] Jaga be famous")
~jan-: from first name *Jan:* Janisław ("[may] Jan be famous")
jar-: "sharp, severe": Jarogniew, Jaromił, Jarmiła, Jarochna, Jaromir, Jaropełk, Jarosław, Jarosz
jutro-: "dawn": Jutrowoj
kani-: "invite": Kanimir
kazi-: "destroy": Kazimierz, *(Czech)* Kazislav

-kraj: "country," in Polish always used as a second element: Dzierżykraj
krasi-: "adorn, beautify": *(Czech)* Krasomysl
krzesi-: "waken, stir": Krzesimir, Krzesisław, *(Czech)* Křěsomysl
kvĕt-: Czech → *kwiat-, kwiet-*
˜kwiat-, kwiet-: "bloom, flower": Kwietosława
˜lato-, leto-: "fly," or "summer": Letosław
˜lech-: from the name *Lech:* Lechosław
lęko-: "slyness, artifice": Łękomir, *(Czech)* Boleluk
leli-: "be unsteady": Lelistryj
licho-: "bad, poor": *(Czech)* Lichoľub
lsti-: "deceive, delude": *(Czech)* Lstislav
lubo-: "loved": Lubomił, Lubomir, Lubosław
lud-: "people, folk": Ludmiła, Ludomił, Ludomir, Ludosław
luto-: "harsh, severe": Lutobor, Lutogniew, Lutomił, Lutomir, Lutosław, Zbylut
mąci-: "trouble, disturb": Męcisław
malo-: "little": Małosław (Masław)
mano-: "delude": Manomir
mieci-: "fling": Mieczysław
-mierz: generally a Polish variant of *–mir,* "peace," its form apparently affected by confusion with the Germanic root *mār,* "famed, renowned"
mil-: "dear, beloved, nice": Bogumił, Bratumił, Daromiła, Dobromił, Drogomiła, Jaromił, Jarmiła, Lubomił, Ludmiła, Ludomił, Lutomił, Miłobrat, Miłogost, Miłorad, Miłosław, Ojcumiła, Radomił, Wszemiła
mini-: "pass": Minigniew
mir-: "peace": Borzymierz, Bożymir, Budzimierz, Chwalimir, Cieszymir, Długomir, Dobromir, Dragomir, Dzierżymir, Gniewomir, Godzimir, Jaromir, Kazimierz, Krzesimir, Lubomir, Ludomir, Lutomir, Mirosław, Niemir, Ostromir, Racimierz, Radomir, Sędzimir, Skarbimir, Sławomir, Włodzimierz, Wojmir, Wolimir, Wyszomir
mne-, nnie-: "to me": *(Czech)* Mnetěch
modli-: "pray": Modlibog
moj-: "mine, my": Mojmir
morzy-: "kill": Morzysław
mści-, msti-: "avenge": Mścibor, Mścigniew, Mścisław, Mściwoj
mysl: "thought, mind": Dobromysł, Myślibor, Przemysł, Przemysław
na-: "on, most": Nawojka
nacze-: "to begin": Naczęmir, *(Czech)* Načěpluk
nad-: "on, over": Nadbor
nam-: "to us": *(Czech)* Namgost
nie-: "not": Niemir
˜nieci-: "kindle, arouse, stir": Niecisław
niega: "rapture, bliss": Dobroniega, Niegosław, *(Czech)* Mironega
nino-: "young, new": Ninomysł

nosi: "bear, carry, bring": *(Czech)* Nosislav

o-: "about, concerning": Osięgniew

ojcu-: "to father": Ojcumiła

ostro-: "sharp": Ostromir

ot-: "from, away": Otjęsław *(Czech* Otĕslav)

pacze-, pako-: "greater, more": Pakosław, *(Czech)* Pačeslav, Pakomil

pęci-: "path," Pęcisław *(Serbo-Croatian* Putislav)

-pełk: "regiment, squad," in Polish used only as a second element: Jaropełk, Świętopełk

po-: prefix expressing a greater degree of something (cmp. *po-* in list of Lithuanian roots): Poznamir

pod-: "under, near": Podsąd, *(Czech)* Podhrad

-polk → -pełk

pozdě-: "later": *(Czech)* Pozdĕrad

pře-: Czech → *prze-,* q.v.

přeja-: "take over": *(Czech)* Přejaslav

přiby-: Czech → *przyby-,* q.v.

prosi-: "ask for": Prosimir, *(Czech)* Prosivoj

prosto-: "simple, direct": *(Czech)* Prostomir

prze-: "through, very": Przemysł, Przemysław

przed-: "before": Przecław

przyby-: "come, arrive": Przybyrad, Przybygniew, Przybysław

puti-: Serbo-Croatian → *pęci-*

raci-: "battle, fight, defend": Racibor, Racimierz, Racisław

rad-: "glad, happy": Domarad, Miłorad, Przybyrad, Radogost, Radomił, Radomir, Radosław, Radowit, Świerad

ředi-: Czech → *rzędzi-*

rodo-: "birth, clan": Rodomił, *(Czech)* Rodoslav

rości-, rosti-: "grow": Rościsław

rzędzi-: "rule": Rzędzisław, *(Czech)* Ředivoj

sam-: "alone, self": Sambor

sby-: Czech → *zby-*

sde-: Czech → *zdzi-*

sedl-: Czech → *siedle-*

sędzi-: "to judge": Sędzisław, Sędzimir, Sędziwój, *(Czech)* Slavisúd

semi-: Czech → *siem-*

sestro-: Czech → *siestrze-*

się-: reflexive pronoun, "himself, herself": Nasięgniew

siedle-: "settlement, abode": Siedlewit, *(Czech)* Svésedl

siem-: "person, family": Siemowit, *(Czech)* Sĕmibor

siero-, siro-: "deprived of": Sierosław

siestrze-: "sister": Siestrzemił, *(Czech)* Sestrohor

siro- → siero-, siro-

skarb-: "to sadden, grieve": Skarbimir, *(Czech)* Skarbimir

skotu-: "cattle, livestock": Skoturad

slaw-: "glory, fame, renown": Bolesław, Bogusław, Bolesław, Borysław, Bratysław, Brodzisław, Budzisław, Chwalisław, Cichosław, Ciechosław, Cieszysław, Czarosław, Czcisław, Czesław, Danisław, Darosław, Długosław, Dobiesław, Dobrosław, Domasław, Domisław, Donisław, Drogosław, Dzierżysław, Dzisław, Fredysław, Gniewosław, Godzisław, Gorzysław, Gościsław, Grodzisław, Gromosław, Grzesław, Grzymisław, Irosław, Izasław, Jacław, Jagusława, Janisław, Jarosław, Krzesisław, Kwietosława, Lechosław, Lesław, Letosław, Lubosław, Ludosław, Lutosław, Masław, Mieczysław, Miłosław, Mirosław, Mścisław, Myślisław, Niegosław, Olesław, Pakosław, Przecław, Przemysław, Przybysław, Racisław, Radosław, Renisław, Rościsław, Rosław, Sędzisław, Sierosław, Sławoj, Sławomir, Sobiesław, Stanisław, Strzeżysław, Svetislav, Tecław, Tolisław, Tomisław, Uniesław, Wacław, Więcesław, Warcisław, Wieczysław, Wielisław, Wieńczysław, Wierosław, Wierzchosław, Wisław, Witosław, Władysław, Włodzisław, Wojsław, Wrocisław, Wyszesław, Zbysław, Zdobysław, Zdzisław, Żelisław

sno-: "dream": Snowid

sobie-: "to himself": Sobiesław, *(Czech)* Soběbor

spyci-: "in vain": Spycigniew, *(Czech)* Spytimir

stani-: "become": Stanisław, Stanimir

stoi-: "stand": Stoigniew, *(Czech)* Doběstoj

strach-: "fear": Strachosław

střězi-: *Czech →* **strzeży-**

strogo-: *(Russian)* "severe": Strogobor

stroj-: "build": Strojsław, *(Czech)* Strojimir

stroni-: "evade, escape": Stronisław

stryj-: "[paternal] uncle": Żelistryj, *(Czech)* Strymíl

strzeży-: "guard, keep watch": Strzeżysław

sud-: *Czech →* **sędzi-**

suli-: "promise": Sulisław

sveti-: *Russ. or Ukr. →* **świat-, świeci-**

světi-: *Czech →* **świąt-, święt-**

sviat-: *Russ. or Ukr.* "holy, mighty" → Polish **świąt-, święt-**

svoj-: *Czech →* **swo-, swoj-**

świat-, świeci-: "light, shine": Svetislav, Svetozar

świąt-, święt-: "mighty": Świętosław, Świętopełk, *(Czech)* Světibor

świe-: *→* **wsze-**

swo-, swoj-: "one's own": Swosław, *(Czech)* Svojboh, Svojmir

tatu-: "father": Tatumir

těch-: *Czech →* **ciech-**

tęgo-: "strong, tough": Tęgomir

ticho-: *Czech, Russ. →* **cicho-**

toli-: "quiet, soothe, calm": Tolisław, *(Czech)* Netol

tomi-: "torment": Tomisław (*Czech* Tomislav)

trpi-: "suffer, endure, bear": *(Czech)* Trpislava

trzebo-: "matter, sacrifice," or "necessity": Trzebosław, *(Czech)* Třebobud

tucho-: "courage": *(Czech)* Tuchorad

twardo-: "firm": Twardostoj

tworzy-: "make, create": Tworzymir, *(Czech)* Tvořislava

uby-: "leave": *(Czech)* Ubyčest

unie-: "better": Uniesław, *(Czech)* Uněrad

uści-: "incite, provoke": Uściwoj

vac-: Czech → **więce-**

vadi-: "hinder": *(Czech)* Vadislav

veli-: Czech → **wieli-**

viache-: Russ., Ukr. → **więce-**

vit-: Czech → **wit-**

vlad-: Czech, Russian → **włod-**

vlast-: Czech, Russian → **włości-**

voj-: Czech → **woj-**

volod-: Ukr. → **włod-**

vrati-: Czech → **wraci-, wroci-**

vrcho-: Czech → **wierzch-**

vše-: Czech → **wsze-**

wid-: "see": Snowid, *(Czech)* Dobrowid

więce-: "more, better": Więcesław, Wieczysław [?], Wieńczysław [?], Wiesław [?]

~*wiecz-, wiek-:* "age, century": Wieczysław [?] (it may be a variant of *Wacław*, however, and if so, it's actually quite old)

wieli-: "order, command," or "great": Wielisław (*Czech* Velislav*)*, Wiesław [?]

~*wieńczy-:* "crown": Wieńczysław [?], (it may be a variant of *Wacław*, however, and if so, it's actually quite old)

~*wiero-:* "faith," or perhaps the first name *Wierusz:* Wierosław

wierzch-: "peak, summit": Wierzchosław (*Czech* Vrchoslav)

wit-: "lord, master": Radowit, Drogowit, Wisław, Witosław, Ziemowit, *(Czech)* Vitomir

włod-: "rule": Włodzisław (later became *Władysław* under Czech influence), Włodzimierz, Wsiewołod, *(Czech)* Bohovlad

wlosci-: "rule": Włościbor, *(Czech)* Vlastimil, *(Czech)* Bohuvlast

woj-: "warrior": Wojciech, Mściwoj, Nawojka, Sędziwój, Sławoj, Wojmir, Wojsław

woli-: "want, desire": Wolimir

wraci-, wroci-: "turn, return": Wrocisław *or* Warcisław, *(Czech)* Vratibor, Vraclav

wsze-: "all, whole, totally": Wszemiła, Sieciech, Świerad, Wiesław [?], Wsiewołod, Wszebor, Wszemiła

-wuj: "uncle," in Polish used only as a second element: Radowuj
wysze-: "higher": Wyszesław, Wyszomir
za-: "past, by, to": Zabor, *(Czech)* Zahost
zby-: "dispense with": Zbigniew, Zbylut, Zbysław, *(Czech)* Sbyrad
~zdoby-: "win, achieve": Zdobysław
zdzi-: "lay, set down, place": Zdzisław, *(Czech)* Sdebor
żeli-: "wish, wish for": Żelisław
żil-: "live": *(Czech)* Domažil
žit-: Czech → *żyt-*
zna-: "know": Znamir
żyro-: "feed": Żyrosław, *(Czech)* Svojžir
żyt-: "live": *(Czech)* Žitomir

Other (French, Italian, Latin, etc.)

As early as King Mieszko, Polish leaders made a conscious effort to keep in touch with what was going on in France, Italy, and other centers of western European civilization. Poland's allegiance to the Roman Catholic Church helped insure that Poland's intellectual life was tied in with that of western Europe. So there was a flow of people and ideas and culture back and forth, and thus one finds Polish names that originated as words or names in French, Italian, Latin, and so forth.

There are not a great many French-derived surnames in Poland, but they do exist, although they have usually been polonized past easy recognition. Bystroń cites a few: *Cordeille → Kordyl, Descourt → Deskur, du Puget → Poszet, de Beaulieu → Deboli,* the son of *de Lesseur* was called *Lesserowicz,* and so on.[32]

As for Italians, over the centuries there has been quite a respectable Italian contingent in Poland. In the Middle Ages it was not at all uncommon to send young Poles to Italian cities to be educated, and for centuries the ultimate recognition of a Catholic seminarian or priest's potential has been to send him to Rome for training. There was also an influential contingent of Italian scholars, architects, artists, diplomats, and craftsmen who came to Poland in the 16th and 17th centuries, beginning during the reign of King Zygmunt I. Zygmunt, whose third wife was Bona Sforza of Milan, was a patron of the arts and culture, and he and his wife made Poland, and especially Kraków, a welcome destination for gifted Italians. Though not large in numbers, these Italians contributed a great deal to Polish culture during that period.[33]

So historically, the links between Poland and Italy have been stronger than one might have expected, and one result is the presence in Polish of at least a few Italian-derived surnames. Some examples are: *Gianotti → Dzianott, Burattini → Boratyni, Gucci → Guczewski* (just tell people your elegant items of apparel are original Guczewskis!), *de Bianco → Debianko-*

wicz. Other names of Italian origin may be harder to recognize because their literal meaning was translated into Polish, e.g., *Montelupi* → *Wilczogórski,* etc.[34] (Please recognize, however, that not every *Wilczogórski* must have come from Italy—"Wolf Mountain" is a toponym that can be found all over Europe in many different languages).

Since Latin was the language of culture and learning wherever the Roman Catholic Church was found, it is not surprising that a few Polish names trace directly back to Latin words. An obvious one is *Magnus,* from the Latin word meaning "great"; this was a term much in evidence when addressing nobility. But there are also names of much humbler origin. *Sartor,* for instance, is the Latin word for "tailor," in Polish *krawiec.* In old records kept in Latin, one can sometimes see a word like *sartor,* a description of occupation, in the process of becoming used as a second name, so that a person might be described as *sartor* in Latin and *krawiec* in the vernacular. Within a generation or two *krawiec* could become the surnames *Krawiec, Krawiecki, Krawczyk,* etc. The same thing could have happened with *Sartor.*

One Latin-derived surname I find particularly fascinating is *Kulpa,* which Prof. Rymut says comes from Latin *culpa,* "guilt, fault." At first I wondered how on earth this word became a Polish surname, but I think I have an idea. Even the humblest Polish peasants went to Mass fairly often (herded into church by order of nobles who wanted their subjects steeped in Christian humility and obedience). They must have heard many times a phrase from the *Confiteor* that is familiar to any Catholic old enough to remember the Latin Mass: *"mea culpa, mea culpa, mea maxima culpa"* (through my fault, through my fault, through my most grievous fault). This is one Latin phrase even the most ignorant Catholic used to know, and a repentant sinner may have used this word, voluntarily or not, as a byname or surname. This is all speculation on my part, but it strikes me as plausible.

Summary

I trust you realize that a scholar deeply interested in the subject of names could take virtually any paragraph in this chapter and produce a whole book dealing with the points made, complete with indications of where I have erred or oversimplified. But I think that would be going into deeper waters than you really care to venture into at this point; if you do want to try the deep end of the pool, there are always the books listed in Chapter Twelve. I simply hope these brief discussions have given you insights into the names and languages of the many people who, whatever their *gente,* were all *natione Poloni.*

Endnotes

[1] Iwo Cyprian Pogonowski, *Poland: A Historical Atlas,* revised edition, Dorset Press, New York, 1989, p. 46.

[2] *Encyklopedia Popularna PWN,* Państwowe Wydawnictwo Naukowe, Warszawa, 1982, pp. 603-606.

[3] Thomas L. Hollowak, *The Rise of Independency Among Baltimore's Polish Catholics, 1868-1898,* M.A. thesis submitted to the Graduate School of the University of Maryland, 1990, pp. 16ff.

[4] Kazimierz Rymut, *Nazwiska Polaków,* Wydawnictwo Naukowe DWN, Kraków, 2001, Volume I, p. LXXI.

[5] Bystroń, *Nazwiska Polskie,* pp. 178ff.

[6] Ibid., p. 180.

[7] Ibid., p. 186.

[8] Ibid., pp. 186-187.

[9] Ibid., pp. 188-189.

[10] Rymut, *Nazwiska Polaków,* p. LXXIII.

[11] Andrzej Bańkowski, *Etymologiczny słownik języka polskiego,* Wydawnictwo Naukowe DWN, Warszawa, 2000, Volume 1, page 513.

[12] Alexander Beider, "Jewish Surnames in the Russian Empire," *Avotaynu,* Fall 1992, pp. 4-7.

[13] Benzion C. Kaganoff, *A Dictionary of Jewish Names and Their History,* Schocken Books, New York, 1977, pp. 56-57.

[14] Rabbi Shmuel Gorr, *Jewish Personal Names: Their Origin, Derivation and Diminutive Forms,* Avotaynu, Inc., Teaneck, New Jersey, 1992, pp. 18, 36.

[15] Beider, "Jewish Surnames," p. 6. I have taken the liberty of giving these names in their most common Polish spellings rather than as in the article cited, because the Polish spellings seem more relevant here than the transliterated Russian renderings given in the *Avotaynu* piece. For accuracy, I checked the spellings Beider gave for these names in *A Dictionary of Jewish Surnames from the Kingdom of Poland.* In that book, he spells names Polish-style; whereas in his *Dictionary of Jewish Surnames from the Russian Empire,* he renders names in English phonetic spellings of their Russian forms. In *A Dictionary of Jewish Surnames from Galicia,* he gives names in their German spelling, but notes the Polish versions whenever appropriate.

[16] Kaganoff, *A Dictionary of Jewish Names.,* pp. 24-27.

[17] Bystroń, *Nazwiska Polskie,* pp. 254-257.

[18] Beider, "Jewish Surnames," p. 1.

[19] Bystroń, *Nazwiska Polskie,* pp. 57-58.

[20] Ibid., p. 177.

[21] Rev. Antanas Saulaitis, S.J., "*Genealogija* Profile," and "Lithuanian Personal Names: Brief History," *Genealogija,* Summer, 1992, pp. 6-8.

[22] Cited courtesy of Mr. David Zincavage—who points out that his own surname is an Anglicized form of *Sienkiewicz* (or perhaps *Zienkiewicz*), a patronymic ultimately from the name *Simon.*

[23] Prof. Casimir Dobilas, "What's so different about Lithuanian women? (Their names, of course!)," *Lithuanian Heritage,* Sept./Oct. 1995, p. 22.

²⁴ Rima Medelis, "Women's Names," *Lithuanian Heritage,* May/June 1996, p. 16.

²⁵ Rima Medelis, "Using Two Personal Names," *Lithuanian Heritage,* Sept./ Oct. 1995, p. 18.

²⁶ This derivation, and the analysis of **Dowgird,** are based on material from the Instytut Języka Polskiego, Pracownia Antroponomiczna, by Prof. Aleksandra Cieślikowa and kindly shared by Mr. Zincavage.

²⁷ Rymut, *Nazwiska Polaków*, p. LXIX.

²⁸ Bystroń, *Nazwiska polskie*, p. 174.

²⁹ Jeff Picknicki, "The Origin and Meaning of Ukrainian Surnames," *Polish Genealogical Society Newsletter,* Spring 1990, pp. 3ff.

³⁰ Ibid., p. 6.

³¹ Bystroń, *Nazwiska polskie,* p. 143. Also for more on the influence Russian sometimes had on Polish names, see Jonathan D. Shea & William F. Hoffman, *In Their Words: A Genealogist's Translation Guide to Polish, German, Latin, and Russian Documents, Volume II: Russian,* Language & Lineage Press, New Britain CT, 2002, especially pp. 10–13 and 23–29.

³² *Ibid.,* pp. 194-195.

³³ A particularly good introduction to the subject of Italians in Poland is the chapter on Italians by Wojciech Tygielski in the book *Pod wspólnym niebem: Narody dawnej Rzeczypospolitej,* ed. Michał Kopczyński and Wojciech Tygielski, Museum of Polish History in Warsaw and Bellona SA, Warszawa, 2010. ISBN 978-83-11-11724-2. A translation in English is expected to be published in 2013.

³⁴ *Ibid.,* p. 105.

Chapter Ten:

"I'm a Pole, Not a Polack!"

I know that to many Polish-Americans, "Polack" is an extremely offensive word, and I hope my use of it here will not anger them. Obviously I would not devote this much time and trouble to writing a book on the names of people I want to insult. I am hoping it is obvious, therefore, that I'm using the term here to make a point. For Poles, there is no prouder boast then the simple statement *"Jestem Polakiem!"*—I am a Pole! It's a dirty shame that in this country, ignorance and bigotry turned the Poles' own name for themselves, *Polak,* into a slur!

This is not the only English word for Poles that began as a simple name and became a taunt. In a 1907 scholarly paper article on Polish settlers in Portage County, Wisconsin, historian Albert Hart Sanford made an interesting comment: "As German children dislike being called 'Dutchman,' so Polish children are tormented by the use of the word 'Polack' or 'Polander.' The latter word has come to have a peculiar accent, 'Po´-land´-er,' which carries with it insinuation of disrespect, implying social inferiority. The word is, however, in good usage; but one avoids employing it in polite conversation with intelligent Poles."[1]

What this shows, of course, is that what bothers people is not so much the word itself as the way it's used. No one in his right mind would get upset with Shakespeare for writing in *Hamlet* (Act I, Scene I, lines 60-63): "Such was the very armor he had on/ When he the ambitious Norway combated;/ So frowned he once, when, in an angry parle,/ He smote the sledded Polacks on the ice." While some say this line reads "smote the sleaded Pollax on the ice," referring to a leaded pole-ax, there are numerous other references in the play to "Polacks"—Hamlet's father had fought the Poles, and Fortinbras is doing so as the play unfolds—and it's clear Shakespeare was using the word in the simple, non-judgmental meaning of "Poles." That's probably how "Polander" started, too. But after Polish immigrants noticed a few dozen times the tone and expression of Americans when they said "Polack" or "Polander," they did not have to speak English fluently to realize they were being treated with contempt. And being Poles, they wouldn't put up with it!

I would like to quote a rather long passage from the Albert Sanford paper mentioned earlier because I think it raises many points that are valid for the Polish-American experience in general:

> All authorities agree that the Polish farmer has opened to cultivation areas that would not have been touched by other nationalities, and that he thrives and advances from poverty to prosperity on lands where American farmers would starve... The high birth-rate among

the Poles and the desire of the majority of the Polish young men to own land, renders certain the continuance of this process. Moreover, the Poles display good business foresight in purchasing farms, very often giving a mortgage which they almost uniformly redeem.

We have here an interesting instance of a stock possessing lower standards and greater industrial efficiency displacing other stocks who are unwilling to pay the price necessary to obtain equal results. There is undoubtedly a tendency on the part of the Poles to adopt higher standards, but this fact does not as yet seem to render them less able to supersede their neighbors.

So far, so good. Poles are industrious and thrifty—hardly observations anyone could object to.

Another strong influence besides the purely economic one works in the same direction. This is social in nature. The concentration of Polish farmers in parts of Portage County is evidence of a clannish spirit, which is more marked in this than in other nationalities. The Polish ward of Stevens Point gives evidence of the same spirit. This is also seen in the fact that intermarriage between Poles and other nationalities is quite uncommon. The separateness of the Polish people is likewise marked in their failure to mingle socially with people of other nationalities. They show little desire for this kind of intercourse. The feeling of their non-Polish neighbors also acts as a barrier to the free and natural mingling of these classes upon an equal social basis. This fact stands in strong contrast to the freedom with which the German, Irish, Norwegian, and English intermingle and intermarry. When asked why this difference exists, the non-Polish farmer answers, "The Poles are different from the rest of us," or, "They are an inferior class of people," or, again, "We have nothing against the Poles, but we do not like them." While there seems to be little reluctance to conduct business with the Poles, there exists little social sympathy on either side. As a result of these conditions, non-Polish farmers are more willing to sell out to the Poles when they become numerous in their neighborhood...

Reading this, you can't help getting a bit angry, but you don't know who to get angry at. The historian is reporting the state of affairs as he sees it, there's no point getting mad at him. But those non-Polish farmers—did it ever occur to them that Poles' clannishness was the result, and not the cause, of the way they were being treated? Sanford goes on to say:

Because of this clannish spirit, also, the process of Americanization among the Poles is slow. The national feeling is strong and it is fostered by their church. The Poles are noted for their faithful adherence to the Roman Catholic Church, and the history of their spread in Portage County indicates the remarkable activity of the church in caring for their needs. The church does not encourage the social intermingling of Poles with non-Poles, and it discourages their intermarriage.

Any discussion of Poles is going to mention religion sooner or later. Whether immigrants from Poland were devoted followers of the Roman Catholic Church, or adherents of the Polish National Catholic Church, or Protestants, or Jews, religion always seems to be a guiding star of their lives. So was use of the Polish language, as Sanford continues:

Adherence to the use of the Polish language is another evidence of racial conservatism, and this also is encouraged by the church. The parochial schools constitute a force working in the same direction. In the country parishes but a small portion of the time in school hours is given to studies involving the use of the English language; but in the parochial school in Stevens Point, English is employed to a great extent. In the city the Polish language is going out of use much faster than in the country. It is a common statement that the language is being corrupted, and that no one, not even the priest, can speak pure Polish. A recent arrival from Warsaw, who is a university graduate, makes this statement emphatically. In some of the remote country parishes, however, children are growing up without the ability to speak the English language. It is a common occurrence to have adults sworn in this country, who are testifying in court, ask for an interpreter. On the other hand, there are numbers of Polish children in Stevens Point who cannot speak Polish; sometimes the latter are ashamed to be known as Poles among their playmates in the public schools, and so purposely avoid learning the language of their forefathers.

An American tendency which is frowned upon by some of the Polish priests is that of altering surnames to make them more easy of pronunciation. Generally, the owner of an Americanized name continues to be known by his original surname among his fellow countrymen.[2]

If you had to choose one text to provide a capsule illustration of the Polish experience in America, these paragraphs would serve as well as any. Hard work, clannishness, the Church, the language—pretty much a roll call of the features other Americans have found prominent among Polish immigrants. Of course, things have changed since 1907; usually by the second and certainly the third generation, the children of Polish immigrants had become thoroughly Americanized. But if you want a picture of what your ancestors had to deal with, I think this text provides a fairly accurate one.

Even more illuminating, in my opinion, is what can be read between the lines. I don't mean to malign Sanford—he was apparently an intelligent man who felt admiration for the people he was writing about—yet some of his comments just seem to rub the wrong way. Granted, it's not fair to judge a 1907 text by the hypertrophied sensitivities of today. But I do think it's interesting how the sentiments long connected with the issue of immigration in America find expression, albeit genteel and refined, in this passage. What I hear behind his matter-of-fact, non-judgmental observations, are whispers echoing in the background, the things coarser and crueler people said. He speaks of "the high birth-rate among the Poles," but I seem to hear others saying "They breed like rabbits." He speaks of the Poles' clannishness, but you know there were those who complained "They all stick together, they think they're too good for us." He discusses Poles' retention of the Polish language, but I hear mutters of "Why can't they learn English?" He points out Poles' devotion to the Catholic Church, but is there any question some railed against "those Papists and their outlandish religion"? And unfortunately, these are sentiments Poles—and most other immigrant groups—have had to contend with in America.

Of course, it would be naïve of us to think some immigrants, including Poles, didn't do the same thing once they got a toehold in American society. The comedian Billy Crystal has a good line about his grandfather's attitude. He has a mental picture of his grandfather at Ellis Island: as soon as they let him in, Crystal says, he can see his grandfather turning around and yelling in a thick accent, "All right, all you foreign bastards, get the hell out of here!"

Well, the subject of this book is Polish surnames, not the social and cultural history of Poles in America—and as you may have noticed, I got back on track by ending the quotation from Sanford with a reference to Polish surnames. So let's get back to talking about them. But first, for anyone who'd like to read more on the subject of Polish-American history, here is a brief list of some works specialists in the field have written:

Bukowczyk, John J., *A History of the Polish Americans*, revised edition, Transaction Publishers, New Brunswick (U.S.A.) and London (U.K.), 2998, ISBN 978-1412806800, Library of Congress Catalog Number 2008015351. As of this writing, it is also available as an eBook from Google Books, and much of the book can be previewed online <http://books.google.com/books/about/A_History_of_the_Polish_Americans.html?id=_YIlKNT2F7MC>.

Kruszka, Wacław, *A History of the Poles in America to 1908,* edited, with an introduction by James S. Pula; translated by Krystyna Jankowski; associate editors, M. B. Biskupski & Stanley Cuba; assistant editors, T. Lindsay Baker... (*et al.*). Washington, D.C.: Catholic University of America Press, © 1993-, ISBN 081320772X. The original work was in Polish *(Historya Polska w Ameryce)* and comprised 13 volumes, the first five with topical chapters providing an overview of Polonia, the rest providing information on local Polish American settlements in each area of the country. I have not seen this English-language edition, which appears to be an ongoing publication, but since it is so recent it should be relatively easy to find.

Obidinski, Eugene Edward, and Zand, Helen Stankiewicz, *Polish Folkways in America: Community and Family (Polish Studies Series, Vol. 1)*, paperback, University Press of America, 1987, ISBN 978-0819158819.

Pacyga, Dominic A., *Polish Immigrants and Industrial Chicago: Workers on the South Side, 1880-1922*, University of Chicago Press, 2003, ISBN 9780226644240. Much of it can be previewed with Google Books <http://books.google.com/books/about/Polish_Immigrants_and_Industrial_Chicago.html?id=pSPzsIKMO44C>.

Thomas, William I., and Znaniecki, Florian, *The Polish Peasant in Europe and America*, Vol. I, xv + 1115 pp., Vol. II, 1135 pp., with an index.[3]

Wytrwal, Joseph Anthony, *Poles in American History and Tradition*, (1st ed.) Endurance Press, 1969.

Zaretsky, Eli, ed., *The Polish Peasant in Europe and America, William Thomas and Florian Znaniecki: A Classic Work in Immigration History*, Urbana: University of Illinois Press, 1996, ISBN: 9780252064845, 152 pp. If you can't get hold of Thomas and Znaniecki's original work, this selection of abstracts from it should be available and affordable. Some selections can be previewed with Google Books <http://books.google.com/books/about/The_Polish_Peasant_in_Europe_and_America.html?id=HOLITuv6UvkC>.

In recent years, far more information has become available on this subject—not just books, but websites, newsgroups, groups on Facebook, and so on. I doubt I need to tell you that an online search for "Polish American history" will give you far more resources to work with than just the ones mentioned above. If you want to get off to a good start studying the subject, however, I believe consulting some or all of these works will prove helpful.

Notes on Polish Names in America

I don't have to tell you that Polish names intimidate Americans. Someone once wrote to ask me how to pronounce the name *Chrząszcz,* and I was tempted to answer, "Don't even try if you're not Polish!" Even if the spelling didn't baffle us, the Poles routinely combine sounds that simply do not go together in English. To pronounce *Chrząszcz* correctly, you have to put together the light guttural sound of Polish *ch* (kind of like an *h* with attitude) + the *rz* sound (as of "zh" in *Zhivago*) + the nasal "on" sound of *ą* + the "sh" sound of *sz* + the "ch" sound of *cz,* and there you have it: "hzho[n]shch." This is enough to make an American recoil in horror; yet a Pole would say "It's pronounced just the way it's spelled," and he'd mean it! Poles grow up hearing and making these sounds constantly, and it's a little hard for them to understand why anyone else would have trouble doing so.

I should add that in my experience, many Poles do realize their language is hard for foreigners to learn; I think more than a few take pride in that fact. I have heard some say, "The only people smart enough to be able to speak Polish are the Poles!" If you're interested in one attempt to quantify how hard Polish is to learn, in comparison with other languages, this Wikibooks item may interest you: <http://en.wikibooks.org/wiki/Language_Learning_ Difficulty_for_English_Speakers>.

It seems to me one reason Polish is difficult for English-speakers to master is that there's a fundamentally different approach to language at work here. English and the other Germanic languages have a preference for short, simple words. Winston Churchill understood this; notice how his most memorable lines bristle with short words that pack a punch. We instinctively dislike wordy statements—"It would be advisable for us to consider an immediate relocation from this particular locality" is downright comical compared to "Let's get outta here!" It seems to me Slavs, on the other hand, enjoy the act of pronouncing the words in their languages. They see absolutely no reason to truncate everything into short grunts. To a Pole, such names as *Fred* and *Joe* and *Jim* seem rather flat and colorless, far less majestic than names that roll off the tongue, such as *Bolesław* and *Stanisław* and *Wojciech*. It's to be expected that confusion would result when a Pole came to a country where English predominates and told the locals "My name's Brzeszczyński, it's spelled just like it sounds!"

Richard Coski of Ashtabula, Ohio once submitted to the *Bulletin* of the Polish Genealogical Society of America® an interesting story about how his family's surname was changed. He wrote: "The original spelling of the surname was *Niedzialkowski* when my paternal grandfather had joined the U. S. Cavalry and was assigned duty out West after the Indian Wars. The company paymaster sergeant had so much trouble pronouncing *Niedzialkowski* that he abruptly took the opportunity to tell my grandfather, 'If you expect to get paid, your name is *Coski* from now on.' My grandmother had to officially change her surname in court in order to collect the Army widows pension after my grandfather's death (ca. 1936). Of course, like most immigrants, he used both *Coski* and *Niedzialkowski* after leaving the cavalry, depending on the situation at the time."[4] Family stories such as this often prove inaccurate, but there's no reason to doubt this one. This sort of thing surely happened again and again as Polish names collided with Americans' linguistic habits.

In fact, surnames weren't the only ones to get mangled; first names didn't always survive the collision intact, either. I've never forgotten how, years ago, researcher Kathi White in Buffalo told me of a machinist named "Hieronim Kaczmarek" who ended up being listed in the 1910 Buffalo city directory as "Heroin"! There's no reason to think anyone was trying to be unkind or uncooperative here; this sort of thing will happen when people struggle with unfamiliar names.

More Manglings, Intentional and Otherwise

I can recall an example from recent experience. A friend of mine, a born-and-bred American, has occasionally traveled on business to the town of Odolanów in Wielkopolskie province. His ancestry is Slovak, so it's not as if Slavic names are utterly unfamiliar to him. Now, the correct way to pronounce *Odolanów* sounds roughly like "oh-doe-lawn´-oof"; the accent is on the next-to-last syllable, and the first two *o* sounds are halfway between the *o* in English "on" and the one in English "owe." My friend, a very intelligent man, has been in Odolanów, surrounded by Poles pronouncing the name correctly again and again—but every time he refers to it, he calls it "oh´-duh-luh-now"! Obviously he saw the name written down many times before he ever went there, and his English-influenced speech patterns imprinted that pronunciation in his brain. He hasn't changed it, despite having been there and heard the name pronounced correctly. He even does it around me, and he knows I'm a bit of a nut regarding Polish names (he regards that as a strange but essentially harmless quirk of my personality). It's not lack of intelligence or empathy that dictates his way of saying this word. It's just that ingrained linguistic habits are hard to break!

Sometimes Polish names changed in America simply because Poles got tired of fighting to make people say their names right, or found it advisable for business reasons to use a name people could pronounce and remember. Many a name just changed by force of repeated and consistent mispronunciation, so that Polish *Sądowski* ("sond-off´-skee") became *Sandusky* because that's the closest Americans could get to the original. I often find that once you do figure out what the original name was and compare it to the form it evolved to in this country, it becomes very clear how and why it changed. But that sort of deduction doesn't work so well backwards: having the changed form, and trying to decipher the original form from it, frequently gets you nowhere.

Also, some Poles undoubtedly changed their names on purpose. Consider this: many of them left Europe because they were starving, or they wanted to avoid serving in the military forces of the hated Russians or Prussians or Austrians. After all, why should Poles get shot just because the Kaiser and Tsar were having a tiff? Well, they knew deportation from the United States back to Europe was a real possibility. I'm sure some of them realized that, if they gave their right names and places of origin, they might very well end up right back where they started from—maybe starving, maybe hearing a sadistic Russian officer say, "So, smart boy, you thought you could dodge our draft, did you? You'll love Siberia!" This gave them incentive to lie a little about their names and homes, and you have to figure some of them did so.

I also have heard of several cases where one member of a family quarreled with the others, and changed his name so he wouldn't be associated with them any more! Sometimes the change was minor, maybe *Grabowicz* to *Grabowski*. Sometimes it was major, a completely different name. I don't know how often this happened, but I know it did happen sometimes.

I'm sure there are other factors I've overlooked, but this brief list explains to some extent why we often find our names difficult to trace. When I think about it, maybe we should be amazed, and grateful, that our ancestral names aren't harder to find!

I hear quite often from researchers who suspect the names they have are incorrect and want to know what the original Polish forms were. Sometimes I can help them, as my experience and familiarity with Polish phonetics and naming patterns will suggest a likely match. "Barshodziej" immedi- ately calls to mind *Bartodziej;* "Dabrovolskytes" is probably a slightly mis- spelled form of Lithuanian *Dabrovolskaitė*, from Lithuanian *Dabrovolskas* or *Dobrovolskas*, adapted from Polish *Dobrowolski* or Belarusian equivalents such as *Дабровольскі* or *Дабравальскі*. Other times, the names are just so distorted that I can't come up with one likely candidate. Very often, there is no exact match, but numerous names are close enough to be possibilities. Several names could end up as "Krisncszyn," for instance, but no one stands out as the best choice.

If you have one of those mangled names, the best practical advice I can give is to move heaven and earth to get the most accurate spelling you can! I know that's easier said than done—trying to read the writing in records is an art in itself—but getting the right form of the name is important. Most researchers come up with three or four spellings of what's clearly the same name. Keep all of them, compare records, and try to use the information in this book to eliminate unlikely spellings.

And if I may give a bit of advice, at the risk of outraging people who paid good money for this book, focus more on the name of the **place** your ances- tors came from. The right forms of your ancestral surnames are valuable; but the right name of the place where they were born or lived is essential. That's because in most areas, whether in Poland or elsewhere, the records of most value to genealogists were drawn up and kept locally. If you know the right place, you can hope to access local records, either through online sources or a trip to the locality. Then chances are good you will spot your relatives, whether you have their surname right or not, just by going through the entries and looking for names and dates that fit. But if all you have is a surname, it's like you're wandering around all over Poland, asking plaintively "Does any- one know where my Kowalski ancestors are?" Good luck with that!

Back to surnames. In Volume II there are occasional notes to help you with questions about name forms and spelling; and the notes on pages 11–12 and on page 196 may be useful. Just don't give up! What seems hopeless today may clear up tomorrow—but only if you keep plugging away.

You Can Be a Phonetic Detective!

While I can't cover every possible eventuality, I can offer a few pointers that will help you recognize many clues for a suspected variant spelling when you encounter them. We all like to play detective—here's your chance!

First and foremost, never use your eyes alone on surnames. Always bring your voice and your ears in to work on the case. Your eyes, unaided, are not likely to penetrate the disguise *Antonavage* is wearing. But if your voice and ears have practiced a bit of Polish pronunciation and you say that name out loud, you may hear the similarity to *Antoniewicz*. Similarly, saying *Yastrzemski* and *Jastrzębski* ("yahss-chemp´-skee") out loud makes the connection easier to grasp. Try to pronounce the American form of the name by Polish phonetic values, and say double vowels separately, so that *Zaenz* or *Zaiontz* sound like "zah´-enz, zah´-yonts" and lead you to *Zając.*

Granted, you may overdo it and end up linking American names with Polish words that have no actual relationship with each other. But your research will give you clues which associations are right and which are wrong. Just write down your chief suspects and then see if any of them show up in your family's records. To beat my detective analogy to death, make the forms appearing in the records stand in a line-up, and see if any match the description you've drawn up of the perpetrator.

Finally, cultivate an awareness of correlations between American spellings and Polish forms. Vowels are hard to pin down, but consonants tend to follow certain patterns, dictated by similarity of sound. Polish *cz* → English *m* or *l* would be a pretty weird change; but Polish *cz* → English *ch, sh,* even *j* is more than possible. An eye (and ear!) for these patterns will suggest that *Korchmar* just might come from Polish *Karczmarz.*

Those experienced in genealogical research will recognize what I am describing as the principles behind the development of Soundex systems. There are several of these, and they all work on the notion of coding a name into a number predicated on similar consonant sounds; a name that has the same code number as another is a possible variation of that name. The whole point of these systems is to bypass the vagaries of human spelling by concentrating on the more stable elements of the original pronunciations. Particularly interesting is the Daitch-Mokotoff Soundex System; designed primarily for work with Jewish surnames, it's not perfect for Polish phonetics, but is still better than just guessing. It is described and used in such Avotaynu publications as Beider's *Dictionary of Jewish Surnames from the Kingdom of Poland.* Even better is Beider-Morse Phonetic Matching <http://stevemorse.org/phonetics/bmpm.htm>. Such systems can help a frustrated researcher enormously.

For those who don't want to delve into Soundex systems, I have listed a few common variation patterns below. I'm sure I've overlooked some, but then you wouldn't want me to hog all the fun, would you? Draw up your own list, and pretty soon you'll be the resident expert on Polish surnames!

VARIANT SPELLINGS DUE TO FOREIGN INFLUENCES

Possible Equivalents

Polish *ą* → German *an,on*
    English *a, on, om*

Polish *c* → German *z, tz*
    English *ts*
Polish *ć, cz* → German *tsch*
    English *ch, g*

Polish *ch* → English *h*
Polish *d* → English *t*
Polish *dzi* → English *j*
Polish *ę* → English *am, an, em, en*
Polish *h* → English *g*
Polish *j* → English *i, y*
Polish *k* → English *c*
Polish *ł* → English *l*
    (sometimes just omitted)
Polish *ó* → English *o, u*
Polish *ów* → German *au*
Polish *rz* → English *r, sh, zh*
Polish *ś, sz* → English *s, s[c]h*

Polish *w* → English *f[f], v*
    (also omitted sometimes)
Polish *z, ś, ż* → English *r, s, z*

Examples

Łączek → German **Lontzek**
Rączko → English **Ronczko**
Sądowski → English **Sandusky**
Racław → German **Ratzlaff**
Płock → English **Plotsk**
Karczmarz → German **Kretschmer**
Czerwiński → English **Chervinsky**
Bartosiewicz → Engl. **Bertasavage**
Chojnacki → English **Hojnacki**
Radkowski → English **Ratkowski**
Kędziorski → English **Kanjorski**
Rękosiak → English **Renkosiak**
Halicz → English **Galich**
Jastrzębski → English **Yastrzemski**
Katkiewicz → English **Catcavage**
Jabłoński → English **Yablonski**
Jabłczyński → English **Yabchinsky**
Jaskólski → English **Jaskulski**
Kraków → German **Krakau**
Rzeźnik → Engl. **Resnick, Reznick**
Oświęcim → German **Auschwitz**
Szymański → English **Shimansky**
Warszawa → English **Warsaw**
Grabów → Engl./German **Graboff**
Lewandowski → Engl. **Levandosky**
Żelichowo → English **Selchow**
Zubrzycki → English **Subritzky**

Endnotes

[1] Albert Hart Sanford, M.A., "Polish People of Portage County," from a copy of *Proceedings, 1907,* Wisconsin Historical Society, reprinted in the Fall 1988 and Spring 1989 issues of the *Polish Genealogical Society Newsletter;* this excerpt is footnote 25 on page 12 of the Spring 1989 issue. As of this writing, the article is available online at <http://content. wisconsinhistory.org/u?/tp,47161>.

[2] Ibid., p. 12. See pages 280–283 in the original article online.

[3] This information comes from an article by Jean Jurkiewicz in the Fall 1991 issue of the *Polish Genealogical Society Newsletter.*

[4] "Polish Surnames," *Bulletin,* Polish Genealogical Society of America®, Fall, 1994, p. 8.

Chapter Eleven:

"You Want Polish Names? How About 341,055 of Them!"

Kazimierz Rymut began his 1991 first edition of *Nazwiska Polaków* by pointing out a problem for students of Polish onomastics: "Writing a work on the surnames used in Poland, even a popular-educational work such as this, is neither simple nor easy. What surnames do Poles use today? We do not know. To this point, there has been no compilation of contemporary surnames."[1]

His point was well taken. I can say from experience, it was frustrating to work on the first edition of this book without knowing which names were common and which were rare. All names are important, of course, especially if they're yours! But if I had some firm indication of whether a particular name was borne by 10 people or 10,000, I could better concentrate my efforts on explaining those most likely to interest my readers. Also, data on distribution would reveal at a glance which names were concentrated in a particular area and which were widespread throughout Poland. That, in turn, may tell you something useful about their meanings and origins.

When he wrote those words, Rymut probably knew he was to head a project that would solve the problem he pointed out. In 1992, the first volumes appeared of the *Słownik nazwisk współcześnie w Polsce używanych*, "Dictionary of Surnames in Current Use in Poland." (In some ways, I prefer "directory" as a translation of *słownik* in this particular title. But "dictionary" is the standard English rendering of *słownik*, so perhaps using that translation is less confusing). The finished work filled ten volumes and listed a total of 811,720 "linguistic units," as Rymut once called them, because many of the names were obviously minor variants of other, more common names. It represented a significant contribution to the field of Polish onomastics.

Rymut had been allowed access to the database of PESEL (*Powszechny Elektroniczny System Ewidencji Ludności*, Universal Electronic System for Registration of the Population), and that was the source of his compilation. All Polish citizens are assigned a PESEL identification number (somewhat like our Social Security number) for use in applying for passports, medical care, tax declarations, etc. Rymut was allowed to use data on surnames and province of residence only, current up to the end of 1990.[2] The *Słownik nazwisk* listed each surname in the database, the total number of times it appeared, and gave a breakdown of its distribution among Poland's 49 *województwa* or provinces during the period 1975-1989.

Naturally, shortly before Rymut started work, the Polish administrative setup was radically redesigned, with the 49 provinces transformed into 16; the new setup went into effect in 1990. Rymut decided it would be less confusing to use the still familiar 1975–1989 provinces, rather than deal with the new setup while people were still getting used to it.

This set of books attracted a lot of attention, and not just from linguists and onomasticians. I think Rymut was a little surprised just how much attention his work received from genealogists. Within a few years of the books' publication, the Dom Polonii in Pułtusk received Rymut's permission to make the books' data available online via a searchable database at <http://www.herby.com.pl/indexslo.html>. The search options included use of wild cards, ? to stand for any one letter, * to stand for any combination of letters. These options greatly facilitated using the database. Then Tomasz Nitsch of Genpol.com created an applet that would take data from the Dom Polonii site and generate a map illustrating the data <http://genpol.com/module-Mapa.htm>. The searchable database and Tomasz Nitsch's map applet are both still functioning as of this writing, and can be very helpful to researchers who take the time to figure out how they work.

As I said, the 10-volume set listed 811,720 surnames; but that number is misleading. I quoted it in previous editions largely to give people some idea why I couldn't possibly hope to include every Polish surname in this book. It's instructive to take a look at a sample page *Słownik nazwisk*.

This map shows the 49 województwa of Poland during the period 1975–1989 and gives the abbreviated names for each used in the Słownik nazwisk.

Borocki 12, Gd:4, Pr:7, Wr:1
Borocz 1, Tb:1
Boroczkowska 1, Wł:1
Boroczowska 0
Boroda 68, Wa:4, Bs:41, El:3, Go:1, JG:2, Su:6,
   Wr: 11
Borodacka 0
Borodacz 103, BB:1, Cz:1, Gd:2, JG:26, Lg:22,
   Ol:3, Op:7, Sz:8, Wb:3, Wr:21, ZG:9
Borodaj 12, Ka:2, Lg:9, Sz:1
Borodajewska 0
Borodajkiewicz 7, Gd:2, Ks:1, Sz:4
Borodajko 69, Wa:3, By:2, Go:3, JG:1, Ka:10, Kr:1,
   Sz:7, Wb:40, Wr:2
Borodaka 1, Bs:1
Borodakiewicz 1, Ka:1
Borodako 12, Wa:1, Bs:1, JG:S, Ko:2, Lg:3
Borodarz 0
Borodas 1, Lg:1
Borodaśko 1, Wa:1
Borodawczenko 0
Borodawka 3, Kr:3
Borodawkin 2, Tb:2
Borodawko 20, Gd:13, Ka:7
Borodecki 6, BB:1, Ka:4, Su:1
Borodej 33, Wa:7, Ch:18, Ło:4, Wb:2, Wr:2
Borodejko 1, Gd:1
Borodejuk 16, Wa:7, BP:5, Ło:4
Borodenko 6, By:1, Go:2, Lu:1, Op:1, Rz:1
Borodeńko 117, BB:35, By:29, Go:1, JG:11, Ka:5,
   Kn:6, Kr:1, Op: 1, Rz:4, Sz:6, Wb:13, Wł:5
Borodicz 6, Ka:2, Ki:2, Os:2
Borodij 23, Wa:9, By:3, Ol:1, Za:3, ZG:7
Borodijczuk 5, Rz:5
Borodijuk 31, Wa:1, BP:18, Ch:8, Sr:4
Borodin 18, Wa:1, Bs:1, JG:6, Lg:4, Pl:5, Sz:1
Borodit 1, Wa:1
Borodiuk 39, BP:18, El:9, Gd:6, Go:3, Lg:2, Su:1
Borodko 32, Wa:2, BP:7, JG:5, Łd:1, Ol:3, Su:12,
   Sz:1, ZG:1
Borodnik 0
Borodnos 0

Borodo 102, Wa:6, El:4, Gd:4, Go:5, Kl:5, Kn 1,
   Ko:4, Ol:18, Pl:3, Po:5, Sd:2, Sł:4, Sz:7, To:5,
   Wr:1, ZG:28
Borodolenko 1, Bs:1
Borodowicz 0
Borodowkin 0
Borodowski 2, Ch:1, Wr:1
Borodrzyczak 0
Borodula 0
Borodulenko 7, Bs:7
Borodulia 1, Op:1
Borodulin 22, Bs:10, Ol:7, Ra:4, Wr:1
Borodycz 49, Lg:1, Wr:48
Borodyjuk 10, BP:4, Sł:6
Borodyn 16, JG:10, Op:l, Wb:4, Wr:1
Borodynko 31, Ko:1, Ol:7, Po:4, Su:5, Sz:4, ZG:10
Borodynowicz 0
Borodyń 9, JG:1, Ko:4, Kr:1, Wb:3
Borodysz 0
Borodzej 1, Ch:1
Borodzenia 10,Wr:10
Borodzi 3, Wa:3
Borodzic 2, Pt:2
Borodzica 0
Borodzicz 173, Wa:13, Bs:20, By:6, El:21, Gd:19,
   JG:12, Ka:4, Ki:8, Ko:1, Kr:2, Lg:4, Lu:6, Łd:2,
   Ol: 17, Pt:2, Sł:1 , To:1, Wb:15, Wr:20
Borodziej 214, Wa:8, BP:57, Bs:13, BB:6, Ch:45,
   Cz:l, El:5, Gd:1, JG:l, Ka:10, Kr:1, Lu:3, Rz:3,
   Sk:l, Sł:1, Su:14, Sz:4, Tb:9, Za:12, ZG:19
Borodziejuk 0
Borodzienko 0
Borodzienkow 1, Pt:1
Borodziewicz 51, Wa:6, JG:6, Ko:1 Ls:3, Łd:5,
   Ol:15, Sz:10, Wr:5
Borodzik 13, Wa:12, Ło:1
Borodzin 0
Borodziński 42, Wa:26, Bs:12, Ch:1, Gd:3
Borodzisz 7, Gd:5, Wr:2
Borodziuk 491, Wa:17, BP:29, Bs:39, Ch:6, El:6,
   Gd:25, Go:7, JG:13, Ka:10, Ko:5, Kr:10, Lg: 5

436

Sample page from the Słownik nazwisk. Note the many names with frequencies of 0 or 1, and the minor differences between some of the names.

Keep in mind that Poland is about the size of New Mexico; according to my encyclopedia, New Mexico has 33 counties, and Poland had 49 provinces; so it's probably safe to say the average pre-1990 Polish province was smaller than the average county of New Mexico. These provinces were named for their capitals—the capital of Białystok province was Białystok, of Krosno province was Krosno, etc. (This is considerably less confusing than in the United States, where Ft. Worth, Texas is the county seat of Tarrant County).

Chapter Eleven: "You Want Polish Names? How About 341,055 of Them!" – 199

In the province breakdown, provinces with no residents by a particular name were omitted, and provinces were listed by alphabetical order (although the abbreviations used may obscure that fact—"Tb," Tarnobrzeg, does properly precede "Ta," Tarnów), except that the figure for the capital city province of Warsaw is always given first.

One thing that strikes people when they see a sample page from the 1990 edition of the *Słownik nazwisk* is the realization just how many different surnames can be formed from one root. In the sample on page 199, most of those names almost certainly derive from Ukrainian or Russian борода [*borodá*], "beard," corresponding to Polish *broda*. Notice how slight the differences are between some of them: *Borodyn* vs. *Borodin*, *Borodiuk* vs. *Borodziuk*, *Borodenko* vs. *Borodeńko*—in the latter case you have to wonder if the former isn't just a misspelled version of the latter. You can't really appreciate how the profusion of suffixes, dialect differences, names of foreign origin, and other factors affect Polish surnames until you look at a list like this.

Another thing that strikes most readers is the vast number of rare names—of these 70 names, 17 have a frequency of "0," and 12 have a frequency of "1." I suspect the "0" needs explaining. In PESEL's 1990 data banks, a name was given as having frequency "0" when it did show up in the database, but the information on it was incomplete. Thus, for instance, as of 1990, there was at least one Polish citizen named *Boroczkowska*, but some of the data in her file was missing; perhaps she had died by 1990, perhaps her place of residence was omitted, and perhaps the data was simply corrupted somewhere along the line. Here is the breakdown by name frequency vs. how many names appeared that often:[3]

Frequency	Number of names		Frequency	Number of names
0:	203,552		7:	9,639
1:	317,806		8:	8,293
2:	41,612		9:	7,279
3:	23,057		10 to 25:	56,159
4:	17,814		26 to 50:	30,500
5:	14,229		51 to 100:	24,346
6:	11,211		100+:	44,723

Thus there were 203,552 instances where names had a frequency of "0," Clearly this category accounts for a huge chunk of those 811,720 names! Rymut mentions that a lot of these names appear to have been corrupted when they were keyed into the computer, so it's hard to say just how much significance they should have. You see there were also 317,806 names that showed up with a frequency of "1," so just "0" and "1" accounted for more than 520,000 of those 811,720 names. In fact, surnames borne by 26 or more people accounted for slightly less than 100,000 of those 811,720 names— which means the other 700,000 were pretty rare.

Forward into the 21st Century!

As time passed, Rymut recognized some flaws and shortcomings in the work, due largely to problems with the original 1990 data. Anyone who worked with it recognized that many of the spellings were suspect, probably due to errors keying in data. There were, for instance, listings of two people named *Zielilski* and two others named *Zielizski*. You have to suspect all four were really named *Zieliński*. There are many such dubious forms, and it was clear the data could stand to be cleaned up. Furthermore, it was incomplete: it only covered about 93% of the population, leaving out some three million Poles. So the original data source itself was inaccurate and incomplete.

Also, Rymut recognized that he and his colleagues had made some methodological errors. For instance, they had lumped together names ending in *-ski* and *-ska* under the *-ski* form; likewise, names ending in *-cki* and *-cka* were all given under the *-cki* form, and those ending in *-zki* and *-zka* under the *-zki* form. In many cases, this was appropriate—but they overlooked a significant number of legitimate surnames deriving from nouns ending in *-ka*, such as *Załuska*. The *Słownik nazwisk* showed no one named *Załuska*, but 2,455 people named *Załuski*. Many of those 2,455 were, as one might expect, females bearing *Załuska* as the feminine form of the surname *Załuski*. But at least some were males and females whose name was *Załuska* as an independent name, not the feminine of *Załuski* at all. We can be certain of this because data from 2002 showed 1,965 Polish citizens named *Załuska*, of whom 509 were males and 1,456 females, as well as 883 Polish citizens named *Załuski*, all of them male.[4] Without drowning you in statistics, the point is that names ending *-ski* and *-ska*, *-cki* and *-cka*, *-zki* and *-zka* cannot be combined under the masculine form without creating a significant inaccuracy, especially for those who might want to study the data in the future.

Rymut had also eliminated many surnames of obvious foreign origin, which, at first glance, seems reasonable. Later, he admitted that he did not take into account the likelihood at least some of the people bearing those names would remain in Poland and become citizens—so their names should be included, to give a complete picture. Granted, it is somewhat jarring to see surnames such as *Rodriguez* and *Yamazaki* included in a listing of Polish surnames. But dumping them compromises the integrity of the data.

Because of these and other factors, Rymut wanted to publish an updated and more accurate version of the *Słownik nazwisk*. Funding for compiling and printing another massive set of books was not so easy to come by, however. I suggested he might want to publish the updated version as a CD-ROM, because publishing in that form is enormously less expensive and more versatile. He asked for help acquiring some funding for the project, and I put him in touch with the Polish Genealogical Society of America®, which is always looking for worthwhile publications with genealogical relevance to sponsor. The result was the publication in 2002 of a CD-ROM called the *Słownik naz-*

wisk używanych w Polsce na początku XXI wieku / Dictionary of Surnames in Current Use in Poland at the Beginning of the 21st Century, co-published by the Polish Academy of Sciences, Polish Language Institute, and the Polish Genealogical Society of America®, Kraków–Chicago 2002.

Borodaj 14, WrGł: M. 4, F. 4, KaBę: F. 1, KamGl: M. 1, KamPi: M. 3, F. 1
Borodajkiewicz 6, GdmGn: F. 1, SzmSz: M. 3, F. 2
Borodajko 97, WrDz: M. 33, F. 37, WrOl: F. 1, WrmWr: F. 1, ToŚw: F. 1, WaWa: F. 2, OpNy: F. 1, GdGd: M. 1, F. 1, KaGl: M. 7, F. 3, KamGl: F. 1, SzMy: M. 2, F. 1, SzSg: F. 1, SzLo: M. 2, F. 2
Borodajko-Żbikowski 2, WaWa: M. 2
Borodakiewicz 2, KamGl: M. 1, F. 1
Borodako 11, WrZg: M. 3, F. 3, WrmLe: F. 2, BsmBs: M. 1, SzDr: F. 2
Borodawka 6, KrmKr: M. 1, F. 5
Borodawkin 1, RzmTa: F. 1
Borodawko 20, KrCh: M. 2, F. 3, GdGd: F. 3, GdmGd: M. 5, F. 2, GdmGn: M. 2, F. 1, KamKa: F. 1, SzDr: M. 1
Borodecka 5, KaCi: F. 1, KamJs: F. 3, KamZo: F. 1
Borodecki 3, KamJs: M. 1, KamZo: M. 2
Borodej 28, WrmWa: F. 1, WrmWr: F. 1, LuCh: M. 4, F. 2, LumCh: M. 5, F. 4, WaWa: M. 4, F. 3, BsmLo: M. 1, F. 3
Borodejuk 16, LuBP: M. 1, F. 2, WaPr: M. 2, F. 4, WaWa: M. 1, F. 2, BsLo: M. 1, F. 3
Borodenko 7, WrZą: M. 2, F. 3, LuPu: F. 1, RzRz: F. 1
Borodeńko 115, WrBo: M. 5, F. 5, WrDz: M. 4, F. 1, WrWa: M. 3, F. 3, ToBy: M. 1, F. 1, ToNa: M. 11, F. 14, TomBy: M. 3, F. 1, TomWl: M. 3, F. 2, LuBg: F. 1, OpKr: M. 1, F. 1, RzRz: M. 4, F. 2, KaBi: M. 4, F. 5, KaŻy: M. 3, F. 4, KamBi: M. 7, F. 11, KamTy: M. 1, F. 1, PomKn: M. 4, F. 3, SzGn: M. 3, F. 1, SzmSz: M. 1, F. 1
Borodicz 3, KamCh: F. 1, KiSk: M. 1, F. 1
Borodij 16, TomBy: M. 2, F. 1, LuHr: M. 1, F. 1, ZGŻg: M. 3, F. 2, WaWa: M. 1, WaWo: M. 2, F. 2, OlLi: F. 1
Borodijczuk 4, RzRz: M. 1, F. 3
Borodijuk 28, LuWł: M. 4, F. 5, LumBP: M. 8, F. 6, ŁoZd: M. 2, F. 2, WaPr: M. 1
Borodin 26, WrJG: M. 2, F. 6, LomLo: F. 1, WaWa: F. 1, KaBL: M. 3, F. 1, KamTy: F. 3, PoZł: M. 1, F. 2, SzWa: M. 3, F. 2, SzmSz: M. 1
Borodiuk 37, LuBP: M. 7, F. 6, WaLo: M. 3, F. 3, GdWe: M. 2, F. 1, GdSz: M. 3, F. 2, GdmGn: M. 1, F. 3, OlmEl: M. 1, F. 2, SzCh: M. 2, F. 1
Borodko 30, WrmJG: F. 3, LuBP: F. 3, LumBP: M. 4, F. 2, ZGZr: F. 1, WaWa: M. 1, OpOp: F. 1, BsSu: F. 1, OlGi: M. 3, F. 8, OlmOl: M. 2, F. 1
Borodniczenko 1, RzmPm: F. 1
Borodo 98, TomTo: M. 3, F. 2, ZGKr: M. 11, F. 10, ZGMi: M. 2, F. 1, ZGSD: M. 1, F. 1, ZGŻg: F. 1, ZGmZG: M. 1, F. 2, WaWa: M. 2, F. 3, WamSd: F. 2, OpmOp: M. 1, GdmGn: M. 2, F. 2, OlBr: M. 1, F. 3, OlmOl: M. 7, F. 10, PoKr: M. 1, F. 5, PoPi: M. 1, F. 1, PoŚm: M. 3, F. 2, PomKn: F. 1, SzGn: M. 4, F. 4, SzPo: M. 1, SzSł: M. 3, F. 1, SzmKs: M. 1, F. 2
Borodowicz 1, ŁoŁa: M. 1
Borodowska 1, WrWo: F. 1
Borodulenko 12, BsSo: M. 4, F. 8
Borodulin 21, WrmWr: F. 1, WaBb: M. 1, F. 2, WaPs: M. 2, F. 1, BsBs: M. 2, F. 5, BsmBs: M. 2, F. 1, OlOs: M. 2, F. 1, OlmOl: F. 1
Borodulin-Nadzieja 1, WrmWr: M. 1
Borodycz 51, WrLi: M. 2, F. 2, WrŚr: M. 2, F. 4, WrTr: M. 2, F. 2, WrWo: M. 2, F. 2, WrWr: M. 5, F. 6, WrmWr: M. 8, F. 7, TomTo: M. 1, KrMi: F. 2, SzWa: M. 2, F. 2
Borodyjuk 8, LuBP: M. 1, F. 1, LumBP: M. 1, GdSl: M. 1, F. 1, GdmSł: M. 2, F. 1
Borodyn 18, WrJG: M. 2, F. 2, WrKł: F. 1, WrLw: M. 1, F. 3, OpKr: M. 2, F. 1, KamDG: M. 2, F. 2, SzDr: M. 1, F. 1
Borodynko 20, ZGNS: F. 1, ZGŻr: M. 2, F. 2, ZGmZG: M. 2, F. 2, OlmOl: M. 1, F. 3, PoPo: F. 1, PomPo: M. 1, F. 2, SzmSz: M. 2, F. 1
Borodyń 10, WrKł: M. 2, F. 2, WrŚw: M. 1, F. 3, SzDr: M. 1, F. 1
Borodyńko 8, WaWa: F. 2, WamOl: M. 1, F. 1, OlGi: M. 2, F. 2
Borodzenia 12, WrTr: M. 4, F. 8
Borodzi 4, WaWa: F. 2, WaWZ: M. 1, F. 1
Borodzicz 191, WrJa: F. 1, WrKł: M. 1, F. 2, WrŚw: M. 6, F. 7, WrWr: M. 4, F. 2, WrZg: M. 6, F. 9, WrmWr: M. 7, F. 2, ToBy: M. 1, F. 2, TomBy: M. 1, F. 3, TomTo: M. 1, LuKr: M. 2, LumLu: F. 1, LomLo: M. 1, F. 4, ŁomTo: M. 3, F. 1, WaWa: M. 4, F. 4, BsBs: M. 3, F. 1, BsMo: M. 2, F. 1, BsSo: M. 10, F. 8, BsmBs: M. 4, F. 5, GdGd: M. 9, F. 4, GdWe: F. 1, GdmGd: M. 4, F. 4, GdmGn: M. 4, KamJs: M. 2, F. 2, KiSk: M. 4, F. 3, OlBa: M. 13, F. 9, OlEl: M. 5, F. 1, OlLi: M. 3, F. 2, OlOs: F. 1, OlmEl: M. 3, F. 6, SzBi: F. 1, SzSg: M. 1
Borodzicz-Smoliński 1, WaWa: M. 1
Borodziej 197, WrmJG: F. 1, WrmWr: F. 1, LuBP: M. 4, F. 6, LuCh: M. 4, F. 5, LuKs: M. 1, LuPa: F. 1, LuŚw: M. 2, F. 1, LuTo: M. 7, F. 3, LuWł: M. 33, F. 27, LuZa: F. 1, LumCh: M. 3, F. 8, LumLu: F. 1, ZGZG: M. 1, F.

Polish Surnames: Origins & Meanings – 202

This compilation used data from PESEL as of September 2002, covering some 38 million Polish citizens. It gives masculine and feminine forms of adjectival surnames separately, to get past the *Załuska* problem mentioned above. It also breaks the data down by województwa and powiaty per the current setup in Poland. So the data is not only more accurate than the data in the original *Słownik nazwisk*; it also shows distribution on a more detailed level.

Researcher Roman Kałużniacki has done some statistical analysis of the data, and found that it covers a total of 341,055 surnames. That's a big drop from the 811,720 names in the 1990 version. But if you factor out all the misspellings and bad data, it's not too hard to believe you'd end up with 341,055 names. As always, there are pluses and minuses with the "new, improved" version. The info you get is more detailed, more reliable, but it's also sanitized. You don't have the wild and woolly inaccuracies of the 1990 data, but you also miss out on names that might have been legitimate and were in the process of dying out. Rymut pointed out that some of the rare names were borne by people who had died recently, or were maiden names of women who had married recently. They were rare in 1990, and by 2002, they had died out—but some of them, at least, had been valid. I prefer working with the 2002 data; but I often check the 1990 data, just to cover all the bases.

If you wish to do the same, the individual page from the CD reproduced on page 202 covers most of the same names shown on page 199. The names with counts of 0 have disappeared; the names that remain can be traced down to the powiat level—which may or may not be helpful in a given instance. The biggest drawback of the 2002 data is dealing with the abbreviations that designate województwo and powiat, such as WaWa and GdmGd. The first two letters designate one of the 16 województwa. The abbreviations refer to the cities that serve as provincial capitals, presented in this order:

1. Wr = Wrocław, capital of Dolnośląskie province
2. To = Toruń, capital of Kujawsko-pomorskie province
3. Lu = Lublin, capital of Lubelskie province
4. ZG = Zielona Góra, capital of Lubuskie province
5. Ło = Łódź, capital of Łódź province
6. Kr = Kraków, capital of Małopolskie province
7. Wa = Warszawa, capital of Mazowieckie province
8. Op = Opole, capital of Opolskie province
9. Rz = Rzeszów, capital of Podkarpackie province
10. Bs = Białystok, capital of Podlaskie province
11. Gd = Gdańsk, capital of Pomorskie province
12. Ka = Katowice, capital of Śląskie province
13. Ki = Kielce, capital of Świętokrzyskie province
14. Ol = Olsztyn, capital of Warmińsko-mazurskie province
15. Po = Poznań, capital of Wielkopolskie province
16. Sz = Szczecin, capital of Zachodniopomorskie province

The powiaty are a little tougher. As of 2002, there were 315 powiaty, as well as 65 cities with powiat status. The latter are distinguished with an *m* after the province abbreviation and before the powiat abbreviation; the rest are designated with two-letter abbreviations. Thus, "GdmSł M. 2, F. 1" means there were 2 males and 1 female by that name living in Słupsk city powiat of Pomorskie province, of which the capital is Gdańsk. This is not very user-friendly, especially for someone who didn't grow up in Poland and doesn't know offhand what sizable town in Pomorskie province might be abbreviated "Sł." Rymut provided a list of all the abbreviations in his Introduction; but it is a bit tedious having to refer back to them constantly. Still, it's hard to blame him; I can't suggest a better way to come up with over 400 abbreviations that will be immediately recognizable, especially to non-Poles.

Consider the first entry of the page reproduced on page 202:

Borodaj 14, WrGł: M. 4, F. 4, KaBę: F. 1, KamGl: M. 1, KamPi: M. 3, F. 1

With a little effort, we can decipher this. As of 2002, there were 14 Polish citizens named *Borodaj*. Of those 14, four males and four females lived in Dolnośląskie province (Wr), Głogów powiat (Gł); one female lived in Śląskie province (Ka), Będzin powiat (Bę); one male lived in Śląskie province, Gliwice city powiat (mGl); and three males and one female lived in Śląskie province, Piekary Śląskie city powiat (mPi).

Now we know the name is quite rare in modern Poland, and is found only in southwestern Poland. If you have ancestors by this name, this information does not exactly lead you right to their front door; but at least it helps you focus on a specific area. In fact, there is a further point of interest about this name we will discuss in a moment.

This gives you a notion of what Rymut's CD-ROM has to offer. Sadly, it is no longer for sale. The Polish Genealogical Society of America® sold out its supply, and as of now, does not intend to offer it any longer. No doubt one can find and buy copies secondhand; but it will take a little searching.

To the Internet!

Many genealogists today think everything they need is available, instantly, for free, online. That is a load of crap. But there's no denying, a lot of great stuff is available, if you know where to look for it and how to make use of it; and the amount is increasing all the time. Whenever you have a question or problem, it makes sense to check online for possible help.

If the thought of getting hold of a copy of the 2002 CD-ROM intimidates you, let alone deciphering the data it contains, I'm glad to say much of this info is online as of this writing, and has been for some years now. It is on the website of Moikrewni, the Polish division of a company called MyHeritage. The URL you want for Polish names is:

<http://www.moikrewni.pl/mapa/>

From that page, you can enter the name of the surname you want in the box labeled "Mapa nazwisk" (Surname map). Or you can click on the appropriate letter of the alphabet near the bottom of the page, and then zero in on the name you need by selecting the relevant entry from a series of lists. This approach takes longer than inputting the name directly; but it has the advantage of not requiring correct spelling with Polish characters. Just keep choosing from the available options till you get to the page with your name. If you prefer the direct approach, the URL you need will almost always consist of "http://www.moikrewni.pl/mapa/kompletny/" followed by the name in question and the extension ".html." So the page for *Borodaj* is here:

<http://www.moikrewni.pl/mapa/kompletny/borodaj.html>

Whichever way you get to the page you want, it's worth the effort. The data is presented in Polish, but is not hard to understand. Even better, the data is presented in a color map that helps you grasp the distribution readily.

Now, if you're familiar with the way the Internet works—or the whole world, for that matter—you know there are going to be pluses and minuses to this. One is that the Moikrewni pages only list the 10 powiaty in which the name was most common. The accompanying color map, however, covers all the data for each name; the color coding is explained by a key in the lower left corner of the map. On the map itself, position your cursor over a powiat and its name appears; that's how you tell which is which.

I should also warn you that the algorithm used to extract and map data from the database does not always parse the data correctly, probably because of inconsistencies with how that data was formatted. As a result, the numbers and the coloring you get are sometimes off a little. The discrepancy is not usually too large; but it is frustrating to know the full data is available but not always portrayed. Besides, knowing how things go in this world, the data that gets dropped will turn out to be just what you need.

Still, you get the top 10 powiaty; you get a rather nice color map that can be copied, saved, printed, and shared; and the site names the powiaty for you—no searching through lists to figure out what "KamGl" means! This is an example of the Internet doing exactly what computers are best at: presenting complex data in a way humans can exploit.

Now, in this book of mine, all that info on those sample pages reproduced on page 199 and 2002 (and a bit more) boils down to one entry:

Borod- *{f,u}* < Ukr. борода [*borodá*], "beard," cmp. Polish names in **Brod-** [R,U]; Baradziej (604, cmp. Blrs. барада [*baradá*], "beard"), Boroda (53), Borodacz (119), Borodeńko (115), Borodo (98), Borodzicz (191), Borodziej (197), Borodziuk (582)

As you see, I chose to include mainly those surnames borne by at least 100 or more Poles; I also included *Boroda* because I had enough room to do so without adding an extra line, and when possible I like to include the name that most clearly shows the root from which the others are derived. I could have included "Borodajko (69)" as well; but Volume II is already monstrous as it is, and I had to draw the line somewhere. So I usually confined myself to listing the most common names that came from a particular root.

Good Points and Bad Points

Now that you've had a sample of the *Słownik nazwisk* and its 2002 update, we can discuss what these works do and do not offer researchers.

The main merit of these works is obvious: they provide massive amounts of hard data on surnames. At a glance you can learn how common your name is and where in Poland it is to be found. How useful this is to you varies from case to case. For instance, if your name is *Nowak,* all either *Słownik* tells you is that it is a very common name. Consider this breakdown of the 1990 data:

Nowak 220217, Wa:8843, BP:464, Bs:408, BB:4349, By:7980, Ch:610 Ci:416 Cz:7306, El:1406, Gd:3987, Go:2928, JG:2514, Kl:5673, Ka:28985, Ki:12541, Kn:3624, Ko:2021, Kr:12234, Ks:12541, Lg:2396, Ls:4897, Lu:3125, Ło:384, Łd:6846, NS:3429, Ol:1680, Op:5919, Os:906, Pl:5404, Pt:4286, Pł:1731, Po:19416, Pr:1024, Ra:4124, Rz:3509, Sd:1582, Sr:3584, Sk:2073, Sł:1786, Su:554, Sz:4748, Tb:3897, Ta:5486, To:1857, Wb:3798

With some names, you can detect a geographical pattern that tells you something useful. In this case, the provinces with large numbers of Nowaks were simply those with the largest populations; so there is no really helpful pattern.

With other names, the data can be quite revealing. If you are interested in the name *Lademann,* for instance, knowing that 632 of the 685 Poles by that name lived in Gdańsk province, by the 1990 data. Note, incidentally, that this is one case where the 1990 data is a good place to start, because that statistic is rather striking; the 2002 data is more exact and paints the same picture, but the concentration in the Gdańsk area is not as easy to spot until you take a look at the Moikrewni map at <http://www.moikrewni.pl/mapa/kompletny/lademann.html>.

Another good example is the 1990 data for *Lorbiecki:*

Lorbiecki 650, Wa:9, By:242, El:20, Gd:259, Go:2, Ka:13, Ko:4, Kr:1, Pr:4, Rz:1, Sr:6, Sł:68, Sz:11, Tb:4, To:6

A look at the map on page 198 (or, of course, the relevant Moikrewni page) shows that the provinces where this name was most common—Bydgoszcz, Gdańsk, and Słupsk—were all in northwestern Poland, and specifically, in the region of Kashubia. This fact suggests an association with the Kashubian ethnic group. Knowing this, you can begin to look for more information about this particular group, which may lead you to the Kashubian Association of North America.⁵ Instead of searching all over for people of the same name who may or may not be related to you, you've defined a specific group of people in a specific area, and identified an organization of researchers who share a common interest with you and just might be able to share a lot more!

If you're interested in a surname that turns out to be quite rare, the *Słownik* can sometimes be even more helpful. For instance, the 1990 data for the name *Kotzwander* shows there were only 16 Poles by that name, and all 16 lived in the province of Opole; the 2002 data shows 18, all in Opolskie province, and 11 of them in Opole powiat. If you descend from someone named *Kotzwander,* this has got to be good news!

Your next step might be to consult the Polish telephone directory for Opole province. Phones in private homes are not quite as common in Poland as in the United States, and cell phones are tremendously popular; so telephone directories are not a sure thing. Still, you may find at least one *Kotzwander* listed—and if so, the odds are good he or she is related to you. It certainly wouldn't do any harm to write or call and ask.⁶

So these are some of the virtues of the two versions of *Słownik nazwisk.* They provide incredible amounts of data, just waiting for you to have the ingenuity to make use of them. What are their defects (at least, considered from our point of view)?

The first one is obvious: any compilation dealing with more than 30 million people is going to include plenty of corrupt and inaccurate data. All those names in the 1990 data with a frequency of "0" prove that. Even the 2002 version, while inspiring considerably more confidence, is not free of error.

But the main flaw of the *Słownik nazwisk* is that, for our purposes, it came 100 years too late! Can you imagine how much more useful for us a similar compilation from 1890 would be? The last century has muddied the waters considerably for researchers. There are obvious factors such as the Holocaust—my experience translating records for Jewish researchers is enough to convince me there were far more Jewish surnames, and far more people bearing them, before 1939, to say nothing of the millions of Polish Christians who died under Nazi and Soviet oppression.

There are also less obvious factors. Compare the boundaries of Poland in 1919 versus the modern ones, as shown in the map on page 208, and you realize that both versions of the *Słownik*—which of necessity deal only with those living within the current boundaries of Poland—lack data on vast numbers of people with Polish ancestry who live in Lithuania, Belarus, and Ukraine. The map shows how Poland's pre-1939 borders (shaded) were shifted westward after 1945 (the current boundaries are outlined in black). From a historical and genealogical point of view, people living in those eastern regions were long considered citizens of Poland, whatever their ethnic identity. Data on their names would have been extremely valuable to researchers.

This map shows roughly the borders of Poland after World War I (shaded) and now. The whole country was shifted westward to suit the purposes of the communists.

Furthermore, the post-World War II era brought enormous changes in terms of who lived where. We saw in Chapter Seven (pages 94-95) that millions of Germans left Poland—many against their will—to move west. There were other mass relocations to muddy the waters. Especially prominent was *Akcja Wisła* (Operation Vistula), the communist government's program uprooting people suspected of pro-Ukrainian sympathies and support for the Ukrainian Insurgent Army. This operation forced some 200,000 people to pack up on almost no notice and moved them from southeastern Poland to the "recovered territories" of western Poland, those taken from Germany and given to Poland after World War II. Operation Vistula explains why both editions of the *Słownik nazwisk* show large concentrations of people with clearly Ukrainian surnames living far to the west of where you'd expect to find them, in areas such as Wrocław, Opole, and Katowice.[7]

Do you remember a few pages ago when I talked about the surname *Borodaj*, which appears only in southwestern Poland today? Well, it's a good example of the confusion caused by Operation Vistula. The name is clearly of East Slavic origin, deriving from the Ruthenian or Ukrainian word for "beard," *боро∂а* [*borodá*], not the Polish word, *broda*. So what are these folks doing in Silesia? Almost certainly, they were among those displaced by Operation Vistula. The bad news is that they do not live where their ancestors did. The good news is that the communists had a habit of keeping excellent records as they committed atrocities; there are records of those forced to relocate. Matthew Bielawa wrote a fine article on using those records, for the Spring and Fall 2003 issues of *Pathways and Passages*, the journal of the Polish Genealogical Society of Connecticut and the Northeast. It is required reading for anyone who has reason to believe his family was uprooted in these postwar relocations.[8]

So there are things about the *Słownik nazwisk* that we would change in an ideal world, even the updated and improved 2002 edition. But I can't imagine how the kind of directory we want could be compiled. Not only did many of the records we'd need perish in the course of war and turmoil; we also have to remember that as for much of the partition era, "Poland" did not exist, officially. Compiling any sort of surname listing for all of pre-World War I "Poland" would mean trying to find, read, and correlate massive stacks of documents drawn up under three different Empires (Russia, Prussia, and Austria-Hungary) in several different languages (mainly German, Latin, Polish, and Russian). The practical difficulties involved in such a project would make the job a nightmare! I honestly don't think it can be done.

The final problem with both editions of the *Słownik nazwisk,* as far as we are concerned, is that they tantalize us by proving that data we need exists, but is not available. The PESEL data banks clearly have first names, addresses, all sorts of information that might help us find living relatives. But getting access to it is no day at the beach. The Polish government agency that administers the program—*Ministerstwo Spraw Wewnętrznych i Administracji* or *MSWiA*, Ministry of Interior and Administration—is not overly cooperative when genealogists request information from the PESEL records. This is not really hard to understand. They have official duties to perform; they were never meant to be a clearinghouse of information for genealogical researchers; and requests for such information would probably overtax a staff that already has enough to do. Also, the Polish government in general has always been anxious to protect its citizens' privacy. That's the main reason the LDS was not allowed to microfilm Polish parish records less than 100 years old, to avoid infringing on the privacy of persons still living. We can only hope that as time goes on, the Polish government will begin to see that making this data available to researchers will benefit Poles by helping them reestablish contact with relatives living far away and anxious to renew ties with the homeland. But for now ... well, let's just say I'm not holding my breath.

Summary

Although, from the genealogical researcher's point of view, there are some drawbacks to the two editions of *Słownik nazwisk* and their online manifestations, they are nonetheless valuable source of data for those who can put it to good use. Doing so depends largely on your ingenuity and persistence. But I hope this chapter has helped you determine what this work might offer you if your surnames number among those 341,055 "linguistic units."

Endnotes

[1] Kazimierz Rymut, *Nazwiska Polaków,* Zakład Narodowy im. Ossolińskich —Wydawnictwo, Wrocław, 1991, p. 5.

[2] Kazimierz Rymut, ed., *Słownik nazwisk współcześnie w Polsce używanych,* Instytut Języka Polskiego, Kraków, 1992, 83-85579-25-7, vol. I, pp. v-vi.

[3] Ibid., vol. I, pp. viii-ix.

[4] *Słownik nazwisk używanych w Polsce na początku XXI wieku / Dictionary of Surnames in Current Use in Poland at the Beginning of the 21st Century*, CD-ROM co-published by the Polish Academy of Sciences, Polish Language Institute, and the Polish Genealogical Society of America®, Kraków–Chicago 2002, pp. 12875–12876 (file T-Z.pdf, pp. 1335–1336).

[5] Kashubian Association of North America (KANA), address as of this writing: KANA, Kashubian Association of North America, P.O. Box 27732, Minneapolis MN 55427-0732, website <http://ka-na.org/>.

[6] Searching Polish telephone directories has always been a challenge. Print versions are not distributed as freely as in the United States, and can be difficult to get hold of. Polish privacy laws affect how much information you can get on individuals. And Poles are just as fond of cell phones as we are—maybe more so, because getting a landline installed has always been a tedious process. As far as I know, there are no cell phone directories.

The Polish Genealogical Society of Connecticut and the Northeast (8 Lyle Road, New Britain CT 06053-2104, <http://www.pgsctne.org>) has a nearly complete collection of directories for individual provinces and can search them for specific names for a fee. It's slow going if you don't know which locality to look in. There is no master alphabetical list of names, only listings by locality that have to be searched, one by one.

As for online directories, they have come and gone frequently in the last decade. The one that seems to be most stable is <http://www.ksiazka­telefoniczna.com/>. The page with the title "Abonenci prywatni" (private subscribers) allows you to input *imię*, "first name," *nazwisko*, "surname," *miasto*, "town/city," *ulica*, "street," and *województwo*, "province." Whether you find someone depends on whether they have a landline or cell phone, and whether they have chosen to be listed or unlisted. So, any way you slice it, there are no guarantees—but it can't hurt to try!

[7] William F. Hoffman, "The Mystery of the Misplaced Ukrainians: Solved," Polish Genealogical Society of America *Bulletin,* Fall, 1994, p. 12.

[8] Matthew Bielawa, "Researching the Documents of PUR: Polish, Genealogical Research of Repatriates and Resettlers after World War II into the Newly Acquired Western and Northern Polish Territories," *Pathways & Passages*, Spring 2003, Vol. 19, No. 2, pp. 1–9, and Fall 2003, Vol. 20, No. 1, pp. 19–23. To order a back issue, go to <http://www.pgsctne.org/publication4. html> or write to the Society at 8 Lyle Road, New Britain CT 06053-2104.

Chapter Twelve:

"Where Do I Go From Here?"

In English we have an expression for a particularly complete work, one that leaves nothing to be desired—we say it's "the last word" on a subject. It would be pleasant for my ego to think I have produced "the last word" on the subject of Polish surnames, at least in English. But that seems an unlikely and even silly thing to hope for. I don't want to be the last person ever to write a book on this subject; and future writers will surely learn from my mistakes to produce works superior to this.

It seems much more reasonable to hope that this book is a good "first word," one that will promote interest in the subject and help researchers get off to a good start. But for the book to represent a good start, the research must proceed beyond what is offered here. Logic, as well as custom, compels me, therefore, to list the sources I have used in compiling this book, as well as other resources you can consult to extend your study of Polish surnames.

Since it is not easy to find books on this subject, I have given as much information as possible to help you locate copies. The following are some of the better suppliers of the works mentioned in the list beginning on p. 212.

Amazon Books—I doubt I need to tell anyone about Amazon. It is always the first place I check when I'm looking for books, and I don't think I'm the only one who does so. <http://www.amazon.com>.

Avotaynu, 155 N. Washington Ave, Bergenfield NJ 07621, USA, phone 201-387-7200, website <http://www.avotaynu.com>. Avotaynu specializes in helping Jewish researchers trace their roots, but its publications are helpful to anyone interested in central and eastern Europe.

Polish Art Center, 9539 Joseph Campau, Hamtramck MI 48212-3437, United States, phone 1-888-619-9771, <http://www.polartcenter.com/>.

Polish Bookstore & Publishing Co., Inc., 161 Java St., Brooklyn NY 11222, phone 718-349-2738, <http://www.polbook.com/>.

The Polish Bookstore, <http://thepolishbookstore.com>, e-mail <sales@ThePolishBookstore.com>.

Polish Genealogical Society of America®, 984 N. Milwaukee Ave., Chicago, IL 60642-4101, <http://www.pgsa.org>. As a look at the following list will show, the PGSA has published a number of works helpful for the study of Polish surnames and for Polish genealogical research in general.

Polish Museum of America, 984 N. Milwaukee Ave., Chicago, IL 60642-4101, <http://www.polishmuseumofamerica.org/>. The Museum's Library has an outstanding collection of works on all things Polish. It does not lend out most of its materials, so you will have to go to Chicago to use them; but if you're in Chicago, you should visit the Museum. It's wise to write or call in advance for information on hours, location, etc.

Polish Reference Works (in English or Polish)

Abramowicz, Zofia, Citko, Lila, and Dacewicz, Leonarda. *Słownik historycznych nazw osobowych Białostocczyzny* [Dictionary of Historical Personal Names of the Białystok Region]. Volume 1, Białystok: Instytut Filogii Wschodniosłowiańskiej Uniwersytetu w Białymstoku, 1997, Volume 2, Białystok: same publisher, 1998. ISBN 83-905750-1-9. This Polish-language work provides insight into surnames found in northeastern Poland, which may be of Belarusian, Lithuanian, Polish, or Russian linguistic origin.

Baker, T. Lindsey. "The Moczygemba Family of Texas and Poland." The *Polish Genealogical Society Newsletter,* Spring 1988, p. 1.

Bańkowski, Andrzej. *Etymologiczny słownik języka polskiego* [Etymological Dictionary of the Polish Language]. Volume 1, A–K; Volume 2, L–P. Warszawa: Wydawnictwo Naukowe DWN, 2000. This work requires considerable knowledge of Polish, and knowledge of several other languages is helpful. The author is very opinionated, and his work provoked considerable controversy; but his lively discussions of word origins are fascinating. Unfortunately, it seems unlikely the final volume of his work will be published, and we may never have a chance to read his analysis of words beginning R through Ż.

Brückner, Aleksander. *Słownik etymologiczny języka polskiego* [Etymological Dictionary of the Polish Language]. Warszawa: Wiedza Powszechna, 1970. This is a Polish-language dictionary with entries on the derivations of numerous Polish words and comparisons with words from other languages from the same roots. Although subsequent scholarship (not surprisingly) has cast doubt on some of the author's analysis, this work remains the only complete etymological dictionary of the Polish language. Others have been begun, including that of Andrzej Bańkowski (see previous item), but only Brückner's was completed.

Bubak, Józef. *Księga naszych imion* [Book of Our First Names]. Wrocław-Warszawa-Kraków, 1993. This Polish-language reference offers the nonspecialist origins and derivations of most common Polish first names.

Bubak, Józef. *Słownik nazw osobowych i elementów identyfikacyjnych Sądecczyzny, XV-XVII w.: imiona, nazwiska, przezwiska* [Dictionary of Personal Names and Identifying Elements of the Sącz region, 15th-17th Centuries: First Names, Surnames, and Bynames], two volumes. Kraków: "Universitas," 1992. ISBN 83-7052-033-2. A Polish-language reference for personal names seen in the region of Nowy and Stary Sącz in southeastern Poland, this two-volume work draws on 38 manuscript and two printed sources from the years 1488-1700. It quotes entries from records that mention names and in most cases gives derivations.

Bystroń, Jan Stanisław. *Dzieje obyczajów w dawnej Polsce, w. XVI-XVII* [The History of Customs in Ancient Poland, 16th-17th Centuries], Volume 1. Warszawa: Państwowy Instytut Wydawniczy, 1960. An English translation of extracts from chapter seven, "Chłopi" ("The Peasants") appeared in the *Polish Genealogical Society Newsletter,* Spring 1991. This is a fascinating study of 16th- and 17th-century Poland's social conditions.

Bystroń, Jan Stanisław. *Nazwiska Polskie* [Polish Surnames]. Lwów-Warszawa: Książnica-Atlas, S. A. Zjedn. Zakłady Krtograf. i wydawnicze T.N.S.W., 1936. A Polish-language work that requires fluency in that language, this book is a prose exposition of the history and processes whereby Polish surnames were formed and developed. It does not provide great detail on many surnames (although there is a useful index to specific names discussed), but concentrates instead on general principles, citing selected names as illustrations. Decades of research since its publication has made it somewhat updated; but it is still a good basic work on the subject of Polish surnames.

Bystrzycki, Tadeusz, ed. *Skorowidz miejscowości Rzeczypospolitej Polski* [Index of Localities of the Polish Republic]. Two volumes. Przemyśl: Wydawnictwo książnicy naukowej, 1934. This source is particularly valuable for finding communities located in those areas that were in Poland between World Wars I and II, but later were incorporated into the Soviet Union, and are now in Belarus, Lithuania, and Ukraine. It is available from numerous libraries, including a number of online digital libraries, for instance, <http://www.wbc.poznan.pl/dlibra/docmetadata?id=12786&from=publication>.

Chojnacki, Władysław. "American Polonia Seeks Its 'Roots.'" *Polish Genealogical Society Newsletter,* Fall 1984–Spring 1985. This article, translated from Polish, presents a brief survey of the state of Polish-American genealogical research at that time.

Cieślikowa, A. "W. F. Hoffman, *Polish Surnames: Origins & Meanings"* (review), issue XL, *Onomastica,* Kraków 1995. Prof. Cieślikowa gives a very even-handed review of the strengths and weaknesses of the first edition of this book.

Cieślikowa, Aleksandra, Malec Maria, and Rymut, Kazimierz. *Słownik etymologiczno-motywacyjny staropolskich nazw osobowych* [Etymologically Motivational Dictionary of Old Polish Personal Names]. Seven volumes by different authors, analyzing different categories of personal names found in the reference work *Słownik staropolskich nazw osobowych* (see Taszycki, Witold, below). ISBN for the whole set: 83-85579-63-X. The seven volumes are:

Volume 1: *Odapelatywne nazwy osobowe* [Personal Names from Appellatives], compiled by A. Cieślikowa with Janina Szymowa and Kazimierz Rymut. Kraków: Wydawnictwo Naukowe DWN, Polska Akademia Nauk, Instytut Języka Polskiego, 2000.

Volume 2: *Nazwy osobowe pochodzenia chrześcijańskiego* [Personal Names of Christian Origin], compiled by M. Malec, Kraków: Polska Akademia Nauk, Instytut Języka Polskiego, 1995.

Volume 3: *Odmiejscowe nazwy osobowe* [Personal Names from Place Names], compiled by Z. Kaleta with E. Supranowicz and J. Szymowa, Kraków: Polska Akademia Nauk, Instytut Języka Polskiego, 1997.

Volume 4: *Nazwy osobowe pochodzące od etników* [Personal Names Deriving from Ethnic Names], compiled by E. Supranowicz, Kraków: Polska Akademia Nauk, Instytut Języka Polskiego, 1997.

Volume 5: *Nazwy osobowe pochodzenia niemieckiego* [Personal Names of German Origin], compiled by Z. Klimek. Kraków: Polska Akademia Nauk, Instytut Języka Polskiego, 1997.

Volume 6: *Nazwy heraldyczne* [Heraldic Names], compiled by M. Bobowska-Kowalska, Kraków: Polska Akademia Nauk, Instytut Języka Polskiego, 1995.

Volume 7: *Suplement. Rozwiązanie licznych zagadek staropolskiej antroponimii* [Supplement. Solutions to Numerous Puzzles of Old Polish Anthroponymy]. A. Cieślikowa, ed. Kraków: Wydawnictwo Naukowe DWN, 2002.

Czapliński, Władysław and Ładogórski, Tadeusz, editors. *Atlas Historyczny Polski* [Historical Atlas of Poland], 4th edition, Warszawa: Państwowe Przedsiębiorstwo Wydawnictw Kartograficznych, 1977. This work features a series of maps with explanatory text that illustrate historical, social, and economic changes of Poland over the centuries. An English-language version, *The Historical Atlas of Poland,* was issued by the same publisher in 1986, ISBN 83-7000-037-1. I suspect one can find maps online that serve the same purpose adequately.

Dworzaczek, Włodzimierz. *Genealogia.* Warszawa: Państwowe Wydawnictwo Naukowe, 1959. An English-language translation (by William F.

Hoffman) of Chapter Three appeared in the *Polish Genealogical Society Newsletter,* Fall 1985-Fall, 1987, and of Chapter Five in the *Polish Genealogical Society Newsletter,* beginning Spring 1990. This was the first book by a Polish scholar that took genealogy seriously as a legitimate branch of history. Chapters One, Two, and Four cover general material available in any book on genealogy, but Chapters Three and Five concentrate on information relevant specifically to Polish genealogy. While much of the information is dated, anyone serious about studying this subject can benefit from reading Chapters Three and Five. An updated translation of Chapter III is available on the website of the Polish Genealogical Society of America® at <http://www.pgsa.org/PDFs/DworzaczekIII.pdf>

Encyklopedia Popularna PWN. Warszawa: Państwowe Wydawnictwo Naukowe, 1982. Much as I have used this one-volume Polish-language general reference in the past, I have to admit that these days, judicious use of Wikipedia and other online sources probably provides as much information, if not more.

Fisiak, Jacek, ed. *Nowy Słownik Fundacji Kościuszkowskiej Polsko-Angielski / The New Kosciuszko Foundation Dictionary: Polish-English.* New York: Kosciuszko Foundation, Inc., 2003. ISBN 0-917004-27-2 and 83-242-0007-X. While this dictionary lacks many of the archaic terms I needed to study, it has several virtues, including an emphasis on translating Polish terms into American English rather than British. If I'm not mistaken, a newer edition is available, and can be ordered in book form, on CD-ROM, on DVD, and as an online reference. For more information, see the website <http://www.thekf.org/about/dictionary/>.

Hanks, Patrick. *Dictionary of American Family Names,* three volumes. New York: Oxford University Press, 2003, ISBN 978-0195081374. This ambitious and rather expensive set of books gives derivations of a wide variety of surnames that appear in America, including a very respectable selection of the Polish surnames most often encountered here. The Polish names were analyzed by perhaps the finest living expert in the field, Prof. Aleksandra Cieślikowa of the Polish Language Institute in Kraków; and Alexander Beider dealt with Jewish and Ukrainian names. Those interested mainly in Polish surnames that were reasonably common in North America should attempt to get their hands on this.

Hanks, Patrick, and Hodges, Flavia. *A Dictionary of First Names.* Oxford, New York: Oxford University Press, 1995. ISBN 0-19-211651-7. I used an older hardcover edition, but Amazon sells a newer, softcover edition published in 2005, ISBN 978-0198607649. I cannot comment on the newer edition, but the one I used struck me as the best reference I could find on given names, covering those used by many different cultures. Too many other books on the subject are aimed mainly at parents searching for a good name to give their babies.

Hoffman, William F. and Helon, George W. *First Names of the Polish Commonwealth: Origins and Meanings.* Chicago: Polish Genealogical Society of America®, 1998. ISBN 0-924207-06-X. The title pretty much says it all.

Hoffman, William F. "The Mystery of the Misplaced Ukrainians: Solved." *Polish Genealogical Society of America Bulletin.* Fall, 1994, p. 12.

Holewinski, Felix W. "The Nature of Polish Knighthood and Chivalry from the Thirteenth to the Eighteenth Centuries." *The Augustan* XX:3. Reprinted in *Polish Genealogical Society Newsletter,* Spring 1989, pp. 5-6, 10-11, Fall 1989, pp. 25-26, 29, 35.

Hollowak, Thomas L. *The Rise of Independency Among Baltimore's Polish Catholics, 1868-1898.* M.A. thesis submitted to the Graduate School of the University of Maryland, 1990.

Hollowak, Thomas L., and Hoffman, William F. *Index to the Obituaries and Death Notices Appearing in the* Dziennik Chicagoski, *1920-1929,* parts I-II, Polish Genealogical Society, Chicago, 1991, LCCN 91-62265. Besides its genealogical uses, this index is helpful in determining the spellings of Polish surnames.

Hoskins, Janina, *Polish Genealogy and Heraldry: An Introduction to Research,* Washington, Library of Congress, 1987, LCCN 87-6000087. 120 pp. Much has been published in the field of Polish genealogy and heraldry since Ms. Hoskin's book appeared, and it is less useful for genealogy than it once was. It still provides a useful starting-place for learning about available resources on Polish heraldry, a subject that has received less attention in English.

Kaleta, Zofia. *The Surname as a Cultural Value and an Ethnic Heritage: Tracing Your Family Roots.* Warsaw: Instytut Sławistyki PAN, Towarzystwo Naukowe Warszawskie, 1997. ISBN 83-866619-07-4. A book by a Polish scholar in English! Kaleta has six chapters discussing the origins and development of Polish surnames, and a seventh that takes up half the book with a "Dictionary of the Oldest Polish Surnames Endings in *–ski,*" a subject she is particularly well qualified to discuss. I recommend it for anyone with a serious interest in Polish names.

Karłowicz, J., Kryński, A., and Niedźwiedzki, W. *Słownik języka polskiego* [Dictionary of the Polish Language], Warsaw: Państwowy Instytut Wydawniczy, 1952, eight volumes. This is a reprint of the original work, published in Warsaw in 1900 and often called the *Słownik warszawski*, "the Warsaw dictionary," in reference to its place of publication. Professor Rymut recommended it as especially valuable for rare and archaic terms that may be relevant to surname origins. As of this writing, it is available online through the University of Warsaw's digital library <http://ebuw. uw.edu.pl/dlibra/publication?id=254>; you can even download each of the eight volumes!

Kiełbasa, Stanisław. *Dictionary of Polish Obscenities*. 3rd, revised edition. [No place of publication given]: Scythian Books, 1994. ISBN 0-933884-93-1. While I have no interest in filth for filth's sake, anyone who cares about the meanings of words needs some insight into which words are considered offensive. That is particularly true when you consider that quite a few Polish surnames come from those words!

Knab, Sophie Hodorowicz. *Polish Customs, Traditions & Folklore*. New York: Hippocrene Books, 1993. ISBN 0-7818-0068-4. This fine book offers a wealth of fascination information on Polish customs, and its insights on the meanings of various terms are surely worth considering when dealing with surnames derived from those terms. I notice Amazon. com sells an edition newer than the one I used. It was published in 1996, ISBN 978-0781805155.

Konarski, Szymon, with an introduction by Sławomir Gorzyński. *Słownik geograficzny Królestwa Polskiego i innych krajów słowiańskich. Index nazwisk.* [The Geographical Dictionary of the Kingdom of Poland and Other Slavic Lands. Surname Index]. Warszawa: Wydawnictwo DiG, 1995. Polish scholar Szymon Konarski went through the massive Polish-language gazetteer *Słownik geograficzny* (see Sulimierski, Filip, below) and indexed all the surnames he spotted. While not wholly devoid of error (what book is?), this is a useful source because it often allows you to make a firm connection between a surname and a place name derived from it.

Kopczyński, Michał, and Tygielski, Wojciech, ed. *Pod wspólnym niebem: Narody dawnej Rzeczypospolitej*. Warszawa: Bellona SA, 2010. This fascinating book contains chapters on the history of various ethnic groups in Poland, including Lithuanians, Belarusians, Ukrainians, Germans, Jews, Armenians, Tatars, Karaites, Gypsies/Romani, Italians, Scots, and Mennonites, as well as a chapter on the Poles themselves. An English translation by yours truly is scheduled to be published in 2013.

Korzon, Tadeusz. *Kościuszko: Biografia z dokumentów wysnuta* [Kościuszko: A Biography Drawn from Documents], second edition. Kraków – G. Gebethner i spółka; Warszawa – Gebethner i Wolff. A Polish-language biography of Kościuszko by an eminent Polish scholar, of onomastic interest only for its discussion on the origins and development of Ukrainian names, which—not surprisingly—focuses on the *Kościuszko* name. <http://www.wbc.poznan.pl/dlibra/docmetadata?id=3569&from=latest>

Kowalik-Kaleta, Zofia, *Staropolskie nazwy osobowe motywowane przez nazwy miejscowe* [Old Polish Personal Names Based on Place Names], Zakład Narodowy im. Ossolińskich—Wydawnictwo, Wrocław, 1981, ISBN 83-04-00831-9. This Polish-language work analyzes how old Polish toponyms contributed to the development of personal names and cites entries in old records and documents. For English-speaking readers, the book by the same author, listed above as "Kaleta, Zofia," is a better practical choice, as it covers much the same ground.

Lenius, Brian J. *Genealogical Gazetteer of Galicia,* expanded data edition. Self-published, Brian J. Lenius, Box 58, Grp. 328, RR#3, Selkirk, MB, CANADA R1A 2A8, 1999. ISBN 0-9698783-1-1. An excellent source for information on Galicia, with introductory notes, lists of communities by their Polish names, a supplementary community list, lists of Ukrainian and German names, and maps. The primary community/estate list is valuable for surname origins as well, especially when contrasted with the appendix that gives their Ukrainian equivalents. Those seriously interested in researching roots in southeastern Poland or western Ukraine need this book. For more information, see the website <http://www.lenius.ca/Gazetteer/Gazetteer.htm>.

Lippóczy, Piotr, Walichnowski, Tadeusz. *Przesiedlenie ludności niemieckiej z Polski po drugiej wojnie światowej w świetle dokumentów* [Resettlement of the German Population from Poland after World War II in the Light of Documents]. Warszawa—Łódź: Państwowe Wydawnictwo Naukowe, 1982. ISBN 83-01-01858-5. In German, Russian, Polish, and English. As the title explains, this is a multilingual collection of documents dealing with ethnic Germans' emigration from Poland and resettlement in Germany after World War II.

Magocsi, Paul Robert. *Historical Atlas of East Central Europe.* Seattle & London: University of Washington Press, 2002. ISBN 978-0295981468. This superb work is a great help in understanding the geographic and temporal background of the history of the Poles and all Eastern Europeans. Its maps are clear and easy to read, the text concise and informative.

Malec, Maria. *Imiona chrześcijańskie w średniowiecznej Polsce* [Christian Names in Medieval Poland], Polska Akademia Nauk, Instytut Języka Polskiego, Kraków, 1994, ISBN 83-85579-52-4. This is a very helpful Polish-language analysis of Christian names common in medieval Poland, with comparison to forms in Latin, Greek, and other Slavic languages. It is based on names appearing in the work *Słownik staropolskich nazw osobowych* (q. v.).

Malec, Maria. *Nazwy osobowe pochodzenia chrześcijańskiego.* Volume 2 of the series *Słownik etymologiczno-motywacyjny staropolskich nazw osobowych*, ed. Aleksandra Cieślikowa, Maria Malec, and Kazimierz Rymuta. Kraków: Polska Akademia Nauk, Instytut Języka Polskiego, 1995. XXIV + 151 pages. ISBN: 85-85579-68-0. As of this writing, it is available from the bookstore of the publisher at this address: <http://sklep.ijp-pan.krakow.pl/product_info.php?products_id=104>.

Milerski, Władysław. *Nazwiska cieszyńskie* [The Surnames of Cieszyn]. Warszawa: Wydawnictwo Energeia, 1996. ISBN 83-85118-47-0. This is an interesting Polish-language work concentrating on surnames found in the Cieszyn/Český Těšin region, with its mixture of Czech, German, and Polish linguistic and onomastic influences.

Niesiecki, Kasper, *Herbarz Polski* [Polish Armorial], edited and supplemented by Jan Nep. Bobrowicz, Lipsk (Leipzig), Breitkopf & Härtel, 1839. This is a reworked and expanded version of a highly regarded Polish armorial, the *Korona Polska* by Kasper Niesiecki, S.J., published between 1728 and 1744. This 10-volume revision, supplemented by Bobrowicz with notes by writers who lived after Niesiecki, is available in many libraries, including that of Chicago's Polish Museum of America.

Obal, Thaddeus J., *Polish Family Tree Surnames,* volumes II-V, published 1977-1983 by the author (739 Hillsdale Avenue, Hillsdale, NJ 07642-2515). These volumes contain thousands of listings of Polish surnames that researchers are tracing; each volume supplements and updates the earlier ones, but no information is repeated. Separate indices are provided for surnames being researched, names and addresses of those studying them, and the ancestral regions in Poland from which those names came.

Ochnio, Constance, "Don't Let Suffixes Confuse You." *Pathways & Passages,* publication of the Polish Genealogical Society of Connecticut. Spring 1992.

Ortell, Gerald A. *Polish Parish Records of the Roman Catholic Church.* Chicago: Polish Genealogical Society of America®, 1996. ISBN

0-924207-03-5. The 104 pages of this book provide an impressive amount of information not only on Polish parish records but also on Polish society and customs, with particular attention to Galicia.

Pentek, Zdzisław. "The Relationships of the So-Called 'Dutch Populace' in Greater Poland." *Gens,* the publication of the Towarzystwo Genealogiczno-Heraldyczne, Poznań. Translated and reprinted in the *Polish Genealogical Society Bulletin,* Summer, 1991.

Picknicki, Jeff. "The Origin and Meaning of Ukrainian Surnames." *Polish Genealogical Society Newsletter.* Spring 1990.

Pogonowski, Iwo Cyprian. *Poland: A Historical Atlas,* revised edition. New York: Dorset Press, 1989. ISBN 0-88029-324-2. Original edition published by Hippocrene Press, ISBN 0-87052-282-5. An unusual reference that combines passages of text with a series of maps drawn to show Poland's economic, social, and territorial changes through the centuries.

Prinke, Rafał T. "Beyond Names and Dates." *Polish Genealogical Society Newsletter.* Fall, 1987. This article describes the information one can gain about ancestors from terms used in church and civil records.

Przyjaciel ludu Kaszubskiego. A publication of the Kashubian Association of North America (KANA), Kashubian Association of North America, P.O. Box 27732, Minneapolis MN 55427-0732, website <http://ka-na.org/>.

Rekowski, Fr. Aloysius, C.S.S.R. *An Anthology of Kashub-Polish Family Names in Poland, Canada, U.S.A.* Self-published, no publication information available. Perhaps the best way to get a copy is to contact KA-NA (see preceding entry).

Rospond, Stanisław. *Słownik nazwisk śląskich* [Dictionary of Silesian Surnames]. Volumes 1–2, A–K. Wrocław: Zakład Narodowy im Ossolińskich, 1967 and 1973. Silesian surnames are a field unto themselves, and Rospond's work was a valuable contribution to their study.

Rymut, Kazimierz, *Nazwiska Polaków: Słownik historzcyno-etymologiczny* [The Surnames of Poles: A Historico-Etymological Dictionary]. Kraków: Wydawnictwo Naukowe DWN, 2001. This is a Polish-language "popular" work, that is, one that is meant to be intelligible to any educated Pole rather than only to specialists. It consists of several prose passages explaining aspects of Polish surname formation, followed by an index of roots and the names that came from them. The latter part comprises the bulk of the work and does not require a thorough knowledge of the Polish language (unlike the first part)—a good dictionary and a grasp of the rudiments will suffice to let non-Poles understand it fairly well. I should add that Professor Rymut completed a final and expanded edition of this book in 2006, shortly before he died. I bought the rights to translate it into English and publish the translation. I hope to do so in the near future, especially if the response to the third edition of my book shows me people want to see more on the subject. My book draws heavily from his, but his contains a great deal of information I have not included.

Rymut, Kazimierz. *Nazwy miast Polski* [Names of the Cities of Poland], second edition. Wrocław: Zakład Narodowy im. Ossolińskich—Wydawnictwo, 1987. ISBN 83-04-02436-5. A Polish-language work of almost 300 pages providing analysis of the names of towns and cities in Poland.

Rymut, Kazimierz, ed. *Nazwy miejscowe Polski* [The Place Names of Poland]. Kraków: Instytut Języka Polskiego PAN, 1996. ISBN 83-85579-34-6. This is a projected 10-volume work dealing with the forms and origins of the names of places within the current borders of Poland. It is likely to become the standard reference on the subject—which is important to us because so many Polish surnames derive from toponyms. As of this writing, these volumes have been published: I, A-B; II, C-D; III, E-I; IV. J-Kn; V. Ko-Ky; VI. L-Ma; and VII. Mą-N. I can't wait to see the rest!

Rymut, Kazimierz, ed. *Słownik nazwisk używanych w Polsce na początku XXI wieku / Dictionary of Surnames in Current Use in Poland at the Beginning of the 21st Century.* CD-ROM. Kraków–Chicago: co-published by the Polish Academy of Sciences, Polish Language Institute, and the Polish Genealogical Society of America®, 2002. To the best of my knowledge, the CD is no longer available, except perhaps secondhand. See Chapter Eleven for more information on this work, including its availability as an online searchable database at <http://www.moikrewni.pl/mapa/>.

Rymut, Kazimierz, ed. *Słownik nazwisk współcześnie w Polsce używanych* [Dictionary of Surnames in Current Use in Poland]. Kraków: Instytut Języka Polskiego PAN, 1992. ISBN 83-85579-25-7. 10 volumes. The printed books appear to be still available from the publisher. See Chapter Eleven for more information on this work, including its availability as an online searchable database at <http://www.herby.com.pl/indexslo.html>.

Rymut, Kazimierz, "Zasób leksemów w prasłowiańskich imionach złożonych," *Onomastica* XXXVIII, pp. 5–19. This article lists roots used in Slavic dithematic names.

Sanford, Albert Hart, M.A. "Polish People of Portage County" *Proceedings, 1907,* Wisconsin Historical Society. Reprinted in the Fall 1988 and Spring 1989 issues of the *Polish Genealogical Society Newsletter.* As of this writing, the original article is available online at <http://content. wisconsinhistory.org/u?/tp,47161>

Shea, Jonathan D. *Going Home: A Guide to Polish American Family History Research.* [New Britain, Connecticut]: Language & Lineage Press, 2007. Website <http://www.langline.com/GoingHome.htm>. ISBN 978-0-9631579-7-3. This is a splendid work by the foremost expert in the field of Polish-American genealogy. It covers many different aspects of Polish research and culture, including grammar and surnames.

Shea, Jonathan D. *Russian Language Documents from Russian Poland: A Translation Manual for Genealogists.* Orem, Utah: Genun Publishers, 1989. ISBN 0-912811-05-6. This book uses maps, sample documents, and text analysis to teach the reader how to perform the daunting task of deciphering the Russian-language records typically encountered in the Russian partition of Poland. It was a pioneering work, but is hard to find now, and the author himself recommends getting the Russian volume of the *In Their Words* series, which covers the same ground but in much greater detail.

Shea, Jonathan D., and Hoffman, William F. *Following the Paper Trail.* Teaneck, New Jersey: Avotaynu, Inc., 1994. ISBN 978-0962637346. This book uses 59 sample documents to illustrate how to analyze and translate records in German, Swedish, French, Italian, Latin, Portuguese, Romanian, Spanish, Czech, Polish, Russian, Hungarian, and Lithuanian. For more information, see <http://www.avotaynu.com/books/FPT.htm>.

Shea, Jonathan D. and Hoffman, William F. *In Their Words: A Genealogists' Translation Guide to Polish, German, Latin, and Russian Documents. Volume I. Polish.* New Britain, Connecticut: Language & Lineage Press, 2007. ISBN 978-0-9361579-6-6. This book is meant primarily to assist researchers in finding and deciphering Polish-language documents; but it also contains a number of practical pointers on how to deal with surnames, especially as they appear in documents. For more information, see <http://langline.com/ITW_Polish.htm>.

Shea, Jonathan D. and Hoffman, William F. *In Their Words: A Genealogist's Translation Guide to Polish, German, Latin, and Russian Documents. Volume II. Russian.* New Britain, Connecticut: Language & Lineage Press, 2002. ISBN 0-9361579-4-9. This book is meant primarily to assist researchers in deciphering Russian-language documents. But it also contains a number of practical pointers on how to deal with surnames, especially as they appear in documents. As of this writing, it is out of print; but we hope to change that soon. For more information, see <http://langline.com/ITW_Russian.htm>.

Sokolnicki, Juliusz Nowina. "The Noble Clans." *Polish Genealogical Society Newsletter,* Fall 1990, pp. 20, 35-36.

Stanislawski, J. *McKay's English-Polish, Polish-English Dictionary.* Random House: New York, 1988, ISBN 0-812-91691-3. This compact one-volume dictionary has the virtue of being easy to find in American bookstores, and it is surprising how many older terms and usages appear in it that do not appear in Stanisławski's *Wielki słownik* (see next entry), even though that work is in most respects the superior reference.

Stanisławski, Jan. *Wielki słownik polsko-angielski, z suplementem* [The Great Polish-English Dictionary, with a supplement]. Two volumes. Państwowe Wydawnictwo • Wiedza Powszechna • 1980, ISBN 83-214-0107-4. This two-volume Polish-to-English dictionary proved valuable in deciphering some of the rather difficult passages I encountered in the course of this research, and it has the merit of not being too hard to find.

Sulimierski, Filip; Chlebowski, Bronisław; and Walewski, Władysław. *Słownik geograficzny Królestwa Polskiego i innych krajów słowiańskich* [Geographical Dictionary of the Kingdom of Poland and Other Slavic Lands]. Warszawa: Nakładem Władysława Walewskiego, 1880-1902. This is an amazingly comprehensive Polish-language gazetteer for towns and villages in Poland. Obviously it does not include the many changes in names, administrative districts, and population that have occurred since it was published; but it is always worth checking for information on hard-to-find localities in Poland and neighboring countries. It is particularly valuable for information on place names that could have produced surnames, and sometimes cites family names associated with specific places. It can be found in many major libraries, and is available for sale as a CD-ROM from the Polish Genealogical Society of America®; for more information, see <http://www.pgsa.org/>.

Surma, Genowefa. *Nazwy osobowe w opoczyńskiem* [Personal Names in the Opoczno Area]. Gdańsk: Uniwersytet Gdański, 1991. ISBN 83-7017-365-9. This Polish-language work on personal names in the Opoczno region cites entries of names in records, gives the date and context, and supplies the derivation. The sections are divided by categories of name formation, which makes the work better suited for the specialist in Polish onomastics than for the curious amateur. This is the kind of research that shows accurately how a specific family name originated in a specific area at a specific time.

Szulc, Tad. "Poland: The Hope That Never Dies." *National Geographic,* January 1988.

Taszycki, Witold, ed. *Słownik staropolskich nazw osobowych* [Dictionary of Old Polish Personal Names]. Wrocław: Zakład narodowy imienia Ossolińskich, Wydwanictwo Polskiej Akademii Nauk, Ossolineum, 1965-1967, six volumes. This dictionary of old Polish personal names deals with surnames as they were in the process of becoming established. It is a source of fundamental value for any Polish onomastic research, because it is a compilation of earliest appearances of numerous Polish names in documents, citing the records in which the names first appeared, giving the context, date, and spelling.

Teki Dworzaczka [Dworzaczek's Files]. Originally a CD-ROM produced under the direction of Jerzy Wisłocki, Adam Bieniaszewski, and Rafał T. Prinke, it is now available online at <http://teki.bkpan.poznan.pl/>. It contains a massive amount of genealogical information compiled by the late Polish historian Włodzimierz Dworzaczek. It covers Polish nobility living in Greater Poland, i.e., the *powiaty* of Gniezno, Kalisz, Kcynia, Konin, Kościan, Nakło, Poznań, Pyzdry, Wałcz, and Wschowa. It is valuable for surname research because you can key in a name and within a few seconds you have every mention of that name in some 50,000 pages' worth of data! The site is in Polish, however, and requires a fair degree of fluency to use effectively.

Zbichorski, Mirosław. "The Polish Inn in History." *Polish Genealogical Society Newsletter.* Spring, 1992. This article mentions the process by which the names of inns became associated in some cases with their owners, eventually becoming surnames.

Czech Reference Works

Poldauf, Dr. Ivan, ed. *Anglicko-český a česko-anglický slovník* [English-Czech and Czech-English Dictionary]. Praha: Státní Pedagogické Nakladatelství, 1971. ISBN 80-04-25987-1. A 1,200+ page dictionary that I found quite useful in comparing Czech and Polish roots.

German Reference Works

Bahlow, Hans. *Deutsches Namenlexikon* [German Lexicon of Names]. Suhrkamp Taschenbuch Verlag, 1967, 1985. ISBN 3-518-36565-7

<2400>. A German-language compilation of common German surnames with analysis of their meanings and origins. Also available is an English-language translation by Edda Gentry, *Dictionary of German Names,* Max Kade Institute for German-American Studies, University of Wisconsin-Madison, Madison WI, 1994, ISBN 0-924119-35-7.

George F. Jones. *German-American Names.* Baltimore: Genealogical Publishing Co., Inc., 1990. ISBN 0-8063-1271-8. I understand the author has published a 1995 edition, ISBN 0-8063-1481-8. This is a very readable, organized analysis of common German surnames. The first part is a prose explanation of general principles with some examples, and the second gives the meaning of individual surnames with cross-reference to the relevant explanatory text passages in the first part. I must admit, however, that when the analysis in the Kohlheim and Bahlow books differs from that of Jones, I have more confidence in theirs.

Kartenmeister.com, <http://www.kartenmeister.com>. This online resource is very valuable for finding places that were in the Germany Empire before World War I. It allows you to search for German or Polish names, names of *Kreis* or *Provinz*, etc. It also helps you connect with other researchers interested in specific places. The Webmaster, Uwe-Karsten Krickhahn, should be commended for providing a valuable service, and I encourage anyone who can afford to make a donation to do so.

Kohlheim, Rosa and Volker. *Duden Familiennamen: Herkunft und Bedeutung* [Duden Family Names: Origin and Meaning]. Mannheim: Bibliographisches Institut / F. A. Brockhaus A.G., 2000. ISBN 3-411-70851-4. This German-language book is easy to use and provides an impressive amount of information on German surnames.

Kaemmerer, M., editor. *Ortsnamenverzeichnis der Ortschaften jenseits von Oder und Neiße* [Gazetteer of Localities Beyond the Oder and Neiße]. Leer: Verlag Gerhard Rautenberg, 1988. This gazetteer indexes and cross-references the German and Polish names of towns and villages in eastern Pomerania, eastern Brandenburg, East Prussia, and Silesia; it includes only those parts of Posen and West Prussia that were in the Grenzmark Posen-West Prussia and in Regierungsbezirk West Prussia that became part of East Prussia in 1920, and does not include the areas in Posen and West Prussia that became part of Poland after World War II.

Jewish Reference Works

Beider, Alexander. *A Dictionary of Ashkenazic Given Names: Their Origins, Structure, Pronunciations, and Migrations.* Bergenfield, New Jersey:

Avotaynu, Inc., 2001. ISBN 978-1886223127. This book provides 728 pages of information about 735 root names of Ashkenazic Jews, and 15,000 variants that derived from them. This information is extremely valuable for studying Jewish surnames because so many of those surnames developed from given names. An index to the 15,000 variations discussed helps you trace them to the proper root name. In addition to the dictionary itself, there is lengthy thesis on the origins, structure, pronunciation, and migrations of Ashkenazic given names. For more information, contact Avotaynu, Inc., <http://www.avotaynu.com>.

Beider, Alexander. *A Dictionary of Jewish Surnames from Galicia.* Bergenfield, New Jersey: Avotaynu, Inc., 2004. ISBN 978-1886223196. This 624-page book deals with the surnames of Jews living within Galicia, the Austrian partition that included what are now southeastern Poland and southwestern Ukraine. The author lists some 25,000 surnames, indicates in which districts of Galicia they were found, analyzes their meanings, and lists variant forms. For more information, contact Avotaynu, Inc., <http://www.avotaynu.com>.

Beider, Alexander. *A Dictionary of Jewish Surnames from the Kingdom of Poland,* Avotaynu, Inc., Teaneck, New Jersey, 1996, LCCN 96-14963, ISBN 0-9626373-9-4. This book features a lengthy discussion of origins of names of Jews living within the Kingdom of Poland, the dictionary itself, and a Daitch-Mokotoff Soundex listing of the surnames. It does not cover directly surnames of Jews living outside the Kingdom of Poland, but its analysis and history are valuable for descendants of Jews living anywhere in eastern Europe. For more information, contact Avotaynu, Inc., <http://www.avotaynu.com>.

Beider, Alexander. *A Dictionary of Jewish Surnames from the Russian Empire, Revised Edition.* Avotaynu, Bergenfield, New Jersey, 2008, LCCN 92-46252, ISBN 0-9626373-3-5. The 2008 revised edition of this work is even more impressive than the original 1993 version. It comes in two volumes, one over 1,000 pages in length, the other 190 pages. The larger volume includes a 200-page introduction and the dictionary itself, analyzing some 74,000 surnames. Volume 2 indexes those names according to the Daitch-Mokotoff Soundex System. It covers only surnames of Jews living in the Russian Empire, but the analysis and history it provides are useful for descendants of Jews living anywhere in eastern Europe. For more information, contact Avotaynu, Inc., <http://www.avotaynu.com>.

Beider, Alexander. "Jewish Surnames in the Russian Empire." *Avotaynu,* Fall 1992. This English-language article written for the Jewish genealogical quarterly *Avotaynu* gives a valuable introduction to the subject of eastern European Jewish surnames. Beider has since published a number of excellent books on Jewish surnames and given names that are listed in this bibliography. But this article is a concise introduction to the subject.

Feldblyum, Boris. *Russian-Jewish Given Names: Their Origins and Variants.* Teaneck New Jersey: Avotaynu, Inc., 1998. ISBN 978-1886223073. This book draws heavily on a 1911 work by Iser Kulisher designed to help Russian officials deal with the complexities of Russian Jews' given names, which, of course, are vital to the study of Jewish surnames. This choice of sources helped Feldblyum focus on precisely the information descendants of Russian Jews need to deal with those complexities themselves. For more information contact Avotaynu, Inc., <http://www.avotaynu.com>.

Gorr, Rabbi Shmuel. *Jewish Personal Names: Their Origin, Derivation and Diminutive Forms.* Edited by Chaim Freedman. Teaneck, New Jersey: Avotaynu, Inc., 1992. ISBN 978-0962637322. 112 + xvi pages. A compact and useful guide to Jewish names, discussing primarily their Hebrew and Yiddish forms. For information, contact Avotaynu, Inc., <http://www.avotaynu.com>.

Kaganoff, Benzion C. *A Dictionary of Jewish Names and Their History.* New York: Schocken Books, 1977. For years, this book's easy availability and readability made it a popular reference on the subject of Jewish surnames. It has its flaws, however, and Beider's books (listed above) have eclipsed it. It was out of print, but I see that Amazon.com is offering a 250-page paperback version published by Jason Aronson, Inc. in 1996, ISBN 978-1568219530.

Menk, Lars. *A Dictionary of German-Jewish Surnames.* Bergenfield, New Jersey: Avotaynu, Inc., 2005. ISBN 978-1886223202. Menk offers 824 pages of information on the surnames borne by German Jews. The book provides the etymology and variants of each name, and identifies where in the region the name appeared, specifying the town and time period. For information, contact Avotaynu, Inc., <http://www.avotaynu.com>.

Mokotoff, Gary. *Getting Started in Jewish Genealogy.* Bergenfield, New Jersey: Avotaynu, Inc., 2010. ISBN 978-1886223462. The author is the publisher of AVOTAYNU, The International Review of Jewish Genealogy, and is especially well qualified to help researchers of Jewish roots get off to a good start. For more information, contact Avotaynu, Inc., <http://www.avotaynu.com>.

Mokotoff, Gary, and Sack, Sallyann Amdur, with Sharon, Alexander. *Where Once We Walked: A Guide to the Jewish Communities Destroyed in the Holocaust, Revised Edition.* Bergenfield, New Jersey: Avotaynu, Inc., 2002. ISBN 978-1886223158. This reference is valuable for locating small central and eastern European towns and villages whose names can appear in a bewildering variety of spellings. It includes Daitch-Mokotoff index codes to help get past the spelling variations. While most useful for Jewish research, it has a place in the library of anyone who deals with eastern European place names—and the guide to the Daitch-Mokotoff Soundex System explains principles that can be applied usefully to surnames as well. For more information, contact Avotaynu, Inc., <http://www.avotaynu.com>.

Lithuanian Reference Works

Genealogija. The Lithuanian-American Immigration History & Genealogy Publication. a periodical published by the Balzekas Museum of Lithuanian Culture Library, 6500 South Pulaski Road, Chicago, IL 60629. Issues used for this book are Spring 1992 and Summer 1992. Individual articles include: "Lithuanian Pioneers" (Spring 1992); "*Genealogija* Profile: Rev. Antanas Saulaitis, S.J.," pp. 5-8, and "Lithuanian Personal Names: Brief History," Summer, 1992, pp. 6-8 (Summer 1992).

Girvilas, K. A. *Senoviniai Vardai: Etimologijos, pagal K. Kuzavinio ir B. Savukyno etimiologini lietuvių vardių žodyną knygelėje Vardai ir žodžiai, Vilniuje. 1977.* Chicago: Pedagoginis Lituanistikos Institutas, 1986. ISBN 0-936694-57-2. A Lithuanian-language book of etymologies for ancient Lithuanian personal names, with analysis of the various roots used in them.

Jonikas, Petras. "Personal Names." *Encyclopedia Lituanica,* Vol. IV. Boston: Juozas Kapočius, 1975.

Kuzavinis, K., Savukynas, B. *Lietuvių vardų kilmės žodynas* [Etymological Dictionary of Lithuanian Names]. Vilnius: Mokslo ir encyklopedijų leidykla, 1994. This small Lithuanian-language book contains an impressive amount of information on the origins of Lithuanian given names.

Lithuanian Heritage. Lemont, Illinois: Baltech Publishing. This an excellent magazine on Lithuanian culture publishcd bi-monthly. Specific articles cited in this book are: Prof. Casimir Dobilas, "What's so different about Lithuanian women? (Their names, of course!)," Sept./ Oct. 1995, p. 22; Rima Medelis, "Women's Names," May/June 1996, p. 16; and Rima Medelis, "Using two personal names," Sept./Oct. 1995, p. 18. More information is available at this website: <http://www.lithuanianheritage. com/>..

Piesarskas, Bronius, and Svecevičius, Bronius, with a supplement by Ian Press. *Lithuanian Dictionary.* London and New York: Routledge, 1995. ISBN 0-415-12857-9. I bought this one-volume English-Lithuanian, Lithuanian-English paperback dictionary (800 pages) via Amazon.com, and have been very pleased with it.

Vanagas, Aleksandras, ed.; Maciejauskienė, Vitalija; and Razmukaitė, Marytė. *Lietuvių pavardžių žodynas* [Dictionary of Lithuanian Surnames]. Vilnius: "Mokslas," 1985-, 2 volumes. A valuable work on Lithuanian names, which Val Ramonis, editor of *Lithuanian Heritage,* graciously helped me acquire.

Russian Reference Works

Daľ, Vladimir Ivanovich. *Толковый словарь живого великорусского языка* [Explanatory Dictionary of the Living Great Russian Language]. This is one of the most popular and extensive dictionaries of Russian, covering some 200,000 words and 30,000 proverbs. Numerous editions have been published; the one I used most is a four-volume print edition published in Moscow in 1998 by Terra Knizhniy Klub. It is available online in numerous places, including <http://slovardalya.ru/> and <http://dic. academic.ru/contents.nsf/enc2p/>.

Petrovskiy, N. A. *Словарь русских личных имен* [Dictionary of Russian Personal Names]. Moskva: Russkie slovari, 1996. ISBN 5-89216-003-3. This book on Russian first names covers a wider range of information than the Tikhonov book mentioned below. It gives particularly useful information on older and dialect forms, which are often more relevant to Polish surnames than the standard Russian forms on which Tikhonov and his co-authors concentrated.

Tikhonov, A. N., Boyarinova, L. Z., and Ryzhkova, A. G., *Словарь русских личных имен* [Dictionary of Russian Personal Names]. Moskva: Shkola-Press, 1995. ISBN 5-88527-108-9. This Russian-language work gives the most popular Russian first names, traces their derivations, analyzes their common diminutives, and gives appropriate saints' name-days. While less relevant to Polish studies than its Ukrainian counterpart (see the entry for Skrypnyk, L. H. and Dviatkivśka, N. P.'s book under "Ukrainian Reference Works"), it contains a lot of useful information; but it may be hard to find if you don't have a contact in Moscow!

Unbegaun, B. O. *Русский фамилии* [Russian Surnames]. Moskva: "Progress-Univers" Publishing Group1995. ISBN 5-01-004266-5. This work on the origins of Russian surnames has a fascinating history: it was originally written in English and published by Oxford University Press, London, in 1972! I had an easier time getting hold of this translation into Russian than the original English version.

Ukrainian Reference Works

Andrusyshen, C. H., and Krett, J. N. *Українсько-Англійський Словник* [Ukrainian-English Dictionary]. University of Toronto Press, 1995. ISBN 978-0802064219. Ukrainian dictionaries are not easy to come by in this country, and I obtained this 1,200-page reference from Amazon. com. It is especially useful because it lists many terms found in western Ukrainian dialects, which are closer to Polish forms and more likely to be relevant to origins of surnames borne by Poles.

Skrypnyk, L. H., and Dviatkivśka, N. P., *Власні імена людей* [Personal First Names]. Kyiv: Naukova duma, 1996. ISBN 5-12-002638-9. This Ukrainian-language book on common Ukrainian first names and their derivations is hard to find, and I appreciate the aid of Frances Swyripa, Ph.D., Canadian Institute of Ukrainian Studies at the University of Alberta, and my colleague Jonathan D. Shea, M.A, A.G., Housatonic Community College, in procuring a copy.

Index of Subjects

Surnames in normal Roman type refer to individual people or families by those names; surnames *in italics* refer to the surname as a name in itself, considered apart from the families or individuals who bore it. As a rule, I did not include specific surnames in this index unless I felt a discussion in Chapters One through Twelve gave information that does not appear in Volume II or might shed additional light on a name.

Numbers given after listings of subjects refer to page numbers in Volume One where that subject is mentioned or discussed. Numbers in ***bold italics*** indicate a page where the term in question is defined, or pages where the main discussion of the subject appears.

Bańkowski, Andrzej 185, 212
Batory, Stefan 139
beards 122
Beider, Alexander 140, 143, 145, 185, 215, 225, 226, 227
Beider-Morse Phonetic Matching 195
Belarus *x*, 51, 52, 95, 127, 129, 130, 141
Belarusian-influenced names 7, 35, 142, *162-164*, 212
Belarusians 104, 150, 169, 217
ben (in Jewish patronymics) 142
Berliner 7
"Beyond Names and Dates" 220
Białowieża 118
Białystok 199, 203, 212
Bielawa, Matthew 210
Bieniaszewski, Adam 224
birds, terms for *111-112*, 123
Biskupiec, Warmińsko-Mazurskie province 76
Biskupski, M. B. 190
Bniński 82
Bobowska-Kowalska, M. 214
Bobrowicz, Jan Nep. 219
Bohemians 127, 130
Bojko 105
Bona Sforza → Sforza, Bona
Book of Our First Names → *Księga naszych imion*
boroda vs. *broda* 200, 204, 205
Borzyszkowy 26, 27
Boyarinova, L. Z. 229
Bremen 13
Bretan, Pat *xii*
Brody 122
Brückner, Aleksander 212
Brzeziński 77
Bubak, Józef *xii*, 212
Budge 104
Buffalo city directory 192
Bukowczyk, John J. 190
Bulletin, Polish Genealogical

Society of America® 196, 210, 220
Byczyński 103
Bydgoszcz 76, 108
Bystroń 122
Bystroń, Jan Stanisław *xii*, 4, 8, 26, 28, 29, 38, 40, 56, 72, 73, 101, 111, 125, 126, 150, 164, 185, 186, 213
bynames 23, 26
Bystrzycki, Tadeusz 213
Bzdawka 108
c and *ć* 10, 12, 13, 14, 21, 31
-ca 35
Canadian Institute of Ukrainian Studies at the University of Alberta 230
Carbon County, Pennsylvania 151
Carroll, Lewis 102
Carrot Top 121
Carter, Eileen *xii*
Castro, Fidel 122
Cavalry, U. S. 192
ceremonial positions 4
Central Statistical Office 95
Český Těšin 219
-ch- 34
-chak 167
chałupnik 92
changing names 135, 145, 150, 162, 192-194
characteristics, personal 22, 23, *121-123*
Chicago 92, 132, 211
Chicago Bulls 103
Chlebowski, Bronisław 90, 223
Chojnacki, Władysław 8, 213
Chołochwość 6, 7
Chonoles, Michael *xii*
Christian Names in Medieval Poland → *Imiona chrześcijańskie w średniowiecznej Polsce*
Chrząszcz 191
-chuk 31, 167

Girvilas, K. A. 228
given names 2, 3, 4, 12, 22, *51-70*,
    91, 141, 165
Glowacz, Kathy *xii*
Going Home: A Guide to Polish
    American Family History
    Research 222
Golembiewski 6
Golochvoščius 6
Golokhvoshch 6
Google Books 190-191
goral 105
Gorr, Rabbi Shmuel 143, 185, 227
Górski 78
Gorzyński, Sławomir 217
Grabowski 44
Grądziel 102-103
grammar, Polish 15
grammarians 9
Grand Duchy of Lithuania →
    Lithuania
Greater Poland (German name
    Großpolen, Polish name *Wiel-*
    kopolskie) 27, 35, 224
Greek Catholic Church 53
Großpolen→ Greater Poland
growing things 23, *118-121*
Grunwald 129
Grzqdziel 102-103
Gumpertz, Dr. Y. 143
Gutowski 93
Gypsies 104, 217
h/g in East Slavic languages → *g/h*
    in East Slavic languages
Hajduk 140
Hamburg 13
Hamlet 187
handwriting, Polish 14-16
Hanks, Patrick 26, 29, 215
Hardy, Thomas 74
Haskell, David *xii*
Hebrew 141
Helon, George W. 216
Heraldic Names → *Nazwy heral-*

dyczne
Herbarz Polski [Polish Armorial]
    126, 219
Historical Atlas of East Central
    Europe 218
Historical Atlas of Poland → *Atlas*
    Historyczny Polski
History of Customs in Ancient
    Poland, 16th-17th Centuries
    → *Dzieje obyczajów w dawnej*
    Polsce, w. XVI-XVII
History of the Poles in America to
    1908 190
History of the Polish Americans
    190
Historya Polska w Ameryce 190
Hitler 95, 163
Hodges, Flavia 215
Hoffman 134
Hoffman, Dustin 74
Hoffman, Fred 1, 2
Hoffman, William 1
Hoffman, William F. 1, 21, 101,
    186, 210, 214, 216, 222
Holewinski, Felix W. 73, 90, 216
Hollowak, Thomas L. 185, 216
Holowak 6
Holowiak 7
Holowka 7
Holy Orders 4
Holyrood, Kansas 76
Hoskins, Janina 216
Housatonic Community College
    230
Hrodna, Belarus 163
Humpty Dumpty 9
Hungarian names *139-140*
Hungarians 105, 139
hypocoristic names *33*,
-i 32
-ic 35
-ica 35, 40
-ich 42
-ickas 151

CPSIA information can be obtained at www.ICGtesting.com
Printed in the USA
LVOW070410311012

305194LV00002B/1/P